T0366421

ASHOKA

ASHOKA

Portrait *of a* Philosopher King

PATRICK OLIVELLE

Yale UNIVERSITY PRESS

New Haven and London

First published in 2023 in the United States by Yale University Press
and in India by HarperCollins Publishers India.

Yale University Press books may be purchased in quantity for
educational, business, or promotional use. For information, please e-mail
sales.press@yale.edu (U.S. office) or sales@yaleup.co.uk (U.K. office).

Photographs courtesy of Wikimedia Commons.

Typeset in 11.5/15.2 Crimson Text at
Manipal Technologies Limited, Manipal.
Printed in the United States of America.

Library of Congress Control Number: 2023933125
ISBN 978-0-300-27000-6 (hardcover : alk. paper)

A catalogue record for this book is available from the British Library.

This paper meets the requirements of ANSI/NISO Z39.48-1992
(Permanence of Paper).

10 9 8 7 6 5 4 3 2 1

𑀘𑀧𑀥𑀸𑀬𑁂 𑀮𑀺𑀧𑀺𑀓𑀭𑀸𑀬𑁂

चपडाये लिपिकराये

capaḍāye lipikarāye

To Chapada,
and to his fellow scribes, engravers and stonemasons,
whose toil and sweat made it possible for Ashoka's messages
to be read by us twenty-two centuries later

Contents

Abbreviations

MRE	Minor Rock Edict
MRI	Minor Rock Inscription
MPI	Minor Pillar Inscription
PE	Pillar Edict
RE	Rock Edict
SepEd	Separate Edict

Preface

THIS PORTRAIT OF KING ASHOKA IS AIMED PRINCIPALLY AT THE informed and curious public. As such, its target audience is not the scholarly community. Although it is based on sound scholarship, I have tried to avoid scholarly jargon as much as possible. Some technical points of scholarship are relegated to the footnotes, and I have, for the most part, steered clear of diacritical marks so frequent in scholarly writing. My wish is that a wide range of readers, including scholars, may find something worthwhile and interesting in it.

The twenty-first century has generated a renewed interest in Ashoka. Harry Falk's monumental work *Aśokan Sites and Artefacts* published in 2006 has become an indispensable resource for anyone working on Ashoka. My own interest in Ashoka developed around the same time. I organized two conferences, one in Austin, Texas, in 2006, and a much larger international conference in Delhi in 2009. The latter was sponsored by the University of Texas at Austin, Jawaharlal Nehru University's Centre for Historical Studies, the Indian Council of Historical Research, the American Institute of Indian Studies and the India International Centre, pointing to the institutional interest in furthering research into Ashoka and his times. These conferences resulted in two volumes: *Aśoka in History and Historical Memory* (Olivelle 2009) and *Reimagining Aśoka: Memory and History* (Olivelle, Leoshko and Ray 2012). In 2012, another book on Ashoka appeared—*Ashoka: The Search for India's Lost Emperor* by

Charles Allen—whose focus was the nineteenth-century discovery of Ashoka. Dilip Chakrabarti's study of the geography of Ashokan edicts, *Royal Messages by the Wayside: Historical Geography of the Asokan Edicts*, appeared in 2011. Nayanjot Lahiri's important biography of Ashoka, *Ashoka in Ancient India*, was published in 2015. Other recent works include Ashok Khanna's *Ashoka the Visionary: Life, Legend and Legacy* in 2020 and a very personal rendering by Irwin Allan Sealy, *Asoca: A Sutra*, in 2021. After this book was sent to press, Nayanjot Lahiri's new book, *Searching for Ashoka: Questing for a Buddhist King from India to Thailand*, tracing Ashoka's influence across Asia came out (Lahiri 2022); and Herman Tieken's (2023) *The Aśoka Inscriptions*. Unfortunately, I have not been able to fully incorporate their material into this volume. Mine is the latest in this spate of books on the great emperor, and I hope it will present this sensitive and complex person in a new light, a light derived from his own words.

Many friends and colleagues have assisted me in numerous ways during the period of this book's gestation and writing. Three, however, must be singled out. Ramachandra Guha not only invited me to write this volume in the series Indian Lives, of which he is the editor, but also read the entire manuscript with care and eye for detail and provided me with valuable feedback. Without his invitation I would never even have thought of writing this book. Thomas Trautmann generously read the whole manuscript and, with his unparalleled historical knowledge, provided invaluable suggestions for improvement. Joel Brereton read my translations of Ashoka's writings with the keen eye of a philologist; they are all the better for his interventions. So did Gregory Schopen, and his observations have made the translations sharper. Michael Gagarin provided a fresh translation of Ashoka's Greek Edicts, and Na'ama Pat-El that of the Aramaic Edicts. Pankaj Chakraborty of Kolkata produced the excellent map of Ashokan sites. The many others who provided help in various ways include Rajeev Bhargava, Donald Davis, Harry Falk, Oliver Freiberger, Janice Leoshko, Timothy Lubin, Claire Maes, Susmita Basu Majumdar, Richard Salomon, John Strong and Herman Tieken. We stand tall because we stand on the shoulders of those who have tilled this ground before. To all of them I extend my gratitude. Their names dot the notes and bibliography. Finally, I want to thank the editors of HarperCollins India for their friendly support during the long editorial process, especially Udayan Mitra, Prema Govindan, Tanima Saha and the copy editor Shreya Chakravertty.

All the translations of Ashokan inscriptions cited in the book are my own, unless otherwise stated. The full translation of the entire Ashokan inscriptional corpus is given in the Appendix.

I have dedicated this book to a group of forgotten individuals, the 'little people' whose labours are seldom recognized—stonemasons, engravers and scribes—whose toil has preserved Ashoka's words for us to read. We know the name of only one, Chapada, whose work is found in the south using the Brahmi script but who was a native of the north-west, because he wrote his name in his native Kharosthi.[1] There are others—sculptors, artists, quarry workers, engineers and simple labourers—whose collective work created the magnificent pillars and capitals that are ascribed to Ashoka, and who go largely unrecognized. These artistic masterpieces are as much the product of these anonymous workers as they are Ashoka's. Let us spare a thought for these unsung heroes of Ashoka's legacy.

Patrick Olivelle

---

1   For a discussion of the role played by Chapada, see Falk 2006: 58.

Prologue

THE MANY ASHOKAS

REIMAGINING THE PAST TO IMAGINE AND THUS CONSTRUCT THE present is a deeply human trait. Our minds edit our memories. This imagining is done sometimes intentionally, but in the main unconsciously, by individuals and groups, be they social, political, or religious. Memory is complex and pliable; it is never a simple and straightforward presentation of the past unconnected to the demands of the present. Memory both selects and suppresses features of the past and adds newly 'remembered' features in creating a narrative that serves the needs of the present.

So it was with the memory of Ashoka, the third-century BCE king, who ruled over a larger area of the Indian subcontinent than anyone else before British colonial rule. The fame of Ashoka spread far and wide both in India and in other parts of Asia, a fame that prompted diverse reimaginations of the king and his significance. Such reimaginations in various strands of Buddhism and in Brahmanical Sanskrit texts, both within India and in regions of South, Southeast, Central and East Asia, produced 'many Ashokas'.[1]

In a seminal remark, the historian Robert Lingat notes: 'There are in reality two Aśokas—the historical Aśoka whom we know through his inscriptions, and the legendary Aśoka, who is known to us through

---

1   I borrow this expression from Paula Richman, ed., *Many Rāmāyaṇas* (Berkeley: University of California Press, 1991).

texts of diverse origins, Pali, Sanskrit, Chinese, and Tibetan.'² Although essentially correct, there are two problems with Lingat's assessment. First, it is simplistic to contrast the 'historical' with the 'legendary'. The portrait of Ashoka I have constructed in this book is based on Ashokan inscriptions and artefacts; yet it contains a heavy dose of interpretation, translation, imagination, narrative, perhaps bias, and, within the constraints of my own abilities, even artistry. Others using these same sources would have, and indeed have, written different biographical narratives. The 'legendary' is not simply false and to be dismissed; it is the reimagination of the past to serve present needs, something inherently human. These narratives were meaningful and important to the persons and communities that constructed them. Their purpose was not to do history in the modern sense of the term, but to do something that was much more significant to them in their own time.

The second issue with Lingat's remark is that it posits a dichotomy. There are actually not two but several Ashokas, including modern ones. Just as the ancient Ramayana narrative has been appropriated, reimagined and retold in different languages in different parts of India and Asia, so Ashoka has been narratively appropriated and reappropriated at different times by different peoples. That is the legacy of Ashoka.

I will turn to that legacy at the end of my narrative. Briefly, though, there are at least three major strands of the Ashokan story in ancient South Asia. The first was constructed by Sri Lankan Buddhist chroniclers spanning the first 500 years of the common era in the *Dipavamsa* and the *Mahavamsa* written in Pali. The theme around which this narrative is woven is the legitimation of Sri Lankan Buddhism of the Theravada tradition by establishing strong historical connections to Ashoka. He is credited with bringing Buddhism to Sri Lanka by sending his own son, Mahinda, and daughter, Sanghamitta, as missionaries, as well as a sapling from the Bodhi tree under which the Buddha gained enlightenment.³ He

2   Lingat 1989: 19.
3   This was observed by Hermann Oldenberg in his introduction to the edition of the *Vinayapiṭaka* (p. 4), noting that the story of Mahinda and Sanghamitta was 'invented for the purpose of possessing a history of the Buddhist

is also credited with holding a Buddhist council in Pataliputra to purge Buddhism of deviant doctrines and practices and to restore the pure and pristine form of Buddhism, which happens to be the 'doctrine of the elders', the Theravada, that took root in Sri Lanka.

The second strand is found in texts of the northern Buddhist traditions written principally in Sanskrit. Its best constructed narrative is the *Ashokavadana* composed around the second century CE and translated into Chinese in 300 CE.[4] This biography of Ashoka exerted a strong influence on the Ashokan traditions in Central and East Asian countries. It is, however, silent on the two prominent features of the Sri Lankan chronicles: the third council of Pataliputra and the bringing of Buddhism to Sri Lanka by Ashoka's children. Nevertheless, they both share the vision of Ashoka as the fulfilment and capstone of the Buddha's mission. Thus, the famous epic poem on the Buddha's life, the *Buddhacharita*, written by the monk Ashvaghosha in the second century CE ends not with the death of the Buddha but with Ashoka's construction of over 80,000 stupas across the Indian landscape, in all of which the Buddha's ashes were entombed. This triumphalist construction project is presented as the final victory of Buddhism in the land of its birth.

The third narrative—if it can be called a narrative at all given the lack of detail—is found in later Brahmanical sources, especially in the Puranas. As opposed to the idealized portrayal of Ashoka in the various Buddhist narratives, the Puranic version is barebone. The *Matsya Purana* version, for example, simply states that Kautilya will anoint[5] Chandragupta as king, and he will be succeeded by Ashoka, who will reign for thirty-six years.[6]

There are also the unarticulated versions of the Ashokan story that occur both in Brahmanical Sanskrit literature, as well as in some Buddhist traditions of kingship—what the Buddhist scholar Max Deeg

---

institutions in the island, and to connect it with the most distinguished person conceivable—the great Asoka'.

4   Translated with a detailed study by John Strong 1983.
5   Statements of the Puranas are always given as prophesies regarding what will happen in the future.
6   See Pargiter 1913: 26.

has called the 'model ruler without a name'.[7] Scholars have noted that
the subtext behind many major Brahmanical writings, including the
Mahabharata and the law book of Manu,[8] is the Ashokan social and
political reforms, which challenged the centrality of Brahmins within the
social structure and political ideology—what has been called 'Brahmanical
exceptionalism'. Ashoka, however, is never mentioned in them by name.
These Brahmanical texts presented arguments and constructed narratives
to support Brahmanical exceptionalism, the epic heroes Rama and
Yudhisthira being Brahmanical counterpoints to the Buddhist Ashoka.

These narrative reimaginations of Ashoka were carried out purely
through historical memory and fertile imagination; the narrators had little
or no access to Ashoka's inscriptional and architectural remains. They
could not read the messages Ashoka had left for posterity in the many
rock and pillar inscriptions written in a script that they could no longer
decipher. But the memory of Ashoka's connection to the inscriptions
and the pillars appears to have continued. The Chinese pilgrim Fa-hsien,
for example, travelling in India round 400 CE, came to Sankasa and
saw there a pillar 'shining bright as lapis lazuli' with a lion on top. The
locals informed him that it was erected by Ashoka.[9] But Ashoka's words
remained silent.

All this changed in 1837. That was the year James Prinsep, a British
colonial officer posted to India, succeeded in deciphering the Brahmi
script in which most of the Ashokan inscriptions were written. The ability
to read and understand the very words of Ashoka created a new Ashoka,
the 'inscriptional Ashoka'. Prior to that year all we had were the Buddhist
hagiographical Ashokas and the Brahmanical antagonistic Ashokas.

The modern scholarly construction of this inscriptional Ashoka,
however, was not easy or straightforward. Some of the inscriptions had
sustained damage over the two millennia they stood in the open exposed
to rain, sun and wind. Others posed linguistic challenges to reading

---

7   See Max Deeg 2012.
8   See Fitzgerald 2004: 135–39. Nick Sutton (1997) devotes an entire paper to
    this topic.
9   James Legge 1886: 50–51; see Irwin 1973: 715.

and understanding. There may have also been errors introduced by the scribes and engravers who mediated between Ashoka's messages and their inscribed forms we possess. Yet, in spite of all the difficulties, this is the precious gift of Ashoka. He has bequeathed to us his very words, something quite rare in the ancient historical record.

There have been, and there continue to be, scholarly debates and disagreements about both the readings and the meanings of Ashokan inscriptions, as well as about their overall significance for the life and message of Ashoka and his imperial project. I will have occasion to refer to them throughout this book, as also in my translations of the inscriptions given in the Appendix. In his exhaustive Ashokan bibliography published in 2006, the historian Harry Falk[10] lists around 1,600 books and articles on Ashoka that have appeared in print over the past century or so; many more have been written since then. The scholar of epigraphy Richard Salomon offers a word of caution: 'Despite having been intensively studied for over a century and a half, the Aśokan inscriptions remain problematic in several respects, and many points of interpretation are still controversial.'[11] So, even with the access we have today to the very words of Ashoka, there have emerged 'many inscriptional Ashokas', not as divergent as the pre-inscriptional Ashokas, but nevertheless containing significant differences.

One other significant ramification of the new inscriptional Ashoka was his adoption by the Indian freedom movement spearheaded by Jawaharlal Nehru, for whom Ashoka provided raw material for his nation-building project. The peace-loving emperor who unified India over two millennia ago and left his words of wisdom for future generations indelibly written on stone, he thought, could serve as a model for the nascent nation, for the new India dedicated to peace and prosperity. This can be called the 'nationalist Ashoka' if we remove the pejorative connotations from the term 'nationalist'. As new nations are created—the United States of America and the modern nation-state of

---

10 Harry Falk 2006: 9–54. For a bird's-eye view of Ashokan scholarship, see
    Allchin and Norman 1985; and Romila Thapar 2012.

11 Richard Salomon 1998: 136.

India are examples—the nation-building process demands national heroes
and mythic narratives. The United States had the revolutionary war, the
'founding fathers' and the written constitution. As the newly independent
India looked for past heroic and exemplary figures, Ashoka and Ashokan
artefacts became an obvious choice. Ashokan emblems decorate the major
symbols of the modern Indian state: the wheel—at once the wheel of
the war chariot of the world conqueror (*chakravartin*) and the wheel of
dharma set in motion by the Buddha—occupies the centre of the Indian
flag. The lion capital that stood atop the Ashokan pillar at Sarnath, where
the Buddha preached his first sermon containing the Four Noble Truths,
now adorns Indian currency and state emblems.

Ashoka also penetrated the consciousness of the Indian populace.
This can be seen in the large number of boys who were and are being
named 'Ashok', a name that was rare before the twentieth century.
When prominent Indian entrepreneurs wanted to found an 'Ivy League'
kind of institution of higher education in India in 2014, they called it
Ashoka University. We also have a television adaptation called
Chakravartin Ashoka Samrat (2015), and Ashoka is featured in the well-
known illustrated biographical series by Amar Chitra Katha (2005).
The name has become so paradigmatically Indian even in the diaspora
that a major character in the popular American comic strip *Dilbert* is an
Indian expat named Asok, an intern who is 'a brilliant graduate from the
Indian Institute of Technology, the stereotype of the cerebral Indian in
popular American culture, and first Indian comic character to win hearts
globally'.[12]

The inscriptional Ashoka had a deep impact also on world historians
of the early twentieth century, given how unique his message was among
the great rulers of the past. The excitement among them is captured by
H.G. Wells in his *Outline of History*:

> Amidst the tens of thousands of names of monarchs that crowd the
> columns of history, their majesties and graciousnesses and serenities
> and royal highnesses and the like, the name of Aśoka shines, and

---

12 See: https://en.wikipedia.org/wiki/Asok_(Dilbert); accessed 28 May 2021.

shines almost alone, a star … More living men cherish his memory today than have ever heard the names of Constantine or Charlemagne.[13]

There has been, however, a tendency among scholars writing on Ashoka—
especially those writing biographies of him—to blend deliberately or
unconsciously the two Ashokas, borrowing interesting details of the king's
life from his hagiographies when they needed to flesh out the meagre
information found in Ashoka's own inscriptions.[14] Even Nayanjot Lahiri's
recent biography, *Ashoka in Ancient India*,[15] admirable in many respects, is
not immune to this pitfall. The eminent historian of ancient India, Romila
Thapar, warned against this over half a century ago:

> Buddhist sources from Ceylon [Sri Lanka], Tibet and China contain
> fairly detailed accounts of his life. The Aśokan edicts were therefore
> interpreted on the basis of information provided by these sources.
> It is indeed unfortunate that in reconstructing his life and activities
> these and other religious sources were regarded as reliable and
> complementary evidence to that of his own inscriptions.[16]

I will heed her warning.

---

13 Wells 1951: 402.

14 The most obvious example is Ananda Guruge's (1993) biography, which he
    calls 'definitive'. Even Harry Falk (1997: 115), a meticulous scholar, slides
    into the hagiographical histories in interpreting an inscription: 'To practise
    saṃnivāsa does not necessarily imply sexual intercourse, as seen above in the
    case of the monks "living together"; but in the case of Aśoka and Vidiśādevī
    the term certainly implies such a notion. Nowhere else in Aśoka's biography
    do we hear of his arranging *saṃnivāsa*: it is restricted to his time in Ujjayinī.
    His marriage to his chief queen (*mahesī*) Asandhimittā is not described in
    the chronicles. Later, when Aśoka went to succeed his father on the throne,
    Devī did not move with him to Pāṭaliputra. Her children played a role in the
    spread of Buddhism, but Mahinda was never brought into state politics.' All
    these details of Ashoka's marriages and dalliances, and his children and chief
    queen, are not in the inscriptions but derived from Buddhist sources.

15 Lahiri 2015.

16 Thapar 1960: 44.

So, in the following pages, I too will be engaged in creating a new Ashoka, following the footsteps, though not the methods, of many modern biographers, beginning with the British historian Vincent Smith in 1901.

One may question, however, whether a biography in the full sense of the term is even possible in the case of Ashoka. I think not. There is such a dearth of reliable information about his life and activities. We do not even know for sure when he was born, when he ascended to the throne or when he died, or, for that matter, his true name. Writing about Alexander of Macedonia, who lived two generations before Ashoka and was a contemporary of his grandfather Chandragupta, the historian Robin Lane Fox concludes that it is impossible to write a biography of that Greek emperor because we do not have sufficient authentic material on his life. 'Augustine, Cicero and perhaps the emperor Julian,' Fox asserts, 'are the only figures from [Graeco-Roman] antiquity whose biography can be attempted, and Alexander is not among them.' He calls his book on Alexander 'a search, not a story'.[17]

We are both better off and worse off in the case of Ashoka. Worse off, because, as opposed to Alexander, histories of whose life and exploits were written based on more than twenty accounts authored by his contemporaries, there is not a single account of Ashoka written by his contemporaries, and no historical biographies, except for the Buddhist hagiographies written at least 300 years later. Ashoka's chancery had no chroniclers or, if there were, their work has been lost without a trace. Better off, because we can hear Ashoka's own voice speaking in his numerous inscriptions, something we do not have for Alexander.

Mine, then, will not be a conventional biography, but more a portrait of the man as it emerges from his own writings and from the art and architecture he pioneered. It will be, in Fox's words, 'a search, not a story'. The hope is that others will carry forward this search, which may lead to further insights and discoveries relating to this unique figure in world history. I will refer to the Buddhist hagiographies and other ancient Indian writings, such as Kautilya's *Arthashastra*—all of them postdating

_____

17 Robin Lane Fox 2004: 11.

Ashoka by several centuries—only in passing when they throw some light on the inscriptional evidence and its social and historical background. Nevertheless, we need further historical information not available from the inscriptions themselves in order to put them into context and understand them within their contemporary historical context. For this I will use non-inscriptional sources, especially Greek sources, such as the surviving fragments of the book by Megasthenes, the Seleucid envoy to Chandragupta's court in Pataliputra, bearing on the Maurya rulers. Historical reconstruction is always an approximation; one can never reach certainty. We have to deal with the possible, the plausible, and, hopefully, the probable in envisaging that background. At the end of it, we will have to acknowledge that this is the best we can do. The old scholastic philosophers of medieval Europe had a wise saying: *Qui nimis probat nihil probat*, 'Who proves too much proves nothing.' Too much certainty where certainty is wanting undermines historical writings. When it comes to Ashoka, certainty is a rare commodity.

We do not need the certainty and hyperbole of the hagiographers, however, to perceive the unique personality of Ashoka. H.G. Wells is right to consider him unique, shining, 'almost alone' among ancient [or even modern!] rulers. I refrain from calling him 'great' or 'the greatest', terms that are much abused these days and have lost their value. I call him unique, because he is singular; there is no one remotely like him in world history. He stands alone. He was not just a king with strong religious convictions, but a king who was deeply introspective, a person who, as Richard Salomon once remarked, was perhaps the lone king in world history who was strong enough to say 'I'm sorry.'

Ashoka wanted not only to rule his territory but also to give it a unity of purpose and aspiration, to unify the people of his vast and heterogeneous empire not by a cult of personality, as numerous kings of antiquity did, often by claiming divine status, but by the cult of an idea, a moral idea encapsulated in the term 'dharma' serving as the lynchpin of a new moral order. He aspired to forge a new moral philosophy that would be internalized not only by the people of his empire, but also by rulers and subjects of other countries, through an ambitious programme of mass moral education. He was attempting to forge a universal moral philosophy that can underpin a theory of international relations, where practising dharma can bring—or so he thought—international conflicts to an end. Indeed, some major modern political philosophers have attempted to mine the ideas of Ashoka to build a modern non-Western theory of international relations.[18]

This is the world of Ashoka—a new, and hopefully a bit more adequate, rendition of the inscriptional Ashoka—that I invite the reader to enter and to discover, to savour this unique and complex personality and, through his eyes, to gain a new perspective of India in the third century before the Common Era.

ASHOKA BY ANY OTHER NAME

What is the name of Ashoka? Asked that way, it is a tautology; the answer is contained in the question. We could ask instead: What is the name of the Indian king who wrote the inscriptions and erected the inscribed pillars in the third century BCE? Asked that way, the answer is not obvious or clear.[19] The following discussion is a bit technical, and I beg the reader's indulgence.

Several of Ashoka's inscriptions contain the three-word title: 'The Beloved of Gods, King Piyadasi' (*devānaṃpiye piyadasi lājā*), or an abbreviation of it (Fig. 1). In all of Indian literature, the epithet 'Beloved of Gods', used self-referentially by Ashoka as already noted, is found for the first time in Ashoka's inscriptions. The consensus is that it is a royal title. Scholars, therefore, often translate it non-literally as 'His Majesty'. That it was an honorific title is beyond doubt. In Rock Edict VIII, Ashoka refers to former kings also with this title, indicating that he viewed it as a generic designation for his royal predecessors. Ashoka's grandson, Dasharatha, left behind three inscriptions in which he used it as his own title.

---

18 See Rajeev Bhargava 2022; some insights also in Olivelle 2022.

19 For Romila Thapar's discussion on this topic, entitled 'The Titles of Aśoka', see Thapar 1961: 226–27.

Yet, in later Sanskrit usage *devānāṃpriya* is used for mockery, generally indicating that the person so addressed is a fool. The historian Harmut Scharfe has suggested that this Indian expression may have derived from a parallel Greek one, 'friend of the king', which was an honorific title that Hellenistic kings bestowed on subordinate rulers owing them allegiance.[20] The Greek historian Grant Parker, however, has noted that this Greek expression does not appear in inscriptions, and it is highly unlikely that the Mauryan rulers considered themselves in any way inferior or owing allegiance to the Western Hellenistic kings. The linguist Madhav Deshpande, furthermore, has shown numerous Vedic precedents to this expression.[21] We must acknowledge, though, that this is a rather curious and unique appellation, which did not last too long after the Mauryas, becoming an expression used in jest or sarcastically.

I will discuss the second term, *piyadasi* (Sanskrit: *priyadarśin*), presently. It was probably the personal name of the king. Some inscriptions shorten the title, omitting one of the first two terms. The name Ashoka, however, is nowhere to be found, except in four isolated cases. If we had only the inscriptions and not the later Buddhist hagiographies and Puranic accounts, we may well have called him Piyadasi, and the title of the present book would have carried that name.

So where does the name Ashoka come from? In Ashoka's inscriptional corpus, it is found four times in a cluster of Minor Rock Edicts in the south (what is today Karnataka), twice in Minor Rock Edict I and twice in Minor Rock Edict II. Most versions of the Minor Rock Edicts carry only the title 'Beloved of Gods'. These four outliers appear to have been inscribed later by scribes or patrons who wanted to connect the name 'Ashoka' to these inscriptions. They also contain other modifications to the original wording of these edicts. We see that the two at Maski and Gujarra give the name of the king in the genitive (*devānaṃpiyasa asokasa*), meaning that what follows is the message 'of the Beloved of Gods, of Ashoka', while all others, and more original versions, are in

---

20 See Scharfe 1971.

21 For a detailed historical investigation of this title, see Deshpande 2009.

the nominative: *devānampiye hevaṃ āha* ('The Beloved of Gods says thus'). The two versions of Minor Rock Edict II at Nittur and Udegoḷam bearing the name Ashoka also present an unusual form, writing *rājā* (king) before Ashoka, when normally *rājā* comes after the king's name, for example, *piyadasi rājā*. All this creates the impression that the name Ashoka was something that was appended to the original text as issued by the king himself.

Recently, Ashoka's authorship of the inscriptions has come under greater scrutiny. The historian Christopher Beckwith, for example, takes Ashoka to be an obscure king elevated to his historical stature by Buddhist hagiographers.[22] This is an outlier and no mainstream Ashokan scholar would subscribe to that view. Further, such a sceptical view is belied by the inscription of Rudradaman made around 150 CE. Significantly, this inscription is written below the famous Ashokan inscription on the large rock surface above an artificial reservoir below Mount Girnar, Gujarat. Rudradaman was aware of Ashoka's inscription below which he is inscribing his own and refers to the construction and repair of the same reservoir undertaken by Chandragupta and Ashoka: and he, indeed, uses the name Ashoka. So, a king just 300 years after Ashoka not only was aware of this name but also knew about Ashoka's construction activities.

It is true, nevertheless, that Ashoka was not the king's preferred name; he liked to call himself, and, I think, liked others to call him 'Piyadasi'. So, we have to conclude that he had two names. Is it unusual for a king to have two names? Some have argued that Piyadasi was his 'coronation' name, that is, the name he took upon becoming king; or an epithet or pseudonym.[23] The name Ashoka, however, receded to the background,

---

22 Beckwith 2015: 125–37, 226–50.

23 Tieken (2002: 36) is inclined to take *piyadasi* as a title, just like *devānampiya*. Monica Smith (2016: 378) calls it a pseudonym. Kubica (2013: 725–26): 'If Aśoka was the proper name of the Emperor, then why would he use the title devānaṃpriya piyadassi rājā (in Greek version Πιοδάσσης) in his inscriptions?' I agree with Benveniste (1964), who argues that the name Piyadassi (Priyadarśin), which is usually translated as a qualifier meaning: 'with friendly look' is in reality a proper name, not a qualifier, and that it was the personal name of the king, while Aśoka was his nickname, which 'may

except within the Buddhist tradition and in Indian historical memory. Given its Buddhist connections, it could be argued that Ashoka was his 'Buddhist' name, that is, the name he assumed after his conversion to Buddhism and when he became an Upasaka, a devout lay Buddhist. But we have little evidence that laypersons who became Buddhists took on a 'religious' name. The Sanskrit term *aśoka* literally means 'non-sorrow', and thus could mean someone who does not bring sorrow, someone who is without sorrow, and the like.

The best solution to the problem, given the current state of knowledge, is to acknowledge that the emperor had two names, however he may have acquired them. This is not unique to Ashoka. We know that Ashoka's father was named Bindusara.[24] That is how he is known in Indian sources. But Greek texts refer to him as Amitrochates, or in Sanskrit, Amitraghāta ('killer of enemies'), and it is likely that this is the name under which he carried out diplomatic activities. It is noteworthy that the names of father and son both begin with the negative/privative particle 'a'—Amitraghāta and Ashoka. We do not know whether Ashoka's grandfather, Chandragupta, also had a second name. None has come down in the tradition, and even Greek sources call him by that name.

Which brings us to Piyadasi, the name preferred by Ashoka. What was its meaning and why did Ashoka show a fondness for it? The meaning of this compound word is not altogether clear: *piya* (Sanskrit: *priya*) means dear, pleasant, or someone/something that is dear; so, beloved. The second word *dasi* (Sanskrit: *darśin*) could mean seeing, seen, or, if formed from the causative form of the verb, 'made to see'. At issue here is the relationship of the two words in the nominal compound. Sanskrit grammar gives two possibilities: in one, called tatpuruṣa, the two words are substantives, and if the compound is dissolved the first member would be put in a declensional form: for example, 'seeing of what is dear' or 'seeing the dear'. The other possibility, which I prefer and is more

---

well have been a name taken by the king after he came under the influence of the Buddha's doctrine'.

24 Here also we come across several versions of this name: Vindusāra, Bhadrasāra, Nandasāra: see Pargiter 2013: 28; Thapar 1961: 17–19.

likely, is called karmadharaya. Here, the first member of the nominal
compound adjectivally qualifies the second: for example, a dear sight. So
it could mean something like pleasant/pleasing/lovely to see, or—as often
translated—'of benign countenance'. The question about whether Piyadasi
was an epithet or a personal name, I think, has now been resolved with
the discovery of several Greek and Aramaic inscriptions, which are for
the most part translations from the original Prakrit. In them, even though
all the other terms, including *devānaṃpiya* and *lājā*, are translated to the
corresponding Greek and Aramaic, Piyadasi is not. It is phonetically
reproduced in Greek or Aramaic letters. They retain a version of the
original, which clearly shows that the scribes and translators accepted the
term as the king's personal name and saw no need to translate it.

Further confirmation of this conclusion comes from a long-
misunderstood inscription at Panguraria, which Harry Falk has analysed
carefully.[25] It says that King Piyadasi, while he was still a prince (*kumāra*)
came to that spot, probably along with his consort, while on a pleasure
tour (*vihārayātrā*). This seems almost like a nostalgic graffiti that Ashoka
wanted to write here to recall some fond memories from his youth. This
is the pleasure or hunting trips that Ashoka would condemn in his later
inscriptions, when he encouraged dharma tours or pilgrimages.

Whether Piyadasi was a name given to him at birth or one he chose
later in life, I think the nice alliterative iteration of the middle two words
of his appellation—*devānaṃpiye piyadasi*—must have appealed to his
aesthetic sensibilities as a writer. Further, the first and last words begins
again with the alliterative 'd'. The first compound word *devānaṃpiye*,
moreover, contains four syllables that Indian poetics calls 'heavy', while in
the second, *piyadasi*, with three or four[26] 'light' or short syllables. Ashoka
must have liked the poetic impact of his title. I will have occasion to point
out similar rhetorical flourishes in his writings.

The question as to how and why the name Ashoka came to dominate
later literature, both the Buddhist and the Brahmanical, and pushed

---

25 See Falk 1997.

26 As written all four are short syllables, but the penultimate syllable is, perhaps,
    long, given that the original was *piyadassi*.

Piyadasi to near oblivion, remains unclear. Buddhists clearly preferred that name, and their usage may have influenced the more general memory of the emperor.

I could—probably should—have used Piyadasi in the title of this book. But, then, nobody would have known whom I was talking about. The victory of 'Ashoka' over 'Piyadasi' is total and irreversible.

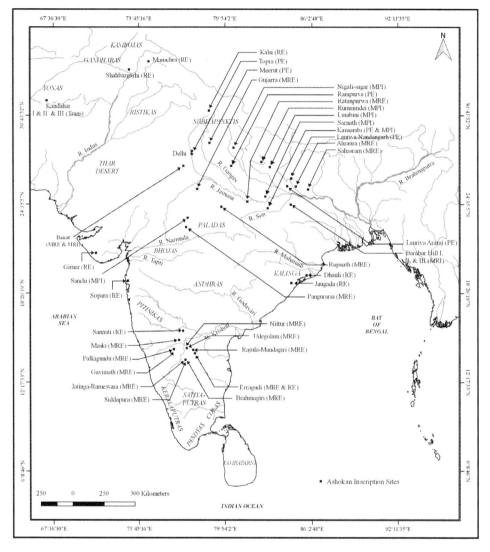

Map of Ashokan inscription sites and geographical names

Legend:

MPI: Minor Pillar Inscription
MRE: Minor Rock Edict
MRI: Minor Rock Inscription
PE: Pillar Edict
Trans.: Translations in Aramaic and Greek

Chart 0.1
Ashoka's Timeline

Regnal Year	Month	Year (BCE)	Events
0	March	268	Royal consecration
1	March	267	Prisoner release
2	March	266	Prisoner release
3	March	265	Prisoner release
4	March	264	Prisoner release
5	March	263	Prisoner release
6	March	262	Prisoner release
7	March	261	Prisoner release
8	March	260	Prisoner release
	Oct–Nov		Kalinga War
	Dec		Becomes an Upasaka
9	March	259	Prisoner release
	Dec		Visits the Sangha
			Becomes zealous, 'striving'
10	March	258	Prisoner release
	October		Sets out on an eight-month tour
	11th regnal year		Visits Bodh Gaya, place of Buddha's enlightenment
11	March	257	Prisoner release
	June	257	Minor Rock Edict I
12	March	256	Prisoner release
	13th regnal year		Begins issuing the Rock Edict series

Regnal Year	Month	Year (BCE)	Events
			Donates two caves of Barabar Hills to Ajivikas
13	March	255	Prisoner release
	14th regnal year		Establishment of dharma–mahamatras
14	March	254	Prisoner release
	15th regnal year		Enlarged Stupa of Buddha Konakamana at Nigliva
15	March	253	Prisoner release
16	March	252	Prisoner release
17	March	251	Prisoner release
18	March	250	Prisoner release
19	March	249	Prisoner release
	20th regnal year		Donates the Supriyeksa cave to Ajivikas
20	March	248	Prisoner release
	21st regnal year		Visits Lumbini, donates stone fence
			Visits Buddha Konakamana at Nigliva
21	March	247	Prisoner release
22	March	246	Prisoner release
23	March	245	Prisoner release
24	March	244	Prisoner release
25	March	243	Prisoner release

Regnal Year	Month	Year (BCE)	Events
26	March	242	Prisoner release
	27th regnal year		Exempting some animals from slaughter
			Pillar Edicts I–VI
27	March	241	Prisoner release
	28th regnal year		Pillar Edict VII
28	March	240	Prisoner release*
29	March	239	Prisoner release*
30	March	238	Prisoner release*
31	March	237	Prisoner release*
32	March	236	Prisoner release*
33	March	235	Prisoner release*
34	March	234	Prisoner release*
35	March	233	Prisoner release*
36	March	232	Prisoner release*
	37th regnal year		Death of Ashoka*

* Not derived directly from the inscriptions but are estimates derived from other sources.

PART ONE

Rājā
Ashoka the King

MODERN SCHOLARLY DISCUSSIONS, MUCH LIKE ANCIENT BUDDHIST hagiographies, frequently present Ashoka as a Buddhist king and the king responsible for spreading Buddhism across India and beyond. Writing in 1901, Vincent Smith, the earliest modern biographer of Ashoka, notes that interest in Ashoka's story 'is mainly psychological and religious, that is to say, as we read it, we watch the development of a commanding personality and the effect of its action in transforming a local Indian sect into one of the leading religions of the world'.[1] His assessment is echoed even by contemporary scholars.[2] Apart from the fact

---

1 Cited in Chakarbarti 2011:3.

2 In a recent study, the archaeologist Monica Smith makes similar remarks about Ashoka being instrumental in spreading Buddhism across India: 'Ashoka's autobiographical endorsements served to spread the doctrine of Buddhism beyond its Gangetic origins to a larger audience' (Monica Smith et al. 2016: 378). She notes that Buddhism 'was a small and relatively unknown sect prior to the royal support that it received from Ashoka' (Ibid: 389). Similar sentiments, although expressed with greater reservation, are found in Lahiri 2015. The British demographer Tim Dyson (2018: 27), speaking about the Indo-Aryan influences on and the origin of the Sinhala language in Sri Lanka, also accepts hagiographical information as historical fact: 'This seems to have occurred roughly two centuries before Ashoka's son, Mahinda, was sent from Pataliputra to convert the island to Buddhism.'

that the last statement is misleading, such views make the most significant identity of Ashoka, that he was first and foremost a king—an identity that he highlights at the beginning of almost all his inscriptions when he identifies himself as *rājā*, king—recede into the background. Ashoka was not a Buddhist king but a king who happened to be a Buddhist.

Ashoka's royal identity ought to be brought back to the foreground. Ashoka was, indeed, the king of such a large and diverse territory that he deserves the title 'Emperor'. As far as we can tell from the distribution of his rock and pillar inscriptions, his empire stretched from what is today Afghanistan in the west to Bangladesh in the east, from Nepal in the north to at least Karnataka in the south. Given that the Chinese and Roman empires had not yet emerged, and the Achaemenid empire had disintegrated after being subjugated by Alexander, the empire over which Ashoka ruled was at the time probably the largest in the world in terms of territory and population.

Like most ancient kings, Ashoka inherited his kingdom from his father and grandfather. A review of his royal and cosmopolitan background and upbringing is important for locating him in history and understanding his life and activities. As a child and young man he was likely exposed to a wide array of cultures and languages, both from within India and from the countries of western Asia—Persian, Greek and perhaps even Egyptian. To this background I now turn.

1

Maurya

TWO MOMENTOUS EVENTS OCCURRED IN THE LAST QUARTER OF THE third century BCE, events that shaped the political landscape of South and West Asia. It was this new political landscape that Ashoka inherited and, to some extent, which shaped his political and moral philosophy. The first was the conquest of West Asia by Alexander of Macedonia, and the second was the seizure of the prosperous and powerful Magadha kingdom along the Ganges by Chandragupta Maurya, Ashoka's grandfather.

Alexander was just twenty-nine years old when he marched from Greece into West Asia, conquering all before him, from Egypt to Persia, introducing the Greek language, culture and mores to the regions bordering India in the far northwest. One of Alexander's biographers[1] surmises that Alexander's ambition to conquer the world up to the 'Eastern Ocean, edge of the world as the Greeks conceived it' was probably 'the posthumous guess of his soldiers'. He cites, however, Arrian's assessment that Alexander 'would not have remained content with any of his conquests ... he would always have searched beyond for something unknown, and if there had been no other competition, he would have competed against himself'.[2] He was a man whom the ancient Indian political theorist Kautilya, author of the celebrated *Arthashastra*, would have easily recognized as embodying the ideal of a king always in search

---

1   Fox 2004: 332–34.
2   Fox 2004: 13.

of conquests (*vijigīṣu*). Alexander, moreover, was as much an explorer as
a conqueror. He wanted to march across the Hindu Kush into the fabled
land of India where, according to Greek myth, honey dripped from trees,
ants dug up gold, and wool grew on trees. His Indian campaign began in
327 BCE and ended two years later when, at the Indus tributary river of
Beas, his troops refused to go any further. Alexander himself died soon
thereafter in 323 BCE. The territories he conquered, including the north-
western provinces of India, were divided among his generals. These
Hellenistic kingdoms and peoples were called '*yona*' (derived from Ionia)
by the Indians.

Into this turbulent political landscape left in the wake of Alexander's
withdrawal and death entered Chandragupta. In the north-eastern region
of Magadha (broadly modern Bihar) a dynasty called Nanda had ruled
for some time from its capital, Pataliputra (modern Patna). At some
point—the details are murky—Chandragupta wrestled power from the
last Nanda king. By the time Chandragupta took control, Magadha had
emerged as a strong kingdom aided by its strategically advantageous
location along the fertile Ganges plain with large population centres.
There is scholarly disagreement about Chandragupta's pedigree and
when and how he came to power and inaugurated the Mauryan empire.
The various dates proposed range from 324 BCE to 313 BCE.[3] Although his
personal connection to the Nanda dynasty is unclear, it appears possible
that he was related to it through his mother, from whom is probably
derived the matronymic Maurya. An old tradition recorded in Buddhist,
Jain and Brahmanical sources refers to a wise and cunning Brahmin
named Chanakya who provided the political and military strategy for
Chandragupta's success. It is the subject of the only historical Sanskrit
play, *Mudrarakshasa* by Vishakhadatta.[4] These traditional sources view
Chandragupta as coming from a lower social class; in Vishakhadatta's
play Chanakya regularly addresses the king as '*vṛṣala*', a term referring to
a person of low birth and often used as a synonym of Shudra.

---

3   See Thapar 1961: 15–16. Eggermont (1956: 180) suggests 317 BCE, and also
    gives a useful timeline for the period; Fussman (1982: 621) gives 313 BCE.

4   For the legend of Cāṇakya, see Trautmann 1971.

Meanwhile in the Punjab, it appears that a king named Poros, who had made an alliance with Alexander, ruled the territory as his satrap. In the turbulent political situation after Alexander's death, Poros was assassinated around 318 BCE. In the wars of succession among Alexander's generals, Seleucus Nikator, who was initially the satrap of Babylonia, extended his power to the territories in north-western India. It was only then, probably around 305 BCE, that Chandragupta, who also had designs on the Punjab, came into conflict with Seleucus. The outcome of that conflict is unclear, but it ended with a negotiated peace treaty in 303 BCE. Seleucus ceded to Chandragupta much of what is today Pakistan and eastern Afghanistan in exchange for 500 war elephants. The historian Paul Kosmin has called this the 'Treaty of the Indus'. It had three major clauses:[5]

(i)   Seleucus transferred to Chandragupta's kingdom the easternmost satrapies of his empire.
(ii) Chandragupta gave Seleucus 500 Indian war elephants.
(iii) The two were joined in a marriage alliance—most likely Chandragupta married a close female relative of Seleucus.

As the historian Thomas Trautmann has documented, the Mauryan rulers after Chandragupta continued to have friendly relations with the Seleucids, who continued to obtain war elephants from the Indian rulers.[6] In the waning years of the fourth century BCE, then, Chandragupta came to rule over a large swathe of land in northern India from Afghanistan to Bengal and emerged as the most powerful king in the subcontinent.

Paul Kosmin also draws our attention to the radical transformation of West Asia after the Wars of Succession following Alexander's death. The imperial ideology of the Achaemenid empire and of Alexander's ambition was 'totality and exclusivity', leaving no room for the coexistence of equal and legitimate powers. In Kosmin's words:

---

5   Kosmin 2014: 33.
6   Trautmann 2015: 235–39.

A diachronic succession of world-empires ... was replaced with a synchronic coexistence of bounded kingdoms. The emergence of a few 'Great Powers' ... gradually developed into a system of peer states, with semiformalized procedures of interaction ... By the third century, a developed and unquestioned international order was operating within the broader Hellenistic world ... Of paramount importance to such a system was the 'border', both in its technical definition and its ideological implications. Kingdoms had to be recognized as spatially limited units, as bounded territories with shared frontiers.[7]

Although evidence is meagre, it is likely that, after securing his north-western border through the 'Treaty of the Indus' with Seleucus, Chandragupta looked southward and undertook military expeditions to other parts of central and southern India to consolidate power and protect trade routes. At his death, probably around 297 BCE, his son, Bindusara, inherited this large and powerful kingdom, which he is said to have further expanded. It has been suggested that he expanded the empire southward and that Ashoka inherited an empire reaching into what is today Karnataka. Evidence for this is sparse, however, the strongest being that Ashoka does not speak about any military expeditions of his own into the southern region.

The capital city of this burgeoning empire was Pataliputra, upon whose ruins stands the modern city of Patna, now the capital of the Indian state of Bihar. Pataliputra was built at the confluence of the Ganges and its tributary, called Erannoboas by Greek writers (Sanskrit: Hiraṇyavāhā), which is the same as the modern Son (Sanskrit: Śoṇa)[8]—both names indicating the reddish or golden colour of its water. Pataliputra was thus bordered by rivers on two sides. The fortified city resembled a parallelogram, given that the Son met the Ganges at an angle.

---

7   Kosmin 2014: 31–32.
8   Today the Son does not flow into the Ganges near Patna but 25 kilometres further west due to geological changes.

Following the 'Treaty of the Indus', a Hellenistic Greek named Megasthenes was sent by Seleucus to Pataliputra around 303 BCE[9] as his envoy to Chandragupta. Upon returning home, Megasthenes wrote a substantive geographic and ethnographic monograph on India called *Indica*. The original is now lost, but he soon became the authority on India for other Greek and Roman historians. Thus, we have extensive fragments of Megasthenes's work preserved in the writings of later authors. The reliability of Megasthenes with regard to his comments on Indian society and culture has been rightly questioned. He seems to have attempted to shoehorn what he observed into the anthropological structures he was familiar with. The historian Klaus Karttunen's estimate of Megasthenes is sober:

> He was not consciously distorting his view of India, but he placed his Indian experience within a Greek ideological framework and projected a Greek utopia on India ... He was, however, selecting precisely those points which correspond well to the Greek conception of an ideal state.[10]

With regard to the physical structures he encountered, however, Megasthenes is more accurate. He gives the precise dimensions of the fortified city of Pataliputra, indicating that he was a good observer and probably had some good informants as well. The accuracy of the dimensions he gives has been supported by the limited amount of archaeological excavations carried out at this site. The old city is buried 6–8 metres under Patna. It is difficult to dig under a modern city and its infrastructure. The antiquity of Pataliputra, however, is confirmed by its wooden defences, something not seen in any other excavated ancient

---

9   For a study of the historical setting of Megasthenes's travel to India, see Bosworth 1996. Cribbs (2017) supports Bosworth's revised history of the contacts between Chandragupta and Seleucus. Trautmann (2021) rejects Bosworth's conclusions, especially because Megasthenes actually visited Chandragupta's capital city of Pataliputra. The best account of Megasthenes is found in Kosmin 2014: 37–53; see pp. 261–71 for the date of Megasthenes.

10 Karttunen 1989: 97–98.

city. These city defences were built before the time of the political theorist Kautilya, who warns kings not to use timber in constructing fortifications, given that they can easily be set on fire by an invading enemy.

The scholar of art and archaeology Dieter Schlingloff has provided the most detailed account[11] of the original city plan of Pataliputra as encountered by Megasthenes in relation to the other major cities of ancient India and the world of the last few centuries before the Common Era. According to Schlingloff's calculations, Pataliputra had a defensive rampart 33.8 kilometres in circumference, enclosing an inner city of 25.5 square kilometres. Alexandria was only one-third its size; Rome, within the Aurelian walls with an area of 13.72 square kilometres, a little more than half its size. Pataliputra was over eleven times larger than Athens. Schlingloff concludes, 'Pāṭaliputra is by head and shoulders far larger than the largest cities of antiquity.'[12] Megasthenes says that there were sixty-four gates and 570 towers along the city wall. Schlingloff observes:

> This distance corresponds almost exactly to the required 54 m [metre] interval between the towers ... That the relation of the number of towers and wall intervals of Megasthenes corresponds exactly to the law confirms the reliability of his city plan.[13]

What about its population? Was it comparable to its physical size? It is, of course, impossible to do a census of Mauryan Pataliputra, and Megasthenes is silent on this point. But we can arrive at an estimate by comparing it with better excavated ancient cities whose population densities can be measured. Schlingloff has done precisely that. He estimates that Kausambi, the next largest city of ancient India, had a population of 90,000–100,000. If we extrapolate from this to Pataliputra, which, according to Schlingloff, was ten times larger than Kausambi, we arrive at approximately 900,000–1 million inhabitants. Even if we bring

11 See Schlingloff 2013: 32–48; see p. 56 for a diagram.
12 Schlingloff 2013: 32.
13 Schlingloff 2013: 33.

that figure down substantially, we still have a very large city of over half a million people.[14] Megasthenes would have been impressed.

The year of Chandragupta's death is uncertain, but 293 BCE has been suggested.[15] He was succeeded by his son, Bindusara, who ruled from 293 to around 268 BCE. The military and diplomatic encounters and connections between the first two Mauryan monarchs and the Hellenistic Greek rulers of the north-western territories, especially Seleucus Nikator, were a significant factor for later Mauryan history and, in particular, for the early upbringing and education of Ashoka. After Chandragupta's peace treaty with Seleucus, it is to be assumed that the two kings had continuing diplomatic contacts. As part of the peace treaty, Paul Kosmin has suggested, Seleucus probably gave a female relative of his in marriage to Chandragupta.[16] It was a common Macedonian/Greek practice to seal treaties with neighbouring rulers with matrimonial alliances. Now, a princess is unlikely to have gone to Pataliputra alone; we can assume that she was accompanied by an entourage of companions and retainers. What is certain, however, is that there must have been a Greek presence in Chandragupta's court. Megasthenes was clearly not a lone traveller. His long and detailed anthropological investigations would have required at a minimum informants and translators.

Similar diplomatic contacts and, perhaps, matrimonial connections were maintained by his son and Ashoka's father, Bindusara, called Amitrochates in Greek sources. They refer to several envoys sent by Hellenistic kings to Bindusara: a diplomat named Deimachus sent by

14 The recent book by Tim Dyson, *A Population History of India* (2018), presents figures different from those of Schlingloff, but Dyson's final rough estimate parallels that of Schlingloff: 'And using just the central assumption of 230 persons per hectare, and areas "within the ramparts" of 1,350 and 2,200 hectares, would imply estimates of 310,000 and 500,000 respectively... Further, it is likely that Pataliputra was one of the world's most populous cities at the time' (Dyson 2018: 22).

15 For these dates, I follow Eggermont (1956: 180). Dates suggested by other authors differ by a few years.

16 See Kosmin 2014: 33. For Greeks in the Mauryan court and the matrimonial alliance between Chandragupta and Seleucus, see also Thapar 1961: 20.

Antiochus I of Syria, and another sent by the king of Egypt, Ptolemy II Philadelphus. One source gives the story of Bindusara writing to Antiochus I with some curious requests:

> Dried figs were so eagerly desired by all men ... that even Amitrochates, the king of the Indians, wrote to Antiochus asking him, says Hegesander, to purchase and send him sweet wine, dried figs, and a sophist; and that Antiochus wrote back: 'We shall send you dried figs and sweet wine; but it is not lawful in Greece to sell a sophist.'[17]

Even if we discount some of the amusing details, it is probable that continuous diplomatic and personal contacts were maintained between the Mauryan court and the Hellenistic kings of West Asia.

Into this Mauryan royal household with strong connections to the Seleucid royal family, in the vast and cosmopolitan city of Pataliputra, was born a boy, and they named him Piyadasi or Ashoka—or both. The date of his birth can only be an estimation, as are so many other details of his childhood and early life. If Ashoka was thirty-four years old[18] when he became king around 268 BCE, his birth year would have been 302 BCE. If this is approximately correct, his grandfather, Chandragupta, was still alive and in charge of the empire when his grandson was born. The regions of the northwest would have been recently annexed to the empire after the 'Treaty of the Indus' with Seleucus in 303 BCE. If Chandragupta died in 293 BCE, Ashoka was about nine years old when his father, Bindusara, succeeded his grandfather as king. Ashoka may even have had some memory of his grandfather. As a teenager or a young man he may have witnessed his father's military campaigns in the Deccan, as well as diplomatic initiatives with the Seleucid court. It is reasonable to assume that, as a prince and possible heir, he underwent military and administrative training.

For our purposes, the important point to note in the upbringing and education of Ashoka is that he was brought up in a cosmopolitan,

---

17 Cited in Hultzsch 1925: xxxv. See also Cribbs 2017: 27.
18 For this estimate, see Thapar 1961: 25.

and probably multicultural, court and city, very much in contact with the Hellenistic Greek world on the western frontiers. Besides marriage alliances with the Seleucids, the large and prosperous city of Pataliputra would have attracted traders, artisans and craftsmen from far and wide. Long-distance trade flourished. War elephants going to the West and warhorses coming from the West. The court and the aristocracy would have been eager for luxury goods—gold, gems, pearls, precious woods.

Unfortunately, we have no information about the education of young Ashoka; in fact, we have no reliable information at all about him prior to his becoming king. Tales about his life and exploits have been spun in hagiographical accounts, which I will set aside. The treatise on political strategy, *Arthashastra* by Kautilya, written two or three centuries after Ashoka, however, shows that curriculum-based education of a prince was the norm. Unlike in the case of Alexander, however, who was trained under Aristotle himself, sources provide no details of young Ashoka's education and training. Yet, some information about the formative experiences of his childhood and teenage years is necessary if we are to understand the path Ashoka took as king, a path that was unique and unconventional. Why did he feel deep compunction after the gruesome war with Kalinga? Kings are supposed to wage war and kill their enemies. They are trained not to be affected by the gore and blood, by the atrocities of war. What made Ashoka different? Why did he feel remorse? Why did he say, 'I'm sorry'? And what made Ashoka undertake his dharma mission aimed at the moral education of his people—perhaps the largest mass education project of the ancient world? What is it that made Ashoka introspective, a thinker? And what made Ashoka a writer—a good writer at that? What made him take to communicating with his people through the medium of the written word, some of it inscribed on stone? There were no Indian precedents. Did his cosmopolitan upbringing introduce him to Persian and Greek writings? Some scholars have even argued that Ashoka invented the very script in which he wrote. Certainly, writing letters and edicts on stone was an Ashokan innovation, completely unknown before him in India. In other words, did his early upbringing have anything to do with why he became a philosopher-king?

I think it is important to understand that upbringing to at least attempt to answer these questions. Without solid facts and evidence, we are left with conjectures—educated, reasonable and judicious conjectures, but conjectures nonetheless. I try to avoid conjectures as much as possible in this book, but I think keeping these conjectural possibilities in mind will permit us to ask different and more informed questions from the materials on Ashoka we do possess. Among these conjectures, the most intriguing is Ashoka's relationship with women of Greek descent who were part of the Mauryan court. I have already referred to the matrimonial alliance between Ashoka's grandfather, Chandragupta, and a female relative of the Hellenistic king Seleucus. A similar alliance is mentioned in Greek sources between Ashoka's father, Bindusara, and Seleucus's son Antiochus I. These princesses and their entourage would have created a significant Greek linguistic and cultural presence in the Mauryan court at Pataliputra.

Chandragupta's Greek wife was technically, though not necessarily biologically, Ashoka's grandmother—in India one traditionally referred to all the wives of one's father as mothers. She may have been alive during Ashoka's early childhood. Bindusara's Greek wife, likewise, would have brought Greek language and culture closer to the young Ashoka. Some of these Greek contacts may explain his familiarity with Antiochus II, who may well have been the brother or close relative of Bindusara's Greek wife. In Rock Edict XIII, for example, Ashoka gives the exact distance of Antiochus's capital from Pataliputra: 600 *yojanas*, or about 4,320 kilometres.[19] This familiarity indicates that he was in regular contact with Antiochus, perhaps with the dispatch of diplomats.

Given this family background, it is reasonable to assume that Ashoka was brought up in a cosmopolitan, multilingual and multicultural environment. He may well have been the first major Indian ruler who had such an upbringing; his father and grandfather did have contacts with Greeks and probably married Greek princesses, but only as adults. His father, Bindusara, may have been already an adult when his own father, Chandragupta, brought a Greek princess and ladies-in-waiting to the

19 See Chapter 2, footnote 45.

palace. This upbringing may explain at least in part the expansive and even universalist vision of Ashoka's moral philosophy.

According to later accounts of Ashoka's life, he was a viceroy during his father's rule at Taxila and Ujjain. In his writings, Ashoka also refers to kumaras or princes resident as viceroys in several urban centres such as Ujjain, Taxila and Tosali. So, it is possible that he may well have been one himself prior to becoming king. The inscriptions themselves, however, are silent on his activities before being anointed king except for one tantalizing hint. According to the credible interpretation of Harry Falk, an inscription accompanying Minor Rock Edict I at Panguraria indicates that Ashoka was precisely such a kumara, probably at the nearby administrative centre of Ujjain.[20] Such appointments would have given Ashoka much-needed administrative and military experience.

We come to know that Ashoka was a Maurya, that he occupied the throne of the Mauryan dynasty founded by his grandfather, from sources other than Ashoka himself.[21] In all his extensive writings, he does not use the term Maurya or mention his father or grandfather; he is completely silent about his ancestors. His practice of beginning his edicts with just his title and name is unprecedented. The Persian counterparts, on which Ashoka may have modelled his edicts, as well as later Indian royal inscriptions, begin with the names of the father, and sometimes grandfather, of the king issuing the proclamation. This genealogy was a way of establishing a king's legitimacy as the son of the former king.

I am Darius the Great King, King of Kings, King in Persia, King of countries, son of Hystaspes, grandson of Arsames, an Achaemenian.[22]

I am Xerxes, the great king, king of kings, king of countries containing many kinds of men, king in this great earth far and wide, son of king

---

20 For a discussion, see Chapter 10 under 'Exemplar of Dharma'.

21 The earliest inscriptional evidence is from Rudradaman's inscription at the rock in Girnar (Gujarat), right next to Ashoka's own Rock Edicts. Written around 150 CE, Rudradaman refers to 'Ashoka the Maurya' as one of the people responsible for the repair of the adjoining lake.

22 Darius, Behishtan [DB], Column 1. Translation from http://www.avesta.org/op/op.htm#db1; accessed 6 May 2022.

Darius, an Achaemenian, a Persian, son of a Persian, an Aryan, of
Aryan stock.[23]

It was a common practice in India to identify people by listing their
fathers and grandfathers, or sometimes their mothers, as in the clearly
pre-Ashokan *Bṛhadāraṇyaka Upaniṣad*.[24] The Satavahana kings of the
Deccan in the first century BCE give the names of their mothers: Son of
Gautami, Son of Vasishti, and the like. Rudradaman also writes the names
of his father and grandfather. During the Gupta period, Samudragupta in
the fourth century CE, writing his own inscription on the same pillar at
Allahabad containing Ashoka's edicts, gives this genealogy:

> Maharajadhiraja Shri Samudragupta, son of Maharajadhiraja Shri
> Chandragupta, born of the Mahadevi Kumaradevi, daughter's son of
> the Licchavi (king), grandson of the Maharaja Shri Ghatotkaca, and
> the great grandson of Maharaja Gupta.

Ashoka's simple introduction of himself also stands in stark contrast
to the bombast of other kings: 'The Beloved of Gods, King Piyadasi
declares.' Why did Ashoka not mention his father or grandfather in
the introductions to his inscriptions?[25] Was it simply an unconscious
omission? That is difficult to accept, given the general inscriptional
practice and the examples from Persia. Was it a deliberate attempt to
separate himself from his ancestors, to cancel his pedigree? If so, why?

One conjecture is that the battle for succession that preceded Ashoka's
accession to the throne may have left him bitter and hostile towards his
ancestors. Did his father favour one of his brothers? There are detailed
descriptions of the bloody and gruesome battle that Ashoka waged against

---

23 Daiva Inscription of Xerxes. Translation from https://www.livius.org/
sources/content/achaemenid-royal-inscriptions/xph/; accessed 6 May 2022.
24 See Patrick Olivelle, *The Early Upaniṣads* (New York: Oxford University
Press, 1998), p. 163.
25 One other ancient king who does not reveal his parents is Khāravela in
the Hathigumpha inscription. Whether this exception proves the rule,
or whether Ashoka's reticence fits into a broader pattern requires further
research.

his brothers in Buddhist hagiographies. The only safe assumption is that there was a period after the death of Bindusara when there was an interregnum, and an internal tussle may have gone on among the sons of Bindusara before Ashoka came out victorious.

Another, and perhaps more likely, possibility is that Ashoka wanted to turn a new page in Indian history, to inaugurate a new form of moral kingship. He states repeatedly, as we will see, that what he is doing is unprecedented, something that none of his predecessors was able to accomplish. He contrasts repeatedly his innovative work in promoting dharma to that of past kings; he is doing what they failed to do or never thought of doing. The omission of a genealogy may have been one way of signalling this break with the past. As the historian Upinder Singh notes: 'The absence of a genealogy in his inscriptions shows that he was not interested in looking back. He looked forward to his successors following his new model of kingship.'[26] Ashoka intimates that he is turning a new page in the annals of imperial governance.

When all is said and done, however, we must acknowledge that we may never know for sure why Ashoka fails to mention his parents or grandparents. He does not claim legitimacy from his Mauryan ancestors or upbringing—he seems eager to let that past sink into oblivion. His legitimacy comes from his own virtue and devotion to his subjects, not from his blood relationship to previous kings. He is eager to inaugurate a new era—perhaps he thought of it as 'the era of dharma'. Yet, his disregard of his father and grandfather stands in stark contrast to what he preaches as dharma, one of whose central tenets, as we will see in Chapter 9, is obedience to and reverence of mother and father—filial piety. Did he not notice this dissonance between his doctrine and practice?

Ashoka is a complicated figure. He is much more complex than the monochromatic and one-dimensional portrait presented by Buddhist hagiographers and sometimes even by modern scholars. We will encounter the complexity of his personality frequently in the following pages. It is this very complexity that makes him such a fascinating figure in the annals of ancient history.

---

26 Upinder Singh 2017: 45.

2

Ruler

ASHOKA WAS ANOINTED KING AROUND 268 BCE.[1] HE WAS PERHAPS around thirty-four years old then, a young man with military skill and administrative experience. One event in his life that Ashoka refers to most frequently is his royal consecration or anointing. All the dates recorded in his inscriptions are calculated from this event: for example, 'twelve years after my royal consecration'. There has been some doubt among scholars whether these are current years or expired years, that is, whether it is 'in the twelfth year' or 'after twelve years'. The discovery of the Greek and Aramaic versions of Ashoka's inscriptions has put this debate to rest. Ashoka used expired years in his dating.[2]

What does 'anointing' mean? The original term is *abhiseka* (Sanskrit: *abhiṣeka*). This term can refer to any kind of bathing, pouring of a liquid or its sprinkling, always within a ritual setting.[3] Within the Vedic ritual tradition there is an elaborate rite for installing a king called *rājasūya* lasting several days and involving animal sacrifices. A section of this ritual is called *abhiṣeka*, the ritual pouring of consecrated water on the body of

---

1 As I have already noted, the dates given should be taken with a pinch of salt. They are only approximations.

2 See Thapar 1961: 32; Scerrato in Carratelli and Garbini 1964: 23.

3 For the ritual of *abhiṣeka* of a deity in a temple setting, see Ferro-Luzzi 1981.

the king.[4] Is this what Ashoka had in mind? Seems unlikely, given the weak presence of Vedic ritual tradition within Magadha, the Maurya heartland,[5] and the aversion of Mauryan kings, especially Ashoka, to the sacrificial killing of animals.[6] The term probably refers to a rite that contained the ritual pouring of consecrated water on the king's head, a rite that ritually constituted the new royal status of the king. We do not know, however, the exact form of this rite or of its component parts.

The claim is often made, as we have already seen, that Ashoka was the 'Buddhist ruler' of India.[7] That Ashoka was the ruler of India who happened to be a Buddhist is closer to the truth. Further, we need to be careful about the use of the term 'India' to refer to the Mauryan imperial territory. If it even vaguely or implicitly refers to what is today the nation-state of India, then it is deeply anachronistic; during that period there was no sense of belonging to a politically united India. The only indication of a geographical notion of the Indian subcontinent that Ashoka had is found in his use of the term 'Jambudvipa' (rose apple continent) in Minor Rock Edict I. The term probably referred to the subcontinent as a geographical unit. As a matter of convenience, I will continue to use 'India' only to refer to the Indian subcontinent as a geographical entity within which existed diverse ethnic, linguistic and religious groups. We will investigate later what influence Ashoka's close connection to Buddhism may have had in the way he governed. But here, my focus is on Ashoka as a ruler: the manner of his personal rule, the state bureaucracy that permitted him to govern a large territory, the armed forces, economic management and the like.

---

4   See *Kātyāyana Śrautasūtra*, XV.1–10. The Brahmanical tradition also recognized that a man is constituted as 'king' (*rājā*) only through his ritual *abhiṣeka* or anointing: see Medhātithi's commentary on Manu 7.1; Vijñāneśvara on *Yājñavalkya Dharmaśāstra* 1.312 (introduction) and 2.1.

5   This has been demonstrated by Bronkhorst 2007.

6   See Chapter 9.

7   Irwin (1983: 247) expresses the common view that Ashoka was the 'first Buddhist ruler of a united India'. See Chapters 5 and 7.

TERRITORY AND POPULATION

What was the extent of Ashoka's empire? It would have been impossible
to answer this question had it not been for the presence of Ashoka's
edicts inscribed on stone. No other contemporary source provides any
information. The premise is that Ashoka would have had some authority
over the areas where his edicts were inscribed and displayed. Either he
had direct control over the region, or those who had control recognized
the authority of Ashoka and wanted to carry out his orders and wishes.
His style of governance through appointed officials that we will discuss
below also shows that he had direct control over much of his territory. His
stone inscriptions have been discovered in Kandahar (Afghanistan) in the
northwest, around the India–Nepal border in the north, in Gujarat in
the west, in Odisha in the east, and in Karnataka and Andhra Pradesh
in the south. That amounts to the entire Indian subcontinent, except
for the southernmost regions of Tamil Nadu and Kerala, and includes
what is today Pakistan and at least the eastern parts of Afghanistan.
Archaeological evidence points to a Mauryan presence in what is
present-day Bangladesh.[8] The issue, however, is how imperial control
was exercised over this vast area. One can draw lines from Ashoka's
capital Pataliputra to each of the edict sites. Did he exercise control over
each point on that line? That is hard to prove, and quite unlikely. As we
will see, in a decentralized state, you want to control what is important
from a strategic and economic point of view, but not everything and
everyone everywhere. That would have been unnecessary and expensive.
Nevertheless, Ashoka is right when in Rock Edict XIV he observes: 'My
territory is vast.'

His territory was, indeed, geographically vast. But what about
the population? Did he also rule over a vast population? Sources to
determine the demography of Ashoka's empire are almost non-existent.
There can only be broad-scale estimates, such as those proposed by the
demographer Tim Dyson and the historian Sumit Guha regarding the
size of populations of ancient India over long stretches of time. For the

---

8   This has been argued by the archaeologist Jean-François Salles (2012).

period 320–220 BCE, broadly coinciding with Ashoka's reign, Dyson gives an estimate ranging from a low of 15 million to a high of 30 million, while Guha gives an estimate of 20 million or less. Dyson confesses that these numbers are educated guesses.[9] The numbers look more or less right, when we consider that the total human population of the world around 200 BCE is estimated to have been around 150 million. Dyson also estimates that 'by around 200 BCE a third of the subcontinent's population may have lived outside the Ganges basin'.[10] If this is correct, then about two-thirds of the population—10–15 million—may have lived in the Ganges basin, which was the heartland of the Mauryan empire and at the time the most densely populated region of the Indian subcontinent.

Ashoka himself uses an interesting term—having the same form in both Sanskrit and Ashokan Prakrit—to refer to the territory of his empire: *vijita*. The term literally means 'conquered' but acquired the common meaning of a territory under imperial rule. He uses this term in its etymological sense to refer to his conquest of Kalinga in Rock Edict XIII given below. The term also points to the political history of such territories, which were, at least ideally, obtained through conquest. Ancient Indian texts, especially Kautilya's *Arthashastra*, often refer to a king using the Sanskrit term '*vijigīṣu*', 'person seeking conquest', a term etymologically related to *vijita* and to more common terms such as '*jaya*' and '*vijaya*' (victory). It also reveals the ancient Indian ideology of kingship: the martial quest for conquest and victory and an expansionist foreign policy define the very essence of a king. This conception of kingship, as I have noted, would have been familiar to Alexander. In his first decade of rule, Ashoka too fitted this mould, as did his father and grandfather. A pacifist king—such as the one advocated by the later

---

9   Dyson 2018: 263. In a personal communication, Professor Dyson notes: 'As I discuss in the text, I think that a reasonable "guesstimate" for the subcontinent's population at that time is 15–30 million. But this is just an educated guess drawing on the work of several other writers.' Guha (2001: 30) notes 'that the total population around 150 CE would not exceed 20 million, and might be substantially lower than that'.

10 Dyson 2018: 21. This estimate is based on C. McEvedy and R. Jones, *Atlas of World Population History* (Harmondsworth: Penguin Books, 1978).

Ashoka—would have been considered an oxymoron by political theorists of the time.

The four wheels around the Ashokan capital of Sarnath beneath the famous four lions—which have become the symbol of the modern Indian nation-state—symbolize the dual nature of Ashoka's reign. On the one hand, the wheel (*chakra*) in ancient Indian symbolism signified the wheel of a war chariot. It was a metonym for conquest and victory, and thus a material symbol of the ideal of the king as 'seeking conquest' espoused by Kautilya. It was, indeed, a fitting symbol for an emperor who ruled over much of the Indian subcontinent, an emperor who came as close to fulfilling the ideal of the *chakravartin*, 'the wheel-turner' or universal emperor, as any in Indian history. On the other hand, the Buddhist symbol-makers gave the image a new twist: the wheel that is turned is not that of the war chariot but of the Buddha's doctrine, the 'wheel of dharma', the *dharmachakra*. It was the wheel of dharma that the Buddha set rolling when he preached his first sermon at Sarnath, and it is fitting that Ashoka chose Sarnath to locate his famous and exquisite lion capital with its wheels. Are these the wheels of dharma or the wheels of the war chariot, or both? The ambivalence is telling and probably intended.

This ambivalence is present in Ashoka's expansionist policy that brought him into conflict with a region of north-eastern India called Kalinga, roughly the region of modern Odisha (Orissa). Ashoka does not tell us what Kalinga was—whether it was a kingdom, and, if so, who ruled it, or why he waged war against it and wanted to incorporate it into his empire. The Brahmanical tradition had a very low opinion of the region. A text written a couple of centuries after Ashoka cites a memorable verse: 'When someone travels to the land of the Kalingas, he commits a sin through his feet.'[11] In his long and self-revelatory writing about this war in Rock Edict XIII, Ashoka does not tell us why he attacked Kalinga, does not give a *casus belli*. Perhaps he did not think it necessary if he was following the normal expansionist ideology of kingship; or he may not have found it politically expedient to question his original decision.

---

11 *Baudhāyana Dharmasūtra* 1.2.15.

It is likely, however, that major trade routes to the south went through this region, and it is possible that the ruler of Kalinga did not want to submit to Ashoka's demands without a fight. Kalinga also had resources that were coveted by the Mauryas. The information provided by Kautilya in his *Arthashastra*, for example, indicates that Kalinga produced some of the best war elephants, an especially valuable commodity as one of the main components of an Indian army.[12] The reasons may have been many—the resources of Kalinga, the trade routes that traversed its territory, a recalcitrant king—but Ashoka wanted Kalinga badly.

The attack took place eight years after his royal anointing, that is, probably around October or November after the rainy season of 260 BCE (see Chapter 5 for the chronology). Ashoka launched his attack with overwhelming force, evidenced by the enormous number of casualties suffered by the people of Kalinga. The little fragments of information we have come from Ashoka's Rock Edict XIII, written sometime in or a little after 256 BCE. There, he reminisces about his Kalinga war and expresses regret at the loss of life it entailed and the immense suffering it inflicted on the population. This is where Ashoka says publicly, 'I am sorry,' holding before him a mirror of self-reflection. Regret and remorse are not emotions commonly associated with ancient monarchs and emperors. Between the war and the writing of the edict, Ashoka had become what today we would call a Buddhist and espoused an ethic of non-injury, not killing—ahimsa. So, the fragmentary information we get of his Kalinga war is through the lens of a remorseful king. Here is his long and detailed statement in Rock Edict XIII:

Eight years after the royal consecration of the Beloved of Gods, King Piyadasi, the Kalingas were conquered. People deported from there numbered 150,000; those killed there totaled 100,000; and almost that many died.[13] Thereafter, now that the Kalingas have been secured, the

---

12 *Arthashastra*, 2.2.15. For a detailed study of the war elephant and the forest ecology that supported wild elephants, see Trautmann 2015.

13 The meaning of the term '*bahutāvatake*' is not altogether clear. It could also mean: 'many times that number'. The meaning adopted is confirmed by the Greek translation of this edict in Kandahar II.

intense study of dharma, love of dharma, and instruction in dharma occupy the Beloved of Gods.

This is the regret that the Beloved of Gods has after conquering the Kalingas. For, conquering an unconquered land entails the killing, death, or deportation of people. That is deemed extremely painful and grievous by the Beloved of Gods. But this is deemed even more grievous by the Beloved of Gods, that Brahmins or Sramanas, or other Pasandas or those staying at home and dwelling there who are well cared for—among whom are established obedience to authority, obedience to mother and father, obedience to elders, and proper regard to friends, companions, associates, and relatives, and to slaves and servants, and firm devotion—that they endure there the injury, killing, or deportation of their loved ones. Even people who are well cared for and whose love is undiminished, when misfortune strikes their friends, companions, associates, and relatives, it causes injury to those very people. This is the common plight of all human beings, and it is deemed grievous by the Beloved of Gods.

There is no land, furthermore, except among the Greeks, where these classes—Brahmins and Sramanas—are not found. Yet even where they are not found, there is no land where human beings are not devoted to one Pasanda or another. Therefore, of the number of people who were killed, died, and were deported among the Kalingas—today even one hundredth or one thousandth part of that would be deemed grievous by the Beloved of Gods.

Here is the king publicly acknowledging the destruction caused by his war on Kalinga and expressing his regret and remorse. This public acknowledgement of remorse by a king for an act of violence against other human beings is, as Richard Salomon has remarked, unique in Indian epigraphic history. 'In fact,' he notes, 'after reading thousands of Indian inscriptions over some 35 years, I have yet to find a single comparable reference to the evils of war and virtues of peace and gentle persuasion.'[14]

---

14 Salomon 2007: 56.

Ashoka presents himself here as a king very different from the royal ideal advocated by Kautilya. Yet, if we read this confession closely, Ashoka never says that he wished he had never carried out the conquest of Kalinga. He expresses regret at the carnage but not at the conquest itself. He is not wedded to pacifism, as the rest of this inscription clearly points out. There he warns those who may have hostile intentions, especially the 'untamed' forest peoples called *āṭavika*, who always lived outside and independent of organized state structures, to be careful; if provoked he has sufficient power to crush them. He is reluctant to use force, but he does not abjure it either.[15] The following paragraph stitches together the first part of the edict dealing with the war and remorse, and the second part discussing conquest achieved through dharma, which he recommends to his sons and grandsons.

And further, should someone commit an offense today, if it can be forgiven the Beloved of God thinks he should be forgiven. And even the forest people living within the territory of the Beloved of Gods— he conciliates them also and persuades them to be favorably disposed. And he also tells them of the remorse, as also the power, of the Beloved of Gods, so that they may become contrite, and never engage in killing.[16] For, what the Beloved of Gods wishes for all creatures is this: freedom from injury, self-restraint, impartiality, and gentleness.

I think here Ashoka gives us a clue as to why he waged war against Kalinga: the authorities and/or the people of that region had 'committed an offense'. He does not tell what the offence was, but they did commit

---

15 Violence was integral to political power, not just in gaining and maintaining that power, but also in governance that is concomitant with political power. Justice and punishment go hand in hand. For a detailed and excellent survey of political violence and violence in the service of politics, see Upinder Singh 2017.

16 So here Ashoka is asking the forest people (*aṭavi*) to be like him—to be remorseful of past deeds and to keep to the path of ahimsa. Others have translated as 'and may not get killed', thus making this a statement about Ashoka's ability to kill the forest people if they do not behave. I think both grammatically and contextually this interpretation is less likely.

an offence against the state. Today, Ashoka tells his audience, he is prone to forgive such offences, with the caveat 'if it can be forgiven'. Back then, the implication is, he dealt with such offences harshly. His mind is elsewhere, however; he is seeking a different kind of conquest now, and to that theme he devotes the rest of his edict.

Internal security required Ashoka to deal with forest peoples,[17] and perhaps other elements within his territory deemed socially undesirable. Ancient Indian political theory viewed the suppression of thieves and highway robbers as the central obligation of a king. Most ancient texts on kingship defend the legitimacy of taxes by presenting them as payments for keeping homes and villages safe from thieves and robbers. Further, long-distance trade would have been impossible if trade routes were not secure. These texts present the stereotype of forest people as robbers and brigands.

Circling back to the Kalinga war, let us look at the numbers that Ashoka provides: 100,000 killed, almost as many dead as a result or in the aftermath of the war, and 150,000 taken captive and deported. Ashoka does not reveal how these people died, except that some were killed during the battle itself, while others died as a result of the war. Nor does he reveal who were killed, but the references to various innocent people who were affected shows that many of the dead were non-combatants. So, the total number of people in Kalinga directly affected by the war was over 350,000. What percentage of the Kalinga population did that constitute?

It is next to impossible to accurately estimate the population of Kalinga during the time of Ashoka. Sumit Guha gives an estimate of 975,000,[18] which may be on the high side. But, even if we come up with an exaggerated number of, say, 1 million, the dead alone would have constituted over 20 per cent of the population; and over 35 per cent if we

---

17 For discussion of forest dwellers in the Maurya period, see Parasher-Sen 1991, 2004.

18 Guha 2001: 30.

include those taken captive. Dyson,[19] however, warns us against taking the figures given by Ashoka literally; ancient kings generally inflated the number of people killed in their battles. We see a similar exaggeration in Rock Edict I, where Ashoka gives the number of animals killed for meat in years past: 'Formerly, in the kitchen of the Beloved of Gods, King Piyadasi, many hundreds of thousands of creatures were slaughtered every day to prepare stews.' It is difficult to take this number literally or to imagine so many animals being killed each day in his kitchen or abattoir. Ashoka here uses hyperbole as a rhetorical device, I think, to create revulsion in his audience about the enormous numbers of animals killed for meat in his palace before his conversion to the practise of ahimsa. In a similar manner, probably, Ashoka gives high numbers in round figures of those killed in the Kalinga war, because he wanted his readers to understand the magnitude of the tragedy his war caused. We should, I think, take these numbers seriously, though not literally. Nevertheless, even if we discount the exact figures given by Ashoka, the number of people killed and the fact that the dead included non-combatants would probably make Ashoka's war—by today's standards—a genocide.

That should not surprise us, however, for conquests of antiquity frequently entailed such genocidal wars, where not even women and children were spared. Robin Lane Fox notes the genocide committed by Alexander's troops in Multan after Alexander was grievously wounded: 'Macedonians were pouring in to avenge a grievance and ... they massacred the men of Multan, down to the last of the women and children.'[20] About the Roman destruction of Carthage in 146 BCE, the historian Ben Kiernan comments: 'Its policy of "extreme violence", the "annihilation of Carthage and most of its inhabitants", ruining "an entire

---

19 In a personal communication, Professor Dyson comments: 'About all I can say with reference to the specific issues that you raise is that I am always skeptical of numerical claims made by historical figures. In particular, in most cultures there is a tendency towards exaggeration when discussing military victories. And, of course, there is also great uncertainty about the size of the total Kalinga population.'

20 Fox 2004: 380.

culture", fits the modern legal definition of the 1948 United Nations Genocide Convention.'[21] As Kalinga and the conquests of Alexander show, Carthage was not the exception but the rule.

If the conquest of Kalinga was this bloody, we can be sure that the wars waged by Ashoka's father and grandfather to consolidate their power over much of India were equally gruesome. The difference is that Ashoka acknowledged it, regretted it and apologized for it. He was living in an era and an area where killing as such—not just killing other human beings but also any living being—was becoming morally unacceptable according to the teachings of newly emergent religions such as Buddhism and Jainism. Ashoka was a king with a conscience, and his conscience was moulded by a new ethic emerging precisely in the area where he grew up, in Magadha. So, the genocide of Kalinga reveals a king more complex than any in antiquity: a fierce warrior and brutal oppressor, but also a contrite penitent.

Ashoka was a penitent but not a pacifist. We saw traces of his willingness to use force in his message to the forest people within his territory. He sends a similar message to people living in the border regions outside his territory in his Separate Edict II:

It might occur to the frontier people outside my territorial jurisdiction: 'What are the king's intentions with respect to us?' This alone is my wish with respect to the frontier people—they should gain the conviction:

This is what the Beloved of Gods wishes: 'They should not fear me but have confidence in me. They will obtain happiness alone from me, not grief.'

They should also know this:

Beloved of Gods will forgive us what can be forgiven.

At my behest, they should practice dharma and gain this world and the next.

---

21 Ben Kiernan, 'The First Genocide: Carthage, 146 BC', *Diogenes* 203: 28. This study is part of the Genocide Studies Program at Yale University, https://gsp.yale.edu/sites/default/files/first_genocide.pdf; accessed 27 December 2021.

The question uppermost in the minds of these frontier people is what designs Ashoka has on their land. They may have heard of what he had perpetrated in Kalinga. Is the same fate in store for them? Ashoka wants to allay their fears—he is a new man now with stronger ethical principles. They should have faith in him, be confident that he will treat them well and procure happiness for them. But there is a sting in the tail. 'The king will forgive what can be forgiven.' Left unsaid is what will happen if these frontier people do things that in Ashoka's eyes cannot be forgiven.

Ashoka shows a sound knowledge of the peoples and polities lying outside the boundaries of his empire, a topic to which I will turn in the section on diplomacy. In Rock Edict II, he mentions five polities on his southern frontiers: Colas, Pandyas, Satiyaputras, Keralaputras and Tamraparnis, the last being Sri Lanka. Beyond the north-western frontier, he had strong personal connections to the Greek king Antiochus, and also mentions his neighbouring kings Tulamaya, Antekina, Maka and Alikasundale (Rock Edict XIII). And, in the same edict, he mentions ethnic groups located in the north-western and southern regions of his own empire: the Kambojas, the Nabhakas and Nabhapanktis, the Bhojas and Pitinikas, the Andhras and Paladas (for their geographical locations, see the Map).

Ashoka thus had a pretty good idea of the extent of his own territory and its boundaries, of the ethnically distinct groups living within his territory, and the peoples and kingdoms outside his empire. As we saw in Chapter 1, the 'Treaty of the Indus' and the independent Hellenistic kingdoms of West Asia may have provided a blueprint for Ashoka's own conception of an empire within borders 'as spatially limited units, as bounded territories with shared frontiers'.[22]

The exception to this territorially bound view of empire is Ashoka's dream of conquest through dharma and conquest of dharma, a victory of an idea rather than an army, a path he implores his sons and grandsons to follow.

---

22 Kosmin 2014: 32.

GOVERNANCE

Romila Thapar notes that 'the Mauryan state ushered in a new form of government, that of a centralized empire'.[23] She argues against those who wanted to claim that this empire was in fact a loose confederation. A close reading of Ashoka's inscriptional corpus shows that she is right, at least in terms of how the Mauryan rulers, and Ashoka in particular, viewed their authority and the structures of governance they constructed. The king's authority was absolute, and his writ extended to the farthest corners of the empire. That, at least, was the theory.

But how do you govern a vast, multi-ethnic and multilingual empire when you cannot make a phone call or send a text message, and the fastest mode of travel is on horseback? This was a problem faced by all ancient polities that sought to rule a large territory. The Mauryan empire was no exception. At some point, the territory becomes simply too large to be governed directly from the centre. The historian Gérard Fussman, in an important study of the structures of governance in the Mauryan empire, gives some eye-opening statistics about the time it would have taken for a message from the capital Pataliputra to reach various nerve centres of the empire and for a reply to be received.[24]

Based on the figures derived from the Mughal empire, Fussman estimates thirty days to travel from Pataliputra to Kandahar or to the southern outpost of Suvarnagiri—and that is an optimistic estimate, because the medieval Mughals had a much better communication network than the Mauryas did over a millennium and a half earlier. For a message to be sent and a reply to be received, therefore, may have required about two months. For cities within northern India, such as the important north-central city of Ujjain, travel times would have been shorter; it would still have taken several weeks. And all that is only during the months of the dry season. During the monsoon rains, a season that can last up to four months, travel would have been difficult at best and often impossible. Traversing swollen rivers, given that bridges were

---

23 Thapar 1961: 94.

24 Fussman 1987–88: 43–72; the original French version of this study was published in Fussman 1982.

unknown in ancient India, was difficult and dangerous. Some scholars have questioned Fussman's assessment, however, taking it to be overly conservative.[25] Nevertheless, the overall point of Fussman is well taken. It was difficult, if not impossible, to control a far-flung empire directly from the centre.

How can an empire function without speedy communications? The answer for the Mauryan empire, as for the Persian, was a strong central authority with a strong army, but with a decentralized bureaucracy. A large amount of independence in governance and in taking decisions and initiatives must have devolved to provincial governors and even to mid-level local bureaucrats and military officers. This is evidenced in several of Ashoka's inscriptions containing messages to senior and mid-level bureaucrats such as the mahamatras and rajukas.

The historian Upinder Singh observes a scholarly shift in the study of empire: 'The hypothesis of a highly centralized polity has made way for a more realistic and textured view of the Maurya empire.'[26] Scholars have suggested various models for conceptualizing this interesting combination of 'absolute authority' vested in the emperor and the de facto decentralization of the exercise of that authority.[27] Without getting into the weeds, it appears highly likely that governance under Ashoka was decentralized in many respects, with the emperor setting broad policy and reserving the right to intervene and to issue orders that had to be obeyed by all government agents. The language and tone of the inscriptional edicts make that abundantly clear. The view expressed by Gérard Fussman reflects by and large the historical reality of the exercise of imperial power:

> One can thus assume that, contrary to general opinion, the Mauryan Empire functioned according to the same rules as other Indian empires of comparable size (Gupta, Mughal and British), with a

25 Personal communication from Sumit Guha.
26 Upinder Singh 2012: 131. The decentralized administrative structure of the Mauryan empire has been argued most forcefully by Fussmann 1987–88.
27 See, for example, Stanley Tambiah's (1976) 'galactic polity'; Monica Smith's (2005) 'network model' discussed by Namita Sugandhi (2013).

central absolute power, personal, that is, dependent on the personal activity of the sovereign, relying on the army and on efficient officers; with a regional administration organized in a non-systematic fashion exercising royal authority, with more liberty the further away from the royal power and putting into practice the king's orders only when they fitted in with the local reality; with larger provinces directly administered by royal agents; with traditional local powers (tribes, cities, feudal kingdoms), which, in many areas (taxes and rents, codes of justice, customs, languages, culture and religious practices, etc.) continued to function as autonomous bodies under the more or less strict supervision of Imperial officials.[28]

Going beyond the theoretical models of governance in an ancient empire, there is limited yet important information about the governance structure and bureaucracy contained in Ashoka's own writings. His references to government officials are neither systematic nor comprehensive. Yet they give us some insight into how his government was organized—or at least how he envisaged the organization of the government structure. At the top of the bureaucratic hierarchy stands a category of official called the mahamatras. There were many of them—we do not know how many—and, like the modern category of 'minister', this term did not directly refer to specific roles or functions of the mahamatras, but rather to their status as the most senior officials in the bureaucracy. Below the level of mahamatra, Ashoka makes references to four kinds of officials: yuktas, rajukas, rastrikas and pradesikas. Given that in Rock Edict XIII Ashoka lists all except the rastrikas in that order, it seems reasonable to assume that the order indicates seniority in rank. The rastrikas are mentioned only once, in Minor Rock Edict II, and there the rajukas are told to issue orders to rastrikas. Ashoka speaks most frequently about the rajukas,

---

28 Fussman 1987–88: 71–72. The historian H.P. Ray (2008) notes the multiplicity of entities exerting power locally within the Maurya provinces: 'Rather than viewing the state as the sole center of control and authority, what is being visualized in this paper is a disaggregation of the model, with the state one of several nodes of power in society. Other nodes included merchants, landowners, and religious functionaries.'

who, he says, govern many hundreds of thousands of people and operate principally in the countryside (Pillar Edict VII).

Outside this barebone bureaucratic structure, there is also an administrative officer called the kumara. The word means 'prince' and clearly refers to a royal personage, a close relative of the king, although not necessarily the king's very own son. In Pillar Edict VII, for example, Ashoka makes a distinction between his 'boys', that is, his own sons, and 'other princes'. The kumaras ranked above the mahamatras, and, given that they were blood relatives of the king, they could be called viceroys. They acted in the name of the king.

The inscriptions mention several such princes—one located in Ujjain in today's Madhya Pradesh, another in a place called Tosali in Odisha, and one in Taxila in the northwest (Separate Edict I). An official identified as 'āryaputra' (literally: 'son of an Arya') at Suvarṇagiri in Andhra Pradesh was also possibly such a prince.[29] The functions of the princes are not spelled out, but Ashoka sends instructions to those at Ujjain, Tosali and Taxila. The prince at Suvarṇagiri, on the other hand, was asked to send instructions to the mahamatras of Isila. These point to broad areas of authority for the princes, and the title 'governor' that some scholars have attached to them seems appropriate. At Tosali the governor's office included both the prince and several mahamatras (given in the plural).

The mahamatras operated both at the central level in Pataliputra and in provincial centres. They are mentioned eleven times in the inscriptions. In Pillar Edict I, Ashoka refers to 'frontier mahamatras', who were probably in charge of border security and also dealt with peoples and polities in the neighbouring regions. In addition to those who were part of the normal governmental apparatus, we have two other kinds of specialized mahamatras: those in charge of dharma (dharma-mahamatra), referred to seven times, and those in charge of women, mentioned just once. It is clear that the mahamatras represented the highest level of state bureaucracy, apart from the emperor and the princes. What is less clear, however, is precisely what they did, and what their responsibilities were. It appears that those stationed in population centres outside the

---

29 Minor Rock Edict I, cover letter appended to the version at Brahmagiri.

capital were responsible for administering a large province, assisted by subordinate officers working under them. Thus, the two Separate Edicts are addressed to the mahamatras of two centres, Tosali and Samapa, with instructions as to how they should deal with the populations under their care. The mahamatras residing in Pataliputra probably provided the central administrative apparatus. At least some of them constituted the ministerial council, called the Parisad, to which disputed or controversial matters were brought. In Rock Edict VI, Ashoka instructs them to bring such matters to his attention immediately, even if they have to interrupt his other activities. Ashoka is here attempting to show his officials that he is a hands-on ruler always concerned about the welfare of his subjects. He distinguishes himself in this, as in other matters, from his predecessors.

> In times past, this practice did not exist: to bring up at any time the affairs that needed attention or related information. But this is what I have done.
>
> At all times—whether I am eating, in my inner chambers, in my private quarters, at the farm, in a vehicle, or in a park—everywhere informants should inform me about the people's affairs. And everywhere I myself attend to the affairs of the people.
>
> Whatever order I issue orally, furthermore, whether it relates to a donation or a proclamation, or else to an urgent matter that is assigned to the mahamatras—in connection with such a matter, if there is a dispute or deliberation in the Council, it should be reported to me immediately everywhere and at all times.
>
> Thus have I ordered.

Some mahamatras had specialized portfolios. This is most evident in those responsible for the propagation of dharma, appropriately called the dharma-mahamatras. In Rock Edict V, Ashoka announces that this class of officials did not exist prior to him. He created it in 255 BCE: 'Now, in times past dharma-mahamatras did not exist at all. But, thirteen years after my royal consecration, I established the dharma-mahamatras.' Likewise, in Rock Edict XII, he speaks of mahamatras supervising women. It is not totally clear who these women were but, given that the context is the inspection of religious groups called Pasanda (see Chapter 11), they may have been female members of these organizations, such as Buddhist nuns. There were other kinds of mahamatras with different roles, and Ashoka refers to some officers as 'other classes' in this edict.

An officer called nagaravyohalaka, who appears to have been a kind of city judicial officer, is mentioned in Separate Edict I: 'At the direction of the Beloved of Gods, the mahamatras of Tosali, who are the judicial officers of the city, are to be so instructed.' The syntax of the sentence without a copula between the two terms seems to suggest that these mahamatras are the judicial officers of the city, that is, the judicial functions were carried out by them. Here also Ashoka instructs judicial officers to carry out their duties even-handedly, just as he does in the case of the rajukas in the extract cited on the next page.

Of the other classes of state officials listed by Ashoka in Rock Edict III—yuktas, rajukas and pradesikas—we have most information about the rajukas. The first, the yukta, was probably an officer higher in rank than the rajuka.[30] Ashoka recalls the instructions he had sent twelve years after his royal consecration (256 BCE) to these three classes of officers: they were to tour the territory under their charge every five years. It is unclear whether this was a new initiative of Ashoka or whether he was simply adding a new task to an existing custom: he tells them to preach dharma in addition to their other assignments. At its conclusion, Ashoka instructs his Council to order the yuktas to make a record of the instructions: 'And the Ministerial Councils shall order the yuktas to register this—providing the rationale and keeping to the letter.'

Ashoka provides greater details about the rajukas in the long Pillar Edict IV written twenty-six years after his royal consecration, that is, in 242 BCE. The excerpt from this edict given on the next page shows that the rajukas exercised authority over a relatively large area, probably in rural districts, as the expression 'people of the countryside' (jānapada) used in the edict indicates. Ashoka says that they have been put in charge of

---

30 Kauṭilya's *Arthashastra* (2.8.23; 2.9.34) refers to an officer called yukta, and at 2.8.23 to an officer called upayukta, probably the deputy of a yukta.

'many hundreds of thousands' of people. That is a large population for a
mid-level bureaucrat, although this may be one more example of Ashokan
hyperbole. Besides their other tasks, the rajukas carried out judicial
functions. In legal proceedings and in imposing punishments, they had
independent authority, but Ashoka asks them to be impartial in exercising
their judicial powers. They had the authority to impose even the death
penalty, and Ashoka tells the rajukas to grant a stay of three days between
judgement and execution, allowing time for the convicted person's
relatives to help the convict to prepare himself for what awaits after
death.[31] This edict also highlights Ashoka's repeated public avowals that
all he cared for was the welfare and happiness of his subjects, an ethic and
mindset that he wished to inculcate in his bureaucrats. The independence
Ashoka gives to his rajukas, and *a fortiori* to his mahamatras, supports the
view of decentralized power within the empire, always subject, however,
to the final and absolute authority of the emperor.

> Within the population, my rajuka-officers take care of many hundreds
> of thousands of living beings. I have given them independent authority
> to grant rewards and to impose punishments, in order that rajuka-
> officers may carry out their tasks with confidence and without fear
> and bestow welfare and wellbeing on and grant favors to the people
> of the countryside. (Pillar Edict IV)

The edict continues, noting that the independence he has granted to the
rajukas is not limitless. They have to obey the emperor's orders and the
instructions of his personal emissaries. These officials are called simply
purusas, 'men', and they probably constituted a trusted core of imperial
representatives whose words should be taken as the emperor's own.
They may have been sent to the various administrative centres of the
empire with orders from the emperor. In this passage from Pillar Edict
IV, Ashoka tells the rajukas that they must obey his 'men' as well.

> The rajuka-officers must also submit to me. They will also submit to
> my personal emissaries who know my wishes. And these emissaries

---

31 On the issue of capital punishment under Ashoka, see Chapter 9.

will also exhort them, so that the rajuka-officers will be able to gratify me.

Just as one feels confident in entrusting one's child to a proficient nurse, knowing, 'She is a proficient nurse. She is able to take good care of my child,' so I have appointed the rajuka-officers for the welfare and wellbeing of the people of the countryside.

That the rajuka-officers, being fearless and confident, may carry out their tasks unperturbed—for this reason I have given them independent authority to grant rewards and to impose punishments. For this is what is to be desired: there should be impartiality in judicial proceedings and impartiality in imposing punishments.

There appears to be a subtext to what Ashoka is telling the rajukas here. Why is he compelled to say: 'The rajuka-officers must also submit to me. They will also submit to my personal emissaries who know my wishes'? What compelled him to write this letter? Did he receive information that some rajukas were going rogue and not respecting imperial instructions and requests? We have a similar instruction in Separate Edict I, where Ashoka speaks of his intention to send emissaries to make sure that officials in outlying districts carry out his instructions: 'And also for this purpose I will dispatch every five years a mahamatra who is neither harsh nor fierce, and who is gentle in his actions in order to find out whether they are acting according to my instructions.' I think Ashoka is trying to cajole the officers rather than castigate them, appealing to their noble impulses. They and Ashoka are embarked on a joint mission to further the welfare and happiness of the people who have been entrusted to their care. But the subtext is worrisome: trouble may have been brewing in some parts of the empire and Ashoka was becoming aware of it.

As he reflects on the demands of good governance, Ashoka invokes two long-standing tropes to define his relationship and obligations to his subjects, as well as to the officials responsible for running the government. One is the notion of debt, and the other is the relationship of father to child as the model for the relationship between king and subject.

Debt is a concept central to both commercial transactions and jurisprudence. The very first title of law in ancient Indian legal treatises is non-payment of debt; it was probably the main reason people went to court. Ancient Indian religious philosophy, furthermore, imagined human social and religious obligations as debts, transferring a legal concept into theological discourse. In the Vedas, a man is seen as being born with three debts: to gods, Vedic seers and ancestors. One discharges these debts by offering sacrifices, learning the Vedas and procreating children.[32] Such metaphoric use of debt may have become common in other areas of discourse as well. Ashoka uses debt to define the relationship between government officials and the king, and between the king and subjects. Ashoka's duties as king constitute the debt he owes to his subjects. He is required to discharge that debt, to be freed from that debt. But he can do that only through the help and cooperation of the officials running the state apparatus. And that is the debt these officials owe to the king. So, debt binds the king, his officers and the people into a large interdependent network. Ashoka uses this language first in Rock Edict VI:

> And whatever striving I have made, it is for this: that I may become freed from *my debt* to creatures, that I may procure wellbeing for them in this world, and that they may attain heaven in the next.

In both the Separate Edicts, Ashoka returns to this topic, urging his officials to help him discharge his debt to the people by discharging their own debt to him. In Separate Edict II he informs them:

> For this purpose, am I instructing you—that I may be freed of *my debt* through this, namely, by instructing you and by informing you of my wish, which is my firm resolution and unshakable pledge... After I have given you my instructions and informed you of my wish, I will have done my duty for the country. For you are up to this task: to inspire confidence in them, to procure welfare and wellbeing in this world and the next. Acting in this manner, moreover, you will attain heaven and be freed from *your debt* to me.

---

32 For a detailed discussion of this theology of debt, see Olivelle 1993: 46–53.

Separate Edict I focuses specifically on the debt state officials owe to the king:

Whoever among you looks at it the same way should tell each other:

Look, such and such are the instructions of the Beloved of Gods. Carrying them out fully yields great reward, while failure to carry them out fully brings great misfortune. For, by carrying them out improperly one gets neither heavenly favors nor royal favors.

The average performance of this task brings a double reward; how much more, then, when it is carried out to an exceptional degree! If you carry it out fully, however, you will attain heaven and you will be freed from *your debt* to me.

Ashoka presents himself as a model for his bureaucrats. He works incessantly and strenuously for the welfare of his people. He is the hands-on chief executive totally devoted to his duties at all times, during day or night. That was not the case with previous kings, he adds.

In times past, this practice did not exist: to bring up at any time the affairs that needed attention or related information. But this is what I have done.

At all times—whether I am eating, in my inner chambers, in my private quarters, at the farm, in a vehicle, or in a park—everywhere informants should inform me about the people's affairs. And everywhere I myself attend to the affairs of the people. (Rock Edict VI)

Beyond military power and governmental apparatus, there has to be something else, a particular glue, that binds the people of a country and gives them a sense of belonging. The 'imagined community' of the political scientist Benedict Anderson needs some raw material to be imagined. For the Mauryan empire it was perhaps provided by Ashoka. I will dwell on this later in the chapter, but what I want to highlight here is Ashoka's attempt to depict the empire as a family, with himself as its father, to naturalize a contingent political entity by conceiving it as a natural reality. This is not something novel in Indian history; many kings have presented themselves in that light. The Sanskrit term 'prajā', meaning both 'subject' and 'progeny', with its double entendre permits Ashoka to stress the familial bonds governing the relationship between the king and his subjects. Ashoka goes to great lengths to present himself as a father ever solicitous about the welfare of his children, the people of his empire.

In the edicts cited above regarding the debt he owes, we noted his fatherly concern for the welfare of his people. An emotionally charged instruction bearing on this is found in Pillar Edict IV. He is speaking to his rajuka officers:

> Just as one feels confident in entrusting one's child to a proficient nurse, knowing, 'She is a proficient nurse. She is able to take good care of my child,' so I have appointed the rajuka-officers for the welfare and wellbeing of the people of the countryside.

And in Separate Edict II he returns to the same theme:

> All men are my children. Now, what I desire for my children, namely, that they be provided with complete welfare and happiness in this world and the next, the same do I desire for all men.

Ashoka takes the trope of father one step further. The king is unable to look after all his children, that is, all his subjects, personally. So, he entrusts them to his officers, who are experienced and loving nurses, to look after his subject-children. The political relationship between state and people is now transformed into a familial relationship between father and children.

In addressing people living in polities bordering his empire, Ashoka attempts to present himself as a father figure to them as well. In Separate Edict II he instructs his officials to tell these people of the borderlands of the emperor's affection for them.

So, by doing this you must fulfil your task and reassure them, in order
that they [the frontier people] may gain the conviction:

The Beloved of Gods is just like a father to us. The Beloved of
Gods has compassion for us just as he has for himself. To the Beloved
of Gods, we are just like his own children.

The role of a benign ruler included the benevolence Ashoka exhibits
to the worst elements of society, those who have fallen foul of the law
and been imprisoned. The fate of prisoners is a recurring theme in the
inscriptions. Ashoka appears to brag a bit about his fatherly concern
for them, saying in Pillar Edict V: 'It has been twenty-six years after my
royal consecration, and during this period prisoners have been released
twenty-five times.' He seems to have followed the custom of releasing
prisoners on each anniversary of his royal consecration. He expresses his
concern about prisoners to his officials: they must keep to the middle way
and not be too harsh or too lenient. They must be impartial in carrying
out judicial responsibilities. Ashoka is here anticipating the modern legal
mantra: justice without fear or favour. But justice must be tempered by
mercy. In Rock Edict V, he instructs his dharma-mahamatras to look
after the interests of prisoners and to set free those who deserve freedom:

They are occupied with prisoners to render them support, to remove
obstacles, and to set them free when it is found: 'This one has to care
for family and children'; or 'This one has an obligation'; or 'This one
is elderly'.

Treating people fairly and mercifully appears to be a standard for
governance. Ashoka tells his sons and grandsons in Rock Edict XIII to
'find pleasure in kindness and lenient punishment'. In Separate Edict I, he
tells his judicial officers 'at all times see to it that the people of the city are
not shackled or subjected to torture without sufficient reason'.

Many questions, however, remain unanswered in these scattered
statements about the officials who constituted the formal structure of
governance. We are not even sure where officials such as the rajukas
were stationed: throughout the empire or only in some strategically

important areas? We know from Ashoka's warnings to forest people mentioned earlier that there were regions within his empire where groups lived independently and with little interaction with or supervision by the state bureaucracy. Another issue that we can raise without hope of resolution is what kind competition and rivalry there may have been among the senior levels of the bureaucracy, especially with the creation of the new bureaucratic layer of the dharma-mahamatras thirteen years after Ashoka's royal consecration (Rock Edict V). Their authority was wide: they could probe the affairs of almost everyone everywhere, even of the families of his own brothers and sisters. It is easy to imagine the kind of animosity this moral police may have created among the established mahamatras.

One central aspect of the state that is hardly mentioned in Ashoka's inscriptions is the economy. To manage his vast empire and to maintain a large bureaucracy and a standing army must have required a lot of money. It can be raised only from a strong economic base and an efficient system of taxation. Ancient Indian states depended broadly on three kinds of revenue streams: taxes and duties on agricultural produce and on merchandise bought and sold by traders, income from state monopolies such as mining and the manufacture of products such as salt and liquor, and income from state participation in agriculture and farming. Ancient Indian states can be described as mixed economies, where a large segment was left for private enterprise, while the state participated in and controlled some profitable areas of economic activities.[33] We get little information about any of this from Ashoka's inscriptions.

No mention is made even of revenue officers, without whom taxes could not have been collected. We can surmise that officers such as the rajukas and pradesikas were also revenue officers, although Ashoka never mentions these aspects of their duties. One of the few places where we get a glimpse of the taxation policy is in his inscription at Lumbini, the birthplace of the Buddha (Fig. 3). The inscription has been misunderstood

---

33 For the economic activities undertaken by the state, see Kautilya's *Arthashastra*, Book II and Trautmann 2012.

for a long time, but Harry Falk has finally provided a satisfactory interpretation:[34]

> The Beloved of Gods, King Piyadasi, twenty years after his royal consecration, came in person and paid reverence.
>
>   Saying 'Here was born the Buddha, the Sakya sage,' he had a stone fence constructed and a stone pillar erected.
>
>   Saying 'Here was born the Lord,' he made the village of Lumbini tax free and to have a one-eighth portion.[35]

The award of a tax-free status to the village of Lumbini presupposes that the state levied taxes on villages, probably on the produce from their farms and fields.

In two places—Rock Edicts VI and XII—Ashoka uses the term 'vaca' (or vacca), whose meaning is not altogether clear. In Rock Edict VI, Ashoka tells his officers to disturb him anywhere and at any time to bring news about his people. Among the places where he expects his officers to disturb him is vaca. The term here probably refers to a farm. If that is correct, then we have some evidence of farms operated by the royal household. The same term is used in Rock Edict XII with reference to a class of high officials (vacabhūmikā), who may have overseen royal farms. The existence of royal farms and agricultural land is supported by the later testimony of Kautilya, who devotes many chapters of his Arthashastra to this topic. Such farming and agricultural enterprises were a major source of income for the state.

Mining may have been another economic anchor.[36] We know from Greek sources that India had a reputation as a major source of gold. Fanciful tales of large ants digging up gold in India are narrated even by reputed Greek historians. In the Ashokan inscriptions themselves, there

---

34 Falk 2012: 204–16.

35 Falk has argued that the 'one-eighth portion' refers to the remains of the Buddha interred in the Stupa at Lumbini.

36 For a study of ancient Indian mining and state control of it, see Olivelle 2012a.

is mention of a major government centre in the south called Suvarṇagiri, 'gold mountain', with its own mahamatra.[37]

Sources also mention various kinds of forests—elephant forests, hunting forests, forests for produce such as timber, and even for recreation—maintained by the king. These also provided income to the state, as well as ecological benefits to the land.[38] Ashoka mentions elephant forests and fishery preserves in Pillar Edict V. We could reasonably suppose that there were similar economically productive preserves targeted at various significant animals, as well as trees for fruit and timber.

The construction and maintenance of a road network are essential for the state, especially for one as large as Ashoka's. His inscriptions do not deal with road construction, but one little detail does give some hints. In Pillar Edict VII written twenty-seven years after his royal consecration, Ashoka, an old man now, looks back recalling all the good things he has done. They include the planting of banyan and mango trees along the roads to offer shade to men and animals. He also had wells dug at intervals of 8 *krośas* (about 28 kilometres), as well as rest houses and sheds where water was available for the benefit of travelling men and animals. These initiatives assume that his administration was also taking care of road maintenance and providing security to travellers. Megasthenes, the envoy of Seleucus to Chandragupta, notes that officials were expected to 'build roads and place pillars every ten stades [about 1,850 metres], showing the turnoffs and distances', and mentions a Royal Road extending from the capital to the western edge of India.[39]

Ashoka's vocabulary draws an interesting parallel between his dedication to his Buddhist faith and to the welfare and happiness of his subjects. As we will see in Chapter 5, Ashoka proclaims his newfound Buddhist faith in Minor Rock Edict I. Note the repeated use there of the term 'strive', my translation of a term, '*pakaṃte*', which is related to the parallel term '*palakaṃte*'—Sanskrit: *prakramate* and *parākramate*.[40]

---

37 The preamble to Minor Rock Edict I of Brahmagiri and Siddhapura.

38 See Trautmann 2015; Olivelle 2016.

39 See Kosmin 2014: 168.

40 In Minor Rock Edict I, most have the form *pakaṃte*, while Sahasram in Bihar has derivatives from *parā√kram*. The latter is the preferred form in the Major

It has been over two and a half years since I have been an Upasaka. But for one year I did not *strive* vigorously. It was over a year ago, however, that I approached the Sangha and began to *strive* vigorously.

But during that time men in Jambudvipa,[41] who were unmingled with gods, were made to mingle with them. For that is the fruit of *striving*. This can be achieved not only by eminent people, but even lowly people if they *strive* are indeed able to attain even the immense heaven.

This promulgation has been promulgated for the following purpose—so that both the lowly and the eminent may *strive*, that the frontier people also may come to know it, and that this *striving* may endure for a long time.

Ashoka uses the same term in Rock Edict X to describe his effort at securing happiness after death. He recommends it to all his people, with the interesting side comment that such striving is more difficult for people of high standing than for the lowly:

Whatever the Beloved of Gods, King Piyadasi, *strives* to do, however, all that is solely for the sake of the hereafter, so that everyone would have few hazards. But this is the hazard: lack of merit.

This is difficult to do, however, for either a low-class person or a high-class person without utmost *striving*, giving up everything. But between them, it is clearly more difficult to do for a high-class person.

So, it is significant that in Rock Edict VI, he uses the same term to describe his executive functions, his efforts on behalf of his people, and his expectations with respect to his heirs. The use of the same term draws an interesting parallel between his efforts to tread the Buddhist path and his efforts to work ceaselessly and strenuously for the welfare of his people.

Rock Edicts dealing with Ashoka's governmental work.

41 Literally, 'island (or continent) of the rose apple'. The appellation generally refers to the land mass of the Indian subcontinent.

And whatever *striving* I have made, it is for this: that I may become freed from my debt to creatures, that I may procure wellbeing for them in this world, and that they may attain heaven in the next.

Now, this writing on dharma has been inscribed for the following purpose: that it may endure for a long time, that my sons and grandsons may *strive* for the welfare of the whole world. But this is difficult to accomplish without utmost *striving.*

In the same edict, he uses a different word with a similar meaning of exerting oneself strenuously.[42]

For, I am never complacent in *exerting* myself and in carrying the affairs to a conclusion. For, I consider the welfare of all the people as my responsibility. The root of that, again, is *exertion* and carrying the affairs to a conclusion. For there is no task more important than working for the welfare of the whole world.

Ashoka recognizes the requirement of personal integrity of his officials as the bedrock for a successful and compassionate government. He is most explicit in this regard in Separate Edict I in the context of impartiality in judicial proceedings. One cannot be impartial without cultivating personal virtues. Ashoka tells his officials:

… you must aspire: 'We will keep to the middle way.' One fails to act in this manner due to these proclivities: envy, quick temper, cruelty, haste, lack of zeal, laziness, and lethargy. So, you must aspire: 'May these proclivities not develop in us.' The root of all this is being always free of quick temper and haste.

In the final analysis, Ashoka returns to his favourite topic, dharma. It is the love of dharma, acting in accordance with dharma, that makes for successful governance. That is the central message Ashoka delivers to his bureaucracy in Pillar Edict I:

---

42 The term is '*uṭhāna*' (Sanskrit: *utthāna*), with the meaning of rising up, exertion, toil.

What pertains to this world and the next is difficult to procure except through utmost love of dharma, through utmost circumspection, through utmost obedience, through utmost fear, and through utmost exertion. But, indeed, through my instruction this concern for dharma and love of dharma have increased day by day, and they will continue to increase. And my personal emissaries also—the high-ranking, the low-ranking, and the mid-ranking—conform to it and procure it, and they are able to inspire the wavering. So also do the frontier mahamatras, for this is the directive—protecting according to dharma, governing according to dharma, bestowing wellbeing according to dharma, and guarding according to dharma.

THE IMAGINED COMMUNITY

The concept of an 'imagined community' was originally developed in the context of modern nation-states by the political scientist Benedict Anderson.[43] The state needed citizens to have a common identity and belonging. Although ancient societies are far removed from modern nation-states, this may still be a useful category that could provide a lens to investigate an ancient state such as Ashoka's, especially within the context of his efforts to forge a common moral identity based on dharma for his subjects, something I will deal with in Chapter 13. The challenges to any such enterprise are obvious. People living within Ashoka's territory did not even have a map of the empire that would give them a visual representation of it. How would a person living in Karnataka know about his fellow 'citizens' in Kashmir or Bengal? There was not even a single name for what we know today as the Mauryan state. The name *Bharata* used in some Brahmanical sources was probably not part of common linguistic usage, and the term 'Jambudvipa' used by Ashoka himself referred not to a polity but to a landmass within an imagined cosmography.

Although it is difficult to get into someone else's mind and read his intentions, especially someone who lived over two millennia ago, my

---

43 The concept was developed in his book *Imagined Communities: Reflections on the Origin and Spread of Nationalism* (London: Verso, 1983).

own view is that Ashoka desired to provide a common identity to the people he ruled and endeavoured to achieve it, irrespective of whether he succeeded or not. Like many ancient rulers, as we have seen, Ashoka used the model of family to articulate his relationship to his subjects. He was the father, and they were his children. To a degree, the articulation of this relationship 'naturalizes' the artificial and contingent nature of a political entity such as an empire. Ashoka, however, attempted something more than that, to transform a population into a 'people'.

There is no consensus as to whether Ashoka invented the script he used, called Brahmi today, but, as I will discuss in the next chapter, he undoubtedly made it the common script of his empire, except for the far northwest, where he continued to use Kharosthi, a script that had been in use there for some time. For the first time in Indian history, people across most of the subcontinent could, if they were literate, read messages written in the same script—much like the Latin script across medieval Europe. The success of Ashoka's imperial script, in spite of the demise of his empire, is evident: all subsequent Indian scripts—including those of some Southeast Asian countries—are derived from it.

Reading means nothing if you cannot understand the language. Ashoka created a common language as well, what we today call Ashokan Prakrit, in which all his inscriptions are written. This was clearly not the vernacular of most regions of the empire, especially in the far south where a variety of Dravidian languages must have been spoken. In some of the northern regions, various forms of Prakrit may have been the vernacular, but it is possible that these forms were to some degree mutually understandable. Such vernacular variants are visible even within Ashoka's inscriptional corpus. What Ashoka did with his inscriptional language was to create a Koine, a lingua franca, that was comprehensible across the various vernaculars at least by the imperial officers and the literate classes. The standardization of language and script across most of the empire was a central part of a broader imperial ideology.

The upshot of all this is that Ashoka helped spread literacy across the country, at least among a segment of the population. If there was no literacy and if the language of the inscriptions was not comprehensible, then Ashoka's instructions that his inscriptions should be read aloud on specific liturgical days would have made little sense. Who would read them? Who would understand them? He does not ask the officials to explain or interpret them—although some such commentarial expositions probably took place—but to read them out aloud. These three innovations—common script, common language, and literacy—would have given a strong foundation to the new imagined community that Ashoka was trying to build.

Script, language and literacy provide the tools for building a community, but they are not the building itself. There must be something more, a stronger glue, that binds the community imaginatively. How, then, can we theorize this work of Ashoka—both his literary corpus discussed in Chapter 3 and his untiring efforts to convert his subjects to the practise of dharma, as well as the bureaucratic reorganization to achieve that objective discussed in Chapter 10—spanning over a quarter of a century? I suggest below that the category of 'civil religion' may be a useful analytical tool to theorize Ashoka's activities, especially his efforts at creating a moral population devoted to dharma. I will turn to this issue in Chapter 13. The civil religion of dharma, I argue, gave a common religious and moral language—to parallel the common script and language—for the people of Ashoka's empire to communicate with each other and to create a sense of belonging to the same moral empire. This is the 'dharma community' Ashoka sought to build.

DIPLOMACY

Ashoka was fully aware, as we have already seen, that there were countries and rulers bordering his own empire. According to the general principles of ancient Indian political theory, these countries were considered enemy territories. Given the opportunity, they would have been prime targets for conquest either through diplomatic strategy or by military conquest, as we saw in his Kalinga war. The post-Kalinga Ashoka, however, plots a different course.

He takes special note of these foreign countries in several of his inscriptions, referring to them interestingly as *avijita*, literally 'unconquered' lands at the borders, in contrast to his own imperial territory which, as we have seen, he refers to as *vijita*, 'conquered'. These foreign lands are, however, mentioned not in the context of conquest or security, but in the context of Ashoka's various diplomatic and missionary activities. In these statements, we get an inkling of Ashoka's foreign policy and perhaps an inchoate theory of international relations. We also saw above that the independent Hellenistic kingdoms of West Asia provided a blueprint for Ashoka's own conception of an empire within settled borders.

In Rock Edict II, Ashoka refers to some of these frontier lands by name: the Tamil regions of Cola and Pandya, the Satiyaputras (probably a little north of Tamil Nadu), Kerala and Tamraparni or Sri Lanka. These are all on the southern borders of his empire. He then turns to the lands ruled by the Hellenistic king Antiochus, probably Antiochus II, the grandson of Seleucus, and by kings who are Antiochus's neighbours—all these are beyond his north-western borders. We notice here an interesting difference. Ashoka refers to his southern neighbours anonymously using ethnic or geographical names, but in the case of the western Hellenistic regions, he refers to the kings by name. The same pattern occurs in Rock Edict XIII, where besides Antiochus, he mentions four other kings: Tulamaya, Antikini, Maka and Alikasundara. These have been identified as Ptolemy II Philadelphus of Egypt (285–247 BCE), Antigonus Gonatas of Macedonia (276–239 BCE), Magas of Cyrene (death dated to between 258 and 250 BCE), and the last either Alexander of Corinth (252–244 BCE) or Alexander of Epirus (272–255 BCE).[44] Ashoka places Antiochus at a distance of 600 *yojanas*. Acknowledging the ambiguity of the actual length of the ancient Indian measure *yojana* in a given context and taking *yojana* as 7.2 kilometres, we can estimate that Antiochus was at a distance of about 4,320 kilometres, which is close to the actual distance between Pataliputra (Patna) in India and Antioch (Antakya) in Turkey.[45] Did Ashoka know the distance because he was in

44 See Thapar 1961: 41. Karttunen 1989: 100, 1997: 264; Kosmin 2014: 57.

45 The actual distance of a *yojana* in ancient India is ambiguous. Basham (1967: 506) remarks: 'It is therefore clear that there were at least two yojanas, and the distances as given in texts are thus unreliable. It would seem that for practical purposes the shorter *yojana* was more often used than the longer,

diplomatic contact with Antiochus, who may also have been related to him by marriage?

Diplomatic connections with Hellenistic kings of the Middle East were fostered by Ashoka's father, Bindusara, and by his grandfather, Chandragupta, following the Treaty of the Indus. I have already made reference to ambassadors sent by Seleucus to Chandragupta at Pataliputra, and by Bindusara to Antiochus. There was probably also a Greek presence in Pataliputra, as we have noted, and Ashoka may have grown up in a cosmopolitan household. Paul Kosmin comments on the development of an 'international order' and of 'peer states with semiformalized procedures of interaction' in the Hellenistic west, so that regular diplomatic contacts may have become the norm.[46] The Maurya rulers also were part of this 'international order' and may have considered themselves peers of those Hellenistic rulers. No such recognition was given—at least by Ashoka—to the rulers of his southern border territories.

It is quite likely, then, that Ashoka, following in the footsteps of his father and grandfather, established diplomatic relations not only with the Hellenistic kings in the west, but probably also with the rulers of the southern states outside his empire, what is today Tamil Nadu, Kerala and Sri Lanka. None of these diplomatic initiatives, however, are recorded in Ashoka's own inscriptions, which are focused on the propagation of dharma. This singular ancient Indian trait of ignoring its neighbours is noted by Romila Thapar:

> Despite the proximity of the Hellenistic Greeks there is little that Indian sources have to say about them. If the Maurya sent ambassadors to the courts of the Seleucids, Ptolemies, and Macedonians there are no ambassadors journals; nor are there any records of enterprising merchants who may have travelled to and traded at the markets of Antioch and Alexandria. There is a curious lack of interest in exterior

---

especially in earlier times.' The shorter distance Basham alludes to is 7.2 kilometres. Kosmin (2014: 57) takes 600 as between 4,800 and 6,000 miles, which is probably too high.

46 Kosmin 2014: 31–32.

landscapes of other regions which pervades the Indian ethos of earlier times.[47]

There is no Indian Megasthenes.

Ashoka does note, however, that he sent envoys to the rulers of these neighbouring countries to propagate dharma internationally. Significantly, the one place his diplomatic efforts feature prominently is Rock Edict XIII, which deals with his remorse at the carnage caused by his disastrous Kalinga war. Ashoka begins the edict with the bland statement: 'Eight years after the royal consecration of the Beloved of the Gods, King Piyadasi, the Kalingas were conquered.' He picks up on the word 'conquered' (*vijita*) in his discussion of diplomacy: 'This, however, is deemed the foremost conquest by the Beloved of Gods, namely, conquest through dharma.' The conquest he wants to achieve is not the usual armed victory, but the moral victory achieved through the acceptance of the moral code of dharma. Ashoka claims to have won this conquest among the neighbouring countries to the west and the south.

I will deal with this dharma-diplomacy in greater detail later in Chapter 10, but here I want to highlight a few aspects of these missions that go beyond simply preaching dharma. As part of his efforts to propagate dharma both in his own territory and, especially, in border lands, Ashoka engaged in what today we would call foreign aid. In the case of Ashoka, it consisted principally of providing medical material and know-how. He speaks of these medical missions in Rock Edit II:

> Everywhere—in the territory of the Beloved of Gods, King Piyadasi, as well as in those at the frontiers, namely, Codas, Pandyas, Satiyaputras, Keralaputras, Tamraparnis, the Greek king named Antiochus, and other kings who are that Antiochus's neighbors—everywhere the Beloved of Gods, King Piyadasi, has established two kinds of medical services: medical services for humans and medical services for domestic animals.

---

47 Thapar 1987: 32.

Wherever medicinal herbs beneficial to humans and domestic animals were not found, he had them brought in and planted everywhere. Likewise, wherever root vegetables and fruit trees were not found, he had them brought in and planted everywhere.

Along roads he had trees planted and wells dug for the benefit of domestic animals and human beings.

Foreign aid in the service of diplomacy is well known even in modern times. Christian missionaries around the world did not go empty-handed. They also provided two principal kinds of services: medical and educational. Ashoka's diplomatic and missionary activities, thus, fall into a familiar paradigm. Pre-dating modern missions by over two millennia, however, he was the pioneer in this regard.

But why did Ashoka single out medicine as an area where he could provide aid and exert influence? Did these countries lack medical knowledge and material? Did he think that he had better doctors and better medicines than others? It is instructive in this regard to look at the early history of Indian medicine, which later developed into the system of Ayurveda. Scholarship has thrown some light on that early history and its close association with the ascetic traditions, particularly Buddhism, in the region of Magadha, Ashoka's birthplace. The historian of medicine Kenneth Zysk makes the case succinctly:

A close scrutiny of the sources from the ninth century B.C.E. to the beginning of the common era reveals that medical practitioners were denigrated by the brāhmaṇic hierarchy and excluded from orthodox ritual cults because of their pollution from contact with impure people. Finding acceptance among the communities of heterodox ascetic renunciants and mendicants who did not censure their philosophies, practices, and associations, these healers, like the knowledge-seeking ascetics, wandered the countryside performing cures and acquiring new medicines, treatments, and medical information, and eventually became indistinguishable from the ascetics with whom they were in close contact. A vast storehouse of medical knowledge soon developed among these wandering physicians, who, unhindered by brāhmaṇic strictures and taboos, began to conceive an empirically and rationally based medical epistemology with which to codify and systematize this body of efficacious medical information ... Portions of the repository of medical lore were codified in early monastic rules, thereby giving rise to a Buddhist monastic medical tradition.[48]

The development of an empirical medical science and practice within Buddhism and in the heartland of the Mauryan empire may have been a source of pride for Ashoka. Possibly, he received information about the lack of such practical medical expertise both in the outlying regions of his empire and in neighbouring countries. These regions may have been receptive to new forms of medicine and medical technology. If so, we can understand why Ashoka may have engaged in medical diplomacy.

The term 'cikisā' (Sanskrit: cikitsā) in Ashoka's Rock Edict II, a term I have translated as 'medical service', has a spectrum of meanings, including medical treatment, medical practice and medical science. The related term 'cikitsaka' is used frequently in early literature to refer to doctors, both for humans and for animals (veterinarians).[49] Ashoka's own use of cikisā probably encompasses all these dimensions of the term. He probably sent medical practitioners along with their medical knowledge and the plants and herbs needed for the preparation of medicines. We can think of them as medical diplomats, working side by side with their political colleagues to further Ashoka's dharma mission.

SOCIETY

One thing that can be said with certainty about the society—perhaps societies—that comprised Ashoka's vast empire, stretching from Afghanistan to Bangladesh, from Nepal to Karnataka, is that it was diverse. It contained great ethnic, linguistic, cultural, religious, culinary and sartorial diversity. Ashoka's challenge was to mould that diversity

---

48 Kenneth Zysk 1991: 5–6. For an examination of this issue within the context of Magadha, see Bronkhorst 2007: 56–60.

49 For a detailed discussion of early Indian medical practitioners, see Olivelle 2017.

into a single political family, into an imagined community. I want here
to discuss the social structures and roles that existed in Ashokan society,
structures and roles that may have been different in different parts of his
empire.

First, we must acknowledge that in writing his edicts it was not
Ashoka's intention to describe his society for posterity. His writing was
directed at his officials and subjects, and his focus was primarily dharma.
His references to society and social structures are in the form of *obiter
dicta*. We have to read between the lines, to tease out implicit messages,
and especially to listen to the silences. In reading texts, whether on paper
or on stone, we must not simply read the lines of a text, lines that the
author wanted us to read. We must *read between the lines,* read those absent
and implied lines that the author did not want us to read. In them may
lie the most interesting things that a text has to tell us, and also the most
important. We must also learn to read the *silences*—to what Ashoka does
not say. Silences often speak volumes, a topic I will return to repeatedly
in the following pages.

Ashoka reveals that he was aware of the social and religious makeup
of various countries. In Rock Edict XIII, for example, he says that there
is no land where the two classes of religious people—Brahmins and
Sramanas—are absent, but quickly adds an exception. They are not found
in the Greek kingdoms beyond his north-western border. He notes,
however: 'Yet even where they are not found'—presumably in the Greek
territories—'there is no land where human beings are not devoted to one
Pasanda or another.' So, Pasandas, discussed in Chapter 11, are found
even among the Greeks. Here, Ashoka is making a broad-brush statement
about a marked difference in the religions and religious organizations
between his own country and the countries of West Asia.

Moving beyond the religious, however, the pickings are meagre. As I
will discuss in greater detail in Chapter 9, the social groups encompassed
by his notion of dharma are mostly familial or broadly within the family
orbit. These include persons superior to the individual who is the target
of Ashoka's instruction on dharma: mother, father and elders; persons
broadly at the same level: relatives, friends, acquaintances and associates;

religious persons: Brahmins and Sramanas; and inferiors: slaves and servants. This is an interesting social circle and many of those included are unremarkable.

Two categories, however, throw some light on Ashokan society: slaves and servants. The terms used here, in Sanskrit '*dāsa*' and '*bhṛtaka*', point to two servile classes. The latter refers to workers who were paid for their services, but were technically free individuals, although it is impossible to say how truly free they were. Could they leave one master and sell their services to another? Or were they indentured? Slaves, on the other hand, were owned by the individuals who are the target of Ashoka's dharma instructions. Slavery was thus a legally recognized and socially sanctioned institution in Ashokan society, as it was in many other ancient societies. It carried no moral opprobrium, even for Ashoka, who presented himself as a paragon of virtue and moral rectitude. Later Sanskrit legal texts present complex categories of slaves, but one stands out with respect to Ashoka: people captured in war and reduced to slavery. Ashoka in Rock Edict XIII dealing with the Kalinga war lists among the enormous number of war casualties the 150,000 people who were 'carried away'. The word used is '*apavaha*' (Sanskrit: *apavāha*), which has the connotation of not simply deportation, as often translated, but of carrying away by someone, clearly pointing to people being in some way enslaved. These two classes of people probably formed part of the household of the person owning or employing them. They were housed, clothed and fed by the householder. The servants, thus, were not simply self-employed workers who went home in the evening. The legal treatise of Apastamba, belonging roughly to the same period as Ashoka, points out the obligation to feed slaves and servants, using the term '*karmakara*', 'worker': 'If he wants, he may deprive himself, his wife, or his son, but never a slave or worker.'[50]

The picture we get from Ashoka's writings is that his empire was ethnically quite diverse. These ethnic groups were identifiable demographically and had ethnic names. Ashoka mentions nine such groups: Kambojas, Gandharas, Ristikas and Nabhapanktis in the

---

50 *Āpastamba Dharmasūtra* 2.9.11.

northwest; Paladas, Bhojas, Andhras, Kalingas and Pitinikas in the Deccan (see the Map). Unfortunately, he does not provide any information about their cultures, languages and ways of life.

The most instructive aspect of Ashoka's statements about society, however, is what he does not say. His silence says a great deal, especially with respect to ancient Indian social structures. For example, he makes no mention of the social divisions and roles we have been trained to assume existed in ancient India. The picture of ancient Indian social organization given in learned books and popular imagination is the same. It is presented by the historian Gavin Flood in an introductory book on Hinduism: 'Vedic society ... was divided into four classes (*varṇas*), the Brahmans, the Nobles or Warriors (*rājanya, kṣatriya*), the Commoners (*vaiśya*) and Serfs (*śūdra*).'[51] Similar portrayals are found in most textbooks on ancient Indian history, culture and religion. If such a fourfold hierarchical structure existed in Ashoka's India, or if individuals during Ashoka's time identified themselves according to this social classification, Ashoka seems either not to have been aware of it or not to have thought it to be significant. The very term '*varna*' or any of the names of the three *varnas*, Kshatriya, Vaisya and Sudra, are completely absent in Ashoka's vocabulary. His extensive discussion of social relationships in the context of the practise of dharma takes no account of the *varna* system. The only member of that system mentioned by Ashoka is the Brahmin, but he is mentioned in the context of religious organizations called Pasandas and not as a social and demographic group.[52] Further, Brahmins are always contrasted not to the other three *varnas*, but to wandering ascetics or Sramanas, with whom they form what Ashoka regarded as the broad category of religious professionals. If the *varna* system was internalized by the population or the ruling elite, or if it was a way for people to think about social roles and hierarchies, then it would have been natural for Ashoka, at least sometimes, to pair Brahmin with the other three *varnas*,

---

51 Gavin Flood, *Introduction to Hinduism* (Cambridge: Cambridge University Press, 1996), p. 58.

52 For a study of what 'Brahmin' may have meant to Ashoka and perhaps to people living in Magadha, see Lubin 2013.

something he never does. It is *always* the Sramana who is paired with the Brahmin.

What are we to make of it? Simple silence, the absence of any reference, cannot by itself prove that the institution of *varna* did not exist during the time of Ashoka. Yet, we should begin to question whether the sources that present this fourfold social division, sources that are the basis for contemporary textbook descriptions of ancient Indian society, are reliable. They are, for the most part, authored by Brahmins, who have historically been placed at the summit of this fourfold hierarchical structure. Are they presenting an ideology garbed in the clothes of sociology? Is the *varna* system aspirational and prescriptive rather than descriptive? Ashoka's silence, I think, is quite eloquent with respect to the historicity of the *varna* system.

It is not just Ashoka who is silent on this point. As the historian Johannes Bronkhorst has observed, most non-Sanskrit inscriptions before the second century of the Common Era are also silent on the *varna* system:

> The brahmanical vision of society is largely absent in South Asian inscriptions that are *not* in Sanskrit and whose makers or instigators have *no* association with Brahmanism. It is absent from the inscriptions of Aśoka. They refer to none of the four *varnas* except the Brahmins, nor to the system as a whole. The same is true of the early Tamil inscriptions.[53]

Another significant topic relating to Ashoka and his view of society is the role of women and issues relating to gender. He never addresses women directly. His edicts are addressed to government officials, who, we must assume, are men, and to the population in general. He refers to one of his queens in the so-called Queen's Edict, but it deals with a simple matter of bookkeeping. Given the fact that his queen makes donations on her own, and that in imperial record-keeping the expenses are charged to that queen, it is reasonable to assume that she had money and resources over which she had control. He refers to his sisters, along

---

53 Bronkhorst 2011: 64 (original italics).

with his brothers, in Rock Edict V in the context of the duties of the dharma-mahamatras. The most common reference to women, however, is in their role as mothers. A recurring element of Ashoka's definition of dharma is obedience to mother and father, and they are always listed in that order, the mother coming first. A third reference involves Buddhist nuns, the *bhikkuni*, a topic I will discuss in Chapter 6. Finally, Ashoka expresses a stereotypical view of women in Rock Edict IX. He deals there with auspicious ceremonies called *mangala* that people perform on various occasions such as weddings and births (discussed in Chapter 11). Ashoka associates many of these folk practices with women and calls such ceremonies trivial and meaningless.

> People perform auspicious rites of diverse kinds—during an illness, at the marriage of a son or daughter, at the birth of a child, when setting out on a journey. On these and other similar occasions, people perform numerous auspicious rites. At such times, however, womenfolk perform many, diverse, trifling, and useless auspicious rites.

It is clear, if clarity is needed, that the society over which Ashoka ruled was deeply patriarchal. It explains the relative invisibility of women in Ashoka's writings, revealing a society in which women played two principal roles, those of wife and mother. But the presence of independent and unmarried women, represented by Buddhist nuns, who organized themselves into self-sufficient groups outside of patriarchal control, opens the window into another side of women and their roles and aspirations during this period, a woman-centred standpoint that is not found in any other parallel society of the period.

There is one silence, nonetheless, that is puzzling. Ashoka's conception of dharma, as we will see in Chapter 9, is built around the relationships surrounding a person, most likely a man. Ashoka lists these varied relationships, but he omits one that is central: wife. She does not enter the picture. Ashoka does not define how to properly cultivate this husband–wife relationship. This is one more puzzle that Ashoka has left behind.

3

Writer

'MY TERRITORY IS VAST, AND I HAVE WRITTEN A LOT. AND I WILL always have still more written,' says Ashoka in Rock Edict XIV, which is a coda to the anthology of Rock Edicts. Whether he intended it or not, a prominent identity that Ashoka has bequeathed to posterity is that of writer, especially a writer on stone.[1] Reading his writings, I get the feeling that Ashoka enjoyed being a writer. He probably thought he had a knack for writing: he says that he found some of his writings 'charming'. For the most part, I think, he was a good writer; his writings are not lacking in literary merit.

The permanence of writing on stone was what attracted Ashoka to that medium, as he notes at the end of several inscriptions, including Rock Edict VI:

> Now, this writing on dharma has been inscribed for the following purpose: that it may endure for a long time, that my sons and grandsons may strive for the welfare of the whole world.

He makes similar statements in Rock Edict V and Pillar Edict II. Ashoka wanted his writings to be permanent, and in Pillar Edict VII he expresses the hope that his inscribed texts will last until the sun and the moon.

---

1 For comprehensive surveys of Ashok's writings, see Allchin and Norman 1985; Norman 2012b. For a comprehensive list of his inscriptions, see Chart 3.2.

It is his writings, available to us exactly as they were inscribed, that open up this unique individual to our gaze and permit us to sketch his biographical portrait.

Most of Ashoka's inscriptions are written in a script that we call Brahmi, while a few found in the far northwest are in the Kharosthi script. There is scholarly consensus that Kharosthi was invented some time before Brahmi and that it was based on or influenced by the Aramaic script used extensively in the adjoining Achaemenid empire. Both, for example, read from right to left, whereas Brahmi, as also all later Indian scripts, read from left to right. Kharosthi continued to be used in the region of greater Gandhara, centred on the city of Taxila in what is today Khyber Pakthunwa (formerly the North-West Frontier Province) of Pakistan, until about the third century CE, when it gradually fell into disuse.[2] The Brahmi script, on the other hand, had a much more illustrious future, becoming the mother of all later Indian scripts and of even some Southeast Asian ones. Richard Salomon presents a brief conspectus of its history:

> Unlike Kharoṣṭhī, which was always geographically limited and died out at a relatively early period, the Brāhmī script appeared in the third century B.C. as a fully developed pan-Indian national script ... and continued to play this role throughout history, becoming the parent of all of the modern Indic scripts.[3]

Ashoka's inscriptions represent the earliest examples of the Brahmi script. Did the script pre-exist him, or was it invented by him or under his leadership? That is still an open question. Books have been written on it, and scholarly debates surrounding it are ongoing. I will delineate just a couple of issues directly related to Ashoka as a writer. Several scholars have proposed that the Brahmi script used in Ashokan inscriptions was

2   For an extensive discussion of the geographical range and chronology of Kharosthi, see Salomon 1998: 42–56.
3   Salomon 1998: 17.

invented by Ashoka or shortly before him.[4] Although there have been challenges to this thesis, it is still widely accepted. The evidence for earlier examples of the script, such as graffiti on potsherds from southern India and Sri Lanka claimed to pre-date Ashoka, has not gained universal acceptance. Even if the script predated Ashoka, however, it could not have been very old. Brahmi was a new script at the time of Ashoka, and the way it is used in the inscriptions—from the earliest in the Minor Rock Edicts of the south to the latest in the Pillar Edicts of the Gangetic plain—indicates that the scribes and stonemasons were learning the craft as they went along.

The logistics of engraving Ashoka's writings must have been complex and daunting; there was no prior inscriptional tradition within India. Large numbers of scribes and engravers needed to be trained. They remain anonymous. They did not sign their names to their handiwork—except for one enterprising scribe named Chapada, a native of the Gandhara region in the northwest corner of the subcontinent. His native script must have been Kharosthi, for he wrote his signature in that script at the end of a Brahmi inscription in the deep south around Karnataka. Clearly, scribes in Ashoka's employ travelled far and wide to engage in their craft. These are the unsung heroes of Ashoka's inscriptional legacy.

Ashoka as a writer was doubly unique: he wrote the first inscriptions of the Indian subcontinent, and there is a distinct possibility that he invented the script as well. At the very least, he was the first to use it extensively and to spread it and, with it, literacy throughout the subcontinent.

Turning to Ashoka's inscriptions themselves, the reader can get a bird's-eye view of the extant corpus of Ashoka's writings in Chart 3.2 at

4 See Falk 1993; Hinüber 1989; Fussman 1988–89. For a discussion of the debate, see Salomon 1998: 17–31, and especially Salomon 1995, who notes (p. 272): 'The major conclusion shared by the studies of Fussman, von Hinüber, and Falk is that at least the Brāhmī script, and possibly also Kharoṣṭhī, originated in the Mauryan period and not earlier ... [and] that Kharoṣṭhī ... was older than the pan-Indian Brāhmī and influenced its formation.' The 'invention' theory of Brahmi script has been supported by several earlier scholars from Max Müller (see Falk 1993: 163) to Goyal (1979).

the end of this chapter. I have divided these writings into two groups. Group A consists principally of Rock Edicts, found in nine locations, and Pillar Edicts, found in six locations, and two pillar inscriptions. Group B consists of Minor Rock Edicts found in eighteen locations, Separate Edicts found in two locations, two specifically Buddhist texts dealing with monastic life, and inscriptions referring to or recording donations. I have placed the Greek and Aramaic translations in an appendix, Group C (Fig. 4, 5, 6, 7).

By my calculation, Ashoka's surviving writings total 4,614 words. The number of words in each inscription is given in the last column of Chart 3.2. These numbers, however, are approximations at best. There are several obstacles to arriving at an exact count. Many inscriptions are damaged or fragmentary. Some inscriptions, like the Rock Edicts, have different word counts in different locations. Further, Ashoka's writing system does not separate words with blank spaces, as is done in modern systems: letters run sequentially without spaces or punctuations. Imagine the difficulties a reader faces in reading and comprehension if this page was printed without 'white spaces' between words. Modern editors and translators of Ashoka's writings have to find out where one word ends and another begins; and, sometimes, different ways of separating words can produce different meanings. The word count will change accordingly. All that said, the word counts I have given are close enough to be useful; they are, to use a sports metaphor, 'in the ballpark'. A corpus of writing consisting of about four-and-a-half thousand words is not large by today's standards—thanks to printing technologies—and even by the standards of orally transmitted ancient Indian texts that pre-date Ashoka. But they were not intended to be inscribed on stone. Ashoka's writings are engraved and thus had to be concise. Compared to inscriptions left by other ancient Indian kings, Ashoka's corpus is more extensive and covers a broader range of topics.

I call the texts of Group A 'Royal Proclamations' and those of Group B 'Royal Communications'. Although placed in a separate group, the Greek and Aramaic translations are based on the Major and Minor Rock Edicts. The reasons for distinguishing groups A and B and for my nomenclature are found both in their opening statements and in their

contents. The inscriptions generally begin with an ascription of the text
to Ashoka. The title and name of the king, however, are significantly
different in the two groups. Group A has the full title with three terms:
'*devānampiya*', '*piyadasi*', '*rājā*' (or *lājā*)—'Beloved of Gods, King Piyadasi'.
If rendered non-literally in formal English, it would read something like:
'His Majesty, King Piyadasi'. Group B has abbreviated forms of this title,
most frequently just one: *devānampiya*. It is notable that the term is found
in all but one of the inscriptions, the one addressed directly to Buddhist
monks and nuns, where he refers to himself simply as 'Piyadasi, the king
of Magadha'.[5] I think the formal 'proclamations' intended for a wide
audience bear the full and formal title with three components. The less
formal 'letters' sent to various officials have simply *devānampiya*.

In Group A, all seven Pillar Edicts and five of the Rock Edicts (III,
V, VI, IX, XI) have the initial statement: *devānampiyo piyadasi rājā hevaṃ
āhā*—'The Beloved of Gods, King Piyadasi, proclaims the following'
whereas the other Rock Edicts refer in different ways to the king using
the same three terms. They are also found in two brief inscriptions
memorializing Ashoka's visit to Lumbini, the Buddha's birthplace (Fig. 3),
twenty years into his reign, and to the Stupa of Buddha Konakamana
fourteen years into his reign. It is likely that this formal opening in
Royal Proclamations became standard, for late in his career Ashoka uses
it uniformly in all the Pillar Edicts, written twenty-six and twenty-seven
years after his royal consecration. I call these Royal Proclamations not
only because of this formal address, but also because they are intended
for all his subjects. Even the brief commemorative statements at Buddhist
sites are meant for all who visited those places.

This opening statement of Group A shows a possible formal
connection to the edicts of Persian kings, which also begins with a
similar refrain: 'King Darius says'. But the tone and the message are
vastly different. Darius I's long inscription at Behistûn introduces the
king: 'I am Darius, the great king, king of kings, the king of Persia,
the king of countries, the son of Hystaspes, the grandson of Arsames, the
Achaemenid.' With Ashoka there are no boasts of his conquests or of

---

5   In the Bairaṭ inscription: *priyadasi lājā māgadhe*. I will deal with this unique
    form of address in Chapter 6.

the humiliation and killing of his adversaries. So, if there were some influences from the Achaemenid inscriptional traditions, they were formal rather than substantive.

One notable feature of Ashoka's outreach to his people is his initiative to get his messages translated into Greek and Aramaic. Interestingly, neither was probably spoken by the ordinary people of his north-western territories. Greek, however, was the language of the ruling elite who inherited the regions that Alexander conquered, while Aramaic was the official language of the previous Achaemenid empire. The Aramaic translations in particular indicate that these messages, and probably also others contained in diverse inscriptions, were perhaps addressed to officials and not directly to the people at large. As the historian Oskar von Hinüber notes, 'no Aramaic-speaking population' existed in the region.[6] So the outreach was not directly to the people of the region but to the ruling elite. Having his inscriptions in these two languages publicly exhibited was also, and especially, a symbolic statement. As Grant Parker notes:

> Given the historical memory of past Greek power, and the proximity
> of the Seleucid Empire, there was still some symbolic power for a
> monarch to appear to be versed in the Greek language and to have
> Greek subjects under his sway.[7]

It is clear that the texts comprising Group A were intended by Ashoka to be inscribed on rocks and pillars. He says as much in the inscriptions themselves. It is a different matter in the case of the texts comprising Group B. Many, if not most, of them may not have been intended for public display on rock or pillar. Local initiatives were likely responsible for their inscribed forms. In some cases, royal instructions accompanying the texts—sometimes called 'cover letters'—were either misunderstood or interpreted in such a way that the local official thought that the king wanted his missives to be inscribed. Minor Rock Edict I, which is the earliest extant writing sample of Ashoka, was probably intended for

---

6   Hinüber 2012: 196.
7   Parker 2012: 323.

public display. Given that it was inscribed in seventeen locations across a vast area, its engraving on stone could not have been simply attributed to local initiative or misunderstanding. The edict was also circulated by senior officials to subordinate officers within their jurisdictions. We have one such 'cover letter' mistakenly inscribed at Brahmagiri, a letter sent by the prince and mahamatras of Suvarnagiri to the mahamatras of Isila: 'From Suvarnagiri, at the direction of the Prince and the mahamatras, the mahamatras of Isila, after wishing them good health, should be told the following.' The so-called Schism Edict, which I will discuss in Chapter 6, is also inscribed at three locations and thus may have been intended for public display.

The two major classes of texts in Group A—the Rock Edicts and the Pillar Edicts—are also distinguished from other Ashokan inscriptions in that they comprise collections of texts, fourteen Rock Edicts and six Pillar Edicts. Those within Group B are individual texts, even though they exhibit variations and textual emendations when inscribed at different locations. To gain an adequate grasp of their content, therefore, it is important to understand their textual histories.

The first question relates to their authorship. It is generally assumed that they are all authored by Ashoka; they contain, after all, his messages, often in the first person. This, however, is an issue that needs to be problematized, even though the substance of the messages, no doubt, came from Ashoka himself. They were all published under Ashoka's imprimatur. But who actually composed these texts in the form they were inscribed?[8] Were they all composed by Ashoka himself? Did he have the help of a 'speechwriter'? Were some even composed by members of his chancery? Do we have them in precisely the same form in which they were composed, or do they reflect editorial interventions? What implications are there in the fact that most of them, especially the Rock and Pillar Edicts, are presented in collections that look very much like

8   By using 'compose' I sidestep the issue whether Ashoka himself was literate. It is unclear whether he wrote these texts himself or, as seems more likely, dictated them to a scribe. As the Greek parallels show (Welles 1934: xxxix), there may even have been professional letter writers within the Ashokan chancery who could have helped in the composition of the king's official correspondence.

anthologies? And how do we explain the regional differences in language and the vocabulary of identical texts inscribed at different locations? Some of these issues cannot be considered in detail here, but it is helpful to keep them in our minds as we explore Ashoka's writings.[9]

The assumption that the inscribed texts contain the *ipsissima verba* of Ashoka faces several problems. The two Minor Rock Edicts, for example, as inscribed in different locations have been subjected to numerous and obvious editorial interventions.[10] In particular, the longer Minor Rock Edict II, found only in the south, has been subjected to substantial emendations at various sites, including additions and omissions. Some sites have only Minor Rock Edict I, others have both; and again, some present them as two separate documents, while others present them as one. Harry Falk thinks that Minor Rock Edict II may not have been composed by Ashoka himself but by one official or a group of them trying to explain the nebulous phrasing of Minor Rock Edict I: 'He gives a canon of behaviour that everyone can understand and he prescribes exactly who is to instruct whom about what. At the end he says that all this is said in the name of Aśoka.'[11]

The linguist and Buddhist scholar K.R. Norman,[12] furthermore, thinks that texts intended to be inscribed were accompanied by 'cover letters' containing instructions to officials. In some locations, however, the officials either erroneously or deliberately inscribed these instructions as well. Such cover letters were common in ancient Hellenistic imperial inscriptions, which also were often not edicts per se but ostensibly private letters that were, nevertheless, intended for public display.[13] The fact that

9   For a more detailed discussion of these issues, see Olivelle 2012b.
10 This issue has been investigated in detail by Norman (1967a) and Falk (2006). For a synoptic presentation of these edicts, see Anderson 1990.
11 See Falk 2006: 58.
12 Norman 1987a.
13 Welles (1934: 13, 19, 37, 40) gives four such cover letters from Greek inscriptions. Here is an example (37, trans. by Welles): 'Anaximbrotus to Dionytas, greeting. Enclosed is the copy of the decree written by the king concerning the appointment of Berenice, the daughter of Ptolemy son of Lysimachus, as chief-priestess of the queen in the satrapy. Carry out its provisions as "he" thinks best, and see to it that the copies are inscribed on

these 'cover letters' were also inscribed in Greek inscriptions indicates that the engraving of similar letters within Ashokan texts may not have been simply mistakes but perhaps deliberate acts on the part of local officials.

Even in the Major Rock Edicts,[14] which are more uniform in content than the two Minor Rock Edicts, we see editorial interventions in the linguistic differences evident in the texts from different places, not only differences in spelling—such as changing 'l' (like *lājā* for king) in eastern sites to 'r' (*rājā*) in western sites—but also more substantial and deliberate variants in both language and content. These were probably prompted by the regional dialects of Prakrit, different from Ashoka's own native Magadhan dialect prevalent in Pataliputra, where the texts were composed. Scribes in different regions, for example, used different words to translate some common words. A telling example is found in Rock Edict IX, where at different locations no less than four different words are used for 'women'.[15] Perhaps some words used by Ashoka or his secretaries in Pataliputra were not normally used in other regions.[16] Norman has also drawn attention to Rock Edict IX, where at a certain point 'the edict continues in two different versions, which in this paper I shall call "recensions" … An examination of the other thirteen Rock Edicts enables us to say that for the majority of them there were at least two recensions in existence.'[17]

We see editorial interventions also in the two Separate Rock Edicts in Jaugada and Dhauli, edicts that were probably sent to other locations as well although inscribed only at these two. The two texts, one addressed

---

a stone stele and set up in the place where they may best be seen. Farewell. Year 108, Artemisius 19.' For the Greek epistolary tradition, see Exler 1923. See also Hinüber 2010.

14 Some of the material here is taken from Olivelle 2012b.

15 The four are: *aṃbikajanikā, striyaka, ithi* and *mahiḍāyo*. The editor Schneider (1978: 53) thinks the original used by Ashoka was the first, *aṃbikajanikā*.

16 See Norman 1967a. Examples of different vocabulary are: *putra* and *pajā* for son/progeny; *han* and *ālabh* for killing; *kūpa* and *udupāna* for well; *spasu* and *bhaginī* for sister; *sthavira* and *mahalaka* for old person.

17 Norman 1978–79: 78. For the genealogical relation of Rock Edicts found in different sites, see Schneider 1978: 18.

to the mahamatras of Samapa and the other to the mahamatras of Tosali, have many passages in common but also significant divergences.[18] Someone, perhaps at the central chancery, probably took a single text and modified it to suit two different geographical, social and political contexts.

Editorial intervention is most evident in the Girnar versions of Rock Edicts IX and XI (Fig. 4). The Girnar editor, for example, had a fondness for the term 'sādhu' (excellent). Ashoka developed a fondness for this expression and used it in his definition of dharma in Rock Edict III (see Chapter 9). The Girnar editor imports that word also into the definitions in IX and XI:

Chart 3.1
Girnar Edition of Rock Edicts IX and XI

Original Version	Girnar Version
It [dharma] consists of the following:	It [dharma] consists of the following:
proper regard toward slaves and servants, reverence toward elders, self-restraint with respect to living beings, and giving gifts to Sramanas and Brahmins. (Rock Edict IX)	proper regard toward slaves and servants, reverence toward elders—excellent! Self-restraint with respect to living beings—excellent! Giving gifts to Sramanas and Brahmins—excellent! (Rock Edict IX)
Proper regard toward slaves and servants; obedience to mother and father; giving gifts to friends, companions, and relatives, and to Sramanas and Brahmins; and not killing living beings. (Rock Edict XI)	Proper regard toward slaves and servants, obedience to mother and father—excellent! Giving gifts to friends, companions, and relatives, and to Sramanas and Brahmins—excellent! And not killing living beings—excellent! (Rock Edict XI)

---

18 For discussions, see Alsdorf 1962; Majumdar et al. 2019.

The question then arises: who made these emendations and recensions? Were the editorial activities evident in many of the Ashokan inscriptions carried out by Ashoka himself or, as seems more likely, by intermediaries, either individual high officials or committees of such officials? And were at least some of them carried out by scribes or officials at the inscription sites?[19]

Another issue relates to their pre- or extra-inscriptional textual history. Copies of at least some inscriptions written on perishable material such as palm leaf or birch bark were carried to inscriptional sites. There are, for example, mistakes in reading similar Brahmi signs, such as '*i*' and '*ā*' and '*na*' and '*ya*'. As with any other manuscript, these written originals may have undergone changes both deliberate and accidental when copied or inscribed. Further, at least some of them were translated into Greek and Aramaic. The translators often did not translate the full text of the original either because some sections were not relevant to the far north-western corner of the empire or because it contained difficult or unclear terms. Some sections were omitted, and others were paraphrased or abbreviated. So, these 'texts of Ashoka' were, in fact, mediated by the hands of scribes, editors and translators.

Beyond all that, the fourteen Rock Edicts in their inscribed form constitute an anthology. In most cases their written exemplars were sent

---

19 It is interesting to note that in the Greek tradition there was within the royal chancery an office of the *epistolographus* that prepared drafts of royal letters (Welles 1934: xxxix). It is unclear, of course, whether such an office existed within Ashoka's chancery. Given the extensive communications that Ashoka undertook, it is entirely possible that Ashoka had a similar office that may have been responsible for either the drafting and/or the transmission and editing of the Ashokan letters. The only ancient evidence for the composition of edicts (*śāsana*) comes from Kautilya's *Arthashastra* (2.10). The role of the scribe consists of both composing and writing a document after he has listened to the oral directive of the king: 'He should listen with single-minded attention to the king's directive and then compose a document characterized by precision of meaning—in the case of the king, with the respectful mention of the country, sovereignty, genealogy, and name; in the case of someone other than the king, with the respectful mention of the country and name' (*Arthashastra*, 2.10.4).

to the inscriptional sites in several batches.[20] So, at these sites the final anthology was built up gradually, with the addition of several groups of texts. In the western site of Girnar, on the other hand, all fourteen were sent as a single corpus, indicating that by the time of the Girnar inscription the anthology had been completed. These inscriptional anthologies were made sometime after 256 BCE, the thirteenth year of Ashoka's reign.

The six Pillar Edicts, likewise, constitute an anthology.[21] They were inscribed together on the same pillars at the same time. The individual texts comprising the anthology appear to have been composed within a narrow period in or shortly before 242 BCE, Ashoka's twenty-seventh regnal year. As I will discuss in the next chapter, in five sites the texts were inscribed while the pillars were still in a horizontal position. This indicates that the stonemasons responsible for carving the pillars were aware that they had to finish engraving the edicts before the pillars could be transported and placed in their erect positions. The only exception is the Allahabad pillar, where the inscriptions were carved in a circular manner while the pillar was erect. From a variety of indicators, including their positioning on the pillars, it appears that the first three Pillar Edicts form a single text and have been mistakenly taken as three by the engravers. We may thus have not six but just four individual Pillar Edicts in the anthology.[22] Perhaps we should consider the Pillar Edicts as

---

20 See Falk 2006: 111.

21 For a study of the Pillar Edicts as an anthology, see Tieken 2012.

22 See Norman 1987b and Tieken 2012. Pillar Edict VII presents its own problems. Norman (1987b) notes, 'The failure of this edict to reach other sites [than Topra] is one of the great unsolved mysteries of the Ashokan administration.' Another mystery is the fact that, alone among all the edicts, the introductory refrain 'devānaṃpiye piyadassi lājā hevaṃ āhā' is repeated in Pillar Edict VII nine times, with a tenth using the abbreviated form 'etaṃ devānaṃpiye āha'. In all the other edicts this refrain occurs only once, and at the beginning. Such repetitions of the refrain that these are the words of the king are found in Persian inscriptions. However, this is quite unusual for Ashoka, and one may question whether these nine sections were meant to be separate texts or were viewed as a miniature anthology just like the Rock and Pillar Edicts.

a single textual corpus rather than as individual and separate texts. In the case of both the Rock Edicts and the Pillar Edicts, we can ask new and significant questions when they are viewed as anthologies rather than simply as individual texts.

Among these, the first set of questions relates to the textual histories of these anthologies. Given that different sets of texts in the Rock Edict anthology were sent to different sites at different times, it is likely that the individual texts were composed earlier and pre-existed their incorporation into the anthology. If that is so, where and in what form did they exist, and to what purposes were they put during their pre-anthological lives? As important is the question of who created these anthologies, which can be viewed as the production of an Ashokan canon. Who made the selection of texts and what were the criteria used? Who decided which texts to include, which to omit, and how to organize the anthology? Was it Ashoka himself, or was it some other high official or panel of officials entrusted with the task of textual compilation and transmission? And finally, what was left out of these anthologies and why? It seems likely again that there were other messages of Ashoka which, for whatever reason, the compilers did not think appropriate to include in this canon of texts. Even though we may never get adequate answers to these, it is important to keep these questions in mind as we explore the Ashokan literary corpus.[23]

At least some of the editorial activities we detect in these texts were deliberate. Ashoka himself alludes to this in Rock Edict XIV. Some of the records are concise or abbreviated, he says, while others are elaborate; not all the records have been put together everywhere. Some topics are repeated several times, while others are omitted because they are deemed unsuitable for a particular location. It appears that Ashoka was aware of the editorial and anthologizing activities with respect to his letters, and perhaps he authorized some, if not all, of these activities. That some were beyond his control and perhaps disapproved by him is also clear from his

---

23 If Norman (1983: *Collected Papers II*: 263) is correct in thinking that the Separate Edicts were never meant to be inscribed, then there may have been others that were in fact neither meant to be inscribed nor were actually inscribed.

statement at the end of this edict: some records, he says, were abridged for a special reason, but some owing to the fault of the scribes.[24] Further, as we will see later, even some of the individual texts within the Rock Edict anthology appear to have been constructed using pre-existing text fragments.

So, the answer to the question 'Who wrote the edicts?' becomes complicated. At the very least, the way they are presented in the inscribed texts as we have them was mediated by several layers of editorial, anthologizing, inscriptional, and, for some, translational activities. But what is important for our purposes is that the inscriptions contain substantially the thoughts and words of Ashoka himself.

These texts had extra-inscriptional (both pre- and post-inscriptional) lives, that is, they existed and functioned outside their inscribed forms. This is clear both from the anthological nature of the Rock and Pillar Edicts and from some of the comments contained in the inscriptions themselves. In Rock Edict III, for example, Ashoka says: 'Twelve years after my royal consecration, I issued this order.' The original term used, 'āñapitam', refers to an imperial order given orally rather than in writing or inscribing.[25] And what follows appears to be a citation of this earlier order, which must have existed in oral or written form outside this particular inscription. The inscribed text is thus a reproduction of an earlier oral order. The same could be said in the case of Minor Rock Edict II, where also verbs of command, rather than ones for inscribing, are used.

Even after their engraving on stone, some, if not all, of these texts may have had extra-inscriptional lives in the form of ritualized public recitations. This point has been illustrated by the spaces between clusters of words in the Pillar Edicts, spaces that function as punctuation and point to pauses during the public recitation of these messages.[26]

---

24 For a study of scribal errors in Ashokan inscription in, see Norman 1967a, 1975a.

25 When Ashoka wants to command the creation of an inscription, he uses terms such as the causative 'lekhāpitā', cause to be written.

26 Klaus Janert (1973: 142–43) notes: 'In the versions of the edicts under discussion spaces within the lines are frequent and occur particularly after groups of two or more words. It is my conclusion that this spacing can

In the Separate Rock Edicts, furthermore, Ashoka gives specific instructions that these texts were to be read out publicly at specific times, such as the full moon days of the rainy season (June–October) and Tishya days. Ashoka adds that some in his audience may want to listen to his messages on other days as well. These public readings of imperial messages were likely carried out not from the inscribed texts, which were often difficult to access and too high to be read from ground level, but from 'soft' copies available to the officials of these places or from memory.

We have a more explicit statement about the liturgical recitation of an imperial message in the Sarnath Pillar Inscription directed at some mahamatras, who are instructed to keep the Buddhist monastic order unified. Ashoka tells these mahamatras to keep one copy of his message with them. A second copy was to be deposited with the Upasakas, the lay Buddhist patrons. Now, the term used for these copies is also '*lipi*', a term that here refers not simply to inscribing on rock but to writing as such. These portable copies of the text, therefore, were intended to be kept in extra-inscriptional form. In this particular case, it is even unclear whether the text was initially intended to be inscribed at all. This is certainly the case in the so-called Queen's Edict, which was probably 'sent as an appendix to earlier instructions'[27] and was probably not meant to be published.

---

scarcely be anything other than a form of notation for pauses made during the recitation of edicts and which scribes each recorded in this fashion.' See also Janert (1967–68: 511–518, 1973: 141–145). Michael Gagarin (2008: 46–48 on the Dreros inscription) has shown that, in writing ancient Greek legal inscriptions around 500 BCE, scribes placed long, vertical lines between single words or small groups of words, possibly to make it easier for the reader to follow the text. Ashoka's rock inscriptions do not have this feature. Is it possible that Ashoka or his scribes came to know about this Greek convention between the time of his Rock and Pillar inscriptions? Recent scholarship (see Hinüber 2010) also points to a possible exchange of letters between Ashoka and his neighbouring Greek kings, which may also have influenced the composition of Ashokan texts. A similar instruction to make clusters (*varga*) of one, two or three words while writing a royal edict or letter is given in Kautilya's *Arthashastra* (2.10.21).

27 Norman 1976: 57.

What all this points to is that (a) the inscribed texts of Ashoka to which we have access constitute only a portion of the textual production carried out by the emperor; (b) not all of the inscribed texts may contain the words of Ashoka verbatim; and (c) even the texts to which we have access enjoyed a life outside of or parallel to their inscribed life, in the form of portable copies made on perishable material and public readings, perhaps accompanied by oral commentary, carried out by imperial officers.

This leads us to the issue of literary form. Some of these texts are written in the first person using first-person verbs and pronouns. Others are written in the third person. As literature, these two classes of writing fall into two different genres. The first-person texts can be viewed as letters, falling thus into the epistolary tradition. The third-person texts fall broadly into a category that straddles eulogy and didactics, a combination of Acta Regis (Acts of the King) and the king's wishes for his people. These two genres do not necessarily mean that they were written by two different authors. Both could have been authored by Ashoka himself using first- and third-person voices on different occasions. We thus see a first-person sentence embedded within a text written in the third person.

Another issue concerns the locations of the texts and the way they are visually presented to the public. The selection of the inscriptional sites and the way the inscriptions are exhibited were intentional, an examination of which provides further insights into the editorial process behind the engraving of Ashokan inscriptions, as demonstrated by the recent books by Nayanjot Lahiri and Dilip Chakrabarti.[28] It will take us far afield to explore the reasons for each site selection. Briefly, however, the fourteen Major Rock Edicts are located in outlying districts of the empire. Harry Falk notes: 'Rock Edicts are found closer to larger towns. In addition, these large towns seem to be located at the borders of the

---

28 See Lahiri 2015. Readers can find a good general survey of the Ashokan inscriptional sites and of their socio-economic significance in the book by the Indian archaeologist Dilip Chakrabarti (2011).

empire.'[29] This stands in sharp contrast to the Minor Rock Edicts, which are located some distance from human habitations; most are on hills and hillocks with boulders and caves. It is likely that these remote areas were associated during Ashoka's time with folk festivals and pilgrimages. The Pillar Edicts, on the other hand, are located in the heartland of the empire.

Harry Falk points out the significance of the sequence in which visitors encounter the texts as they approach various inscriptional sites.[30] The public display of texts inscribed on boulders and pillars had an iconic quality, especially when we consider that people of the time, who were mostly illiterate, were seeing these 'speaking stones' for the first time. Did these stones assume a religious significance? Many of the inscriptional sites already appear to have had religious significance as centres of folk ritual and pilgrimage. Even today one finds flowers and other devotional material left at inscription sites.[31] One anecdote illustrates the iconic nature of inscribed words even today. An archaeology student at the University of Wisconsin (Madison, USA) inscribed an Ashokan inscription on a boulder near the university as part of her class project. One day she found flowers placed by the boulder.[32]

Richard Salomon notes how unique and atypical Ashokan inscriptions are with reference to what he calls 'the inscriptional habit' of later Indian kings: 'In terms of format, content, and tone, there is practically nothing in the later inscriptional corpus of the Indian world that even resembles Ashoka's inscriptions.'[33] 'Royal inscriptions of a purely exhortatory character are rare,' Salomon adds, 'and in fact are virtually limited to the inscriptions of Aśoka.'[34]

What I have attempted to show above seconds this conclusion, but also gives a possible reason for Ashoka's uniqueness. His inscriptions

---

29 Falk 2006: 111. For a detailed discussion of the edicts found in South India, see Basu et al. 2017.

30 Falk 2006: 111–12.

31 See the picture in Monica Smith et al. 2016: 381.

32 The student, Heather Walder, describes her experience of actually chiselling the Ashokan inscription in Walder 2018.

33 Salomon 2009: 45.

34 Salomon 1998: 111.

consisted of letters and exhortations set in stone rather than the common eulogistic records of a king's glory and achievements. They are sober exhortations on matters relating to morality; no note is made of the king's conquests or power, except in the record of his Kalinga conquest, written to show why wars are evil, to express regret for his actions, and to tell his descendants to aspire to conquest through dharma, rather than to demonstrate his power and glory. The unique nature of these writings justifies our attempt to see them as a different genre of literature than simply edicts or eulogies.

As we will see in subsequent chapters, Ashoka was on a mission. He wanted to convert his subjects, and even people living outside his empire, to living moral lives according to the dictates of dharma. To this mission he dedicated his entire life and the resources of his empire. His new venture as author—writing letters to his subjects and officials and engraving some of them on stone—was undertaken to further that mission. Ashoka was also a smart politician. He knew the importance of 'messaging'. How could he get the people, living busy lives and trying to eke out a living, to pay attention to a distant philosopher-king talking about dharma and morality? He noted that gentle persuasion rather than the heavy hand of the law was a more effective strategy. His writings were meant to persuade rather than command, to nudge an apathetic population to take his teachings seriously.

The last member of each of the two anthologies, as already noted, can be viewed as a coda—a concluding statement about the anthology. Rock Edict XIV is clearly such a coda. It reflects on the Rock Edict anthology and tells the readers why and how they were written and why there may be some defects in them.

This writing on dharma has been made to be inscribed by the Beloved of Gods, King Piyadasi. It is given in greatly or moderately abbreviated form or in greater detail, for not everything is suitable for every place. For, my territory is vast, and I have written a lot. And I will always have still more written. Some of it has been repeated over and over again because of the charm of various topics, so people would act accordingly. Here and there, however, some may have been written

incompletely either bearing the region in mind, or taking a particular
reason into account, or due to the fault of the scribes.

Ashoka raises here some significant points. First, he confesses that his
inscriptions are in abbreviated form in some places, while elsewhere they
are more expansive. He excuses his repetitions—a literary fault looked
down upon by later Indian rhetoricians—on the grounds that he found
certain topics, or perhaps a turn of phrase he invented, to be charming
or 'sweet', something I will turn to below. But the most important
point Ashoka makes is the extensive nature of his writings. The reason
why some have been abbreviated—and perhaps why some have been
completely omitted in some places—is that his writings are vast, as is his
territory. And he promises to write more in the future.

Although not as clear as Rock Edict XIV, Pillar Edict VI probably
serves as a coda for the Pillar Edict anthology. In it, Ashoka recalls that
he started writing on dharma twelve years after his royal consecration.
He did this to promote the welfare and wellbeing of all the people, so he
may lead them to happiness. He pays attention to all classes, and honours
all religious organizations or Pasandas, a topic I will discuss in Part Four.
He concludes by saying that his principal duty is to pay personal visits—
it is unclear whether such visits are to the religious groups he had just
mentioned or to people in general. This coda, unlike the one attached to
the Rock Edict anthology, is less specific and more a reminiscence of his
past quarter-century of activity as king.

This brings us to the extent of Ashoka's writings. The extant corpus
given schematically in Chart 3.2 contains thirty-four texts, plus three
translations, totalling approximately 4,614 words. As I have noted above,
the word counts are approximations. This corpus of Ashoka's writings
is substantial, considering that they are all inscribed on stone, a time-
consuming and laborious enterprise. Further, it is certain that we do
not have all the inscriptions he wrote; every decade or so archaeologists
have discovered a new inscription. Ashoka's statement in Rock Edict
XIV about the large extent of his writings—with more to come in the
future—indicates that, as I have already noted, most of his writings may

have been not inscribed on stone but written on perishable material, the 'paper' of his time.

Most of the inscribed writings of Ashoka deal with his efforts to propagate dharma. There are only a few that deal with the normal running of the kingdom, which would have required the king to communicate regularly with his far-flung bureaucracy. That there must have been such writings is a safe assumption. The surviving texts also suggest that. For example, the so-called Queen's Edict was such a communiqué by the king to his officials about a trivial matter of bookkeeping.

> At the direction of the Beloved of Gods, the mahamatras everywhere should be instructed—
> Whatever gift is given there[35] by the second queen—a mango grove, garden, almshouse, or anything else at all—it is credited to that queen. You should credit to the second queen, that is, Kaluvaki, the mother of Tivala.

This royal command deals with a banal matter, but fortunately we learn two names—the only two Indian names in the whole Ashokan corpus—of a son and a wife. That similar, and perhaps more important, royal communications may have been written by Ashoka is revealed in Pillar Edict IV. There he speaks about the freedom he has given to his senior officials to act independently and about his wish that they act impartially, especially in judicial proceedings. Then he goes on to say that he has previously sent orders to these officials to grant a stay of three days for people condemned to death. Clearly these and similar orders would have been sent in written form to all his senior officials across the empire. Unfortunately, these writings of Ashoka are irretrievably lost.

Given the presence of ambassadors of Hellenistic kings in India and Ashoka's own statements about the ambassadors he sent to four Greek kings, it is not far-fetched to assume that Ashoka sent diplomatic letters

35 The reference of this term (*hetā*) is unclear, but it probably refers to the localities overseen by the mahamatras in which the donations were distributed.

to and received such letters from these Greek rulers. The same could be said in the case of rulers of the southern states bordering his empire, including Sri Lanka. These diplomatic communications, alas, are also lost.

Finally, I want to return to a point I made at the beginning: some of Ashoka's writings have literary merit. In the Prologue I drew attention to the alliterative qualities in Ashoka's very title: devānaṃpiye piyadasi, with the repetition of the two middle words piya. Herman Tieken[36] has drawn attention to Ashoka's use of the term 'sweetness' or charm, in Sanskrit, mādhurya, in Rock Edict XIV to describe the literary merits of some of his compositions. The significance of this term derives from the fact that, a few centuries after Ashoka, the seminal treatise on poetics, Bharata's Natyashastra, gives the aesthetic quality of sweetness (mādhurya-guṇa) as one of the ten qualities of a good literary composition called kāvya.[37] It is likely that this literary genre and its analysis occurred in the Prakrit or Middle Indic long before it emerged within the Sanskrit literary tradition. The linguist and historian Stephanie Jamison notes: 'As it turns out, it is only Sanskrit that lacks the term "kāvya" in this crucial period [last few centuries BCE]; it has been lurking in the Middle Indic all along, and it is likely that both the word and the practice re-entered Sanskrit literature from there.'[38] The presence of a developed poetical tradition within Prakrit, the language of Ashoka, makes it plausible that he may have been aware of poetical conventions.

Unfortunately, alliteration—falling within what Indian theorists called 'sound embellishment' (śabdālaṃkāra)—is impossible to replicate in translation. In Rock Edict X, for example, Ashoka engages in wordplay with the sound 'pal' repeated six times, with other 'p' sounds resonating that alliteration.[39] And sa- of savaṃ is picked up immediately by sakale and by savaṃ at the end. I give here the text with the alliterative sounds in upper-case italics to make it easier for the reader to follow:

---

36 Tieken 2006.
37 Nāṭyaśāstra XVI: 104.
38 Jamison 2007: 142.
39 I thank my colleague Joel Brereton for identifying some of these alliterative features in the edicts.

aṃ cu kichi *PAL*akamati devānaṃ*Piye Piyadasi* lājā, taṃ *SAvaṃ PAL*atikāye vā kiti: *SA*kale apa*PALiSA*ve siyā ti. esa cu *PALiSA*ve e a*P*une. dukale cu kho esa khudakena vā vagenā usaṭena vā aṃnata agenā *PAL*akamenā *SA*vaṃ *PAL*itijitu.

The rhythm of the sound is completely lost in translation:

> Whatever the Beloved of the Gods, King Piyadasi, strives to do, however, all that is solely for the sake of the hereafter, so that everyone would have few hazards. But this is the hazard: lack of merit. This is difficult to do, however, for either a low-class person or a high-class person without utmost striving, giving up everything.

In Rock Edict II, Ashoka uses the strategy of repeating a word at the beginning of a statement, which is picked up again in the middle after a long parenthetical statement. Such repetitions are common in oral compositions. Here the word is 'everywhere'—*savatā* (Sanskrit: *sarvatra*):

> *Everywhere*—in the territory of the Beloved of Gods, King Piyadasi, as well as in those at the frontiers, namely, Codas, Pandyas, Satiyaputras, Keralaputras, Tamraparnis, the Greek king named Antiochus, and other kings who are that Antiochus's neighbors—*everywhere* the Beloved of Gods, King Piyadasi, has established two kinds of medical services: medical services for humans and medical services for domestic animals.

The next two sentences of the same edict repeat the last eight words. Note the repetition of -*āni* as the last two syllables of five words:

> osadhāni munisopagāni ca pasuopagāni ca, **ata atā nathi, savata hālāpitā ca lopāpitā ca.** hemeva mūlāni ca phalāni ca, **ata atā nathi, savata hālāpitā ca lopāpitā ca.**

Wherever medicinal herbs beneficial to humans and domestic animals **were not found, he had them brought in and planted everywhere.** Likewise, wherever root vegetables and fruit trees **were not found, he had them brought in and planted everywhere.**

Examples of such literary embellishments can be multiplied, but they can be appreciated only in the original Prakrit. They do, however, point to Ashoka taking the trouble to make his writing not only meaningful but also have literary charm—*mādhurya*.

Chart 3.2 Ashoka's Inscriptional Corpus GROUP A: Royal Proclamations							
Name	Date	Location(s)	Surface	Script	Language	Person	Word Count[40]
RE I	nd	9[41]	Rock	Br/Ka	Prakrit	3rd Per.	87
RE II	nd	9	Rock	Br/Ka	Prakrit	3rd Per.	84
RE III	12[42]	9	Rock	Br/Ka	Prakrit	1st Per.	64
RE IV	12	9	Rock	Br/Ka	Prakrit	3rd Per.	160
RE V	13?[43]	9	Rock	Br/Ka	Prakrit	1st Per.	179
RE VI	nd	9	Rock	Br/Ka	Prakrit	1st Per.	153
RE VII	nd	9	Rock	Br/Ka	Prakrit	3rd Per.	47
RE VIII	nd	9	Rock	Br/Ka	Prakrit	3rd Per.	66
RE IX	nd	9	Rock	Br/Ka	Prakrit	3rd Per.	168
RE X	nd	9	Rock	Br/Ka	Prakrit	3rd Per.	91
RE XI	nd	7[44]	Rock	Br/Ka	Prakrit	3rd Per.	71
RE XII	nd	7	Rock	Br/Ka	Prakrit	3rd Per.	206
RE XIII	nd	6	Rock	Br/Ka	Prakrit	3rd Per.	425
RE XIV	nd	9	Rock	Br/Ka	Prakrit	1st Per.	61
Major Rock Edicts Total Word Count: 1,862							

40 Words in nominal compounds have been counted separately.
41 Dhauli, Erragudi, Girnar, Jaugada, Kalsi, Mansehra, Sannati, Shahbazgarhi, Sopara. At Sannati, we only have Edicts XII and XIV inscribed on a free-standing stone slab. It is assumed that the first eleven edicts were inscribed on other slabs, but Edict XIII has been omitted, as at Dhauli and Jaugada.
42 The dates given correspond to the year after Ashoka's royal consecration.
43 The edict itself is undated, but he says that he established the office of dharma-mahamatra thirteen years after his consecration. So, the edict must have been composed after that year.
44 Edicts XI, XII, XIII are omitted at Dhauli and Jaugada.

PE I	26	6[45]	Pillar	Brahmi	Prakrit	1st Per.	81
PE II	26	6	Pillar	Brahmi	Prakrit	1st Per.	69
PE III	26	6	Pillar	Brahmi	Prakrit	3rd Per.	66
PE IV	26	6	Pillar	Brahmi	Prakrit	1st Per.	191
PE V	26	6	Pillar	Brahmi	Prakrit	1st Per.	176
PE VI	26	6	Pillar	Brahmi	Prakrit	1st Per.	77
PE VII	27	Delhi-Topra	Pillar	Brahmi	Prakrit	1st Per.	542
Major Pillar Edicts Total				**Word Count: 1,202**			

Buddhist	12	Rummindei	Pillar	Brahmi	Prakrit	3rd Per.	36
Buddhist	14	Nigali	Pillar	Brahmi	Prakrit	3rd Per.	24

GROUP B: Royal Communications							
MRE I	nd	18[46]	Rock	Brahmi	Prakrit	1st Per.	140
MRE II	nd	7[47]	Rock	Brahmi	Prakrit	3rd Per.	103
SEP I	nd	2[48]	Rock	Brahmi	Prakrit	1st Per.	324
SEP II	nd	2	Rock	Brahmi	Prakrit	1st Per.	237
Schism	nd	Sanchi	Pillar	Brahmi	Prakrit	1st Per.	Fragmented
Schism	nd	Sarnath	Pillar	Brahmi	Prakrit	1st Per.	93
Schism	nd	Kausambi	Pillar	Brahmi	Prakrit	1st Per.	Fragmented
Buddhist	nd	Bairat	Rock	Brahmi	Prakrit	1st Per.	107
Queen's	nd	Kausambi	Pillar	Brahmi	Prakrit	3rd Per.	38
Barabar I	12	Barabar	Cave	Brahmi	Prakrit	3rd Per.	12

---

45 Delhi-Topra, Delhi-Mirarh, Lauriyā-Araraj, Lauriya-Nandangarh, Rampurva, Allahabad-Kosam (Kausambi).

46 Ahraura, Bairaṭ, Brahmagiri, Delhi (Bahapur), Erraguḍi, Gavimaṭh, Gujarra, Jatinga-Ramesvara, Maski, Nittur, Palkigundu, Panguraria, Rajula-Mandagiri, Rathanpurwa, Rupnath, Sahasram, Siddapur, Udegolam.

47 Brahmagiri, Erraguḍi, Jatinga-Ramesvara, Nittur, Rajula-Mandagiri, Siddapur, Udegolam.

48 Dhauli, Jaugada.

Barabar II	12	Barabar	Cave	Brahmi	Prakrit	3rd Per.	12
Barabar III	19	Barabar	Cave	Brahmi	Prakrit	3rd Per.	15
Panguraria	nd	Panguraria	Rock	Brahmi	Prakrit	3rd Per.	12

GROUP C: Translations							
Greek	nd	Kandahar	Rock	Greek	Greek	3rd Per.	255
Bilingual I	nd	Kandahar	Rock	Greek + Aramaic	Greek + Aramaic	3rd Per.	72
Bilingual II	nd	Kandahar	Rock	Greek + Aramaic	Greek + Aramaic	3rd Per.	70
All Edicts		**Total Word Count: 4,614**					

4

Builder

RULERS, BE THEY ANCIENT MONARCHS OR MODERN PRESIDENTS, LOVE to build. Their monumental constructions are visual testaments to their power and glory. Monuments from across the ancient world bear witness to this proclivity of powerful persons, and Ashoka was no exception. Ashoka's building programme, however, was unique in Indian history and unparalleled during his time. He was the first to build with stone and, as the art historian Frederick Asher has noted, 'the first identifiable patron of Indian art'.[1] And, as far as we can tell from what has survived, he did not build monuments to himself.

The only surviving Ashokan monuments are the pillars—along with the capitals surmounting them—many bearing his inscriptions. Ashoka calls them *silā-thaṃbe* or 'stone pillars'. It is possible, even likely, that other stone buildings and art works were commissioned by him, but none have been discovered. Much of his attention as a builder may have been directed to his capital city, Pataliputra, but, as I have already noted, this city, sitting beneath modern Patna, has not been fully excavated. So, we are left with the pillars—in the words of Asher 'from the time of Aśoka we are left with a single type of monument, the pillars'.[2]

There are remains of some twenty pillars that probably go back to the time of Ashoka, some of them still standing; of others, only fragments

1   Asher 2006: 51.
2   Asher 2006: 57.

remain.[3] The pillars still standing in one piece measure between 9 and 13 metres in height. They do not stand on an abacus or platform but are buried directly in the ground to a depth of about 2.5 metres. Thus, the pillars visible above ground approximate from 7 and 11 metres. All are round and tapering towards the top. The diameters at the base vary from 1.85 to 0.75 metres, and at the top from 0.95 to 0.55 metres. At least some of the pillars stood on stone base slabs 2.4 metres square or oblong: 2 metres wide and 2.4 metres long. They were placed at the bottom of the pits housing the pillars.[4] Many of the pillars are capped with capitals consisting of bell, abacus and animal. It is unclear whether originally all had capitals because some are in a fragmentary state (Fig. 16).

The shafts of the pillars are monoliths, single, long blocks of stone carved from living rock.[5] Where did the engineering and artistic know-how that went into quarrying these monoliths, weighing approximately 50 tonnes, shaping them into cylindrical shafts, buffing them to a high polish, and transporting them to their locations come from? There is no evidence that these engineering and artistic traditions developed locally over time. Scholars have suggested influence from Persia, where stone was used for elaborate monumental architecture, including pillars, long before Ashoka's time. Persian pillars, however, were integral parts of buildings rather than singular pillars standing all alone. Further, they were quarried as short drums, which were put one on top of another to form a pillar; they were not monoliths. The only other example from

---

3　For a detailed discussion of all the pillars, with locations and dimensions, see Falk 2006: 139–224.

4　There is some controversy about whether all the pillars had such base slabs. Irwin (1973, 1974) argued that older pillars were buried directly in the ground, causing subsidence. Engineers figured out a solution by putting a large base slab below later pillars. This has been challenged by other scholars (Falk 2006: 139). One stump of a pillar found in Patna has a wooden base slab.

5　The hypothesis of Vidula Jayaswal (1998: 222; 2004: 44; 2012: 229–57) that Ashokan pillars, like their Persian counterparts, are composed of several drums placed one on top of the other, and that the polish is achieved by applying a coating of 'crushed pink sandstone with hamaetite pellents' has not found much support.

outside the subcontinent is Egypt, where monolithic obelisks weighing as much as 455 metric tonnes were quarried at Aswan and transported via the Nile to their respective locations. One can see today the unfinished obelisk of pharaoh Hatshepsut (1479–1458 BCE) lying at the quarry at Aswan. Whether knowledge of quarrying large monoliths travelled from Egypt to India is hard to tell, but, as we have already seen, the whole of West Asia, including Egypt, was part of a Hellenistic political and cultural sphere that was in close contact with the Mauryas. Ashoka says that he sent an ambassador to the Hellenistic king in Egyptian Alexandria. In India, as in Egypt, much of the transportation was done by boats or barges along rivers. Indian rulers, however, had the advantage of elephants that could help in pulling large loads.

For the methods of transporting such heavy and delicate pillars, we have some evidence from the medieval re-erecting of Ashokan pillars requiring their transportation. During the Delhi Sultanate, in 1367, Firuzshah Tughluq had the Ashokan pillar at Topra pulled out and erected in Delhi. There are two contemporary sources with information about the technology involved in this activity, including a cart with forty-two wheels and several thousand labourers. These sources are used by the historian Syed Ali Nadeem Rezavi in his description of the transportation of the Topra pillar.[6]

Harry Falk summarizes both the unique nature of the Ashokan pillars and their artistic perfection:

> The pillars of Aśoka seem to appear out of the blue; there are no predecessors anywhere on the subcontinent. The pillars have a certain air of perfection; they are admirably polished, their tapering gives them elegance, their proportions are well-balanced. The threefold capitals have been designed and produced with a quality never to be reached again by later copyists. It requires some skill and experience to produce such pieces of art; another sort of experience is needed to transport them from the quarry to their places of erection, and it requires further expertise to erect the pillars weighing from 8.6

6 See Rezavi 2009–10.

(Lumbinī) to 51 (Vesalī) tons, and finally to top them with capitals weighing a further 2 tons.[7]

Frederick Asher reflects on the unease with the Euro-centric tendency to ascribe all Indian innovations to foreign, especially Greek, influence:

> While it may feel uncomfortable to accept extra-Indian sources for major changes in the history of Indian art, it is undeniable that many of the most inventive periods for the history of Indian art coincide with times that India played a major role in global systems.[8]

It is well to remember, however, that 'nation', 'foreign' and even 'Indian' itself are identities forged in the last few centuries and cannot be projected back to a period over 2,000 years ago. The cultural and linguistic world of what is today Tamil Nadu would have been in some ways more 'foreign' to people living in Kashmir or Gandhara than those of Persia or Syria. That the three early Mauryan kings forged an empire out of these diverse cultural and linguistic landscapes is remarkable. One must also admit a certain cultural 'family resemblance' within the subcontinent. But the movement of people, goods and ideas across the landscape of West Asia and the Indian subcontinent—made possible by the Treaty of the Indus and the emergence of 'peer states' and an 'international order'[9] already discussed—created a cultural cosmopolis in which ideas and technologies could percolate. Artists, craftsmen and architects no doubt travelled in search of work and patronage. We saw in the last chapter that a scribe named Chapada travelled a long distance from the far northwest region of the subcontinent to Karnataka to work as a scribe in Ashoka's employ. Any so-called 'foreign influence' in the construction of the Ashokan pillars must be seen in this light. Ashoka, no doubt, tried to get the best artists, engineers and craftsmen he could find, no matter where they came from. He was cosmopolitan enough not to limit his search to his backyard.

---

7   Falk 2006: 139. Falk also discusses in detail the various theories of foreign influence in the construction of Ashokan pillars and capitals.
8   Asher 2006: 51.
9   Kosmin 2014: 32.

Regarding the stone used in the pillars, scholars have suggested the quarries at Chunar in Mirzapur district bordering the Ganges and at Prabhosa near Kosam bordering the Yamuna as possible sources from which the stone for the Ashokan pillars and capitals were quarried.[10] These quarries were close to waterways, making it easier to transport the stone over long distances. Chunar produces a light beige sandstone, while Prabhosa stone varies from beige to rose with black inclusions. Both types were used by Ashokan stonemasons. Asher notes: 'We can be reasonably sure that most of the Aśokan pillars were centrally produced and then transported to sites of erection. The common stone alone suggests centralized work.'[11]

The twenty or so pillars commissioned by Ashoka were crafted and installed in a relatively short period, from about 256 or later to 242 BCE. This breakneck speed of construction stands in contrast to the Egyptian obelisks, which were manufactured over several dynasties. An obelisk, scholars estimate, took about seven months to carve. Given the novelty of the engineering techniques used, it may have taken even longer for Ashoka's stone-carvers and labourers. The transportation and erection of the pillars probably added several more months. In the case of many Ashokan pillars, furthermore, several inscriptions had to be engraved, most frequently while they were lying flat on the ground. It would be reasonable to assume that each pillar would have taken close to a year to be constructed and erected in place. The Ashokan pillars had a feature that the Egyptian obelisks did not: they were topped by large, exquisitely carved capitals. The quarrying, carving, polishing and transporting of these capitals would have taken several months. It is probable, therefore, that teams of stonemasons, engineers and artists would have worked in tandem at the quarry sites.

There were two methods for inscribing edicts on pillars. In a few, the engraving was done on the erected pillars. In such cases, we have

---

10 There was a time when Chunar was regarded as the sole source of stone for the pillars. But this has been successfully challenged by Falk (2006: 154–57) and Asher (2006).

11 Asher 2006: 61.

the inscriptions going around the pillar in a spiralling manner. In the case of the Major Pillar Edicts, this method was followed only on the Allahabad pillar. In all others, the engraving was done before erection while the pillars were lying flat on the ground. Engraving on prone pillars was done in columns (Fig. 5). This would have been logical, given that the engraver could write one column from top to bottom and then turn the pillar to engrave another column on the new face. Some have just two such columns, while others have four narrow ones. It is likely that such inscriptions were done at the quarry itself, given that many of the stonemasons and other experts would have been resident there. There were, however, several engravers involved, given the different handwritings visible in the inscriptions.[12]

A prominent and conspicuous feature of Ashokan pillars and capitals is their high polish, a polish also found in other Ashokan sites such as the Barabar Cave. It is unique—not encountered before Ashoka and never to be imitated again. How was that polish achieved, and why did it disappear from the architectural and artistic history of India? These are questions currently without good answers. With respect to the technique of achieving the lustrous polish 'giving its buff tones a jade-like finish', the art historian John Irwin remarks: 'The technique for getting this finish, which is known as "Mauryan polish", remains scientifically unexplained. It was not used in India after the first millennium B.C.'[13] This is yet another one of those little, and not-so-little, mysteries surrounding Ashoka.

What is the meaning of the Ashokan pillars? What do they signify? Scholars have searched deep into ancient Indian symbology and delved into the arcane world of primal religious symbols, such as the Axis Mundi, in search of answers.[14] A better and more useful way to frame the question is: Why did Ashoka erect these pillars at enormous cost and effort? What did he seek to achieve? Such questions are grounded in history, and any

---

12 See the explanations of Falk 1993b; and 2006: 146.

13 Irwin 1973, 1974. Falk (2006: 142) also confesses: 'The Mauryan polish as a technical process seems still to be undescribed.'

14 See, especially, Irwin 1976.

answer needs to be substantiated by evidence. We cannot, of course, know for sure why Ashoka in the waning years of his rule thought of assembling architects, engineers, artists and a large workforce—an entire bureaucracy—and spending an enormous amount of money to build a large number of these awe-inspiring pillars of little practical use, pillars that centuries later prompted a pilgrim from China, seeing the pillar at Sarnath, to report that it was 'bright as jade … glistening and (sparkling) like light'.[15] We should not overlook the iconic nature of the Ashokan pillars. Romila Thapar has characterized the pillars with their capitals as 'a form of visual literacy'.[16] Nevertheless, I think we can offer some educated guesses by looking at, among other things, the locations of the extant pillars and the images that are carved on the capitals.

One significant fact emerges from their locations: most pillars are, in one way or another, located in places associated with Buddhist monasteries and pilgrimage routes and practices. Several pillars are located in or near Buddhist stupas, monasteries and places of significance for Buddhism: Sanchi, Sarnath, Lumbini, Kumrahar, Nigali and Gotihava. Sanchi in Madhya Pradesh was an ancient monastic complex, but it was far from the Buddhist and Mauryan heartland. It is significant that Ashoka thought the place important enough to place a pillar there surmounted by a capital with four lions. Sarnath is a significant Buddhist site, the place where the Buddha preached his first sermon. It is also close to the sacred city of Varanasi (Benares). Both the Sanchi and Sarnath pillars carry Ashoka's Schism Edict prohibiting dissension within the Buddhist order. Kumrahar is near the capital Pataliputra and again the site of a monastery. Nigali and Gotihava were birthplaces of two previous Buddhas, Konagamana and Krakucchanda, and an inscription on the Nigali pillar memorializes Ashoka's pilgrimage to the spot twenty years after his royal consecration.

At least six pillars are located along the road from Pataliputra to the Buddha's birthplace, Lumbini, within today's Nepal: Vesali, Araraj,

---

15 Cited in Susan and John Huntington 2014: 47.
16 Thapar 2000: 446.

Nandangarh, Rampurva, Tribeni and finally Lumbini. Harry Falk
presents the distances from one pillar to the next: '43 km from Patna
to Vesālī, 112 km from Vesālī to Ararāj along the Gandak, 23 km from
Ararāj to Nandangarh, 34 km from there to Rāmpūrvā, 63 km from there
to Tribeni, and 60 km from there to Lumbinī.'[17] There may have been
other pillars along the way that are now lost. Interestingly, there are wells
near all these pillars, and Falk comments:

> The line of stations would make sense from an Aśokan point of view:
> the pillars would guide the pilgrim to Lumbinī, from well to well,
> touching many holy places on the way, Vesālī being just one of the
> many sites connected with the vita of the Śākyamuni.[18]

Near the wells, there may have been rest houses for the pilgrims to stay,
as indicated in Pillar Edict VII (iii). Some of the pillars have been moved
from their original locations, and the original significance of those
locations cannot be identified. But these twelve pillars demonstrate a clear
association of pillars to Buddhism and Buddhist pilgrimage.

An examination of the extant capitals also points in the same
direction. The capitals are surmounted by three kinds of animals:
lion, elephant and bull (Fig. 13, 18, 19). There are four addorsed lions
facing the four directions at Sanchi and Sarnath, and one at Rampurva
and Vaishali. There is an elephant at Sankisa, and a bull at Rampurva.
Scholars have made numerous attempts to understand and explain
the significance of these animals, either singly or as a group. These
efforts are predicated on there being a comprehensive plan conceived
by Ashoka for the placement of the animals. This cannot be taken for
granted, and we may never be privy to some of the reasons. The three
animals, however, have symbolic values in ancient Indian culture. The
lion is 'king of animals' par excellence, and often represented the king,
whose 'throne' is called *siṃhāsana*, 'lion's seat'. It was the king's privilege
to ride on an elephant, and it was the premier animal within the royal
army. Kings controlled its habitat, capture and training, as well as the

---

17 Falk 2006: 148.
18 Falk 2006: 148.

trade in elephants among rulers.[19] We saw earlier the exchange of war elephants between Chandragupta and Seleucus Nikator. The bull is a sign of virility and power, and humans and even gods are often compared to bulls in eulogies. Conversely, royal symbols were appropriated by ascetic organizations, especially Buddhism. Both the Buddha and other founders of new religions during this period are called *jina*, conqueror. The Buddha's doctrine is compared to a wheel, a metonym for the war chariot and conquest; and his first sermon is the *dharmacakrapravartanasūtra*, 'the Sutra that set the wheel of dharma rolling'. The Buddha's teaching is *śāsana*, the counterpart of a royal edict. These are all clearly royal symbols used, deliberately I think, to define a new ascetic group and a new religious ideology.

   The symbolism of the capitals, thus, has a dual reference, encompassing the emperor and the Buddha. The four roaring and open-mouthed lions of Sanchi and Sarnath are the most symbolically rich. The preaching of the Buddha is frequently compared to a lion's roar.[20] The art historian Susan Huntington comments:

> The Buddha is often called a 'lion', and his words, 'the voice of the lion', or *siṃhaghoṣa*. It is tempting to suggest that the four addorsed lions, with their open mouths, may have served as a dual metaphor, referring both to Aśoka, whose words were inscribed on the pillar and were to be spread throughout the land, and to Śakya muni [i.e., the Buddha] and his teachings, some of which were first revealed at Sārnāth.[21]

---

19 For a comprehensive account of elephants, their domestication and their use in armies, see Trautmann 2015.

20 For a detailed account of the lion's roar in the Buddhist canon, see Anālayo, 'The Lion's Roar in Early Buddhism: A Study Based on the *Ekottarika-āgama* Parallel to the *Cūḷasīhanāda-sutta*'. *Chung-Hwa Buddhist Journal*. Taipei: Chung-Hwa Institute of Buddhist Studies, 22 (2009): 3–24.

21 Huntington and Huntington 2014: 47. For the symbolism of the lion within the Buddhist context, see also Irwin 1973, 1975.

The elephant in a special way is associated with the conception of the Buddha when his mother dreamt of a white elephant entering her womb. As we will see, the double entendre here and elsewhere was probably intentional on the part of Ashoka. This is what I have called Ashoka's 'strategic ambivalence', when language and symbols are used in such a way that they could be read differently by different people. This fluidity of meaning is deliberate and beneficial to Ashoka's dharma mission and to his ongoing commitment to Buddhism.

If the polish of the pillars has given rise to admiration, surprise and puzzlement, so have the exquisite carvings of the pillar capitals, especially the four lions of the Sarnath capital. They also carry the same 'Maurya polish' as the pillars. How such mature sculptural artistry was achieved has puzzled art historians, especially when we consider the fact that it has no known precedent within India. The beauty of the sculpture, nevertheless, is something we can appreciate, irrespective of its history or origin. Charles Allen, one of several recent writers on Ashoka, notes:

> There is no finer demonstration of the state of sculpture at the time of Ashoka than the Sarnath lion capital. It is no exaggeration to speak of it as the work of a Mauryan Michelangelo, a craftsman whose mastery over his material was as complete as anything produced by the Assyrians, the Persians, or the Greeks.[22]

Ashoka probably commissioned other monumental stone structures. The only one of clear Ashokan origin is the stone fence he had constructed at Lumbini around the sal tree under which the Buddha was born. Harry Falk[23] has argued that this stone fence was later transferred by Buddhist monks to Sarnath, where it now stands. It is carved out of a single block of sandstone, just as the Ashokan pillars and capitals, and polished to a fine gloss. Falk estimates that the block from which the fence was sculpted weighed as much as 22 tonnes. The production and transportation of such an enormous structure would have required imperial approval and resources.

---

22 Allen 2012: 335.
23 Falk 2012: 204–16.

Reviewing the activities of Ashoka as a builder, one prominent feature that stands out is his focus on building monuments that contributed to his central mission of propagating dharma and his commitment to Buddhism. On the monumental pillars were inscribed his Pillar Edicts, paralleling his Rock Edicts spread throughout the empire. The pillars were iconic representations of dharma spelled out verbally in the inscriptions. Ashoka in his Pillar Edict VII refers to them as *dhaṃma-thaṃbāni*, 'dharma-pillars'. Soon after their creation, the pillars themselves appear to have become cult objects at least within the Buddhist tradition, but perhaps more broadly as well. A sculpture dating to the first century BCE at Sanchi shows two women with their arms and heads touching a pillar in a posture of veneration, a pillar that resembles an Ashokan pillar but with an oversized wheel at the top (Fig. 12). This is probably a visual portrayal of the veneration of the Buddha's message represented by the pillar and wheel.

A final Ashokan artefact that also has the Maurya polish and the refinement noted in the pillars and capitals are the Barabar Cave dwellings. Ashoka donated these to Ajivika ascetics. As I will note in Chapter 11, these artificially excavated caves were probably executed by the same masons who mastered the craft of sculpting the capitals, as well as by their counterparts responsible for the pillars. Falk calls these caves breathtaking: 'the walls shine like mirrors.'[24]

∼

At the beginning of this chapter I said that Ashoka's building programme is unique in Indian history and unparalleled during his time. He was the first to build with stone and, as Frederick Asher notes, 'the first identifiable patron of Indian art'.[25] But Ashoka was unique in other ways also, and not just in India.

Both in his activities as ruler and writer and in his work as builder, Ashoka cuts a rare figure among ancient monarchs both in India and across the world. In all these activities, but especially as writer and builder, he does not trumpet his triumphs and conquests. The elegant pillars and

24 Falk 2008: 245.
25 Asher 2006: 51.

gorgeous capitals must have evoked wonder and excitement. But Ashoka never boasts about his patronage of these artistic wonders. Instead, he simply engraved his dharma messages on them and left it at that. Ashoka here underscores the claim he makes in Rock Edict X:

> The Beloved of Gods, King Piyadasi, does not consider glory or fame as offering great benefits, with this exception—whatever glory and fame the Beloved of the Gods, King Piyadasi, seeks, it is so that in the present and in the future the people may observe obedience to dharma and follow my teaching of dharma. It is for this reason, the Beloved of God, King Piyadasi, seeks glory or fame.

PART TWO

Upāsaka
Ashoka the Buddhist

N EXT TO HIS IDENTITY AS KING, THE MOST CENTRAL, THE MOST
defining identity of Ashoka was his explicit claim to be—what
we would call today—a Buddhist. He proclaims this identity in the very
first words he left to posterity, Minor Rock Edict I. In it, he uses the
technical term '*upasāka*' to identify himself. Although this term is used
with reference to lay devotees of various religions, such as the Jains, in
this edict it clearly refers to Buddhist laypersons, and more particularly
to persons who are deeply committed to the Buddhist doctrine and
practice, who take that practice seriously and make it a central focus
of their lives. They may also have a close personal relationship to the
Buddhist monastic order, the Sangha.[1] Ashoka's Buddhist faith is also
explicit in his donative inscriptions at Lumbini, where the Buddha
was born (Fig. 3), and at Nigliva, the birthplace of a previous Buddha,
Konakamana, as also in the two inscriptions (Bairat and Schism Edicts)
dealing explicitly with the Buddhist Sangha (see Chapter 6). At Bairat,
Ashoka is explicit in his confession of his Buddhist faith: 'It is known

---

1   A variant reading is found in Minor Rock Edict I as inscribed at Maski,
    although the reading is not without uncertainty. There, Upasaka is replaced
    by *budhasaka* (i.e., Buddha-Sakya)—probably a common designation for
    people who followed the Buddha's path, Sakya referring to the clan to which
    the Buddha belonged.

to you, Venerable Sirs, my esteem of and faith in the Buddha, Dharma and Sangha. Whatsoever, Venerable Sirs, the Lord Buddha has spoken, all that has been well spoken indeed.'

The central identity of Ashoka as a Buddhist needs to inform our investigation and interpretation of the written documents and artefacts he has left behind. We have already seen the distinctly Buddhist stamp on the monumental pillars he erected across a vast swathe of northern India. He does not always speak as a Buddhist; most frequently he speaks as king and as a promoter of morality, dharma. But his Buddhist identity, even when not open and explicit, is never far removed. Sometimes, in the effort to demonstrate that Ashoka's dharma is not simply the Buddhist dharma, scholars have erred on the opposite side by downplaying or ignoring his Buddhist identity. Ashoka, as I have noted, is a complex character.

5

Deepening the Faith

UCH HAS BEEN WRITTEN ABOUT THE 'CONVERSION' OF ASHOKA TO Buddhism. It is the cornerstone of Buddhist hagiographies of Ashoka. Conversion, according to this narrative, transformed him from the 'cruel Ashoka' (*caṇḍa aśoka*), the sadist who delighted in giving pain to and torturing people, to the 'righteous Ashoka' (*dharma aśoka*), the pious Buddhist. This Damascene event is certainly a good storyline and makes for great hagiography. Historically, however, it is specious. Ashoka's inscriptions themselves do not point to a cathartic conversion experience, and Romila Thapar is correct in her assessment that 'there was no sudden conversion but rather a gradual and increasingly close association with Buddhism'.[1] I will attempt to come up with a reasonable timeline for Ashoka's turn to Buddhism, a timeline that may also have a bearing on our understanding of Ashoka's later inscriptions dealing with dharma.

BECOMING A BUDDHIST

The most detailed account we have of Ashoka's association with Buddhism is in Minor Rock Edict I, the earliest of his writings to come down to us. Its account is still sketchy and contains puzzling statements that have spawned numerous interpretations but little consensus. This is geographically the most widespread of Ashoka's inscriptions

---

1   Thapar 2000: 424.

(see the Map). It has been discovered in eighteen locations throughout
the subcontinent including the far south, around today's Karnataka
and Andhra. Being the first of his writings, one detects some level of
experimentation; neither the officials in charge nor the scribes had done
anything like this before. The edict has been subject to numerous editorial
interventions either by local officials or by scribes in charge of inscribing
the text on rock surfaces. The edict reads in full (Fig. 14):

The Beloved of Gods proclaims the following—

> It has been over two and a half years since I have been an Upasaka.
> But for one year I did not strive vigorously. It was over a year
> ago, however, that I approached the Sangha and began to strive
> vigorously.
> But during that time men in Jambudvipa,[2] who were unmingled
> with gods, were made to mingle with them. For that is the fruit
> of striving. This can be achieved not only by eminent people, but
> even lowly people if they strive are indeed able to attain even the
> immense heaven.
> This promulgation has been promulgated for the following
> purpose—so that both the lowly and the eminent may strive, that
> the frontier people also may come to know it, and that this striving
> may endure for a long time. And this matter will spread and spread
> immensely—spread at least one and a half times more.
> This promulgation has been promulgated on completing 256.

The first thing to note in this message is that Ashoka announces
here—as far as we can tell for the first time in public—that he has been
an Upasaka for two and a half years. His use of this technical term, which
is used here clearly in the Buddhist sense, is noteworthy. The same can
be said regarding Ashoka's use of the technical term 'Sangha' to refer to
the Buddhist monastic order. He must have expected his audience, both

---

2   Literally, 'island (or continent) of the rose apple'. The appellation generally
    refers to the land mass of the Indian subcontinent.

his officials and the members of the public who read or listened to the edict, to understand its meaning, for he makes no attempt to define or explain the terms. Nor do the local officials and scribes—except perhaps in Maski, discussed below—who, in other circumstances, do make editorial comments. Why would he have had such an expectation? Remember that this is the most widespread of all Ashoka's edicts. Did he expect people in all these remote corners of his empire to be familiar with the Buddhist technical vocabulary? I deal with this question in Chapter 7. We must assume, however, that Buddhism by this time was sufficiently widespread for the term to have been either in common use or at least widely known. That the edict was intended for the far corners of his empire is indicated both by the widespread inscriptional sites and by his reference to 'frontier people' who are included in his target audience.

The problem with this technical term is revealed in the version of this edict found in Maski in Karnataka in southern India. At Maski, the officials or scribes may have been of the opinion that people would not have understood the meaning of Upasaka, or they thought the term in their manuscript was corrupt. So, they changed it to a more common term: 'budhaśake', that is, Buddha-Sakya—at least that is the likely reading, although the characters here are not totally clear. It may even be, as has been suggested,[3] that the original *upāsaka* was changed later by an editor to give this reading. It appears that these individuals interpreted Upasaka not in its narrow technical sense but more broadly as simply a person devoted to the Buddha.

Ashoka says that for a whole year after he became an Upasaka he did not 'strive', a term that is central to the edict and is repeated six times in this short text. The original term is '*pakaṃte*', sometimes rendered '*palakaṃte*' (or a version of these). The first relates to the Sanskrit *prakramati* and the second to *parākramati*. Interestingly, both these terms have strong martial connotations—military attack, showing courage in battle. Once again here we find Ashoka using military/royal terms to define a Buddhist undertaking. In both contexts, Ashoka must strive, be bold and exert himself. In Ashoka's inscriptional corpus cognates of these

---

3   See Anderson 1990: 59.

terms are used in Major Rock Edicts VI and X. In the former the topic is Ashoka's zeal in working for the welfare of the people. Reports relating to the affairs of the people, he tells his officials, should be sent to him immediately, no matter what he is doing or where he is. He also expresses the hope that in the future his sons and grandsons may similarly strive for the welfare of the whole world. He concludes that such a goal is very difficult to achieve without 'utmost striving'. In Rock Edict X we have an even closer parallel to the use of this term in the Buddhist context. Here Ashoka is talking about the striving needed to accumulate merit for the next world and to eliminate any demerit or sin. He concludes this text by saying: 'This is difficult to do, however, for either a low-class person or a high-class person without utmost striving, giving up everything. But between them, it is clearly more difficult to do for a high-class person.' In these examples the term appears to refer to exertion and effort directed at accomplishing a moral goal, the goal of personal growth. The meaning of the term in Minor Rock Edict I must be the same or similar, although there it may have a somewhat more Buddhist tinge.

Ashoka credits his visit to the Sangha with his newfound fervour and zeal. He does not identify the monastery or where it was located, but we can be confident that it was in or near the capital city of Pataliputra. The visit certainly was not a casual one to greet the monks. He went there for a specific purpose, for spiritual instruction and guidance. This visit became a turning point in Ashoka's life. Without that visit we may not have had the numerous Ashokan inscriptions and artefacts, and our knowledge of ancient Indian history would have been impoverished. What did the monk or monks say or do to make Ashoka a zealot in the best sense of that term—a man full of zeal, full of striving? Ashoka gives us no clues as to the nature of his interactions with the monks, but it is reasonable to assume that it involved some kind of instruction in Buddhist doctrines and practices.

All this led to his 'striving'. But here too Ashoka does not tell us what this striving entailed. Is it directed at living a moral life, as indicated by his later edicts dealing with the propagation of dharma? Is it directed also at some specifically Buddhist practices, for example, visiting Buddhist places of worship on special occasions such as full moon days, or reciting and observing the five Buddhist precepts, or even engaging in some form of meditation? Sometimes Ashoka is infuriatingly brief—he stops when we want him to continue, to tell us more.

Instead, he changes the topic and talks about a time when 'men in Jambudvipa, who were unmingled with gods, were made to mingle with them'. This, he says, was the result of his striving. Two things stand out here. For the first—and the last—time, Ashoka mentions a geographical region named Jambudvipa, 'the island of the rose apple'. It is an appellation generally given to the Indian subcontinent, and the use of the term indicates that Ashoka had some idea that his empire extended over all or most of the subcontinent. What 'mingling with the gods' means has occupied the minds of scholars for the better part of two centuries, and still there is little consensus. It is, nevertheless, the direct result of the 'striving' advocated by Ashoka. This appears to indicate that it refers to some kind of spiritual attainment, rather than something worldly or ceremonial. Perhaps, this striving assures that humans will mingle with the gods after death.[4] Immediately afterwards, he mentions that the goal of striving is the attainment of 'the immense heaven'. That there must be some sort of metaphoric language used here is implied in the Greek version based on this edict located in Kandahar, where the reading is 'everything thrives on the whole earth'.[5] Some kind of paradisiacal state on earth seems to be intended.

The edict also gives an insight into Ashoka's intended audience: it included people of low social standing. He says that the striving he is speaking about 'can be achieved not only by eminent people, but even lowly people if they strive are indeed able to attain the immense heaven'. A similar sentiment is expressed in Rock Edict X, where Ashoka shows a

---

4   Norman 2012a: 119: 'I take it to mean that he had succeeded in bringing men to heaven, where of course they will be reborn as gods, i.e. mixed with other gods.' John Strong (2012) connects the theme of the commingling of gods and humans to the Buddha's descent from heaven and the honouring of the relics. Wright (2000: 335) takes the statement 'as a metaphor for a Buddhist regeneration here on earth': Ashoka's work paves the way for people to be with the gods in the next life.

5   See Gaál and Tóth 2018.

preference for the little people: 'This is difficult to do, however, for either a low-class person or a high-class person without utmost striving, giving up everything. But between them, it is clearly more difficult to do for a high-class person.' It is, however, unclear whether lowly or low-class refers to the poor or to those in socially lower positions, or to both. For the first time in his edicts, he also talks about people living outside but near the borders of his own empire. The outreach he is making includes these frontier people as well.

Ashoka makes a prediction that 'this matter' will spread far and wide, that his programme of education in 'striving' will be successful. What I have translated as 'matter' reads in the original '*aṭhe*' (Sanskrit: *artha*), one of the most frustrating terms in the Sanskrit language because of its vast semantic range. What does *artha* refer to? What is this 'matter' or 'thing'? I think it is logical to connect it with the 'striving' mentioned in the previous sentence. Ashoka hopes and expects that his preaching about the importance of striving for everyone, both those at the top of the ladder and those at the bottom, including those who may live outside his own territory, will be successful.

The edict concludes with the number 256, which appears to be related to the date of the edict: 'This promulgation has been promulgated on completing 256.' This is another Ashokan riddle that most scholars working on Ashoka have attempted to solve, mostly without success. The original term '*vyuṭhenā*',[6] which I have translated as 'on completing', is ambiguous. Some have taken it to mean that Ashoka was 'on tour' and away from home. But the evidence from other ancient sources, such as Kautilya's *Arthashastra*, makes it clear that the meaning I have adopted is the correct one. The historian J.C. Wright's assessment, I think, is correct: 'It seems that the actual intention of the MRE [Minor Rock Edict] dating was no longer understood anywhere at the time of its inscription

---

6   For the interpretation of the term '*vyuṭhenā*' as referring to the 'lighting up' in the morning of an Uposatha day, see Falk 2013. For other interpretations of the term (with variants), see Norman 1983, who accepts the interpretation that Ashoka was away from home. See Wright 2000 (especially p. 327) for my interpretation that it means 'completed'.

on rocks.'[7] Even the officers and scribes working on engraving this edict were unclear about its meaning, and some attempted to emend the text to produce a clearer meaning. This is not the place to review all the scholarly attempts to make sense of 256, but I think the solution based on the 'military month' of thirty-two days provides the best result.[8] Thus, 256 translates to eight months constituting the dry season when travel, whether military, commercial or religious, was possible, before the onset of the four-month rainy season. This was also the period when itinerant ascetics, such as the Jains and Buddhists, were expected to wander before settling down in one place to spend the rainy season. If this interpretation is accepted, then Ashoka composed this edict at the end of a trip lasting eight months and just before the onset of rains.

If this calculation is correct, then Ashoka issued the edict in the middle of June, the beginning of the rainy season. There is good evidence, furthermore, that it was issued ten years after his royal consecration, that is, in the eleventh year of his reign.[9] In Kandahar I, both the Aramaic and Greek translations state that Ashoka began his dharma mission after ten years, that is, in the eleventh year of his reign. If we take 268 BCE as the year of his royal consecration—if another date is preferred, then the relative dates would have to be adjusted—then we can move back from that date to calculate the year when Minor Rock Edict I was issued: 258 BCE. But first we have to figure out the month of his royal consecration.

Although there is some uncertainty, we can assume that it was in the bright half of the lunar month of Chaitra, generally falling in mid-March. The reason is that the Vedic ritual of royal consecration (*rājasūya*) within which the central component was the pouring of sacred water on the king's head, the *abhiṣeka*—the term used by Ashoka—was carried out during this month. Chaitra is the first month of spring in the Indian

---

7   Wright 2000: 331.
8   For a history of scholarly interpretations of this number, see Wright 2000.
9   See Falk 2006: 55. Wright (2000: 338) says that this edict was issued in the '13th regnal year', but does not spell out how he arrives at this date. This date would imply that it was written five years after the Kalinga war, whereas Ashoka himself says that he wrote some of the Major Rock Edicts twelve years after his royal consecration.

calendar, and it may well have been a custom even outside of the Vedic ritual context to have auspicious rites performed during that month. So, if Ashoka's royal consecration was in the middle of March 268, then June of the eleventh year, when Minor Rock Edict I was written, would be June 258 BCE.

We can now calculate the time when Ashoka became an Upasaka, which, he says, happened a little over two and a half years before writing his edict. That would have been around December 260 BCE. He became zealous in the practise of his Buddhist faith one year after, that is, in December 259 BCE.

With these dates in mind, we can return to the war Ashoka waged against Kalinga discussed in Chapter 2. It is worth recalling some of the details, because Ashoka's conversion to Buddhism is closely linked to the horrors of that war. In both Rock Edict XIII and its abridged translation into Greek in Kandahar, the war is said to have taken place eight years after his consecration, that is, in the ninth year of his rule beginning around March 260 BCE. We need, however, to pin down the month he started his military offensive. Although some exceptions are given in later sources, military strategists sought to avoid the rainy season extending from mid-June to mid-October for military campaigns, a time when travel with heavy equipment and animals was difficult and often impossible. The roads became muddy, and rivers swollen. Crossing them posed dangers to men, animals and equipment. Remember that there were no permanent bridges over rivers in ancient India; rivers had to be forded. Winter months were avoided due to the likelihood of inclement weather. So we have two windows for military operations: between mid-March and mid-June, and between mid-October and mid-December. The ideal month recommended in later texts is the lunar month of Margasirsa, which begins in the middle of November. Both possible dates for the Kalinga war fall before yet very close in time to when Ashoka became an Upasaka, that is, in December 260 BCE. I think the November date is more likely. Ashoka expressed deep regret at the suffering and loss of life that the war entailed. It is possible to imagine—although there is no certainty—that the suffering he caused the people of Kalinga and the deep personal remorse he felt may have influenced his pivot to Buddhism. The chart below provides an outline of the dates relating to the first ten years of Ashoka's reign.[10]

Chart 5.1
Ashoka's Conversion: Timeline

Royal consecration	March 268 BCE
Kalinga war	April–June or October–December 260 BCE
Becoming Upasaka	December 260 BCE
Becoming zealous	December 259 BCE
Minor Rock Edict I	June 257 BCE

GOING ON PILGRIMAGE

Returning to Ashoka's eight-month travel before writing Minor Rock Edict I, a couple of obvious questions emerge. What was the purpose of this travel? What sorts of places and people did he visit? A clue is found in Rock Edict VIII, in which Ashoka talks about converting royal pleasure excursions into religious pilgrimages. And significantly, he gives the year when he started this practice by going out to what Ashoka calls 'saṃbodhi'. This term means literally enlightenment or full enlightenment. There is a difference of opinion as to whether Ashoka means to say that he set out on an inner journey to become enlightened, or that he went to the place where or the tree under which the Buddha gained enlightenment. I opt for the latter.[11] This tree (*Ficus religiosa*) is even today called Bo-Tree (Bodhi Tree) in Sri Lanka. Ashoka says that his journey to the place of the Buddha's enlightenment, today's Bodh Gaya, took place ten years after his royal consecration, that is, in his eleventh regnal year. This was precisely the year in which Ashoka issued his Minor Rock Edict I, which we have been examining.

---

10 A similar conclusion is reached by Gaál and Tóth 2018: 92.

11 Ashoka's visit to the Bodhi tree is visually represented at Kanaganahalli where, as Monika Zin (2022: 546) has noted, 'the two panels thus depict Aśoka's visit to the *bodhi* tree in Bodhgaya. The narrative of Aśoka's pilgrimage to the *bodhi* tree was familiar to the artists who created the Kanaganahalli *stūpa*, as well as to its visitors.'

So, we now can set the scene. Ashoka undertook a tour during the dry season of his eleventh regnal year, 258 BCE, during which he visited Bodh Gaya, and at the conclusion of his pilgrimage—that is, at the end of the eight-month dry season and the beginning of the four-month rain retreat—Ashoka issued his edict. Here is Rock Edict VIII, which describes his pilgrimage:

> In times past, Beloveds of Gods [= kings] used to set out on recreational tours. During these, hunting and other such enjoyments took place.
> But, the Beloved of Gods, King Piyadasi, ten years after his royal consecration, set out to Enlightenment. Through that came about the dharma-tour.
> During it the following take place: paying visits to Sramanas and Brahmins and making gifts to them, paying visits to elderly people and providing monetary support to them, paying visits to people of the countryside, providing instruction in dharma and in germane questions about dharma.
> This gives greater enjoyment to the Beloved of Gods, King Piyadasi; the other is but a fraction.

Even though his 'dharma tour' (*dharmayātrā*) begins with his visit to Bodh Gaya, it is here cast within a wider perspective. His trips include visits to the dual class of religious people, Sramanas and Brahmins, making donations to them, as well as other charitable activities. In a special way, these trips were intended to teach dharma to the general population. The term '*yātrā*' requires some elucidation. It refers to any long journey—not a quick trip to the local store. A journey for pleasure and recreation, such as hunting, can also be called *yātrā*. The term, however, took on a more specifically religious meaning as a pilgrimage when people journeyed to places of religious significance. Even in later India such religious pilgrimages are called *yātrās*. In this edict, as in others, Ashoka wants to contrast his activities to those of past kings. His *yātrā* was not for pleasure but for dharma—or, it was for pleasure, but a totally different kind of pleasure, for spiritual pleasure, as he notes at the conclusion of his edict.

On other occasions also Ashoka visited various places of importance in the Buddha's life. He visited Lumbini, the Buddha's birthplace, later in his life, twenty years after his royal consecration. He erected a pillar there and wrote a brief inscription to memorialize the event (Fig. 3):

> The Beloved of Gods, King Piyadasi, twenty years after his royal consecration, came in person and paid reverence.
>
> Saying 'Here was born the Buddha, the Sakya sage,' he had a stone fence constructed and a stone pillar erected.
>
> Saying 'Here was born the Lord,' he made the village of Lumbini tax free and to have a one-eighth portion.

As I have already noted in Chapter 4, a fence probably surrounded the sal tree under which the Buddha was born, a long-lived tree that possibly was still there during Ashoka's time. He also made the village of Lumbini free from taxes, which meant that the taxes that would have normally gone to the king were now redirected to support the monks who lived there and who looked after the birthplace of the Buddha.

The tricky part of this edict is the last word: *aṭha-bhāgiye*. It has previously been misunderstood as referring to the tax-exempt status of Lumbini, thus making it not completely tax-free but only free of one-eighth of the tax due. As Harry Falk has remarked, this makes Ashoka niggardly, and it does not sound right. The new meaning suggested by Falk is that a 'one-eighth portion' of the Buddha's remains was given to Lumbini to be interred there. If this is correct, as it appears to be, then we have inscriptional evidence of Ashoka redistributing the bodily remains of the Buddha. This lends some support to the later Buddhist hagiographical account that Ashoka divided the original remains of the Buddha and distributed it across the subcontinent.

The Buddhist pilgrimages of Ashoka included places sacred to Buddhas who were thought to have preceded the historical Buddha.

One was to the birthplace of a Buddha named Konakamana.[12] Ashoka, fourteen years after his royal consecration, enlarged the stupa found at this place to double its original size, and later visited the place personally. It is unclear whether this was his first visit, but it is probable that in the twentieth year he visited the birthplaces of both the historical Buddha and Buddha Konakamana, perhaps as part of the same pilgrimage. During his second visit, moreover, Ashoka erected a stone pillar to memorialize the occasion and had an inscription carved on the pillar. This is today called the Nigali Sagar Pillar.

The erection of stone pillars to mark places of significance to Buddhism is a hallmark of Ashoka's building activities, as I have noted in Chapter 4. Harry Falk has remarked in the context of the Ashokan pillars: 'In some way or other all of them seem to be connected either with places of the Buddhist *Sangha* or were parts of an itinerary leading to the birthplace of the Buddha himself.'[13]

The three or so years leading up to and following the Kalinga war constituted a watershed in Ashoka's personal biography. He would have been engaged in diplomacy and busy with preparations for war against Kalinga for the better part of 260 BCE. The war ended probably late that year. Ashoka was deeply affected by the carnage he had caused. It is likely that he had dabbled in Buddhism for a while, but now he felt a sense of urgency. A few months after the war, probably around December 260 BCE, he formally became a Buddhist Upasaka. We do not know whether this step involved a public ceremony or ritual, but Ashoka remembered the date well, as he recalls it in Minor Rock Edict I. It would take him another year, December 259 BCE, to develop what he calls 'striving', a single-minded focus on and commitment to his Buddhist faith. During the first half of 258 BCE, the months following his new commitment, he must have entered a new phase of life. Did he get instruction from Buddhist monks on the moral and meditative practices of Buddhism? Did they read and

12 For this Buddha, see Hultzsch 1925: 165, n. 6.
13 Falk 2006: 55.

explain to him Buddhist texts? As we will see in Chapter 6, he appears to have become well-versed in Buddhist scriptures, so much so that he was bold enough to recommend a scriptural reading list to the monks.

Around October 258 BCE at the end of the rainy season, Ashoka took a decision to go on tour. Such imperial tours to visit important places in the territory and to speak with senior officials in the provinces may have been a long-standing practice. They may have included recreational and pleasure activities, such as hunting, mentioned in Rock Edict VIII and in Ashoka's graffiti at Panguraria. But Ashoka gave the royal tour a new twist: he transformed it into a religious exercise, even imitating the eight-month itinerant lifestyle of a monk.

During this his first religious tour he must have come up with the idea of writing a message to his subjects and having it inscribed on rock surfaces across his territory—a momentous decision that transformed his life and that of his people, as well as the structure and activities of his government. It changed Indian history. His first message was written towards the end of his tour, probably in or around June 257 BCE, although inscribing it on stone may have been carried out in subsequent months. He came up with the idea of having his message inscribed on stone, so it would be visible to the people and last a long time. Nothing like that had been attempted by any Indian ruler before him. He sent his message— what we know as Minor Rock Edict I—to officials in various parts of the empire, and it was also passed around among the officials themselves. The message proclaimed his Buddhist faith and invited his audience to join him in this 'striving'.

6

Exhorting the Sangha

WHEN ASHOKA FIRST ANNOUNCED PUBLICLY THAT HE WAS AN Upasaka, a devout Buddhist layman, he ascribed his newfound zeal in following the Buddhist path to a visit he paid to the Sangha. This technical term in the Buddhist religious vocabulary refers both to the idealized universal Buddhist monastic order and to any particular congregation of Buddhist monks or nuns living in a specific monastic setting. The first meaning is found in its use within the three basic treasures—the triple gem—of Buddhism: Buddha, Dharma and Sangha. But one cannot 'visit' the universal Sangha. Ashoka does not disclose what specific monastery or which specific monks he interacted with in this pivotal visit. In this early encounter, it is clear that Ashoka was the neophyte needing guidance and instruction. That first visit was probably followed by more and more frequent visits that helped deepen his faith, increase his knowledge of Buddhism, introduce him to Buddhist scriptural texts and further his spiritual journey.

I dealt with Ashoka's early interactions with the Sangha in the previous chapter. Here I focus on his dealings with the Sangha after he became a mature and confident Buddhist and took an increasing interest in the organization of Buddhism in general and in the proper functioning of the Sangha in particular.

Ashoka's interest in the Sangha can be seen, on the one hand, as part of his interest in all religious organizations within his empire, organizations that he calls Pasandas. I will examine his relationship to

Pasandas in Part Four. His interest in the Sangha, however, was deeper and broader, given that he was himself an Upasaka, a lay member of the Buddhist Pasanda. Two of his inscriptions deal specifically with the Sangha and reveal Ashoka's desire not just to be a patron and an advisor, but also to exercise control over Buddhist monastic institutions. The first is inscribed on a rock originally discovered in a place called Bairat, about 170 kilometres south of Delhi. It is now housed at the Asiatic Society premises in Kolkata. The second is found in three versions inscribed on three pillars located at Sanchi, Sarnath and Allahabad.

INSTRUCTING THE SANGHA

In the Bairat inscription, Ashoka emerges as a bookworm ready to recommend selected texts to both monastics and laypeople. This is the only inscription where Ashoka addresses monks and nuns directly. Other inscriptions dealing with Buddhism, such as the Schism Edict, are addressed to various officials, even though they deal with the conduct of monks. The Bairat inscription reads (Fig. 8):

> Piyadasi, the king of Magadha, having paid his respects to the Sangha, extends his wishes for your wellbeing and comfort.
>
> It is known to you, Venerable Sirs, my esteem for and faith in the Buddha, Dharma and Sangha. Whatsoever, Venerable Sirs, the Lord Buddha has spoken, all that has been well spoken indeed. But, Venerable Sirs, what I see as embodying the statement: 'Thus the True Dharma will long endure,' I take the liberty to state that—namely, Venerable Sirs, these discourses on Dharma:
>> *Vinayasamukase* (Exaltation of Monastic Disciplinary Rules), *Aliyavasāni* (Lineages of Noble Ones), *Anāgatabhayāni* (Future Dangers), *Munigāthā* (Sage's Poem), *Moneyasūte* (Discourse on Sagehood), *Upatisapasine* (Upatissa's Questions), and *Lāgulovāde* (Advice to Rahula) relating to falsehood,
>
> spoken by the Lord Buddha.
>
> These discourses on Dharma, Venerable Sirs—I wish that large numbers of monks and nuns will listen to them repeatedly and reflect

on them, so also male Upasakas and female Upasikas. For this reason, Venerable Sirs, this has been inscribed, so that they will know my intention.

In this short inscription Ashoka addresses Buddhist monks and nuns, as also male and female lay devotees, the Upasakas. The inscription has a wealth of interesting and important information about Buddhism and Ashoka buried in it which I will try to unpack. First, let us look at Ashoka's vocabulary. It is apparent that he had learned both Buddhist technical terms and the polite ways of address when laypeople are speaking to monks. The term *'bhante'* is used five times in the text at the beginning of each sentence after the introduction. This mode of address, which I have inarticulately translated as 'Venerable Sirs', is a stock term in Buddhist texts when someone is addressing a monk. Its frequent use here shows Ashoka, despite being the king, exhibiting deference to the spiritual superiority of monks.

Then, we have the enquiry about the 'wellbeing and comfort' of monks—the 'How are you?' of the period. The wording, however, is specifically Buddhist. The original language—*apābādhataṃ phāsuvihālataṃ*—is found frequently in the Buddhist canon as a form of greeting when a layperson meets the Buddha or a monk. In the Pali scriptural texts we find a longer and fuller version of this greeting where the layperson asks whether the monk 'is well, not indisposed, of bodily vigor, strong, abiding in comfort'.[1] Ashoka uses the first and the last words of the longer version, although we cannot be sure that such a longer version existed during his time. Or, could the use of the first and the last be an abbreviation, a way of greeting the monks implicitly with the full formula?

He then uses the term *'saddharma'*, a ubiquitous term in Buddhist theological vocabulary to refer to the Buddha's doctrine as *sad*, which means both doctrinally true and morally good and virtuous. I will return to this expression on the next page.

---

1   See *Dīgha Nikāya* (Subhasutta), I: 204 and *Vinaya Piṭaka* (Cullavagga), II: 127. The Pali wording is: *appabādhaṃ appātaṅkaṃ lahuṭṭhānaṃ balaṃ phāsuvihāraṃ*.

1. The words '*devānaṃpiyena piyadasina lājina*' on a pillar in Lumbini

2. 'Dhaṃma' in Brahmi script

3. Lumbini pillar inscription

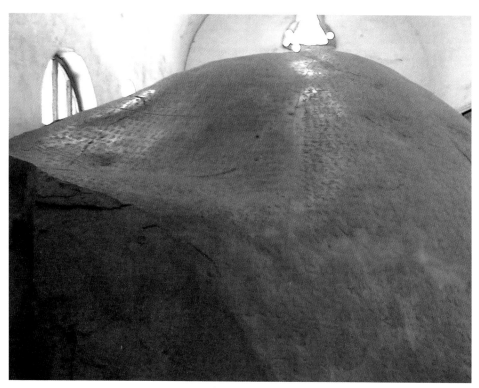

4. Rock edicts at Girnar

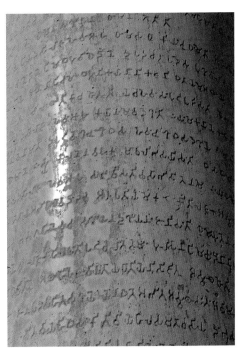

5. Pillar edicts at Lauriya

6. Four scripts of Ashokan inscriptions: Brahmi, Kharosthi, Greek and Aramaic

7. Bilingual edict at Kandahar

8. Ashoka's message to the Buddhist Sangha inscribed at Bairat.

9. An Indian coin with
the Lion Capital, 1954

10. An Indian stamp with
the Lion Capital, 1947

11. First banknote of Independent India, 1949

12. Adoration of a pillar in Sanchi

13. The Lion Capital in Sarnath at the time of discovery

14. Minor Rock Edict I at Gavimath

15. Schism edict at Sarnath

16. Vaishali pillar

17. The Barabar Caves of Lomas Rishi

18. The Lion Capital at
the Sarnath Museum

19. The Bull Capital
in Rampurva

It is also notable that Ashoka's initial self-reference in this letter to Buddhist monks and nuns is quite unique: 'Piyadasi, the king of Magadha.' This is a form of introduction not found in any other inscription. His reference to himself simply as king of Magadha, as opposed to using his formal title of 'Beloved of Gods' (*devānāṃpriya*), may again indicate deference to the monks. We do not have any parallel texts, unfortunately; none is addressed to monks.

He begins his message by trying, I think, to blunt his directive about the scriptural texts that he expects the monks and nuns to study by telling them how much he is devoted to the Buddhist triple gem—Buddha, Dharma, Sangha. He acknowledges that *everything* the Buddha has said—that is, all Buddhist scriptures—is 'well said': they are all worthy of study.[2] But given the objective that the Buddha's 'true (or good) Dharma' (*saddharma*) will endure for a long time, Ashoka wants to recommend seven selected texts of Buddhist scripture for special attention. Note the oblique way he couches his directive. He uses the term '*alahāmi*' (Sanskrit: *arhāmi*), which is a term often used in polite discourse to couch an order as a plea, similar to our saying: 'please', 'you may want to', and the like.

Clearly, Ashoka thinks these seven texts are the best, or at least the most appropriate, in the canonical repertoire; the ones, if studied, will ensure that Buddhism will last a long time. Did he come to this conclusion on this own, or were there monks close to him and having his ear who promoted these texts? Did they have a sectarian slant and promote some factional doctrines and practices? What was the subtext to Ashoka's letter to the monks and nuns? Was there an incident or a set of circumstances that prompted him to write this letter? In any event, here we have evidence that Ashoka took his Buddhism seriously and engaged in intense study of the Buddhist scriptural texts available to him at that time.

A related—and important—question is in what format these texts were available to him. Were they available orally? In which case, he would have had to listen to them as someone, probably a monk who

---

2   This phrase is also found in different formulations in the Pali canon: *yaṃ kiñci subhāsitam sabbam tam tassa bhagavato vacanaṃ*: 'whatever is well spoken is all the word of the Blessed One' (*Anguttara Nikāya*, IV, 164, 8).

knew them by heart, recited and explained them. And did he subsequently learn them by heart? Or were they available in written form? In which case, did he send copies of these along with his message to the Buddhist monasteries? How else would the monks, nuns and laypeople have access to them, unless there were monks and nuns in these monasteries who knew these texts by heart?

Even though there is no general agreement among scholars about the identity of these seven texts and whether we can trace them, at least tentatively, in the extant Pali canon,[3] it is fruitful to see what the content of these texts may have been with an eye to understanding Ashoka's intentions, why he was attracted to these specific texts. The first, *Vinayasamukase* (Exaltation of Monastic Disciplinary Rules), could be the Buddha's very first sermon delivered at Sarnath. In the *Vinaya Piṭaka* and elsewhere this sermon is called *sāmukkaṃsikā dhammadesanā*, 'the most excellent sermon on dharma'.[4] If this identification is correct—and that is far from certain[5]—it would have been quite logical for Ashoka to place this at the head of his list. Not only is it the Buddha's very first sermon, but it also contains the gist of his doctrine: the Four Noble Truths and the Eightfold Noble Path. Note that it was at Sarnath that Ashoka erected a pillar with the most beautiful lion capitals.

The identity of the second text, *Aliyavasāni* (Lineages of Noble Ones), is a bit more certain: the text deals with the ten noble abodes of a monk. These are the ten qualities that he cultivates, and they are given in the *Saṃgīti Suttanta* of the *Dīgha Nikāya*.

(The monk) has got rid of five factors, is possessed of six factors, has set the one guard, carries out the four bases of observance, has

---

3   The Pali canon called *Tipiṭaka* comprises the Buddhist scriptures of the Theravada School dominant in Sri Lanka and Southeast Asia. For a discussion of these identifications, see Schmithausen 1992: 113–17.

4   See *Vinaya Piṭaka*, Mahāvagga, I.7.6; I.8.2.

5   Other scholars have identified this text as the *Pāṭimokkha*, a compendium of Buddhist monastic rules which forms the basis of the Buddhist *Vinaya Piṭaka*. This is unlikely because this compendium is always read out at the Uposatha ceremony. Thus it was unnecessary for Ashoka to single this out for reading.

put away sectarian opinions, has utterly given up quests, is candid
in his thoughts, has calmed the restlessness of his body, and is well
emancipated in heart and intellect.[6]

The text goes on to explain each of these. For example, emancipation
of the heart consists of being free of passion, hatred and illusion; and
emancipation of the intellect consists of his conviction that passion,
hatred and illusion have been eliminated. A significant point here is that
these enumerations remind us very much of the Buddhist method of
mental training using numbers.

We see numbers coming up again in the third text, the five future
dangers (Anāgatabhayāni) found in the Aṅguttara Nikāya.[7] It deals with
dangers that a monk living in the wilderness may face: snakes and other
poisonous creatures, risk of falling down, vicious beasts such as lions and
tigers, criminals and malevolent spirits. Contemplation of these dangers
will prompt the monk to attain quickly those spiritual goals he has not yet
attained. Although directly applicable to monks living in the wilderness,
these are probably meant as warnings also to monks within established
monasteries and to the devout lay folks. The future is uncertain. So, one
must be assiduous in cultivating Buddhist virtues today and not postpone
it to tomorrow.

The next two texts deal with the Muni, the ideal sage of both
Buddhism and the Brahmanical tradition. The first, Munigāthā (Sage's
Poem), deals with the qualities of the ideal Buddhist sage, and the second,
Moneyasūte (Discourse on Sagehood), deals with what makes a sage a
sage.[8] The two are, therefore, related texts. There are two candidates for
the identity of the first: the most obvious is the Munisutta of the Suttanipāta
(verses 207–21); the other possibility is the Sammāparibbājaniyasutta
(Suttanipāta verses 359–75), which is sometimes also called Munisutta.[9]

---

6   Translation in T.W. Rhys Davids, Sacred Books of the Buddhists (London:
    Humphrey Milford, 1921), IV, p. 247.

7   Aṅguttara Nikāya III: 100f.

8   The Prakrit moneyya (Sanskrit: mauneya) is an abstract noun—the state of a
    sage—derived from muni.

9   See Norman 1985: 188.

The first, *Munisutta*, is an elegy of a monk's solitary life, the homeless state, which is contrasted to the life of a householder. The sage lives on food given by others, lives a wandering life, and abstains from sex. The final two verses contrast the two paths:

> The two of them, with far different dwelling place and way of life, are not equal—the householder supporting wife and the unselfish one of good vows. The householder is not fully restrained in respect to killing other living creatures; the sage, being restrained, constantly protects living creatures.
>
> As the peacock with blue neck never attains the speed of the ruddy goose when going through the sky, so a householder does not equal a monk, a sage, living apart, meditating in the forest.[10]

The less probable *Sammāparibbājaniyasutta* (discourse on proper wandering) begins with an interlocutor asking the Buddha the proper way a monk should wander. In fifteen verses the Buddha outlines what sort of mental and moral state would permit a monk to wander properly. The very first of these verses is instructive, because it asks the monk to root out various elements of popular religion, the very first of these being *mangala*, the various rites performed on auspicious occasions, which probably include the interpretation of omens and other signs.

> The Lord said: 'For whom ceremonies (*mangala*)[11] are rooted out, as also meteors, dreams, and signs; the monk who has completely abandoned the blemish of ceremonies—he shall wander properly in the world.

Ashoka also, in his Rock Edict IX, discussed in Chapter 11, disparages such trivial ceremonies (*mangala*) engaged in by people, especially women.

The *Moneyasūte* found in the Pali canon[12] deals with three *moneyyas*, generally taken to mean moral perfections paradigmatic of a sage (*muni*).

---

10 Translation from Norman (1985: 35) with modifications.

11 Norman (1985: 61) translates *mangala* as 'omen'.

12 *Aṅguttaranikāya*, I: 120.

The three are perfections relating to body, speech and mind. Generally, all human activities are viewed as originating from these three, and perfection consists of control or restraint of these activities. The first consists of abstaining from killing, from taking what is not given and from sexual misconduct; the second consists of abstaining from false, divisive and harsh speech, and from idle chatter; and the third consists of abandoning longings and ill will and holding the right views.

The sixth text, *Upatisapasine* (Upatissa's Questions), is probably the *Sāriputtasutta*:[13] Upatissa is another name of Sariputta, the chief disciple of the Buddha. This text has twenty-one verses. In the first eight, Sariputta asks the Buddha some basic questions:

> How many dangers are there in the world ... which a monk should overcome in his secluded lodging? What ways of speech should be his? What virtuous conduct and vows should there be for a monk? Undertaking what training, being attentive, zealous, and mindful, would he blow away his own dross, as a smith blows away the dross of silver?[14]

The Buddha replies with a list of dangers: gadflies, mosquitoes, snakes, human attacks and quadrupeds. This list is similar to the one we saw above under future dangers. The Buddha says that a monk should not be distracted by thinking 'What shall I eat? Where shall I eat?' and the like. One term the Buddha uses with respect to the training of a monk's inner self is instructive. The monk should endure sickness, hunger, cold and heat, and 'he should make firm effort'. The term used here is '*parakkamma*', meaning striving, exertion, endeavour, effort. This, as we saw, is the same term that Ashoka used in Minor Rock Edict I with respect to his own spiritual journey discussed in Chapter 5: 'It was over a year ago, however, that I visited the Sangha and began to strive vigorously.'

The text that is easiest to identify in the extant Pali canon is the last, 'Advice to Rahula'. Ashoka's knowledge of Buddhist scriptural texts is demonstrated here because he is careful to add a qualifier: this text deals

---

13 *Suttanipāta* 955–975.

14 Translation of Norman (1985) with modifications.

with telling lies. There are, in fact, two texts with the same title, only one of which is about speaking falsehoods. That is found in the *Majjhima Nikāya*, 61, while the very next text (62), also titled 'Advice to Rahula', deals with other matters. The 'Advice to Rahula' recommended by Ashoka deals with the evils of telling lies, which destroys a monk's monastic state. The Buddha uses some telling examples to demonstrate the point. He asks Rahula whether he sees the little water remaining in the vessel used to wash his feet, and comments: 'So little is the monastic state of those not ashamed to tell a deliberate lie.' After throwing away that little water, the Buddha tells Rahula: 'So do those who are not ashamed to tell a deliberate lie throw away their monastic state.' His final message to Rahula relates to the purification of bodily, verbal and mental actions, a message we saw also in the *Moneyasūte*.

Ashoka appears to think that these seven texts are the best in the canonical repertoire. But best for what? So the Buddhist dharma will last a long time or forever? How would the study of these seven brief texts do that? The short answer, I think, is that the survival and advance of the Buddhist dharma depends on the continuation and growth of the Sangha. It is for the instruction of the Sangha that Ashoka is sending this reading list.

Two points stand out in this list. First, most of the texts he recommends deal with the development of moral virtue and mental cultivation of monastics and with the difficulties inherent in monastic life. Second, many of the texts deal with numbers. We see the significance of numbers in some sections of the Buddhist canon. For example, the *Aṅguttara Nikāya* arranges the texts according to the numbers contained in them: texts dealing with ones, twos, etc. The scholastic texts called *Abhidharma* also place a value on numbers, as do some of the earliest sermons of the Buddha: the Four Noble Truths and the Eightfold Noble Path.

Ashoka's message concludes with two statements that are interesting for their intent and rhetorical format. In the first he says, 'I wish that large numbers of monks and nuns will listen to them repeatedly and reflect on them, as also male Upasakas and female Upasikas.' In intent, this is clearly a command, and it would have been viewed as such by the monks, nuns and Upasakas who read or heard it. But in format Ashoka uses polite language, as I noted earlier. Here he couches a command as a desire or wish that they listen to and reflect on the texts he has recommended. An order cloaked as a wish is evident also in Separate Edict II where the strategy is used repeatedly: for example, 'This alone is my wish with respect to the frontier people.'

The second statement, likewise, informs them of the reason for getting his message inscribed: 'For this reason, Venerable Sirs, this has been inscribed, so that they will know my intention.' Here the audience is reminded of his intention. In the first statement he uses the verb *icchāmi*, 'I wish (or desire)', and in the second the past participle *abhipretam*, 'intended'. Both show what the emperor's wish and intention are, which surely carried an injunctive meaning and message. And in the frozen form of the stone inscription, they remain a perpetual and constant reminder of the royal command to monastics and laypeople alike.

Ashoka has come a long way from the neophyte of Minor Rock Edict I, just beginning his Buddhist journey and crediting the Sangha for strengthening his efforts and deepening his faith. In the Bairat inscription, he presents himself as a self-confident and mature Buddhist, well-versed in Buddhist scriptures, confident enough to preach to that very Sangha, to give them what amounts to a 'reading list' so as to make them better monks and nuns with a deeper understanding of Buddhist doctrine and practice. How long did it take for him to develop from neophyte to master? Unfortunately, the Bairat inscription is not dated, nor is the companion inscription aimed at the Sangha, the Schism Edict. Given that the Major Rock Edicts were completed sometime in or after the thirteenth year from his royal consecration, and assuming that the Bairat and Schism Edicts were written after that time, we have a window of about ten years: fifteen to twenty-five years after his royal consecration. This would mean that he had been a Buddhist for a minimum of five years, but more likely longer than that when he wrote these messages of instruction and admonition to the Sangha.

Both with respect to the Buddhist Sangha and, as we will see in Part Four, with respect to other religious organizations he calls Pasandas, Ashoka demonstrates his penchant to be intrusive, to get involved in matters that we would normally expect these organizations to handle by themselves. In the above passage, we saw Ashoka's hubris in telling monks which scriptural texts to read, especially when we recognize that he was still a layman and became a convert just a few years earlier. Later we will see his determination to push his dharma agenda not only on members of these Pasanda religious organizations but also on ordinary people. He wanted his messages and intentions to be taken seriously and implemented by everyone, especially by his officials. Ashoka, in his polite language, may show a velvet glove, but underneath there is an iron fist.

ADMONISHING THE SANGHA

Ashoka's intrusive attitude with respect to Buddhist monastic establishments seen in his Bairat inscription is strikingly evident also in his so-called Schism Edict. This edict is extant in three versions inscribed on three pillars—Sanchi, Sarnath and Allahabad. The longest is at Sarnath, and it contains two distinct parts. The first, which constitutes the edict proper, deals with dissension in the monastic community. This part is reproduced in variant forms at all three sites. The second part contains Ashoka's instruction to his officials, telling them what to do with the edict. This is what has been termed a 'cover letter' and may not have been intended to be inscribed.[15] It may, or may not, have been a 'mistake' on the part of the officials to inscribe it, but for historians it is a godsend; we have to be thankful to the Sarnath officials who were wise enough to make this mistake.

The edict is badly damaged at all three locations (Fig. 15). Putting the bits and pieces together, the text has been tentatively restored by Ludwig Alsdorf:[16]

---

15 For further discussion of 'cover letters', see Chapter 3.
16 See Alsdorf 1959. For a study of this inscription, see Tieken 2000, and the three studies by Sasaki 1989, 1992, and 1993.

> The unity of the Sangha has been instituted. In the Sangha no division
> is to be tolerated. Whoever divides the Sangha, be it a monk or a nun,
> that person should be made to put on white clothes and to reside in a
> non-monastic residence.

The intent of the edict is clear: Ashoka wants to maintain the unity and
integrity of the Sangha and expel from it any monk or nun who causes
divisions within it. It is unclear whether this is a general command, or
whether Ashoka was dealing with a specific incident in one or more
individual monasteries. Given the appended instruction to his officials, I
think it is likely to be the former.

The term for dissension used here is 'bheda' and its verbal equivalents.
The disunity of the Sangha would then be called 'sanghabheda', which
is actually an offence within the Buddhist monastic disciplinary code
(vinaya). As the historian of Buddhism Heinz Bechert[17] has shown, such
disunity or dissension with the Sangha does not constitute a 'schism' in
the sense known within Christian history, where schisms normally relate
to diverse interpretations of theological dogma. As we will see, internal
dissension within any kind of Sangha, whether political, corporate or
religious, poses a threat to the very existence of that Sangha.

The Buddhist disciplinary code for the Sangha envisages precisely
such a sanghabheda and provides remedies and punishments for monks
and nuns who engage in such divisive activity. So why would the emperor
interfere with a heavy hand, expelling monks and nuns who foment
dissension, when the Buddhist code itself imposes adequate but lesser
penalties?

Ancient Indian legal codes recognize laws governing the internal
administration of corporate entities under the category of samaya,
corporate law. Even though the extant codes are later than Ashoka,
they probably reflect an older legal philosophy. For legal purposes,
the Buddhist Sangha is such a corporate entity. Indeed, the same term,
'Sangha', is used in the legal literature for non-religious corporations,
such as guilds and trade unions. Here is a provision from the Code

---

17 See Bechert 1982.

of Manu (8.218–19): 'When a man belonging to a village, region, or corporate entity (*saṅgha*) enters into a contract truthfully and then breaks it out of greed, the king should banish that man from his realm.' Similar statements regarding individuals who sow dissension in corporate entities are given also in other legal texts.

So, from a purely legal standpoint, Ashoka's intervention when monks were causing disunity within the Sangha is nothing remarkable. But, ancient Indian law also assumed that corporations would generally police themselves without state intervention. It is only when they were unable to do so, or when a serious crime required corporal punishment or execution, that a corporation might request state intervention. This is where the background to and the subtext of Ashoka's order to his high officials become significant. Did he simply one day think of sending this order? That seems highly improbable. More than likely, there was a particular reason for his doing so. Could it have been requests made by one or more monks or monasteries having the emperor's ear for royal intervention and legal remedy with regard to some recalcitrant monks? Was there a more general breakdown of monastic discipline within the Buddhist Sangha requiring state intervention? Some such situation within the Sangha must have been the reason for Ashoka's order recorded in these inscriptions.

A monk or nun who persists in causing disunity within the Sangha 'should be made to put on white clothes and to reside in a non-monastic residence'. Being forced to wear white clothes symbolized the person's reduction to the lay status; monks wear ochre-coloured clothes. The expelled person is also made to live in 'a non-monastic residence'. The original term '*anāvāsa*' is the negative form of *āvāsa*, which is the Buddhist technical term for a monastic residence, whether it is a permanent monastery or a temporary abode during the rainy season. A permanent *āvāsa* had well-demarcated boundaries.[18] Thus, *anāvāsa* is any place outside those monastic boundaries. In effect, such a monk or nun is reduced to lay status in both dress and residence.

---

18 For further details, see Sukumar Dutt 1960: 102–09.

The Sarnath version of the edict has an additional sentence: 'This decree should be communicated in this form both to the Sangha of monks and to the Sangha of nuns.' The implication is that the edict was not sent directly to the Sangha but to some other person or persons, who would then transmit it to monks and nuns. These persons are identified in the 'cover letter' appended to the Sarnath version of the edict. The Sanchi version adds the clause that the Sangha of monks and nuns remain united 'as long as my sons and great-grandsons, as long as the moon and the sun'. This recalls Ashoka's statement in the Bairat inscription that the Sangha should last a very long time. Internal dissension, Ashoka thinks, is the principal cause for the disintegration of the monastic order.

Turning to the second part of the edict, the 'cover letter' appended to the Sarnath version reveals more of Ashoka's thinking and strategy with respect to the Buddhist monastic order. The letter is addressed to the mahamatras. The fragment preserved in the Allahabad version refers to the mahamatras of Kosambi. It is likely that several versions of the edict and the 'cover letter' were sent to different parts of the country. The execution of the provisions of the edict is thus made the responsibility of these non-monastic state officials.

> The Beloved of Gods says the following—Let one copy of this edict remain with you, deposited in the bureau,[19] and have one copy of it deposited with the Upasakas. And let these Upasakas go on every Uposatha-day so that trust may be developed in this decree; and consistently on every Uposatha-day let respective mahamatras go to the Uposatha-ceremony so that trust may be developed in this decree and attention paid to it.

The term used by Ashoka for 'decree' in this message to the Sangha is 'sāsana'. This term in both Prakrit and Sanskrit means a decree or order of a king. Buddhism, however, borrowed several terms from the 'royal vocabulary' and used them with altered meanings. Thus, sāsana is used

---

19 The meaning of the original term 'saṃsalana' is not altogether clear. It probably refers to a place of assembly where matters of public interest were discussed and public records stored.

regularly in Buddhist texts with the meaning of 'teaching, doctrine', specifically the teaching or instruction of the Buddha. Here, as elsewhere, Ashoka appears to be using strategic ambivalence. His message to the monks and nuns is his royal decree—his instruction, his *sāsana*—with an implication that it parallels the Buddha's own instruction. Monks and nuns accustomed to reading Buddhist texts containing the Buddha's *sāsana* could not have failed to note the implication.

The 'cover letter' concludes with instructions to disseminate the edict in the districts under the jurisdiction of the mahamatras and other officials:

> And as far as your jurisdiction extends, you should dispatch officers everywhere adhering to the provisions of this directive. Likewise, adhering to the provisions of this directive, you should have officers dispatched to all the areas around forts.

Two copies of the edict were to be made, one for the mahamatras and one for the Upasakas. All of them were expected to make sure trust in the edict is developed in a ritual manner on Uposatha days, perhaps by reading it or listening to it being read. It is not completely clear exactly who should develop this trust, but given the topic addressed in the edict it must refer to the members of the monastery. Uposatha refers to new moon and full moon days, which were sacred days in the Buddhist liturgical calendar. On these days Buddhist monks and nuns gathered in assembly to read out the Code of Monastic Rules and to publicly acknowledge any infractions of those rules. Buddhist laity also probably gathered at the monasteries to listen to sermons and to deepen their commitment to the Buddhist lay moral code. The rehearsal of the edict on such a day is unusual, and it probably indicates some form of supervision and invigilation of the monastic communities by both the imperial officials and the Upasakas, who were probably prominent and well-connected lay patrons.

The final addendum to the 'cover letter' goes a step further. It directs the mahamatras to dispatch their subordinates across their jurisdictional region to publicize the edict, and further afield in the border regions where forts may have secured the imperial presence and projected imperial power. A significant point that emerges from the content of the 'cover letter' is that Ashoka is here using the normal elements of state bureaucracy to implement his directives with regard to a specific religious group, the Buddhist Sangha. We have seen in Chapter 2 the creation of a new category of senior bureaucrats, the dharma-mahamatras, to further Ashoka's propagation of dharma, his moral philosophy. One would have expected Ashoka to dispatch some of these officials—as he intimates in Pillar Edict VII discussed in Part Four—to deal with issues relating to the Buddhist Sangha, especially issues relating to discipline and governance. Instead, what we see in this 'cover letter' is the use of the normal state bureaucratic apparatus to advance his programme with respect to the education and supervision of the Buddhist Sangha. All this brings us to Ashoka's propagation of Buddhism and the use of imperial machinery for that purpose, issues I will take up in the next chapter.

Before turning to that, however, I want to go beyond the four corners of Ashoka's own edict to see why, within the context of monastic discipline, he focused on disunity within the Sangha. There are two important documents dealing with this issue that are useful in this regard. The first is Kautilya's treatise on kingship and governance, the *Arthashastra*. Its eleventh book is dedicated to discussing how a king can subvert and conquer a political Sangha, that is, a confederacy. The second is, in fact, a Buddhist text, the Pali *Mahāparinibbānasuttanta* depicting the last days of the Buddha. It contains a long conversation between the Buddha and Vassakara, a minister of King Ajatasattu of Magadha, a conversation that focuses precisely on causing dissension within a Sangha.

The discussion in the *Arthashastra* gives the political background to the Buddha's reply to Vassakara's queries and to the significance of dissension and disunity within a Sangha. One issue that confronts us, however, is chronology. Many scholars have taken this text to have been authored by Chanakya, the Prime Minister of Chandragupta, the grandfather of Ashoka. If we accept that date, then the *Arthashastra* falls broadly within the same chronological slot as the two other texts we are examining. But strong evidence places Kautilya sometime in the first century CE or thereabouts, several centuries after the other two documents, even though some of Kautilya's sources may pre-date him by several centuries.[20] I think, nevertheless, that, with respect to political confederacies, Kautilya is presenting established views of political theory and strategy, views that probably long pre-dated him. The views expressed in the *Arthashastra*, therefore, were probably the accepted political wisdom on the ways monarchs interacted with confederate polities. Kings knew how to deal with other kings, how to wage war against them. But they had difficulty figuring out the confederate polities and politics.

First, as we have already seen, the term 'Sangha' is not simply, and probably not originally, a term referring to the Buddhist monastic order. Indian legal literature, we have seen, uses several technical terms, including Sangha, to refer to various kinds of trade and artisan associations. In ancient Indian political discourse, however, Sangha referred more specifically to a particular kind of polity different from monarchy, a polity that was governed through consensus by leaders of extended family groups and could be called a confederacy. Indeed, the clan of Sakyas to which the Buddha belonged may well have been such a political Sangha. So the Buddha may have been familiar with this kind of polity. The eleventh book of the *Arthashastra* is named 'Conduct Toward Sanghas'. At the outset, Kautilya tells the king he is addressing that a Sangha is the most difficult polity to conquer: 'Sanghas, because they are close-knit (*saṃhata*), are impervious to enemy assaults' (11.1.2). Note the close etymological connection between *saṅgha* and *saṃhata*, both originating from the Sanskrit verbal root *sam √han* (to put together, to join, to bond).

The fact the Sanghas are close-knit and bonded makes them especially dangerous and powerful; hence the need to deal with them surreptitiously and not in open conflict. In the context of a confederate polity, the term '*saṃhata*' is used in the sense of cohesion and unity of purpose forged by family bonds. A Sangha is always and by its very nature *saṃhata* and cannot be easily defeated by traditional military means. The best

---

20 For detailed arguments in favour of this date, see Trautmann 1971, Olivelle 2013, and McClish 2019.

and perhaps the only way to defeat a confederacy is to create internal dissension and disunity, that is, *bheda*. That is when a Sangha is no longer *samhata*, close-knit and united, and thus vulnerable. Sowing dissension is done through various strategies and the deployment of secret agents. Here is one example:

> Secret agents operating nearby should find out the grounds for mutual abuse, hatred, enmity, and quarrels among all members of Sanghas, and sow dissension in anyone whose confidence they have gradually won, saying: 'That person defames you.' When ill will has thus been built up among adherents of both sides, agents posing as teachers should provoke quarrels among their young boys with respect to their knowledge, skill, gambling, and sports.[21]

The centrality of *bheda* or sowing discord as a political strategy, especially with regard to confederacies, is important to understanding the conversation between the Buddha and Vassakara. When there is internecine conflict within a Sangha polity, it is destabilized and weakened from within.

Just like Kautilya's ideal-typical king who is bent on conquest, King Ajatasattu of Magadha was planning an attack on the Vajjis, who constituted a Sangha. The king, however, is cautious, and with reason; Kautilya points to the difficulty of defeating a confederacy in open combat. So, he sends his minister, Vassakara, to talk to the Buddha, because the Buddha knows the future and tells the truth. From his response Ajatasattu would be able to judge whether his expedition will be a success. Vassakara informs the Buddha of Ajatasattu's plan to attack the Vajjis in stark terms:

> The Magadha king Ajatasattu … said this: 'These Vajjis—so prosperous and so powerful—I will annihilate the Vajjis! I will destroy the Vajjis! I will bring them to utter perdition!'[22]

---

21 Kautilya, *Arthashastra*, 11.1.6–7.

22 *Digha Nikāya*, II: 73.

Ajatasattu's boast, however, sounds hollow. He is concerned and wants
to find out the Buddha's prediction. The Buddha's reply to the minister,
given as an aside to his favourite disciple Ananda, is instructive with
regard to dissension and disunity within a Sangha, both political and
monastic:

> So long, Ananda, as the Vajjis will continue to sit together at meetings
> constantly and to hold such meetings frequently, the Vajjis should be
> expected to prosper and not to decline. So long, Ananda, as the Vajjis
> will continue to sit together at meetings in unity (*samaggā*), and to rise
> in unity, and to carry out the affairs of the Vajjis in unity, the Vajjis
> should be expected to prosper and not to decline.[23]

Vassakara's parting words to the Buddha are reminiscent of Kautilya's
advice with regard to the means of conquering a confederacy.

> Venerable Gotama, the Vajjis cannot be subdued by the Magadha King
> Ajatasattu … through war except through instigations and through
> mutual dissension (*bheda*).[24]

As soon as Vassakara had left, the Buddha turned to his monks to instruct
them about the conditions for the welfare of the Buddhist Sangha,
conditions that parallel those for the political Sangha:

> So long, O monks, as the monks will continue to sit together at
> meetings constantly and to hold such meetings frequently, the monks
> should be expected to prosper and not to decline. So long, O monks, as
> the monks will continue to sit together at meetings in unity (*samaggā*),
> and to rise in unity, and to carry out the affairs of the Sangha in unity,
> O monks, the monks should be expected to prosper and not to decline.

Kautilya's and the Buddha's views on how a Sangha can prosper and resist
external assaults are identical. What keeps a Sangha, whether it is political

---

23 *Dīgha Nikāya*, II: 73–74.
24 *Dīgha Nikāya*, II: 76.

or monastic, strong and prosperous is unity, concord and taking decisions by consensus: the *saṃhata* of Kautilya and *samaggā* of the Buddha. This is confirmed by the use of the parallel Magadhan Prakrit form *samage* by Ashoka for the unity and concord he wants to promote within the Buddhist Sangha.

We can now see why Ashoka chose to focus on dissension with respect to the internal discipline of the Buddhist Sangha. Unity and the elimination of dissent and discord are the means of assuring its long-term survival and prosperity.

7

Spreading the Faith

IN THE PREVIOUS TWO CHAPTERS WE HAVE TRACED ASHOKA'S JOURNEY from Buddhist neophyte to self-confident Buddhist lay theologian; today we would even dub him a 'Buddhist activist'. His writings bear witness to his desire for spiritual growth and to his attempts to use his position to ensure that the Buddhist Sangha, and thereby the Buddhist religion, would prosper and last a long time. Did he also use his imperial power to spread Buddhism across his empire and beyond? Was he a Buddhist Constantine, as often claimed?

Later Buddhist narratives see Ashoka as a Buddhist missionary spreading Buddhism both within India and in neighbouring countries. Modern scholars also detect a connection between the spread of Buddhism and Ashoka's patronage. The earliest biographer of Ashoka, Vincent A. Smith, writing in 1901, proposed, 'So far as we can see, the transformation of this little local sect [i.e., Buddhism] into a world-religion is the work of Asoka alone.'[1] That assumption, unfortunately, is echoed by contemporary scholars as well. K.R. Norman, one of the most eminent Ashokan scholars of our time, provides some telling examples, such as: 'Ashoka was the first Buddhist Emperor.'[2] A book by

---

1   Vincent Smith 1901a: 22; see also Vincent Smith 1901b: 854, where he calls Buddhism 'an obscure Hindu sect in the Gangetic valley', which Ashoka raised 'to the rank of a world-religion'.
2   Norman 2012a: 113.

the influential Sri Lankan Buddhist monk Walpola Rahula presents a
similar conclusion:

> This notion of establishing the Sāsana or Buddhism as an institution
> in a particular country or place was perhaps first conceived by Asoka
> himself. He was the first king to adopt Buddhism as a state religion,
> and to start a great spiritual conquest which was called *Dharma-vijaya*
> … Like a conqueror and a ruler who would establish governments in
> countries politically conquered by him, so Asoka probably thought
> of establishing the *Sāsana* in countries spiritually conquered (*dharma-
> vijita*) by him.[3]

Trevor Ling, in his popular book *The Buddha*, has a chapter entitled
'The Ashokan Buddhist State'.[4] A distinguished archaeologist asserts
that Buddhism 'was a small and relatively unknown sect prior to
the royal support that it received from Ashoka',[5] and that 'Ashoka's
autobiographical endorsements served to spread the doctrine of
Buddhism beyond its Gangetic origins to a larger audience'.[6]

Such assertions have no basis in Ashoka's own writings or even in
other historical sources, apart from Buddhist hagiographies. Indeed,
the opposite is probably true, namely, that Buddhism and the Buddhist
Sangha were securely established and widely spread across the Indian
subcontinent by the time Ashoka proclaimed openly that he was a
Buddhist layman. We saw evidence for this in Chapter 5. I can only echo
the conclusion of K.R. Norman:

> It has been said that Aśoka's patronage was responsible for establishing
> Buddhism over a far wider area than could have been imagined before
> the founding of the Mauryan empire. We must note that we can

3 Walpola Rahula 1966: 55.
4 Trevor Ling 1976: 183–212.
5 Monika Smith et al. 2016: 389. See also the comment of the distinguished
   historian A.L. Basham: 'it seems that before Asoka Buddhism was a
   comparatively unimportant feature in the religious life of India' (Basham
   1982: 139).
6 Monika Smith et al. 2016: 378.

find no evidence in the Edicts that there was any greater patronage of Buddhism than of any other sect ... if it is true that Buddhism expanded during the reign of Aśoka, then it seems to me that, rather than this being the result of his patronage, or to his deliberate attempts to propagate it ... it is more likely that it was a result of the peace which he established, leading to greater prosperity and the expansion of trade.[7]

Nevertheless, as we will see, there may have been in Ashoka's writings and artefacts an implicit message to the populations that gave greater visibility and the emperor's imprimatur to Buddhism.

Let us first look at what the Buddhist establishment was like during Ashoka's time. Lacking firm archaeological evidence, we can once again mine Ashoka's own writings for this purpose. The very first inscription of his, Minor Rock Edict I, as we have seen, was written in approximately June 257 BCE, in the eleventh year of his reign. We have already examined this inscription, but let us read it again with this question in mind.

The Beloved of Gods proclaims as follows—

It has been over two and a half years since I have been an Upasaka. But for one year I did not strive vigorously. It was over a year ago, however, that I approached the Sangha and began to strive vigorously.

But during that time men in Jambudvipa, who were unmingled with gods, were made to mingle with them. For that is the fruit of striving. This can be achieved not only by eminent people, but even lowly people if they strive are indeed able to attain even the immense heaven.

This promulgation has been promulgated for the following purpose—so that both the lowly and the eminent may strive, that the frontier people also may come to know it, and that this striving may endure for a long time. And this matter will spread, and spread immensely—spread at least one and a half times more.

---

7   Norman 2012a: 128–29.

Unlike many of the other Ashokan edicts, this one is not addressed to imperial officials. The aim is to teach 'the fruit of striving', which Ashoka had already achieved and which he wants his hearers also to achieve. He wants to make clear that it 'can be achieved not only by eminent people'—like himself, we can assume—but also by lowly, ordinary people. He wants both the eminent and the lowly to embark on this striving, as also the 'frontier people'. This makes it clear that the intended audience includes the lower strata of society, as well as those living in the borderlands.

If this is true, then the opening of the message becomes problematic. He uses two technical terms from the Buddhist vocabulary: 'Upasaka', a devoted Buddhist layperson, and 'Sangha', the Buddhist monastic order. Note that he does not even tell his audience that he has become a Buddhist—a perceived absence, as I have already noted, that made some scribes insert the term 'Sakya', a common term for Buddhists based on the Buddha belonging to the clan of Sakyas. It appears that Ashoka expected his audience of 'lowly people' and 'frontier people' to understand these technical terms. It is unclear whether 'striving' in this context also had a technical meaning, and, if so, whether it would be a term expected to be understood by the people.

Further, this Minor Rock Edict is the one that is most widespread across India from the north to the south. Harry Falk, in his extensive exploration of the geographical spread of Minor Rock Edict I, notes that the inscriptional sites are far from cities and towns, often on hilltops and near caves. He thinks that they may have been strategically placed near sites where there were local religious celebrations and pilgrimages.[8] Ashoka may have been thinking of catching his audiences during their religious activities. If he expected all these people around the subcontinent to understand the technical Buddhist terminology, then there must have been Buddhist monastic establishments and Buddhist lay followers in the vicinity of—or, at least, not too distant from—these locations. In other words, Buddhism must have been already widespread at the time of Ashoka's writing of his first inscription and not 'a small and relatively unknown sect'.

---

8   Falk 2006: 55–58.

Further, Ashoka's exhortation does not say, as some have implied, that people should become Buddhists. He only asks them to 'strive' or 'to become zealous', which, as we have seen, is used by Ashoka also in Rock Edicts VI and X with a broad meaning of making a strong and sustained effort. If, in the context of the current edict, the term has a Buddhist meaning relating to a specifically Buddhist exercise, then the implication is that those who are told to strive are already Buddhists, but, like Ashoka in his early days, they may not have been striving sufficiently to progress along the Buddhist path—or, at the very least, they knew the meaning of the term Ashoka was using.

Ashoka concludes his message with the hope and expectation that 'this matter will spread, and spread immensely'. What 'this matter' means is not spelled out. As I have already noted in Chapter 5, I think the term here refers to the gist of Ashoka's message, that he wants all the people, both those in high positions and those occupying the lower rungs of society, to engage in 'striving'. So, here Ashoka wants this message to be spread far and wide, that more and more people across his empire will come to know his message and practise 'striving'. This is the same message he imparts at the end of Rock Edict X discussed in the context of striving in Chapter 5.

In this, the earliest piece of Ashoka's writings, he openly professes his Buddhist faith and claims to be a devoted adherent with the technical designation of Upasaka. Further, he presents himself as a kind of preacher, telling his subjects, and even those who lived in the frontier regions and may not have been his subjects, that he wanted them to get serious about their Buddhist practice. Can this be seen as the excitement and enthusiasm of a new convert? Or, perhaps, as we will see, a rash decision without considering its political costs? If my calculations are correct, he wrote this message (June 257 BCE) two and a half years after he became an Upasaka (December 260 BCE) and just a year and a half after he engaged seriously in 'striving' (December 259 BCE). If he had continued down this path, he may well have become what the later Buddhist tradition and even some modern scholars ascribe to him, a true Buddhist apostle spreading the

Buddha's message both within his own empire and internationally. But that did not happen.

Between the promulgation of Minor Rock Edict I and the beginning of his Major Rock Edict series in 256 BCE—that is, during a period of approximately one year or one and a half years—Ashoka seems to have taken stock of his religious and ethical mission and changed course. I will discuss this change of strategy in greater detail in Chapter 8. In brief, Ashoka seems to have pivoted to a different imperial strategy—away from the open sponsorship of Buddhism to a new moral philosophy based on Ashoka's own interpretation of dharma. This Ashokan moral philosophy of dharma, as we will see in Chapter 9, turns into an imperial ideology underpinning his imperial project.

First, it is important to remind ourselves that the signature concept of the Ashokan moral philosophy, namely, dharma, is absent in his very first piece of writing. At this stage of his life, soon after his adoption of Buddhism, his focus was elsewhere. This absence is highlighted and amplified in the so-called Minor Rock Edict II, whose central focus is, indeed, dharma. This inscription is found only in a few southern inscriptional sites and never in the north. It is found together with Minor Rock Edict I in five locations, but never alone. Minor Rock Edict II contains a 'definition' of dharma, which we will encounter frequently in the Major Rock Edicts and will be discussed in Chapter 9. Scholars have suggested that the message contained in Minor Rock Edict II was never meant to be inscribed.[9] The term used here by Ashoka is '*ānapayati*', 'orders', rather than '*likhita*', 'written' or 'inscribed'. This message probably contained orally transmitted orders of Ashoka to his officials. It is unclear precisely when such orders were issued, but it is likely that it was after Ashoka's decision to focus on dharma as his central message. This suggests that some of the southern inscriptions of the Minor Rock Edicts were made a considerable time after the edict was originally issued and inscribed in the northern sites. Officials in the south entrusted with making the inscriptions may have been already aware of the new focus

---

9   For a detailed study of the way Minor Rock Edict II was inserted into Minor Rock Edict I, see Falk 2006: 57–58.

on dharma, and thus inserted the oral instructions they had received from Pataliputra when they inscribed these edicts.

When, between March 256 and March 255 BCE, his thirteenth regnal year, Ashoka began issuing his messages that are anthologized in the fourteen Major Rock Edicts, he had shifted his focus to a newly minted moral philosophy centred on the concept of dharma. In these and in the Pillar Edict anthology, the last of which, Pillar Edict VII was issued in 241 BCE, his twenty-eighth regnal year, there is no mention of Buddhism or his affiliation to it, except for a few hints here and there.

Did he then abandon his dedication to Buddhism and to fostering his new faith? I don't think so. We have two inscriptions devoted totally to Buddhist topics written after his pivot to dharma: the Bairat inscription and the Schism Edict, both of which we have examined above. They demonstrate his continued interest in the Buddhist monastic organizations and in strengthening them both intellectually and organizationally. We also have the two Buddhist pillar inscriptions at Lumbini and Nigliva. They do not, however, give us any indication that Ashoka was also actively trying to propagate Buddhism within his empire in the same way as his dharma.

Some indications about his continuing support of Buddhism and Buddhist practices come not in the form of writing but in Ashoka's building activities, which we explored in Chapter 4. These activities span a maximum period of about fourteen years (256–242 BCE), perhaps considerably less. There we asked the question: Why did Ashoka erect these pillars at enormous expense and effort? The answer emerges principally from their geographical locations. Most of them are found in places with strong Buddhist associations and significance. Many, such as those at Sanchi and Sarnath, are located within prominent Buddhist monastic complexes. Others are in places associated with the Buddha's life. Even more telling is the placement of pillars along a pilgrim's way from the Ashokan capital Pataliputra to Lumbini, the birthplace of the Buddha. These pillars, as we have seen, led a pilgrim from pillar to pillar, showing the way to Lumbini. There were wells for water near the pillars. It is not difficult to imagine that there may have also been rest houses by the pillars for pilgrims to rest and spend the night. Very pertinent in this regard is his statement in Pillar Edict VII (iii), expanding on a topic he had already discussed in Rock Edict II:

> Along roads, furthermore, I have had banyan trees planted to provide shade for domestic animals and humans; I have had mango orchards planted; and I have had wells dug at intervals of eight Krosas [about 28 km] and constructed rest houses. I have had numerous watering places constructed at different locations for the benefit of domestic animals and humans.

If Ashoka undertook these construction projects along roads throughout his empire, it stands to reason that he would have done so along a pilgrim's way to the Buddha's birthplace, especially when he had constructed the elaborate pillars to mark the way.

The construction of the elaborate and expensive pillars, along with their decorative capitals, was thus connected closely to Buddhist organizations and pilgrimage practices. This public works project was, therefore, a loud and permanent advertisement for Buddhism and for the emperor's support of it. The range of this construction project is also impressive. From the easternmost pillars near the capital city of Pataliputra to the westernmost in Sanchi, the distance is over 900 kilometres, and the distance from Pataliputra to the northernmost location in Lumbini in southern Nepal is about 350 kilometres. The symbolic value of the pillars, therefore, was spread far and wide in north-central and north-eastern India. The pillars probably had more than a single symbolic value; they would have been subject to different religious and cultural interpretations and appropriations by different segments of the population. Yet, it would have been difficult for anyone to be ignorant of or to ignore their Buddhist overtones.

The ambiguity and multivalence that we saw in Ashoka's architectural symbols are also observable in the semantic spectrum that surrounds his words, especially words of special cultural and religious significance. The most prominent of such words, of course, is dharma. Indeed, a claim can be made that dharma was, and perhaps is, the most central cultural concept of India, cutting across religious, cultural and ethnic divides. As we will discuss in Part Three, Ashoka dedicated much of his public life to the promotion of dharma, which he was careful to define. Even though Ashoka's dharma is not simply the Buddhist dharma, yet the semantic range of the term, as people during Ashoka's time heard it, must have included most prominently the Buddhist dharma.

Whether intentionally or not, therefore, Ashoka's propagation of dharma among his family members, bureaucracy and the population at large must have been viewed at least in some quarters as support for Buddhism. In Buddhist theology the term 'dharma' assumed a more central and dominant position than in any other organized religion of the period. It was, as we have seen, part of the triple gem of Buddhism: Buddha, Dharma and Sangha. The opening refrain of any Buddhist chant is the triple refuge: 'I go to the Buddha for refuge. I go to the Dharma for refuge. I go to the Sangha for refuge.'

Yet, the promotion of dharma is not the same as the promotion of Buddhism. Ashoka uses it as a central but non-sectarian religious and moral concept. He could tell everyone that he supports all Pasandas, the religious organizations of his time: Buddhists, Brahmins, Jains and Ajivikas. And he would have been telling the truth. Yet, as I have already noted, Ashoka engages in what we may term 'strategic ambiguity', where the very ambiguity and multivalence of his words and artefacts were important for his support and propagation of Buddhism. His moral and bureaucratic support would have given an edge to the missionary activities of Buddhist monks and nuns, and his financial support would have helped the construction of Buddhist sacred spaces. Buddhism in the third century BCE had a visible and monumental presence on the Indian landscape that was not matched by any of its religious competitors.

ASHOKA'S BUDDHISM

Within the context of Ashoka's deepening faith and his Buddhist religious education discussed in the context of the Bairat and Schism Edicts, we need to ask the question: What was Ashoka's Buddhism? The answer is important both for the portrait of Ashoka I am drawing, but also for the broader history of Buddhism. Ashoka's inscriptional corpus is a uniquely significant source for the history of Buddhist doctrine and practice.

So what was Ashoka's Buddhism like? What did he believe in? Positively, we get very little information. He did participate in pilgrimages to major Buddhist sites, such as the Buddha's birthplace and the site of his enlightenment. He visited the Sangha and was inspired by the monks to undertake what he describes as 'striving' or 'effort'. But he does not tell us the content of his zealous endeavours. In fact, he tells us precious little about any Buddhist doctrine, belief or ethical practice. Perhaps his insistence on the primacy of not killing living beings—ahimsa—which I will examine in Chapter 9, was inspired by Buddhism,[10] although ahimsa was central also to the contemporary religious tradition of Jainism. As we will see, even the elements of Ashoka's definition of dharma are not specifically Buddhist, and indeed the five precepts of Buddhism find no place in that definition.

I have already spoken about the importance of Ashoka's silences— what he does *not* say—in understanding his cultural world. I talked earlier about his silence with respect to the central social category of ancient India, the four social groups called *varnas* closely connected to the caste system of later times. When it comes to Buddhist doctrine, his silence is deafening. Ashoka mentions none of the central doctrinal tenets of Buddhism as we have come to know them from canonical texts. These include the diagnosis of human ills: that life is ultimately and intrinsically suffering (*duḥkha*), and that this innate suffering is due to human life being subject to repeated births, deaths and rebirths, a cycle that is called samsara. The final goal of the Buddhist path is the extinction of this suffering, the liberation from the cycle of rebirth, which is called nirvana. And the driving force, the energy, that keeps that cycle spinning eternally

---

10 For the centrality of ahimsa in the Buddhist ethics of nature, see Schmithausen 2000, who says: 'Animal ethics is firmly rooted in traditional Buddhism from the outset, and is perhaps the most important contribution Buddhism has to make to a new ethics of nature. As is well known, *not to kill living beings* is the first moral precept or commitment of both Buddhist monks and lay people' (p. 29).

is human action, both the good and the bad, which is called karma. These elements of the Buddhist doctrinal repertoire, especially rebirth and karma, are also central to other major religions of the period, such as Jainism, and have been recognized as key cultural components of the region identified as Greater Magadha by Johannes Bronkhorst.[11] And Magadha was the heartland of Ashoka's empire. Ashoka thus had double the reason to comment on them, both as a Magadhan and as a Buddhist. So why didn't he?

A second area of silence relates to the heart of the Buddhist lay ethic and discipline contained in the five moral precepts, the *pañcaśīla*. These consist of refraining from (1) killing living beings, (2) taking what is not given (that is, stealing), (3) sexual misconduct, (4) false or wrong speech, and (5) intoxicant drinks. Of these, only the first, abstention from killing, is represented in Ashoka's definitions of dharma, although speaking the truth is given in his last statement in the seventh Pillar Edict, as also in Minor Rock Edict II. Why did Ashoka not make the five Buddhist precepts part of his definition of dharma?

I will deal with the latter in Part Three, but here I want to focus on Ashoka's silence regarding the central Buddhist doctrines. Scholars over the past century or so have found Ashoka's silence in this regard puzzling. They have tried various solutions to solve the puzzle—Ashoka was simply an ignorant layman; he thought these doctrines irrelevant to what he was attempting to do with the publication of his edicts; the early Buddhism of Ashoka's time was in its infancy and did not contain these doctrines; original Buddhism was simply a moral philosophy; the higher doctrines were limited to monks seeking liberation, while the laity, then as now, focused on accumulating merit and going to heaven. None provides a satisfactory answer.

Ashoka's central focus was propagating his new dharma. For this purpose, he selected doctrinal and moral elements that would be readily understood and accepted by all the diverse groups within his vast empire. This no doubt can explain some of Ashoka's reticence in delving deep

---

11 Bronkhorst 2007. For a discussion of Ashoka's silence on these central beliefs, see Schmithausen 1992: 137–39.

into Buddhist doctrine. But he did espouse ideas, such as ahimsa, that would have been deeply unpopular in some quarters. That moral stance affected the livelihood of many people including butchers, fishermen and hunters, not to speak of the culinary habits of the people. So, his reticence alone cannot explain adequately his complete silence. The ethics of karma and rebirth, in a special way, would have fit perfectly with his efforts to encourage the population to pursue dharma and the goal of heaven after death. As the sociologist Max Weber remarked, no better theodicy than karma has ever been invented. When such a perfect justification for moral living was available, why did he not use it?

The puzzle remains.

PART THREE

Dharma

Ashoka the Moral Philosopher

Ａ SHOKA WAS A RULER RESPONSIBLE FOR GOVERNING A VAST AND diverse territory and protecting it against enemies, foreign and domestic. He was a writer, the first writer in India to leave behind his writings inscribed on stone for later generations to read and, according to some, the man who invented the script he used, a script he bequeathed to later generations, and which became the mother of all Indian scripts. He was, indeed, a builder, undertaking the largest building project ancient India had seen, commissioning some of the most elegant and beautiful monumental pillars and capitals, one of which, the lion capital of Sarnath, was to become the symbol of the modern Republic of India. He was also a proud Buddhist broadcasting his faith in the Buddha as a lay disciple and attempting to instruct and exhort the Buddhist Sangha. All this, however, did not fully define his identity.

During the last two decades of his life, Ashoka spent the greater part of his time and energy not on visible edifices or dreary imperial administration. During this period, he was single-mindedly devoted to an idea, an idea encapsulated in the term 'dharma' (Fig. 2). If there was a single attribute that defined Ashoka's primary identity, it was his devotion to dharma. And it was the propagation of dharma across the world that he envisaged as his lasting legacy to his own country and to the world at large.

149

Dharma became the cornerstone of a broader civilizational project on which Ashoka embarked sometime before March 256 BCE, in the twelfth year of his reign. This project envisioned a moral citizenry both within his empire and in foreign countries known to him. A central part of this project was to formulate a moral philosophy to which all the people—no matter their social or economic standing, or their religious, cultural or ethical affiliations, no matter what language they spoke or to which polity they belonged—could subscribe and which they could internalize in their own lives. This was the beginning of Ashoka's 'dharma project', and to it he devoted not only his unflinching energy but also a large part of his imperial administration, and possibly his wealth. It is the topic for this part of Ashoka's portrait.

8

Pivoting to Dharma

IT WAS AROUND DECEMBER OF 259 BCE WHEN ASHOKA PAID A VISIT TO some Buddhist monks, or perhaps a single eminent and learned monk, for advice and instruction. That momentous visit was to transform him as a person and as king—we witnessed that transformation in Chapter 5. He had already been an Upasaka for more than a year, but still remained a so-so Buddhist during that period. We do not know what the monk or monks said to him, or what spiritual training he underwent under their guidance. But after that visit, Ashoka tells us, he became a resolute 'striver' on the Buddhist path.

A year and a half later, in June 257 BCE or thereabouts, he had a bright idea: 'Why don't I write a letter to my subjects about the wonderful experience I had a few months ago? Why don't I encourage them to embark on the same path?' This letter is what we have come to call Minor Rock Edict I. With this message inscribed on numerous rock surfaces throughout his empire, and with his vast bureaucracy co-opted to what may have seemed to many of his officials a bizarre quest—a Don Quixote tilting at windmills—he thought he was embarking on a new conquest, not a territorial conquest but a spiritual one. He was intent on making the 'lion's roar' of the Buddha resound across the land.

The year or so that followed his first inscriptional message to his subjects, that is, between June 257 BCE and the spring of 256 BCE—the twelfth year of his reign—was pivotal in Ashoka's intellectual and religious trajectory. This trajectory took a decisive turn sometime during this interlude. Ashoka's public mission turned from the propagation of Buddhism to a campaign of mass education of the population in Ashoka's own brand of moral philosophy anchored in his own interpretation of an old idea, the idea of dharma.

I call this 'pivoting to dharma' not because he abandoned his allegiance to and faith in Buddhism, but because in his public policy of moral education directed at his subjects he breaks decisively from his earlier emphasis on Buddhism, seen in Minor Rock Edict I, and pivots to a policy based on dharma, to a moral philosophy that transcended sectarian divides. This pivoting is expressed most clearly in his messages anthologized in the Major Rock Edict series, which begins tellingly with the expression '*dharmalipi*', a term that can mean at once both writing and inscription dealing with dharma. Although he did not cease to be a Buddhist, from now on his writings concerned dharma, not Buddhism per se. The only place where he mentions Buddhism in this series of fourteen edicts is a reference in Rock Edict VIII to 'setting out to Enlightenment', probably a reference to his pilgrimage a few years earlier to Bodh Gaya, the place where the Buddha became 'Buddha', the Enlightened One.

How and why did this pivot in Ashoka's thinking and approach happen?

We do not know, of course, and there is no way of knowing it for sure. I want to propose a hypothesis, however—conjecture may be more accurate—that I for one find plausible. Ashoka wrote Minor Rock Edict I at the conclusion of an eight-month-long travel, which probably had a religious—more specifically, a Buddhist—motivation and purpose. It was probably during this journey that Ashoka paid the visit to Bodh Gaya he mentions in Rock Edit VIII. So, after eight months on the road and with the zeal of a new convert, he decided to shout out to the world the good news of his newfound faith. He wrote a letter. And in it he does not mention dharma even once. Clearly, at that time, this term, which was to become the obsession of his life, was not uppermost in his mind.

Then he went home, back to his capital, Pataliputra, and to the beehive of administrative activities. It was now the rainy season of 257

BCE. In some of his later writings, he speaks about his Parisad, that is, the council of his most senior ministers, which we discussed in Chapter 2. What did his senior ministers and advisors have to say about this new initiative of the young king? Did they raise objections? Did he consult with other senior advisors? Members of his family? The princes who were viceroys in major urban centres across his empire? Even prominent Buddhist monks? We have no way of knowing. But something must have happened. Some individual or individuals must have made an intervention. Or, did Ashoka himself have second thoughts? Did his thinking during this period move to a wider horizon and to a grander and more creative intellectual project?

Whatever the catalyst, Ashoka moved away from an overtly Buddhist-centred message to one that was neutral with regard to the organized religions of his day—what he calls Pasandas—and that sought to stay above the fray of religious identities and rivalries. The outcome of this period of reflection was the formation and formulation of his moral philosophy of dharma. This pivot may have taken place during that rainy season of forced sedentary life, a life of reflection and thought.

Ashoka began writing about dharma a few months later, sometime after the spring of 256 BCE, the thirteenth year of his reign. This is clearly stated in Pillar Edict VI, written twenty-six years after his royal consecration, that is, fourteen years after he first started writing on dharma. There he says: 'After I had been consecrated for twelve years, I had my writing on dharma inscribed for the welfare and wellbeing of the people.' A case could be made for considering Minor Rock Edict II as Ashoka's first and somewhat tentative and clumsy attempt to communicate to this people his new dharma message. It is telling that this message is inscribed as a supplement or addendum to Minor Rock Edict I centred on Buddhism. In the five locations where both are inscribed together, an astute contemporary reader could have seen Ashoka's pivot away from the explicitly Buddhist message to a more nuanced one dealing with dharma.

We cannot be certain, of course, that this edict, originally sent as an oral communication to imperial officials, pre-dated the Major Rock

Edict series. In my estimation, though, it very likely did. There is an experimental quality to the edict, with several expressions—'ancient standards' repeated twice, and 'attributes of dharma'[1]—never to be repeated in his later writings. The definition of dharma Ashoka provides is also rudimentary, lacking several key features listed in the Major Rock Edicts; and telling the truth listed here as a component of dharma is omitted in later definitions.[2] Several of the statements, moreover, are unclear and garbled, such as elephant-riders and horse-trainers. If Ashoka were living today, we would think that, after getting Minor Rock Edict II composed, he changed his speechwriter. Whatever the cause, the writings in the Rock Edict anthology are more eloquent, and their prose is clearer, crisper and more elegant.

If Minor Rock Edict II was Ashoka's first experiment at preaching his dharma, then we can date it to the winter of 257 BCE or the spring of 256 BCE, with some of the writings included in the Rock Edict anthology coming sometime later in 256 BCE or early in 255 BCE.

As we have seen in Chapter 3, his writings after 256 BCE are for the most part centred on dharma—its meaning and its propagation. These writings were anthologized in what are today known as the Major Rock Edicts. They number fourteen and are currently found in nine locations, although there may have been others that are now lost. A separate set of writings, probably from a time several years after the Rock Edict series, were anthologized in the six Pillar Edicts inscribed in 242 BCE. Another set was anthologized in the seventh Pillar Edict the following year, 241 BCE. In all these, with a few notable exceptions, his teaching about dharma figures prominently.

Just a year after he started writing about dharma, that is, in 255 BCE, he embarked on a new initiative that transformed the upper echelons of the imperial bureaucracy. He created a new class of senior officials in charge of his dharma mission. He called them, naturally, dharma-mahamatras, parallel to the older class of generic mahamatras. This new group of mahamatras was devoted to a single task: preaching Ashoka's

---

1   In the original Prakrit: *porāṇā pakiti* and *dhaṃmaguṇā*.
2   It is listed only in the very last inscription, Pillar Edict VII.

dharma to the population at large and to the organized religious groups called Pasandas. While reporting on this initiative in Rock Edict V, he is quick to point out that none of his predecessors had thought of doing it: 'Now, in times past dharma-mahamatras did not exist at all. But, thirteen years after my royal consecration, I established the dharma-mahamatras.'

The impression one gets from these two great anthologies of Ashoka's writings is that of a man whose passion was the education of his population in the centrality of moral living. It is, he never tires of pointing out, the key to true human happiness in this world and the next. Some scholars have characterized this passion of his as an 'obsession', and there may be some truth to it, especially in his later writings in the Pillar Edict phase. But he was also a strategic thinker, and we see in his writings how he used his communication skills and his command of the vast imperial bureaucracy to further his objectives with regard to the moral education of his people.

In using dharma as the central concept and cornerstone of his moral philosophy, however, Ashoka was not using a blank slate to write his message. Dharma was not an unknown or neutral concept. That term had already acquired theological, ethical and even political connotations, and by Ashoka's time it had had a linguistic and semantic history stretching over a millennium.[3] Given its prevalence and centrality in later Indian religion and culture, however, it is difficult for us from this distance to recognize that this term may not have had the same centrality and valence within religious and philosophical discourse in early India. To understand Ashoka's own appropriation of dharma and his moral philosophy centred on that concept, therefore, it may be useful to explore briefly the early semantic history of this term.

DHARMA BEFORE ASHOKA

The life of dharma, if we can call it that, began with its birth in the oldest literary corpus of India, the *Rig Veda.* The hymns that comprise this collection were composed over several centuries in the second half of

---

3 Several studies on the semantic history of dharma by major scholars are included in the edited volume: Olivelle 2009a.

the second millennium BCE. We can call this the 'birth of dharma' because there are no Indo-European cognates of dharma in any language of that family, including Avestan (an old form of Persian), which is the closest linguistic relative of the old Vedic language. The word was coined in India by Rig Vedic poets.

The basic meaning of the term in its earliest usage is 'foundation', a secure and firm base for the physical world, the ritual system and the moral universe. It is the dharma of the god Varuṇa that keeps heaven and earth apart: 'Heaven and Earth were propped apart according to the dharma of Varuṇa.'[4] It is this connection of dharma with the Vedic gods Mitra and Varuṇa, gods associated with commandments and alliances, that gave it what we would call today a moral dimension, as also its connection to royalty and royal duties. Varuṇa is king, and the divine counterpart of the earthly king. The poet seeks forgiveness for transgressions against the dharma of Varuṇa: 'If by inattention we have erased your dharma, do not harm us because of that guilt, o god.'[5]

If cosmic order is overseen by Varuṇa, social order—the moral and social regulation of human societies—is overseen by kings on earth, who are viewed as representatives of the divine king Varuṇa. In the ritual of the royal consecration, these connections—Varuṇa, dharma and king—are made explicit. Ashoka, as we have seen, marks all dates from his own royal consecration. In this Vedic ritual by which a man is transformed into king, dharma figures prominently. Varuṇa is invoked as the lord or protector of dharma (*dharmapati*), and immediately thereafter the king is explicitly said to be Varuṇa himself with respect to dharma: 'Varuṇa himself, the lord of dharma, makes him [the king] the lord of dharma.'[6]

This connection between dharma and king is made explicit in a passage from a major Upanishad, where dharma is said to be 'above' the king and thus bestowing legitimacy on him:

Dharma is here the ruling power standing above the ruling power. Hence there is nothing higher than dharma. Therefore, a weaker man

---

4   *Rig Veda*, 6.70.1 (translation from Jamison and Brereton 2014).
5   *Rig Veda*, 7.89.5 (translation from Jamison and Brereton 2014).
6   *Śatapatha Brāhmaṇa*, 5.3.3.9.

makes demands of a stronger man by appealing to dharma, just as one does by appealing to the king.[7]

The Sanskrit term for 'ruling power' is '*kṣatra*', from which is derived 'Kṣatriya', a term used for both a king and for the ruling elite. Dharma gives a weaker man power to seek justice from a stronger man, by appealing to the king on the basis of dharma. The connection of dharma to social justice and the legal system responsible for enforcing laws becomes significant when we investigate Ashoka's own use of this term.

The central duty of the king as the lord of dharma, then, is to make sure that he and all his subjects submit to and follow dharma. Thus, dharma is 'the power superior to the ruling power'; dharma stands above the king as the power that confers on him the power to rule. This semantic history provides the background for Ashoka's pursuit of dharma as an imperial project.

So, in the period dubbed the 'middle Vedic', that is, the three or four centuries before 500 BCE, the term 'dharma', on the one hand, became less prominent and somewhat marginal in the theological vocabulary of the Brahmanical texts produced during this period—the Brahmanas and the early Upanishads—and, on the other, its semantic compass narrowed to refer principally to the royal and ethical spheres. In the early prose Upanishads, for example, where we would have expected the concept of dharma to be dominant, it occupies a peripheral position in the discourse, occurring only in five passages. The term dharma became so ubiquitous in later Indian religion and culture that it is common for people, even serious scholars, to assume that it was a central ingredient in Indian civilization from time immemorial. That, however, was not the case. Ashoka, in fact, was in no small part responsible for dharma assuming the centrality it did in Indian history.

This was the semantic backdrop of dharma at the time when the ascetic communities, called Pasandas by Ashoka, espousing new religious doctrines emerged, at first principally in north-eastern India, the heartland of Ashoka's empire.

---

7   *Bṛhadāraṇyaka Upaniṣad*, 1.4.14.

The term dharma becomes a much more central theological concept
in these new religions than it did in the older Brahmanical ritualism and
Upanishadic philosophies. But why? The hypothesis I offer[8] is that the
new religions, especially Buddhism, developed theologies that made their
founders spiritual parallels to world-conquering emperors (*cakravartin*).
The founders of these new religions were imagined as a new kind of
world conqueror through a conquest that was not military but spiritual—
something emulated by Ashoka in his concept of 'conquest through
dharma' (*dharmavijaya*). Further, the new religious discourses used many
of the symbols of royalty, such as the chariot wheel, *cakra*, from which we
get the term '*cakravartin*', the one who rolls the wheel, a metonym for the
war chariot. As we already saw, the Buddha's very first sermon is called
'*dharma-cakra-pravartana-sūtra*', the sermon that set the wheel of dharma
rolling. The founders of the new religions are called '*jina*', conqueror, and
from this term we get the name of the religion 'Jain' founded by Mahavira,
who is *jina*. The Buddha's doctrine is called '*śāsana*', instruction, the
counterpart of a royal edict. I think it is within this broad assimilation of
royal symbols and vocabulary that we can locate the adoption of dharma
by these new religions as their central theological concept. As the king
proclaims and protects dharma, the socio-ethical foundation of society,
so the Buddha proclaims the new dharma, the new foundation of a path
that leads to liberation from earthly suffering.

With the consolidation of these organized religious bodies, the
Pasandas, a century or two before Ashoka, however, the concept of
dharma became a site of contention. Theological battles were fought
over the meaning of this term. In some verses of the Buddhist anthology
Aṭṭakavagga of the *Suttanipāta*,[9] which is considered to represent the
oldest stratum of the Buddhist canon and certainly pre-dates Ashoka, we
have some interesting admonitions to Buddhist and perhaps even other
ascetics. These verses tell them not to engage in debates about which

8   See my two papers: 'Power of Words: The Ascetic Appropriation and
    Semantic Evolution of Dharma', and 'Semantic History of Dharma: The
    Middle and Late Vedic Periods', in Olivelle 2005: 121–54.
9   For an examination of these texts, see Olivelle 2005: 130.

dharma is true or the best; better to leave them alone. Here are a few representative verses:

> They call their own dharma the highest; the dharma of others the lowest.
>   Some call a dharma the highest; others call the same the lowest.
> They call someone from another sect a fool with impure dharma.
> If you do not know my dharma you become an animal; this is how they speak.[10]

Clearly, there was acrimonious and offensive language thrown at each other by members of ascetic sects that had adopted and adapted the term dharma to define their doctrines and messages. We will detect reflections of this acrimony when we discuss Ashoka's advice to the Pasandas in Part Four. He asks them to control their tongues.

It was this fraught terrain that Ashoka had to navigate as he sought to put his own stamp on the concept of dharma and to use it as the cornerstone of a new moral philosophy he was attempting to construct.

Part of my hypothesis about the early semantic history of dharma is that it was Ashoka's extensive use and 'popularization' of the notion of dharma that contributed to its becoming the defining concept of Indian civilization. Upinder Singh has aptly dubbed Ashoka as 'a political prophet of soteriological socialism'.[11] The emperor's use of the term made it impossible for anyone, including the Brahmanical theologians, to ignore it. It was around this time that a new genre of literature devoted to dharma, called the Dharmashastras, came to be created within the Brahmanical tradition. The date of the earliest extant text of this genre, the Dharmasutra of Apastamba, is close to the time of Ashoka.

The frequency of Ashoka's use of the term gives us an inkling into how pivotal it was to the central and defining mission of his life as

---

10 *Aṭṭakavagga* of the *Suttanipāta*, verses 904, 903, 893, 880. On the antiquity of the *Aṭṭakavagga*, see Gomez 1976; Vetter 1990. Note that several of the texts listed by Ashoka in the Bairat inscription are from the *Suttanipāta* (see Chapter 6).

11 Upinder Singh 2017: 49.

emperor. Ashoka articulates his dharma philosophy principally in the two anthologies, the Rock and Pillar Edicts, which together contain approximately 3,064 words. By the standards of early Indian texts, such as the Brahmanas and the Upanishads, this corpus of Ashoka's writings is extraordinarily brief. Yet, in these concise writings Ashoka uses the term dharma a total 106 times, an average of once every twenty-nine words. Its importance to Ashoka—the fact that the word was uppermost in his mind—cannot be overstated.

In the portrait of Ashoka we can recover from his own words, his engagement with dharma occupies the foreground, front and centre. This was his pet project, and he must have spent a sizeable portion of the imperial budget for the various components of his dharma programme. In the following chapters, I will try to flesh out Ashoka's involvement with the definition and dissemination of dharma within his empire and into the neighbouring countries of the south and the west.

9

Dharma as Moral Philosophy

ONE OF THE OLDEST BRAHMANICAL TEXTS TO DEAL SPECIFICALLY
with dharma, the *Āpastamba Dharmasūtra*, a text that was written
around the time of Ashoka, makes this telling remark on how we can
know dharma: 'Dharma and non-dharma do not go around saying: Here
we are!'[1] This epistemological remark was intended to tell his audience
that the 'true' and 'correct' dharma is not self-evident or easy to identify.
It must be sought in the Vedas, the exclusive property of Brahmins, and
in the societal norms established by Brahmin communities. Not just
anybody can weigh in on this important topic, not even if he happens to
be the emperor.

Ashoka, however, would have none of that. Dharma is not the
monopoly of any group or sect. It is universal. He is refreshingly direct
and thoroughly forthright about what, to his mind, dharma is. In most of
his major writings, he explains dharma in great detail. But what is even
more significant is that he offers formal definitions of dharma at least
nine times, from his earliest writing around the year 256 BCE to his last
recorded inscription fifteen years later. As opposed to the Brahmanical
version, Ashoka's dharma is a system of moral behaviour that is based
on—for want of a better word—reason, and is universally applicable
to both the rich and the poor, both the eminent and the lowly, both

---

1   *Āpastamba Dharmasūtra*, 1.20.6.

in his territory and across the world; what Upinder Singh has called 'soteriological socialism'.[2] There cannot be one dharma for Brahmins and another for the rest, one dharma for the rich and the upper classes and another for the poor and the lower echelons of society. Ashoka dismisses the notion of a specific dharma for specific people, the notion of *svadharma* so prominent within the Brahmanical tradition. This universality of dharma is a feature that he shared with—and probably inherited from—Buddhism. He does not, however, answer directly and explicitly Apastamba's epistemological question: what are the sources that reveal the true dharma to us? Ashoka appears to assume that reason can get us there. He presents his definitions of dharma as self-evident and not in need of demonstration or proof.

AHIMSA AS DHARMA

In the various definitions of dharma, as also elsewhere in his writings, Ashoka presents the virtue of ahimsa—not killing living beings, not causing hurt and injury—as the bedrock of his moral philosophy. It is the sole topic of Rock Edict I, which inaugurates his writings on dharma. Although he never uses the precise term 'ahimsa', he uses variant forms with the prefix '-*vi*' giving forms such as *avihisā* (Sanskrit: *avihiṃsā*), not killing/injuring, and its opposite *vihisā* (Sanskrit: *vihiṃsā*), killing/injuring. The addition of this prefix does not change the underlying meaning much, except, perhaps, to make it more intensive. The double meaning of the term is derived from the basic root meaning of striking or smiting, from which we get the extended meaning of slaying or killing. Both meanings—smiting/injuring and killing—are inherent in the term, thus giving rise to its modern interpretation as 'non-violence'.[3]

Other related words used by Ashoka are linked to the Sanskrit term '*ālambha*', whose root meaning is to seize or take hold of, and which is closely associated with the 'taking hold of and tying to the sacrificial post'

---

2   Upinder Singh 2017: 49.

3   For a comprehensive survey of violence in ancient India, see Upinder Singh 2017.

of an animal that is to be sacrificed.[4] This connection between killing animals and sacrificial offering is evident in Ashoka's very first writing on dharma in Rock Edict I, where he says: 'Here no living creature is to be slaughtered and offered in sacrifice. And no festivals are to be held.' The term for 'slaughtered' is '*ālabhitu*' and for 'sacrifice' is '*pajohitaviye*' (Sanskrit: *prahotavya*). The latter is a technical term within Vedic ritual literature for offering parts of an animal in the sacrificial fire. The connection of Ashoka's prohibition of killing animals with ritual animal sacrifices, most often connected to Vedic rituals but not limited to them, is evident in this statement. The term 'here' that opens the proclamation has at least two possible meanings within this context—'here', in this place where the writing is inscribed, and 'here', in my territory. I think within the creative ambiguity that Ashoka often relishes, the term may well refer to both. The prohibition of festivals appears to be also related to the abolition of ritual killing: various religious rituals of a folk kind may have taken place at such festive gatherings. They may also have entailed killing animals for other purposes, such as for selling their meat at the festivals; they may have been bloody affairs, reminiscent of the modern 'wet markets'. And, who knows, there may have been other types of entertainment involving the death of animals, such as cock fights. Betting on animal fights is referred to in later Indian legal texts as *samāhvaya*.[5]

Ashoka is not breaking new ground when he disparages festivals. We have passages in Buddhist texts forbidding monks to attend such gatherings. Apastamba's text on dharma, which is nearly contemporaneous with Ashoka, likewise forbids Brahmins from attending them.[6]

In the statement just cited, the object of slaughter is a 'living being' (*jīva*). In a parallel inscription in Rock Edict IV, we have a somewhat more complex statement with different words used with respect to

---

4   For further discussion of ritual terminology in Ashoka's writings, see Lubin 2013.

5   See Manu's Law Code, 9.221–28; Yājñavalkya's Law Code, 2.203–07; Kautilya's *Arthaśāstra*, 3.20.1–13.

6   *Āpastamba Dharmasūtra*, 1.3.12; 1.32.19–20.

what should not be killed or injured: 'not slaughtering animals (*prāṇa*), not injuring creatures (*bhūta*)'. The three terms—*jīva*, *prāṇa* and *bhūta*— probably have the same or very similar meanings, the first referring directly to the fact that they are living, the second to the fact that they breathe, and the last and possibly the broadest category referring to all beings, but clearly implying that they are also alive. Although some of these categories may refer to plants, which are also alive, the thrust of Ashoka's message is not to kill animals.

Ashoka probably was sensitive to the differing religious and cultural sensibilities of the people across his vast empire. In Rock Edict XIV, as we saw, he explicitly states that he modulated his message in different regions, 'for everything is not suitable for every place'. We saw in our discussion of Ashoka's Buddhism that he may not have included specifically Buddhist doctrines, such as rebirth and karma, in general messages to all his subjects; he wanted his messages to have a universal appeal. In the case of ahimsa, however, he was uncompromising, unyielding and totally consistent. From his earliest statement on dharma to his last, and even in his messages to the people of the north-western frontier regions translated into Aramaic and Greek, he foregrounds ahimsa as a cornerstone of his dharma message.

The reasons why Ashoka was uncompromising in his attachment to the virtue of ahimsa may be many, but the religious milieu in which he grew up, including the influence of Jainism and Buddhism, must have played a large role. There is also a tradition within India that Ashoka's father and grandfather were associated with Jainism and the Ajivikas, religions that placed ahimsa at the centre of their moral teachings. Whatever the reason, Ashoka did not see any reason to modify or abandon this central virtue in his conception of dharma, irrespective of his audience.

Besides including ahimsa prominently in his formal definitions of dharma, I will presently discuss: Ashoka promotes ahimsa in his various proclamations targeting the killing and injuring of animals. He outlines his policy relating to ahimsa succinctly in Pillar Edict II: 'I have conferred various benefits on bipeds and quadrupeds, on birds and aquatic animals, even up to the gift of life.' Ashoka's efforts at alleviating the suffering of all living beings—birds, fish, land animals and human beings—extended to the suspension of various cruel activities, including even some necessary ones such as branding and castration, that cause suffering and inflict pain. These suspensions are ordered especially on days and seasons of special religious or cultural significance. In the passage cited below, the days of Tishya figure prominently.[7] Also called Pushya or Pausha, it corresponds to December–January in the modern calendar, but it also may refer to the lunar asterisms of that name. We find the most detailed account of such orders in Pillar Edict V issued in 242 BCE, twenty-six years after Ashoka's royal consecration. However, he had already stated his unwavering commitment to ahimsa in edicts issued at least fourteen years earlier. Why did he wait so long to forbid the killing of these animals? Was there pushback from various quarters? Did his advisors think that such a ban on slaughter was politically risky? One may never know, but it did take him a long time to come down strongly in favour of ahimsa in the context of killing animals for human consumption.

Twenty-six years after my royal consecration, I made the following species exempt from being slaughtered—parrots, myna birds, whistling teals,[8] sheldrakes, ruddy geese, the red-billed leiothrix, malkohas, Indian oriole, tortoise, soft-shell turtle, water snake, Gangetic dolphin, Samkuja fish, pangolin, flying fox, Simale, Samdaka, Okapinda, turtle dove, white pigeon, and village pigeon, as well as all quadrupeds that are neither useful nor edible.

Those nanny goats, ewes, and sows that are pregnant or nursing the young are exempt from slaughter, as also the young before they are six months old. Cocks should not be caponed. Chaff containing living beings should not be burnt. One should not set a forest on fire without reason or for killing. Animals should not be fed to animals.

---

7   For Tishya and Pushya, see the Glossary.

8   For the identities of the animals listed in this edict, see its translation in the Appendix.

Fish are exempt from slaughter and should not be sold on the three full-moon days at the beginning of each season, on the full-moon day of Tishya, on the three days of the fourteenth and fifteenth of a fortnight and the first day of the next fortnight, and on every Uposatha-day. During these same days other animal species living in elephant forests and fishery preserves should not be killed.

On the eighth day of each fortnight, on the fourteenth and fifteenth days of a fortnight, on the Tishya day, on the Punarvasu day, on the three full-moon days at the beginning of each season, and on festival days, bulls should not be castrated, and goats, rams, pigs, and other animals that are subject to castration should not be castrated.

On the Tishya day, on the Punarvasu day, on the full-moon days at the beginning of each season, and on the fortnight following the full-moon day of each season, horses and bulls should not be branded.

One aspect of the virtue of ahimsa inherent in the term is that it is a negative concept signalled by the privative prefix '*a*': *not*-injuring, *not*-killing. Did Ashoka conceive of this non-aggressive relationship to the animal world purely on a negative basis, as abstaining from injurious activities? There is evidence that it was not. Ashoka considered ahimsa as an external manifestation of the inner virtue of compassion, '*daya*' in the original. In one of the earliest definitions of ahimsa found in Minor Rock Edict II, he frames it this way: 'Living creatures should be treated with compassion.' Ashoka returns to this theme in his Pillar Edicts, where compassion is mentioned twice as a constituent of dharma. In Pillar Edict II: 'Dharma is excellent! But what is the extent of dharma?—Few evil acts, many good deeds, *compassion*, gift-giving, truthfulness, and purity.' In Pillar Edict VII (v): 'For noble acts of dharma and conforming to dharma consist in this—that *compassion*, gift-giving, truthfulness, purity, gentleness, and goodness will increase among the people.' A somewhat different way of expressing the inner virtue of ahimsa is given in Rock Edict IX: 'self-restraint with respect to living beings.'

In two of his inscriptions, Ashoka gets personal. He believed that his personal example is the best way to instruct the people in dharma. In the *Bhagavad Gita*, the famous Hindu text written several centuries after

Ashoka, the main interlocutor Krishna says this about himself and his effort to provide an example for the people to follow: 'For, if I do not tirelessly pursue my tasks, people everywhere would follow my path, …the whole world will fall into ruin.'[9] Ashoka too believed that ordinary people are bound to follow the example set by prominent individuals, especially the king. People may, indeed, ask: 'Okay, you want us to refrain from killing animals. What about you? What about your own kitchen? Any meat dishes served there?' Hunting and eating meat were, after all, paradigmatic activities of kings in ancient Indian lore.

Ashoka takes such possible objections head on. In the very first of his Rock Edict series devoted to dharma that we already examined, immediately after prohibiting sacrificial killings and the holding of festivals, he talks about his own kitchen, how they used to kill large number of animals for meals of the royal household. The number he gives—'many hundreds of thousands'—must be a hyperbole, like the numbers of casualties he gives in the Kalinga war. Yet, no doubt, a large number of animals and birds probably had to be killed to feed the royal household. At the time of writing his edict, Ashoka says, that number had been reduced to just three—two peacocks and a game animal, perhaps a deer. And he promises his audience that he will eliminate even these in the future.

Formerly, in the kitchen of the Beloved of Gods, King Piyadasi, many hundreds of thousands of creatures were slaughtered every day to prepare stews. But now when this writing on dharma is being inscribed only three animals are slaughtered to prepare stews: two peacocks and one game animal, and the game animal also not always. Even these three animals are not going to be slaughtered in the future.

Ashoka took this matter seriously enough to include it in the Greek and Aramaic translations inscribed in the north-western frontier outpost of Kandahar, Afghanistan (Fig. 7). The Greek version of Kandahar I is brief and somewhat generic: 'And the king abstains [from killing] living beings,

9 *Bhagavad Gītā*, 3.23–24.

and other men, as also the king's hunters and fishermen, have refrained from hunting.' The Aramaic version is more detailed: 'In addition to this, with respect to the food of our Lord the King, very little killing is done. Seeing this, all the people refrained [from killing]. And in the case of those who caught fish, those people abjured that. Likewise, with respect to those who were trappers, they have refrained from trapping.'

So, did Ashoka finally become a vegetarian? He never says that he gave up eating meat, although he promises to put a stop to his kitchen staff killing animals. We get some clues from an unlikely source: Sanskrit grammarians. Around the middle of the second century BCE, less than a hundred years after Ashoka's death, the grammarian Patanjali wrote his *Great Commentary* on the seminal grammar of Panini. Patanjali's commentary incorporates an earlier commentarial work by one of his predecessors, Katyayana. The latter either lived during the time of Ashoka and was thus one of his subjects, or he lived very close to him in time. In either case, Katyayana knew or knew about Ashoka. And so did, in all likelihood, Patanjali himself. Katyayana and, following him, Patanjali give a grammatical explanation of a compound word found in common speech: '*śāka-pārthiva*'. Literally, the expression means: 'vegetable-king'. Now, since the literal meaning is impossible—a king cannot be a vegetable—the grammarians posit the elision of an intervening term that would provide the necessary context and meaning. And that term is *bhoji*, 'eating'. The full compound would thus be *śāka-bhoji-pārthiva*, 'vegetable-eating-king'. But, given that most, if not all kings, would have eaten vegetables if they listened to their mothers, the compound must have a pregnant meaning: a king who eats *only* vegetables. So, the compound would really mean 'vegetarian king'. This kind of culinary preference must have seemed quite odd and unique in ancient India, where kings and nobles were fond of meat and the hunt. There is, thus, a strong likelihood that this expression referred to Ashoka; he was the 'vegetarian king'.[10]

If this interpretation of the expression 'vegetarian king' used by ancient Sanskrit grammarians is correct, as it seems to me, then we have external evidence for Ashoka's aversion to killing and meat-eating. He

10 For a long and detailed study of this compound, see Scharfe 1971: 219–25.

set himself as an example by becoming a vegetarian. That appears to have been viewed as strange and anomalous. So, people coined a new word for him—'vegetarian king'.

Ashoka's discussions of ahimsa generally refer to the killing or injuring of animals. That his concern extended to human beings is clear, especially in his writings on the evils of war. His war on Kalinga, as usual, is uppermost in his mind. This is where he apologizes for the carnage he caused. He speaks in Rock Edict XIII about how painful he found all this, how much distress it caused him:

> This is the regret that the Beloved of Gods has after conquering the Kalingas. For, conquering an unconquered land entails the killing, death, or deportation of people. That is deemed extremely painful and grievous by the Beloved of Gods … Therefore, of the number of people who were killed, died, and were deported among the Kalingas—today even one hundredth or one thousandth part of that would be deemed grievous by the Beloved of Gods.

But there is one problem with the ethical principle of ahimsa. If taken to its ultimate limit, to its uncompromising and logical conclusion, it is simply impossible for a human being, let alone a king, to adhere to it. The history of ahimsa in India, both within the ascetical religions of Buddhism and Jainism and in the broadly Hindu–Brahmanical traditions, has been one of hermeneutical gymnastics in efforts to identify and justify exceptions.[11] Buddhism found exceptions through its fundamental ethical postulate of intentionality. If you do not intend to kill, you cannot violate the ahimsa principle. So, you can even eat meat if the animal killed was not intended for you specifically.[12] Brahmanical exceptions abound to exempt both any killing within the context of Vedic rituals and killing in self-defence when someone is about to assault you or your family or property. In these contexts, to use a memorable saying of

---

11 For a study of how the Brahmanical tradition dealt with the issues created by the ethical principle of ahimsa, see Olivelle 2023.

12 For a history of ahimsa in Buddhism, see Jerryson 2013.

the great lawgiver Manu, 'killing is not killing'.[13] Killing in war would also be an exception, within the principle of 'just war' or dharmic war (*dharma-yuddha*). This is the message of the Sanskrit epic Mahabharata, and Krishna's advice to Arjuna and to all soldiers in the Bhagavad Gita (2.37) encapsulates it: 'If you are slain, you will attain heaven; or if you are victorious, you will enjoy the earth.'

In Buddhism too this issue must have arisen, especially in the context of what would be today called 'judicial killing'. Is it morally right to impose capital punishment and other forms of bodily torture and mutilation on criminals? In the Pali Buddhist text *Questions of King Milinda* (*Milindapañho*) this question is raised by the king in his conversation with the Buddhist monk Nagasena. The monk admits that despite the Buddhist precept regarding benevolence and non-injury, a king may punish a thief by cutting off the hands, by torture, and even by execution. Such acts are to be viewed as not arbitrary or the result of the Buddha's doctrine. They are the result of the thief's own actions.[14]

Whether he was aware of these hermeneutical arguments or not—and there is a good possibility that he was—Ashoka himself seems to have carved out several exceptions to his ethical principle of ahimsa. The first is war. Even though he expresses regret at the death and destruction caused by his Kalinga war, he is clear-eyed about the need for a strong military, sometimes even for war and the killing that it would entail. In the case of Kalinga, his deepest regret is for the death and suffering of 'good people', not for death and suffering of people as such. Regarding the hundreds of thousands of people who, he says, were deported, there is nary a word about what happened to them. Were they enslaved, as is usually the case with war captives? Did he or his soldiers continue to keep them as slaves? Did he release them and allow them to return to their homeland and families? He is totally silent on these points.

---

13 Manu's Code of Law, 5.39. For more detailed discussions of this topic, see Halbfass 1983. For a comprehensive study of violence and non-violence in ancient India, see Upinder Singh 2021: 131–77.

14 *Milindapañho*, IV.3.37; T.W. Rhys Davids, *The Questions of King Milinda* (Oxford: Clarendon Press, 1890), p. 256.

In the same Rock Edit XIII where he deals with the Kalinga war, Ashoka also goes off at a tangent to speak to forest peoples living within his territory. These people were by nature independent-minded and fiercely defended their own autonomous ways of life. They were often thorns in the side of the 'civilized' states that sought to tame them. Ashoka recognized this issue and warned them to follow his path of moral self-reflection. If not—well, he reminds them that he has powerful armed forces and can deal with them one way or the other. He can be forgiving if the offences are forgivable, and the offenders repent. This is his advice and warning to forest peoples:

> And further, should someone commit an offense today, if it can be forgiven the Beloved of God thinks he should be forgiven. And even the forest people living within the territory of the Beloved of Gods—he conciliates them also and persuades them to be favorably disposed. And he also tells them of the remorse, as also the power, of the Beloved of Gods, so that they may become contrite, and never engage in killing.[15]

And he adds immediately his devotion to ahimsa: 'For, what the Beloved of Gods wishes for all creatures is this: freedom from injury, self-restraint, impartiality, and gentleness.' The point he wants to convey is that people should not mistake his gentleness, his focus on ahimsa, for weakness. Yet, he invites them to be like him, to give up their violent past, and to give up killing.

Even in his advice to his children and grandchildren, he seems to recognize a king's deep-seated longing for combat, for conquest. At the same time, he recognizes the inevitable slaughter and suffering that war entails. In the same edict, he simply asks his children to exercise moderation and mercy:

> And it is for this purpose that this writing on dharma has been inscribed, to wit, that my sons and grandsons may not think that a

---

15 Others have translated: 'and may not get killed', thus making it a statement about Ashoka's ability to kill the forest people if they do not behave. I think both grammatically and contextually this interpretation is less likely.

new realm is worth conquering, that they find pleasure in kindness and lenient punishment in their own territory, and that they consider the only real conquest to be conquest through dharma, for that is conquest in this world and the next world. And may every pleasure be pleasure through dharma—for that is pleasure in this world and the next.

Not only war, but even the very act of governing a country inevitably entails killing and infliction of pain through judicially imposed corporal punishment, which in those days included cutting of various limbs. Despite his strong commitment to ahimsa, Ashoka never banned corporal or capital punishment. In ancient times, mercy simply dictated beheading, which was called 'clean killing', while other forms of execution involving various forms of torture, including impaling, was called 'colorful killing'.[16] As we can see from the following instruction to his regional officers in Pillar Edict IV, Ashoka only tries to make the execution a little less harrowing, permitting family visits, as also rites and repentance, so the prisoner would find happiness after death.

My practice, moreover, has extended as far as this: for men who are confined in prison, on whom the sentence has been passed, and who have received the death penalty, a stay of three days is granted. Their relatives will make them reflect on what provides protection for their lives. Having been made to reflect on the fact that their lives end in death, they will give gifts for the sake of the world beyond, or they will perform fasts.

ASHOKA'S DHARMA

Ashoka's conceptualization of dharma extends far beyond ahimsa. He is refreshingly direct and explicit in stating what he means by dharma. This

---

16 For a study of Ashoka and capital punishment, see Norman 1975b. I do not agree with Norman's interpretation that the wording of the edict does not imply execution.

he does principally in his missives to his officials, especially to those in the provinces far from the Mauryan heartland and Ashoka's capital and seat of power. He depends on them to spread the word about dharma, to educate the population about the importance of following the Ashokan dharma, and to govern according to the dictates of dharma. John Strong provides a useful summary of the Ashokan dharma: '[W]e may say that Dharma seems to have meant for Aśoka a moral polity of active social concern, religious tolerance, ecological awareness, the observance of common ethical precepts, and the renunciation of war.'[17] For Ashoka, then, dharma was both personal self-cultivation and socially committed action.

In his writings spanning over fifteen years, Ashoka provides nine separate disquisitions that can be viewed as definitions of dharma. Examining them closely and with some care, we can grasp the main contours of Ashoka's dharma, as well as any changes or developments his thinking may have undergone over that period. Here, then, are the nine definitions, arranged more or less chronologically, even though we cannot be totally certain about their absolute or relative chronological order.

Chart 9.1
Definitions of Dharma

1	2
Mother and father should be obeyed. Elders, likewise, should be obeyed. Living creatures should be treated with compassion. Truth should be spoken. These are the attributes of dharma that should be practised. MRE II	Obedience to mother and father—excellent! Giving gifts to friends, companions, and relatives, and to Brahmins and Sramanas—excellent! Not killing living beings—excellent! Spending little and accumulating little—excellent! RE III

17 Strong 1983: 4.

3	4
Not slaughtering living beings, not injuring creatures, proper regard towards relatives, proper regard towards Sramanas and Brahmins, obedience to mother and father, and obedience to the elderly. RE IV	It [dharma] consists of the following: proper regard towards slaves and servants, reverence towards elders, self-restraint with respect to living beings, and giving gifts to Sramanas and Brahmins. RE IX
5	6
Proper regard towards slaves and servants; obedience to mother and father; giving gifts to friends, companions and relatives, and to Sramanas and Brahmins; and not killing living beings. RE XI	[O]bedience to authority, obedience to mother and father, obedience to elders, and proper regard to friends, companions, associates and relatives, and to slaves and servants, and firm devotion. RE XIII
7	8
Dharma is excellent! But what is the extent of dharma?—Few evil acts, many good deeds, compassion, gift-giving, truthfulness and purity. PE II	For noble acts of dharma and conforming to dharma consist in this—that compassion, gift-giving, truthfulness, purity, gentleness and goodness will increase among the people. PE VII (v)
9	
[O]bedience to mother and father, obedience to elders, deference to the aged, and proper regard to Brahmins and Sramanas, to the destitute and distressed, down to slaves and servants. PE VII (vi)	

Although there are differences in the formulations, the governing principle of Ashoka's conception of dharma appears to be a web of relations emanating from the self, relations that must be nurtured and governed by dharma. Dharma in this conception consists of the ethical principles that regulate these relationships. These relational elements are called 'attributes of dharma' in Minor Rock Edict II.

Although there are additional relations mentioned occasionally, the basic structure of Ashoka's dharma consists of five main relationships. In Chart 9.2 I present these as a pentagon surrounding the self. Each side of the pentagon is one face of the self as it confronts significant others within its orbit, others with whom the self develops specific kinds of relationships.

The most central of the five facets relates to those who are superiors, especially mother and father. Besides parents, Ashoka mentions others who could be viewed as 'superiors'. Prominent in this group are 'elders'; the original word is 'guru', a term that encompasses a whole range of individuals including teacher and father, but also those of one's father's generation and older: grandparents, uncles, aunts and the like. Included sometimes within this group are older people of the community and eminent people, including possibly the rich and influential, as also high-ranking officials. The relationship of self to this group is governed by obedience. The original term—in Sanskrit, *śuśrūṣā*—has a semantic range that is broader than simply obedience. The term is derived from a root with the meaning 'to hear' or 'to listen'—with the added connotation of listening to and learning from someone. As we will see in Chapter 12, Ashoka places great emphasis on the importance of religious individuals belonging to different Pasanda groups 'learning' from each other. The word used there, '*bahu-śruta*' (much learned), is also derived from the same verbal root. So, 'obedience' here, like the English 'listen to your parents', implies the willingness of younger generations to learn from and listen to—thus be obedient to in every sense of the term—the older generation. This is what Ashoka in his Minor Rock Edict II refers to as 'ancient standards'; he was in this regard a strong conservative.

Chart 9.2

Components of Dharma

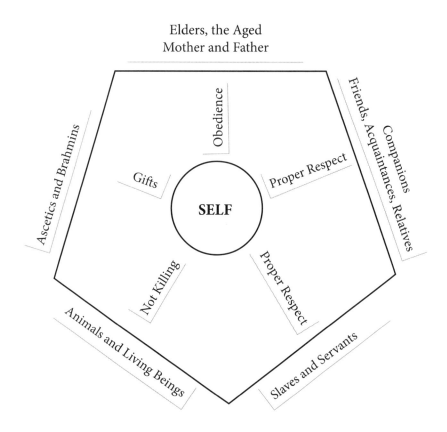

The next facet consists of a group of religious professionals comprising two broad classes: Brahmins and Sramanas. We will discuss these two groups in greater depth in Part Four, but in the context of dharma Ashoka sees them as deserving special consideration by those who wish to pursue dharma. Most frequently, the relation of self to Brahmins and Sramanas is defined by giving gifts—'*dāna*' is the original term—by providing them material support. In the case of Sramanas, most of whom were itinerant mendicants, such support consisted principally

of providing food. As they were supposed to beg for their food every day
and not hoard, people's contact with Sramanas by providing them food
would have been a daily affair. For Brahmins, the kinds of gifts given
are less obvious. They provided many ritual services that would have
entailed the donation of gifts. But, as we will see in the next part, at least
some Brahmins may well also have been itinerant mendicants, identified
in later texts as belonging to the fourth *āśrama* or religious mode of life.
A couple of times, however, the relationship of self to Sramanas and
Brahmins is defined as '*saṃpaṭipati*' (Sanskrit: *saṃpratipatti*), a term that
refers to the proper attitude, regard and comportment with respect to a
particular person or group. This term is connected more frequently with
the next group of people related to the self, namely, friends, companions,
acquaintances and the like. With respect to Sramanas and Brahmins,
the term probably referred obliquely to the obligation to provide them
material support, but perhaps extending to reverence and respect as well.

The third facet consists of a motley array of people. It is interesting
that in most of the iterations the first place in this group is occupied by
friends and the second by acquaintances, while relatives are relegated to
the third position. In Rock Edict IV, on the other hand, only relatives
are mentioned. The whole collection, however, appears to include
people with whom the self has quotidian or regular contact. In contrast
to the first two groups, individuals here are more or less equal in status
to the self. Here also, as in the case of Sramanas and Brahmins, the
relationship is characterized as 'proper regard or deportment', although
Rock Edict III says that gifts should be given to this group, along with
Sramanas and Brahmins, and Rock Edict XIII adds another characteristic:
'firm devotion'.

The three groups we have examined thus far consist of individuals
who are either superior to or on the same level as the self. The fourth
group is clearly of a lower social and economic status than the self and
consists of slaves and servants; very poor people are added to the group in
Pillar Edict VII. The relationship to this group is uniformly characterized
as proper regard. Surely, the notion of 'proper regard' must have been
quite broad and elastic, because the way one related to friends and

relatives must have been quite different from the way one interacted with one's slaves and servants. I think the inner virtue of compassion, which Ashoka alludes to frequently even with reference to officials in the governing bureaucracy, is something that may have governed these kinds of quotidian social interactions.

The fifth and final group consists of all living beings, especially animals. We have already discussed this relationship governed by ahimsa and compassion.

Surveying these five broad groupings, we see a hierarchy in operation. The first group is hierarchically superior to the self, while the second could be in one sense superior—these are religious professionals—but in another sense somewhat equal, given their need for economic support. The third group is clearly at an equal level of status with the self. The fourth and fifth are unquestionably lower in rank than the self, and, in the case of slaves and domestic animals, the self may even exercise ownership over them.

One question that emerges from this survey is whether we can detect a development of thought, a refinement of Ashoka's conception of dharma, in these documents written over a span of about fifteen years. The first thing to note is the remarkable consistency of Ashoka's thinking. The major components of dharma remain stable throughout. There are, however, subtle yet significant changes.

In his last message twenty-seven years into his reign, an aged Ashoka, reflecting back on his decades-long campaign to spread the message of dharma, says that he has tried two approaches. One is coercion, focused on statues and their enforcement. The second is persuasion, getting the people to internalize his message. He says in Pillar Edict VII (vii):

> But this growth in dharma among the people has grown through just two means: through regulations with respect to dharma and through persuasion. Of these two, however, regulations with respect to dharma do little, while a lot is accomplished through persuasion.

This change of tactics is reflected in the very linguistic structure of the first two definitions of dharma given in Minor Rock Edict II and Rock

Edict III. Although we cannot be sure, I think the formulation of Minor Rock Edict II is probably earlier than that of Rock Edict III. In the former we have gerundive forms of verbs with the meaning 'that should or must be done'. Along with other injunctive verbal forms, the gerundive is used frequently in Sanskrit legal literature to enunciate laws, statues and norms. So, we have Ashoka's rule in Minor Rock Edict II: 'Mother and father should be obeyed.' This formulation is abandoned in later iterations, beginning with Rock Edict III.

In the latter, Ashoka says that a particular mode of acting is '*sādhu*'. This term means literally 'good' or 'excellent', but in popular usage, especially within Buddhism, it developed into an exclamation, like the modern 'Bravo!' or 'Great!' If one goes to a Buddhist procession in Sri Lanka today, for example, one will see and hear people lining the road shout out '*Sādhu! Sādhu! Sādhu!*' three times as the Buddha's relic passes by, with the last '*Sādhu*' being lengthened. Such exclamations do not just say that something is good—it says that and much more. It has an emotional resonance. Echoes of such exclamatory and performative use of '*sādhu*' can be detected in Ashoka's use of the term to refer to various ingredients of dharma in Rock Edict III:

> Obedience to mother and father—excellent! Giving gifts to friends, companions, and relatives, and to Brahmins and Sramanas—excellent! Not killing living beings—excellent! Spending little and accumulating little—excellent!

The significant point is that here we see a shift in Ashoka's formulation from commanding to inspiring. With '*sādhu*', he is asking his audience to see how wonderful these virtues are. He is making both an intellectual and an emotional appeal. He never reverts to the gerundives.

Even though Ashoka does not use '*sādhu*' in his later formulations of dharma, an editor at Girnar seems to show a fondness for this term. He inserts it into the formulation in Rock Edicts IX and XI. The readings of Girnar, therefore, are:

It [dharma] consists of the following:

Proper regard toward slaves and servants, reverence toward elders—
excellent! Self-restraint with respect to animals—excellent! Giving
gifts to Sramanas and Brahmins—excellent!

Proper regard toward slaves and servants, obedience to mother and
father—excellent! Giving gifts to friends, companions, and relatives,
and to Sramanas and Brahmins—excellent! And not killing living
beings—excellent!

From a formal point of view, moreover, we see a shift in the Pillar
Edicts from the concrete examples of dharmic conduct to abstract
articulations of virtue. Thus, in Pillar Edict II Ashoka asks the rhetorical
question: 'But what is the extent of dharma?' And he answers with an
enumeration of virtues: 'Few evil acts, many good deeds, compassion,
gift-giving, truthfulness, and purity.' And in Pillar Edict VII (v), he
again enumerates virtues within the context of observing dharma: 'For
noble acts of dharma and conforming to dharma consist in this—that
compassion, gift-giving, truthfulness, purity, gentleness, and goodness
will increase among the people.'

We also witness several substantive and noteworthy changes in
Ashoka's descriptions of dharma. The most notable is the emergence
of slaves and servants as a category of individuals deserving special
attention within the context of dharmic living. They are absent in the
first three definitions, making their appearance in the fourth, Rock
Edict IX. In it, they are listed first and given pride of place: dharma
'consists of the following: proper regard toward slaves and servants'.
It remains in first place in Rock Edict XI as well, and it continues to be
included in all subsequent definitions of dharma, except those with lists
of abstract virtues.

Then there is the strange case of truth-telling. In the very first
definition of dharma found in Minor Rock Edict II, one ingredient of
dharma is: 'Truth should be spoken.' Truth disappears from subsequent
definitions, reappearing as 'truthfulness' in the two Pillar Edict definitions
with lists of virtues. We saw in Chapter 6 that Ashoka's recommended
reading list for Buddhist monastics includes 'Advice to Rahula'. Given

that there are two texts by that name, Ashoka alertly identifies the text
he has in mind with the qualifier 'relating to falsehood'. Ashoka singles
out a sermon of the Buddha relating to the evils of telling lies. Ashoka
was thus aware of the importance of truthfulness even when he does not
include it in his definitions of dharma, probably because in the middle
period of his writings he focused on the importance of properly nurturing
a person's familial and social relationships.

There is one other ingredient of dharma that makes a solitary
appearance in Rock Edict III. There, Ashoka teaches the people the
virtue of 'spending little and accumulating little'. Simple maths will tell
you that if you have a steady income and you go on a spending diet,
the result will be that you have a large and growing bank balance. How
can one spend little, and yet accumulate little? The solution, I think, is
generosity, giving away one's wealth to deserving people—the virtue of
dāna or gift-giving that Ashoka advocates not only in his definitions of
dharma, but also elsewhere in his writings. Although gifts are mentioned
especially in connection with Sramanas and Brahmins, in Rock Edict III
the list of recipients of a person's generosity is considerably expanded:
'Giving gifts to friends, companions, and relatives, and to Brahmins and
Sramanas.' One sure sign of persons who are committed to dharma is
their generosity in giving gifts, as Ashoka notes in his instructions to his
dharma-mahamatras in Rock Edict V:

> 'This one is fervent with regard to dharma', or 'this one is established
> in dharma', or 'this one is devoted to gifts'—thus they are occupied
> everywhere in my territory with dharma-devotees.

Ashoka presents himself as the paragon and exemplar of such generosity.
In Rock Edict VIII he speaks of his 'tours of dharma', going around his
territory to engage in acts of dharma and to spread dharma. Such tours
included 'paying visits to Sramanas and Brahmins and making gifts to
them, paying visits to elderly people and providing monitory support
to them'. He recruited officials from his bureaucracy to help him in the
distribution of gifts by him and by members of his family, as he explains
in Pillar Edict VII (v):

These, as well as many other top officials, are occupied with the distribution of gifts, that is to say, from me and from the queens, and within the whole of my inner chambers. In many different ways they establish spheres of contentment right here[18] and in the provinces. I have ordered them to be occupied with the distribution of gifts from my boys also and from other princes from the queens.

His great wish, he tells us in Pillar Edict IV, is that 'distribution of gifts may increase among the people'.

In stressing the importance of generosity and gift-giving, Ashoka was following a common ethical principle articulated in ancient religious texts from diverse sources. Wandering ascetics, such as Buddhist monks, were mendicants and dependent on the generosity of the people for their very subsistence. Brahmins also depended heavily on gifts given to them, especially in return for ritual services. One early Brahmanical Upanishad has this very succinct praise of gift-giving: 'By gift giving enemies turn into friends. In gift giving is the whole world founded. Therefore, they call gift giving the highest.'[19]

GLEANING FROM SILENCE

So far, we have considered how Ashoka, either formally in his definitions or more broadly in his writings, characterized the main contours of his dharma. We can glean further insights into his thinking, however, if we look at what he chose *not to include* within his conception of dharma—that is, at Ashoka's silences, which we already had occasion to comment on. When we look at the kinds of activities that would be either encouraged as socially and ethically positive, or discouraged as immoral or even criminal, we find that a wide range of human activities are left out from Ashoka's conception of dharma.

Before turning to the moral and immoral activities left out by Ashoka, we can ask him a more basic question: How do you know what dharma

18 That is, in the capital Pataliputra.

19 *Mahānārāyaṇa Upaniṣad*, 523. For a detailed study of gift-giving and hospitality in ancient India, see Jamison 1996.

is? Where did you come by your definitions of dharma? We looked at this issue at the beginning of this chapter, citing the provocative statement of the Brahmanical theologian Apastamba, probably a near-contemporary of Ashoka: 'Dharma and non-dharma do not go around saying: Here we are!'[20] Brahmanical law codes of the period open with the central issue of the epistemology of dharma: How do you know dharma? What are the legitimate sources of dharma? For Brahmins, it was the Vedas and the authoritative practices of Brahmanical communities. For Buddhists, it was the words of the Buddha who, through his transformative experience of enlightenment, had awakened to the ultimate truth. But how does an ordinary king have access to what truly constitutes dharma? Ashoka does not address the issue. He is silent. The best we can say is that he may have seen his definitions as a common moral consensus at least among the religious elite represented by the Pasanda religious communities. He likely assumed that people across his empire, and even those living beyond it, would see the truth of the Ashokan dharma.

Turning to the elements of the Ashokan dharma, let us first look at the criminal code. Ashoka himself hints at a well-developed criminal justice system, which included imprisonment and punishment for malfeasants. Ashoka's bureaucracy undoubtedly included not only the armed forces and civil administrators, but also law enforcement agencies targeting criminal activities. Ancient Indian political thought singled out theft as the paradigmatic social ill. In many discussions and myths about the institution of kingship, the suppression of theft is viewed as the raison d'être of that institution. Taxes are justified on the basis of the king's ability to protect private property. Ancient Indian jurisprudence acknowledges numerous other infractions that can be the basis for judicial intervention. Among these are non-payment of debts, breach of contract, physical and verbal assault, murder, sexual offences including rape, and so on. Yet, Ashoka's dharma takes no cognizance of such crimes. Clearly, it could not have been Ashoka's intention to condone such activities. For him, however, dharma was a higher calling, we must assume; it presupposed such commonplace civic sense and integrity.

---

20 *Āpastamba Dharmasūtra*, 1.20.6.

Given that Ashoka was likely influenced by Buddhism and by his interactions with Buddhist monks in his views about dharma, we would have expected at least some elements of the Buddhist conception of dharma in his own definitions. In Chapter 7, I posed the question as to why Ashoka did not make the five Buddhist precepts part of his definition of dharma. These five precepts, known as '*pañcaśīla*', consist of five prohibitions: (1) killing living beings, (2) taking what is not given (that is, stealing), (3) sexual misconduct, (4) false or wrong speech, and (5) intoxicating drinks. The only one making a consistent appearance in Ashoka's comments on dharma is the first, not killing living beings, while the fourth, being truthful, is mentioned in passing three times.

Both the Buddhists and the Brahmins were strongly against the consumption of alcohol. Abstinence was a prominent element of the religious ethic of the time, and in some sources, such as the Brahmanical law codes, there were also criminal sanctions against drinking. On the opposite end of the spectrum, Kautilya's *Arthashastra* provides what would have been the political or governmental attitude to liquor.[21] There, we find that liquor was not only a commonplace and widely used commodity, but it was also, for the most part, a state monopoly. Obviously, kings knew a good source of income when they saw one and, like some modern states, forbade the private manufacture, transport and sale of liquor, except during certain festivals. Liquor flowed freely at festivals and fairs, which Ashoka, as we saw, mentions with disapproval. Why did he not make abstention from liquor part of his dharma?

The same question may be asked about sexual misconduct, which in most ethical systems is considered far more serious than the consumption of alcohol, and some elements of which, such as rape, deflowering a virgin and adultery, also carry criminal penalties. Within Buddhism and other ascetic religions, where celibacy was a prominent feature of the monastic life, proper sexual behaviour occupied an elevated position within the moral hierarchy. Why did Ashoka not make refraining from sexual misconduct part of his dharma?

---

21 For a detailed history of liquor in India, including legal and moral attitudes, see McHugh 2021.

No clear answers to these and similar questions are given in Ashoka's own writings. He simply ignores these issues. Either they did not occur to him or, more likely, he chose to be silent about them. Why? We can only glean some conjectural—hopefully plausible—answers from clues we find in his corpus of writings. First, once he had pivoted from his initial impetus to preach Buddhism evidenced in Minor Rock Edict I to a new conception of a more universal and inclusive dharma, he may have been inclined to stay clear of anything that was easily and closely associated with Buddhism in the public's mind, such as the five Buddhist precepts. We can certainly understand that. His reluctance to include the criminal code is also understandable: dharma was not meant to be the least common ethical denominator, to simply create a citizenry not prone to crime. Dharma, for Ashoka, presupposed all that. But it was much more than that.

A statement in Rock Edict IV may provide a hint at Ashoka's thinking. Towards the end of this edict, he expresses his hope for his sons and grandsons: 'Abiding in dharma and good conduct (*sīla*), they will provide instruction in dharma. For, this is the paramount task—to provide instruction in dharma. The practise of dharma, however, is not possible for a man devoid of good conduct (*asīla*).' This is the only place Ashoka uses the common term '*sīla*' (good conduct or moral precept) prominent in Buddhist discourse. He relates it to, but distinguishes it from, dharma. It is not possible for a man devoid of good conduct to practise dharma. This conclusion implies that 'good conduct' or *sīla* is a prerequisite for embarking on a life of dharma. Now, as we saw, the five Buddhist precepts are called *sīla*, and such rules forbidding people from engaging in bad behaviour may have been thought by Ashoka to be a moral precondition to following his path of dharma rather than part of his dharma.

Yet, I think there may be more to Ashoka's reluctance to broach these areas of ethics and criminality. As I have attempted to show above in Chart 9.2, most, if not all, of what Ashoka calls 'attributes of dharma' are relational. They concern a person's—the 'self' within the chart—relationships with significant others in his life (yes, for Ashoka, it is always a 'he'). There are no doubt virtues that fall in its orbit, such as compassion, mercy, gentleness, truthfulness, self-control, restraint of speech, purity and so forth. But the relational ethic is placed in the foreground. It appears that Ashoka viewed the proper development of these relationships as the key to a life well lived, promoting happiness in this world and the next. He may have seen this as a 'new' kind of ethic that he had personally discovered or constructed, a new ethic that he could preach even to people outside his own cultural sphere, such as the Greek kings ruling the countries of West Asia.

Even when we accept Ashoka's commitment to a moral philosophy based on the proper cultivation of social and familial relationships, however, there are some surprising and inexplicable omissions. For a start, with the exception of the mother—given within the pair of 'mother–father', much like the gender-neutral English 'parents'—the relationships are male-oriented. It appears that the individual who is the implicit object of Ashoka's instruction—what I have rendered with the gender-neutral term 'self' in Chart 9.2—is, in reality, a male. I will discuss the implicit audience of Ashoka's moral sermons in Chapter 10, but suffice it to say here that this audience is both male and middle or upper class. This 'self' is probably married and head of the household, in control of financial assets. It is he who needs to be told that he must 'listen to' his parents and the elders of his extended family. Young boys or girls will have no option but to do so, given that they are dependent on their parents for their very sustenance.

This adult male, economically productive and financially independent, lives within a web of relationships with significant others, some transient, such as visiting Sramanas and Brahmins, others enduring and stable, such as parents, relatives, friends and slaves. The inclusion of slaves and servants is a clue that Ashoka was addressing individuals of a certain social and economic standing. Within such a context, however, we would have expected other significant relationships to be included, such as those with wife, sons, daughters, sisters, brothers and even grandchildren. These too are passed over in silence, however. The 'Why?' here has, as far as I can tell, no obvious or plausible answer, except perhaps that, in the case of women, Ashoka was operating within a deeply patriarchal system where women rarely broke to the surface of public discourse. As we have already seen, besides the mother in the definitions of dharma, there are only a few occasions where women are mentioned: female relatives in Minor Rock Edict II, Ashoka's queens and sisters, and Buddhist nuns in the Schism Edict and the Bairat Edict.

Finally, going beyond the confines of dharma itself, Ashoka is sometimes self-reflective about the project he had embarked on, placing it within the broader human predicament. The following passage is set within Rock Edict XIII, the most self-reflective of Ashoka's writings where he comes close to apologizing for a war he had started. Perhaps influenced by the Buddhist doctrine that human life is inherently and essentially characterized by suffering, he says:

> Even people who are well cared for and whose love is undiminished, when misfortune strikes their friends, companions, associates and relatives, it causes injury to those very people. This is the common plight of all human beings, and it is deemed grievous by the Beloved of Gods.

Ashoka has a solution to this human predicament. Practising dharma fully and with total dedication brings unending felicity in this world and the next.

10

Preaching Dharma

Ashoka celebrated the twelfth anniversary of his royal consecration in the spring of 256 BCE. The year that followed, the thirteenth year of his reign, was to be a watershed in his life and that of his empire, as also in Indian history. As we saw in Chapter 8, that year Ashoka pivoted away from an overtly Buddhist message to one that was neutral with respect to organized religions—what he calls Pasanda—and that sought to stay above the fray of religious identities and rivalries. That was the moral philosophy of dharma. During that crucial thirteenth year Ashoka turned with his usual zest and zeal to preaching his new dharma to all the people in his vast empire and beyond. Commenting on the duties of a king, he says in Rock Edict IV: '[T]his is the paramount task—to provide instruction in dharma.' This chapter will narrate the story of how that new mission of Ashoka unfolded.

Here is Ashoka writing Pillar Edict VI in 242 BCE, the twenty-seventh year of his reign, now an old man in the twilight of his remarkable career reflecting back on his activities on behalf of dharma:

> After I had been consecrated for twelve years, I had my writing on dharma inscribed for the welfare and wellbeing of the people, so that by not transgressing that writing they may obtain an increase of dharma in various ways.

So, his first writing on dharma proper—as distinct from his first writing as such about his conversion to Buddhism inscribed in Minor Rock Edict I—was done sometime between spring 256 BCE and spring 255 BCE, probably early in that thirteenth regnal year, given that several of his writings are dated to that year. It is likely that the writing referred to in Pillar Edict VI is, in fact, Rock Edict I preaching the virtue of ahimsa and prohibiting the killing of animals. That same year he also wrote Rock Edict III. It is dated and deals explicitly with the dissemination of his teachings on dharma by his government officials:

> Twelve years after my royal consecration, I issued this order. Everywhere in my territory yukta-officers, rajuka-officers, and pradesika-officers should set out on circuit every five years for this purpose: in order to give the following instruction in dharma, as also for other tasks.

A third edict, Rock Edict IV, was also written the same year:

> This has been written for the following purpose: that they should apply themselves to its [dharma's] increase and not countenance its diminution. This was written by the Beloved of Gods, King Piyadasi, twelve years after his royal consecration.

The very same year he donated two cave dwellings in Barabar Hill for use by Ajivika ascetics.[1] That was a busy year for Ashoka. It is likely that the first four of the Rock Edict series were written during that year, because, as we will see, Rock Edict V deals with a major initiative of his that took place the following year, the fourteenth of his reign.

From the numerous writings Ashoka left behind, it becomes clear that he experimented with several methods of disseminating his dharma in his own empire and abroad. We can classify these methods into three groups: (1) writings: Ashoka uses effective written communications, their permanent publication through engravings on stone, and their public

---

1   See Barabar Hill Cave Inscriptions I and II under Miscellaneous Inscriptions in the Appendix.

recitations with commentary by officials as a crucial method to teach dharma; (2) bureaucracy: Ashoka co-opts government officials of various ranks to inculcate dharma among the people in their charge; (3) example: Ashoka believed that the people would follow his example, and he wanted to present himself as both a paragon of a person devoted to dharma and a model for others to follow.

AUDIENCE FOR DHARMA: GENDER AND CLASS

An initial question presents itself as we begin to explore Ashoka's campaigns to propagate dharma: What was the audience, explicit and implicit, for Ashoka's orations on dharma? This is a topic I touched upon in the previous chapter, but it deserves a fuller investigation.

I drew attention there to the lack of representation of women within the web of relationships that anchor Ashoka's conception of dharma. This becomes even more significant when we query the gender of the person whose relationships anchor Ashoka's definitions of dharma—the person whom I have labelled 'self' in Chart 9.2. It is most likely, if not certain, that Ashoka, at least implicitly, pictured this person as an adult male. In the few places where a pronoun is used, it is always in the masculine. Even though many of the relationships that Ashoka identifies can occur in the case of a man as well as a woman, it is quite unlikely within the ancient Indian context that women would own slaves. I think it is a reasonable conclusion that the person to whom Ashoka's orations and the missionary efforts of his officials are directed is a married male head of household, the paterfamilias, and he is also sufficiently wealthy to own slaves—perhaps we can think of Ashoka's dharma as primarily a middle-class morality.

But that would be selling Ashoka short. He and his messages are more complex. Although the married male householder is in the foreground, he does not fill the landscape. That the dharma message of Ashoka was intended also for women emerges from several of his statements. In Pillar Edict VII (v), Ashoka says that his wives and other female members of his family and household are engaged in distributing gifts in order to promote the observance of dharma among the population:

These, as well as many other top officials, are occupied with the distribution of gifts, that is to say, from me and from the queens, and within the whole of my inner chambers. In many different ways, they establish spheres of contentment right here and in the provinces. I have ordered them to be occupied with the distribution of gifts from my boys also and from other princes from the queens, for the purpose of promoting noble acts of dharma and conforming to dharma.

The accounting procedures for gifts from his various queens are the focus of the so-called Queen's Edict.

His dharma-mahamatras, furthermore, were dispatched 'here and in outlying cities, with the inner chambers of my brothers and sisters, as well as with other relatives' (Rock Edict V) to make sure that dharma is observed by his brothers and sisters, and by members of their respective households.

Within the ambit of Buddhism, moreover, Ashoka had plenty of opportunity to note the role of women in the practice and promotion of the Buddhist dharma. In his Bairat letter and the Schism Edict to the Buddhist Sangha, he mentions both monks (*bhikkhu*) and nuns (*bhikkhuni*), and in the Bairat letter also lay Buddhist devotees, both male and female Upasakas. So, Ashoka was clearly aware of the commitment of women to the practice of the Buddhist faith, both as nuns and as committed lay women. Buddhist nuns, we must remember, constituted the *only* voluntary organization for and by single celibate women outside the control of family patriarchy, the only organization that presented women with an alternative to traditional marriage.

I noted above the probability that uppermost in Ashoka's mind when he was writing his letters on dharma was the male paterfamilias making a comfortable living, with a household that included servants and slaves. From a socio-economic point of view, such individuals clearly constituted the most important segment of the population, and Ashoka must have been keen to convert them to his new dharma-based moral philosophy. Their conversion would have a ripple effect, bringing the lower economic classes into the fold. Yet, there are statements that show Ashoka's sensitivity and concern for what he calls the 'lowly people'. In the very first sample of his writing to have survived, Minor Rock Edict I, Ashoka is keen to point out that the 'striving' he advocates is not reserved for the rich and powerful. 'This can be achieved,' he says, 'not only by eminent people, but even lowly people if they strive are indeed able to attain even the immense heaven.' In the same message Ashoka goes on to state its purpose: 'This promulgation has been promulgated for the following purpose—so that both the lowly and the eminent may strive, that the frontier people also may come to know it, and that this striving may endure for a long time.' His outreach extended even to the 'frontier people', who may have been considered even lower than the 'lowly people' within his territory. Upinder Singh highlights the breathtaking freshness of Ashoka's dharma:

> But the most amazing news of all must have been the king's repeated announcements, enunciated through oral and written word, that everyone, whether high or low, could attain heaven by following dhamma. Although the Buddha and Mahavira had said this sort of thing earlier, this was the first (and the last) time that an emperor was making such announcements. Ashoka was a political prophet of soteriological socialism.[2]

There is a moving declaration in Rock Edict X that reminds one of similar statements from ancient religious leaders, a statement that has received little attention from scholars. Ashoka thinks that it is actually easier for the lowly people to practise dharma than for the rich and eminent: 'This is difficult to do, however, for either a low-class person or a high-class person without utmost striving, giving up everything. But between them, it is clearly more difficult to do for a high-class person.' This parallels the aphorism of Jesus that 'it is easier for a camel to go through the eye of a needle than for a rich man to enter the kingdom of God', or the beatitude that says: 'Blessed are you poor, for yours is the kingdom of God.'[3] The *Bhagavad Gita* speaks of God accepting even a leaf offered with love

---

2   Upinder Singh 2017: 49.
3   Gospel of Matthew, 19.24; Gospel of Luke, 6.20.

and devotion.[4] And, of course, there is the great example of the Indian ascetical traditions, including Buddhism, where mendicants are vowed to total poverty and depend for their very sustenance on the generosity of the people.

The intended audience of Ashoka's dharma included rulers and people living beyond the borders of his empire. He envisaged his dharma as having a universal appeal. I will deal with the universalist aspect of Ashoka's messaging with respect to dharma presently. Here I will only allude to the fact that Ashoka conceived of his dharma as a universal moral philosophy that can and should be adopted by the people of the whole world. Ashoka sees this as his 'world conquest', not through the might of arms but through the power of an idea. In what seems like a hyperbolic boast, but which nonetheless reveals his thinking, Ashoka claims in Rock Edict XIII to have already accomplished much of this task:

> Even where envoys of the Beloved of Gods do not go, after hearing the discourses on dharma, the ordinances, and instruction in dharma of the Beloved of Gods, they conform to dharma, and they will conform to it in the future. In this manner, this conquest has been secured everywhere. In all cases, however, the conquest is a source of joy. So, joy has been secured by the conquest through dharma.

WRITING TO PROMOTE DHARMA

Ashoka was the first, and perhaps the last, Indian king to use writing as an instrument of good governance and mass education. At the beginning of his long Pillar Edict VII (i), he casually mentions how this came about.

> Here's what occurred to me. I will promulgate dharma-promulgations. I will prescribe dharma-prescriptions. Having listened to that, people will comply, they will be lifted up, and they will assuredly grow through growth in dharma. For this purpose, I have promulgated dharma-promulgations and decreed diverse kinds of dharma-

---

4   *Bhagavad Gita*, 9.26.

prescriptions, so that my numerous personal emissaries, who are occupied with the people, will exhort them and fully explain to them.

He does not say when this idea came to him, but it was probably sometime in 256 BCE, the thirteenth year of his reign. As we saw in Chapter 3, he wrote a large number of letters to his officials, some of which were anthologized in two major series: Rock Edicts and Pillar Edicts. The purpose of these letters was to enlist these officials in an unprecedented undertaking: a programme of mass education and training of the entire population of the empire so that they may adhere to the dictates of dharma. But Ashoka also expected his words to have a direct effect on the population, to persuade them—rather than command them—to follow the path of dharma. That was the reason for the quasi-ritual public readings of his edicts.

In the very first of his Rock Edict series, Ashoka calls his inscriptions 'dharmalipi', writings on dharma. The term 'lipi' can refer to writing on any surface, such as a palm leaf. But it refers more specifically to engravings on stone. Both meanings probably lurk behind the term, thus precluding a single precise translation. What is clear, however, is that Ashoka thinks of his writings as directed principally, if not exclusively, at providing instruction on dharma. The principal duty of a king, according to him, is to be a teacher. His imperial officials are to be his teaching assistants, at one point compared to nurses in whose care he has left his subjects, his children. It appears, further, that he thinks of his writings—especially the permanence and iconic nature of the inscribed texts—as having an almost talismanic effect on those who view and/or read them. He is especially concerned that his sons and grandsons, the future rulers of his empire, will be equally committed to dharma and its propagation. Here are some examples of that concern and of his hope that his stone inscriptions would spur his heirs to maintain and expand his dharma mission.

And the sons, grandsons, and great-grandsons of the Beloved of Gods, King Piyadasi, will further make this practice of dharma increase until the end of the eon. Abiding in dharma and good conduct, they will provide instruction in dharma. (Rock Edict IV)

Therefore, if my sons and grandsons, and my descendants beyond them until the end of the eon, abide by this in the same manner, they will do the right thing … For the following purpose has this writing on dharma been inscribed—that it may endure for a long time, and thus my children may act in conformity with it. (Rock Edict V)

Now, this writing on dharma has been inscribed for the following purpose: that it may endure for a long time, and thus my sons and grandsons may strive for the welfare of the whole world. But this is truly difficult to accomplish without utmost striving. (Rock Edict VI)

The very last of his messages written in 241 BCE, his twenty-eighth regnal year, echoes the same words:

Now, this has been done so that it may endure as long as my sons and grandsons, as long as the moon and sun, and so that people may defer to it. For, by deferring to it in this manner one gains this world and the next. (Pillar Edict VII [vii])

The medium on which Ashoka displayed his writings to the public was also intended to give them an aura of solemnity, if not sacrality. We must remember, as we saw in Chapter 3, that written documents were either non-existent or very rare before Ashoka. So, the mere display of written words on large rock surfaces and imposing pillars must have, to say the least, created a stir among the population.

But Ashoka had another trick up his sleeve. Not long after he started inscribing his writings on dharma, he started on an expensive and unprecedented building project, which we examined in Chapter 4. He commissioned the complicated construction and erection of monolithic polished stone pillars topped with exquisitely carved capitals. Then he had his series of Pillar Edicts engraved on them, so that people would see his iconic writings on these awe-inspiring pillars. Early Buddhist art shows that Ashoka's pillars had become cult objects, with persons in poses of veneration (Fig.12). And Ashoka calls his pillars '*dharmastambha*', Pillars of Dharma.

The inscribed inscriptions may also have been thought to exert a talismanic effect on future generations. We see this in ancient Buddhist donative inscriptions. These are often engraved under the statue where they can never be read.[5] Scriptural passages are also interred within Buddhist stupas. There is an efficacy to the written word that far outpaces its reading. Inscriptions continue to speak in a sort of frozen sermon. They continue to have an efficacy through time.

Ashoka also knew how to use language to create the impact he wanted on his audience. I have already noted his use of compound words where the first member is 'dharma' to refer to a wide range of things, activities, attitudes and emotions. It is noteworthy that in the two anthologies of his writings on dharma, the Rock and Pillar Edicts, the word 'dharma' is used on its own outside of a compound infrequently: four times in the Rock Edicts and six times in the Pillar Edicts. In the latter, four of the occurrences are in a single passage of Pillar Edict I, where Ashoka instructs his senior officials that their conduct should be according to dharma (using the instrumental case of the word: *dharmeṇa*): 'protecting according to dharma, governing according to dharma, bestowing wellbeing according to dharma, and guarding according to dharma'. In contrast, dharma is used in thirty-three compounds, where dharma qualifies as an attribute or quality of the object or activity designated by the second member of the compound. I give these compounds in the chart on the next page.

---

5   Gregory Schopen has commented on these: 'To judge by their placement, however, it would appear that a large number of early Buddhist donative inscriptions were never intended even to be seen, let alone read' (Schopen 2004: 387). To the question 'why such inscriptions were written at all', Schopen answers that inscribing the name has the efficacy of leaving the donor behind as a permanent presence at the very site of his or her donation. Indeed, one might note, the earliest donative inscriptions of India are from the time of Ashoka.

Chart 10.1
Tentacles of Dharma

Prakrit	Sanskrit	Translation	Reference
dhaṃmakāmatā	*dharmakāmatā*	love of dharma	RE XIII, PE I
dhaṃmaguṇa	*dharmaguṇa*	attributes of dharma	MRE II
ahodhaṃmaghose	*ahodharmaghoṣa*	sound of 'Ah! Dharma!'	RE IV
dhaṃmacalane	*dharmacaraṇa*	practice of dharma	RE IV, SEP II
dhaṃmathaṃbha	*dharmasthambha*	dharma pillars	PE VII
dhaṃmadāne	*dharmadāna*	gift of dharma	RE IX, XI
dhaṃmaniyame	*dharmaniyama*	regulation regarding dharma	PE VII
dhaṃmanisite	*dharmaniśrita*	fervent with regard to dharma	RE V
dhaṃmapaṭīpati	*dharmapratipatti*	observance of dharma	PE VII
dhaṃmapalipucchā	*dharmaparipṛcchā*	questions about dharma	RE VIII
dhaṃmapaliyāyāni	*dharmaparyāya*	orations on dharma	Bairat
dhaṃmamaṃgale	*dharmamaṅgala*	auspicious rite of dharma	RE IX
dhaṃmamahāmātā	*dharmamahāmātra*	dharma-mahamatra	RE V, VI, XII, PE VII
dhaṃmayātā	*dharmayātrā*	dharma tour	RE VIII
dhaṃmayuta	*dharmayukta* (?)	devoted to dharma	RE V
dhaṃmalati	*dharmarati*	pleasure through dharma	RE XIII
dhaṃmalipi	*dharmalipi*	writing on dharma	RE I, V, VI, XIII, XIV, PE I, II, IV, VI, VII
dhaṃmavaḍhi	*dharmavṛddhi*	increase of dharma	RE V, PE VI, VII
dhaṃmavāye	*dharmāvāya*	study of dharma	RE XIII
dhaṃmavijaye	*dharmavijaya*	victory of/through dharma	RE XIII

dhaṃmavuta	*dharmavṛttam* (?)	dharma discourse	RE XIII
dhaṃmasaṃvibhāge	*dharmasaṃvibhāga*	distribution of dharma	RE XI
dhaṃmasaṃthave	*dharmasaṃstava*	praise of dharma	RE XI
dhaṃmasaṃbadhe	*dharmasaṃbaddha*	bond through dharma	RE XI
dhaṃmasāvanāni	*dharmaśrāvaṇāni*	proclamations of dharma	PE VII
dhaṃmasusūsā	*dharmaśuśrūṣā*	obedience to dharma	RE X
dhaṃmādhithāne	*dharmādhiṣṭhāna*	establishing dharma	RE V
dhaṃmānugahe	*dharmānugraha*	favour of dharma	RE IX
dhaṃmānupaṭīpati	*dharmānupratipatti*	observance of dharma	PE VII
dhaṃmānusathi	*dharmānuśasti*	instruction in dharma	RE XIII, PE VII
dhaṃmānusāsana	*dharmānuśāsana*	instruction in dharma	RE IV
dhaṃmāpādāna	*dharmāpādāna*	noble acts of dharma	PE VII
dhaṃmāpekhā	*dharmāpekṣā*	concern for dharma	PE I

The constant repetition of 'dharma' in association with thirty-three kinds of objects, activities and emotions instils in the reader or listener the centrality of dharma within the lives of individuals, groups and society itself. Dharma signifies all that is good and noble, summarized in the oft-repeated exclamation '*sādhu*'—good, excellent, lovely, splendid.

Ashoka's writings and the way he expected his bureaucracy and the people at large to relate to them point to what may be described as a 'cult of dharma'. In this cult, his writings inscribed on stone, especially the two major anthologies of the Rock and Pillar Edicts, came to assume the role of scripture. Ashoka also appears to have established an annual liturgical calendar during which these scriptures were read aloud along with explanatory sermons by government officials to the people gathered for the event. In both the Separate Edicts he expresses his wish that his writing should be read and listened to by the people every four months on the especially sacred Tishya days:

This writing, furthermore, should be listened to on the day of the Tishya constellation. Even in between the days of the Tishya when an opportunity presents itself, even a single individual may listen to it. And acting in this way, you will be able to carry it out fully. (Separate Edict I)

And this writing should be listened to during every four-month season on the days of the Tishya constellation. Even in between the days of the Tishya when an opportunity presents itself, even a single individual, if he so wishes, may listen to it. (Separate Edict II)

The individuals entrusted with the responsibility of conducting these services with the public reading of Ashoka's writings and commenting on them are senior officials in the imperial bureaucracy. In Pillar Edict VII (i) Ashoka reminds these officials about this central task:

For this purpose, I have promulgated dharma-promulgations and decreed diverse kinds of dharma-prescriptions, so that my numerous personal emissaries, who are occupied with the people, will exhort them, and fully explain to them. Also, rajuka-officers, who are occupied with many hundreds of thousands of living beings—they too have been ordered by me: 'In such and such manner, exhort the people to be devoted to dharma.'

The days of public recitation were probably observed as religiously significant times of the calendar by the people long before Ashoka thought of using them for broadcasting his dharma message. Further, he placed restrictions relating to killing or hurting animals on these days, something we have discussed in Chapter 9. The combination of such restrictions on normal life of the public and probably ceremonial reading of Ashoka's writings would have added a further layer of sacrality and authority to these writings.

GOVERNANCE AND DIPLOMACY IN THE SERVICE OF DHARMA

Self-reflective as always, Ashoka speaks openly about his activist style of governing in his instructions to his officials in Separate Edict I:

Whatever I set my eyes on, that I seek to carry out through action and
to realize through appropriate means. And I consider this to be the
principal means in this matter—to give you instruction.

Ashoka recognizes that his messages, even those inscribed on stone, could
reach only a tiny fraction of the population of his vast empire. He needed
a message multiplier, individuals who could mediate between him and
his people and thereby amplify his message. As he says in his Separate
Edict I, he found that multiplier in his state bureaucracy. He placed his
governmental apparatus in the service of dharma.

     The fourteenth year of Ashoka's reign, that is, sometime between
the spring of 255 BCE and the following spring, was pivotal in the
transformation of his bureaucrats into ambassadors of dharma. It
was during this year, Ashoka tells us in Rock Edict V, that he had the
revolutionary idea of creating a brand-new cadre within the most senior
level of his administration. The highest echelon in the bureaucracy was
occupied by the mahamatras. Ashoka created a parallel group called the
dharma-mahamatras devoted to the propagation of dharma. He brags
about this new initiative of his, something no previous king had ever
thought of doing:

> Now, in times past dharma-mahamatras did not exist at all. But,
> thirteen years after my royal consecration, I established the dharma-
> mahamatras.

Even though, as we will see, Ashoka employed all his imperial officers
in his dharma campaign, the dharma-mahamatras were in the vanguard.
Unfortunately, Ashoka does not tell us how these officers were selected,
whether they underwent a special kind of training, and how they interacted
with other elements of the imperial bureaucracy. If they underwent a
period of training, did it include information about the doctrines and
practices of the various Pasandas they were expected to oversee? Were
they members of particular Pasandas, or did they largely belong to
Ashoka's own Pasanda, Buddhism? That the dharma-mahamatras may
have specialized in different Pasanda groups is hinted at in Pillar Edict

VII (iv): 'different mahamatras with different Pasandas according to the special features of each'.

Their seniority in the imperial bureaucracy and their closeness to the emperor must have made it easier for them to be both intrusive and taken seriously. As we will see in Part Four, they were dispatched to look into and look after the various organized religious groups, including the Brahmins and Buddhists. But their mission was as broad as Ashoka's empire was vast. In Rock Edict V, he presents what appears to be a definition of a dharma-mahamatra and provides a glimpse into the geographical areas these officials operated in and the social groups with which they interacted.

They are occupied with all the Pasandas for the establishment of dharma and, by the increase of dharma, for the welfare and wellbeing of dharma-devotees among the Greeks, the Kambojas and Gandharas, the Ristikas and Pitinikas, as also among others along the western frontiers.[6]

They are occupied with Bhatamayas, Bambhanibhiyas,[7] the destitute, and the elderly for their welfare and wellbeing, and for the removal of obstacles from dharma-devotees.

They are occupied with prisoners to render them support, to remove obstacles, and to set them free when it is found: 'This one has to care for family and children'; or 'This one has an obligation'; or 'This one is elderly'.

They are occupied everywhere, here and in outlying cities, with the inner chambers of my brothers and sisters, as well as with other relatives.

'This one is fervent with regard to dharma,' or 'this one is established in dharma,' or 'this one is devoted to gifts'—thus they are occupied everywhere in my territory with those dharma-devotees.

---

6   For the identification of these peoples, see the Glossary and the Map.

7   These two terms, as Schneider (1978: 128) says, are 'still inexplicable and should therefore not be translated at all'. Given that they are grouped with the destitute and the elderly, they may refer to social groups needing the assistance of the state.

These are the dharma-mahamatras.

This long list includes ethnic groups living along the north-western frontier, what is today western Pakistan and Afghanistan. Their remit extended to the innermost spaces of royal households—the original term may be translated as 'harem' or 'seraglio', but I think it does not carry a strict sexual connotation—including those of his brothers and sisters.

Ashoka did not limit his dharma mission to his own territory. He conceived of it as a worldwide mission, and in this he may have been inspired by the Buddhist vision of the Buddha's doctrine, unconstrained by culture and geography and spreading beyond the confines of what Ashoka calls Jambudvipa, the Indian subcontinent. For this larger mission beyond his territory, Ashoka deployed envoys, as we hear in Rock Edict XIII. He uses the term '*dūta*', which is the common term used in Indian texts on governance to refer to ambassadors sent by one king to another. But these were not normal diplomatic contacts. These envoys were charged with the special mission of converting the rulers and peoples beyond Ashoka's territory to the Ashokan 'cult of dharma'. Given the importance of their mission, these envoys were probably recruited from the cadre of dharma-mahamatras.

We do not have independent evidence to determine how successful Ashoka's international dharma missions were. Were they able to find converts in those distant West Asian lands ruled by Hellenistic kings? Were these kings interested at all in Ashoka's dharma and the ethical principle of ahimsa? The historian Francisco Adrados[8] presents a tantalizing possibility of Ashokan influence in a Greek inscription of a king named Antiochus of Commagene (62–34 BCE). Adrados thinks that this inscription is inspired by the Greek translation of an Ashokan edict from Kandahar, which reads:

When ten years had been completed, King Piodasses [=Piyadasi] disclosed piety [Greek: *eusébeia* = dharma] to men. And from that time, he has made men more pious, and everything thrives throughout the whole world.

---

8   See Adrados 1984.

The inscription of Antiochus, as translated by Adrados, reads:

> The Great King Antiochus … Among my worldly goods, I considered
> that *eusébeia* is for all men not only the safest possession but also the
> most pleasurable enjoyment … and during the whole of my reign, I
> have considered saintliness (*hosiótes*) to be my most faithful guardian
> and my most unequalled pleasure.

This is tantalizing, and nothing more. The use of '*eusébeia*' is significant,
but on its own it cannot establish a direct dependence on Ashokan
writings. And this Antiochus is two centuries removed from Ashoka.
Yet, it is interesting to see *eusébeia*, the Greek equivalent of dharma,
emerge as a central concept within a Hellenistic royal pronouncement in
western Asia. Antiochus's statement that he finds 'unequalled pleasure'
in following *eusébeia* parallels Ashoka's statement in Rock Edict VIII that
going on dharma tours gives him greater enjoyment than anything else.

Ashoka did not depend solely on the cadre of dharma-mahamatras
to spread his message. He co-opted all his senior officers for the task.
The most senior of these were the mahamatras. In Separate Edict I,
Ashoka says that he, or the prince viceroys of provincial capitals, would
send mahamatras on circuit every five years. This rule was already
established in the thirteenth year of his reign, 256–255 BCE, with respect
to the senior officers below the mahamatras. In Rock Edict III, Ashoka
gives this clear command:

> Everywhere in my territory yukta-officers, rajuka-officers, and
> pradesika-officers should set out on circuit every five years for this
> purpose: in order to give the following instruction in dharma, as also
> for other tasks.
>
> 'Obedience to mother and father—excellent! Giving gifts to friends,
> companions, and relatives, and to Brahmins and Sramanas—excellent!
> Not killing living beings—excellent! Spending little and accumulating
> little—excellent!'

So, we have this new practice initiated by Ashoka, where senior officers
go on circuit around the geographical area under their charge to preach

dharma. The practice of going on circuit likely pre-dated Ashoka. It was probably connected to both judicial and revenue activities. Ashoka, thus, piggybacks a new layer of activities onto the existing ones. As he tells his officials in Separate Edict I, they should 'set out on a tour without neglecting their own tasks'.

In Pillar Edict IV, Ashoka engages in a lengthy discourse about the provincial officers called rajukas. There, as we saw in Chapter 2, he both warns them and cajoles them to follow his instructions about how they should govern and look after the people entrusted to their care. On the issue of teaching dharma to the people, Ashoka gives us a glimpse as to how this may have been carried out. Simply going to a place and preaching dharma could encounter resistance. This may be the reason why Ashoka tells the rajukas to use as intermediaries those residents in the region who are already devoted to dharma. They may have been neighbours or important people who would command the respect of the residents. Or, the expression 'dharma-devotees' may refer to members of Pasanda groups, who could be recruited to spread the word about the emperor's mission. 'Through dharma-devotees, furthermore,' Ashoka says, '[the rajukas] will exhort the people of the countryside, so that they may gain the benefits of this world and of the next.'

In some instances, Ashoka appears to recruit the 'dharma-devotees' directly to spread the word. Rock Edict IX is a good example, with some gender undertones. This is the edict in which Ashoka inveighs against what he calls trivial rites on special occasions, such as marriage and birth, to bring good luck and prosperity. Ashoka links these rites especially with women: 'At such times, however, womenfolk perform many, diverse, trifling, and useless auspicious rites.' He recommends, instead, what he calls 'the auspicious rite of dharma'. And those who should promote this new rite are the male members of the family:

> Therefore, a father, son, brother, master, friend, companion, or even a neighbor should say: 'This is excellent! This auspicious rite of dharma should be performed until the object is achieved.'

Ashoka's expectation that family members should take the initiative to promote dharma within their families is not limited to the context of

Rock Edict IX dealing with women. In Rock Edict XI the same instruction is given within a broader context:

> A father, son, brother, master, friend, companion, or even a neighbor should say this: 'This is excellent! This is to be carried out.'

In the last of his writings, Pillar Edict VII (ii), late into his reign when he was an old man reflecting on his reign and his activities on behalf of dharma, Ashoka summarizes his three main initiatives:

> Reflecting on this very matter, I have made dharma-pillars, established dharma-mahamatras, and issued dharma-promulgations.

EXEMPLAR OF DHARMA

Ashoka knew that, whether he liked it or not, people would look up to him as an exemplar and model of dharma. Towards the end of his long reign, he verbalizes what is evident from all his writings—he actually wanted to be the paradigm of a person devoted to dharma, he welcomed this role. He says so in Pillar Edict VII (vi): 'For, whatever good deeds I have done, people have conformed to them and continue to adhere to them.' The effect of his personal example, coupled with his programme of public instruction of dharma, on the behaviour of the people is clearly expressed in Rock Edict IV:

> But now, due to the practice of dharma by the Beloved of Gods, King Piyadasi … the kinds of things that did not exist for many hundreds of years, today these same things have increased through the instruction in dharma provided by the Beloved of Gods, King Piyadasi.

Beyond his words and deeds, beyond his officials spreading the cult of dharma, Ashoka became in his own person the symbol of dharma.

Ashoka appears to have been acutely aware that he was for his people, to use the categories of anthropologist Clifford Geertz, a *model of* and a *model for* the new universal religion he was preaching, the religion of dharma, of which he was the founder and high priest. His activities as

emperor were devoted to the propagation of dharma, and in Rock Edict
VIII he contrasts his own activities to those of his predecessors, activities
Ashoka portrays generally in a negative way.

> In times past, Beloveds of Gods [= kings] used to set out on
> recreational tours. During these, hunting and other such enjoyments
> took place.
>
> But, the Beloved of Gods, King Piyadasi, ten years after his royal
> consecration, set out to Enlightenment. Through that came about
> the dharma tour.
>
> During it the following take place: paying visits to Sramanas and
> Brahmins and making gifts to them, paying visits to elderly people
> and providing monetary support to them, paying visits to people of
> the countryside, providing instruction in dharma and in germane
> questions about dharma.[9]

His 'dharma tours' (*dharmayātrā*) parallel the tours he instructs his officials
to undertake to educate the populace in the Ashokan dharma. Did Ashoka
himself in his younger days go on similar excursions that he accuses his
predecessors of undertaking? Did he hunt? The answer is: probably yes.
In the Panguraria Inscription, he seems to record precisely such a tour
he undertook in his younger days while he was still a prince: 'The king
named Piyadasi, when he was a prince and living with his consort, came
to this place while he was on a recreational tour.' It was ten years after
becoming king that he inaugurated the 'dharma tours', and here he seems
to look back with aversion at such royal frivolity.

The passage of Pillar Edict VII (vi) about his three initiatives I cited
above continues by showing the effect of his example—it had the desired
effect:

> Thereby they have grown and will continue to grow by means of
> the following: obedience to mother and father, obedience to elders,

---

9 As Schneider says (1978: 135), the questions are appropriate, because they
   relate to what he has taught. So this is like a quiz at the end of a class.

deference to the aged, and proper regard to Brahmins and Sramanas, to the destitute and distressed, down to slaves and servants.

Ashoka, as we have already seen, likes to compare his activities on behalf of dharma to those of his predecessors. His successes stand in sharp contrast to their failures, as spelled out in Rock Edict IV:

In times past, for many hundreds of years, the following only continued to increase: the slaughter of living beings, the injuring of creatures, disrespect toward relatives, and disrespect toward Sramanas and Brahmins.

That was under the old regimes. All that has now changed 'due to the practice of dharma by the Beloved of Gods'.

The example he was presenting to his people, the example of a life well lived, extends beyond the mere preaching of dharma to acts of kindness and generosity that flow from dharma. In several of his inscriptions he spells out all the good deeds he has done for the benefit not only of his own people but also of people in foreign territories. Just thirteen years into his reign, he notes in Rock Edict II:

Everywhere—in the territory of the Beloved of Gods, King Piyadasi, as well as in those at the frontiers, namely, Codas, Pandyas, Satiyaputras, Keralaputras, Tamraparnis, the Greek king named Antiochus, and other kings who are that Antiochus's neighbors—everywhere the Beloved of Gods, King Piyadasi, has established two kinds of medical services: medical services for humans and medical services for domestic animals.

Wherever medicinal herbs beneficial to humans and domestic animals were not found, he had them brought in and planted everywhere. Likewise, wherever root vegetables and fruit trees were not found, he had them brought in and planted everywhere.

Along roads he had trees planted and wells dug for the benefit of domestic animals and human beings.

And towards the end of his reign, twenty-seven years after his consecration, in Pillar Edict VII (iii) he returns to the same topic as he reflects on what he has done to make travel a bit easier for the people.

> Along roads, furthermore, I have had banyan trees planted to provide shade for domestic animals and humans; I have had mango orchards planted; and I have had wells dug at intervals of eight Krosas [about 28 km] and constructed rest houses. I have had numerous watering places constructed at different locations for the benefit of domestic animals and humans. But this benefit is really trivial. For, previous kings, as well as I, have gratified the people with various gratifications. But I have done this so that they may conform to the observance of dharma.

The last sentence is important, because all these public works have as their goal to encourage the people to follow the dharma.

His numerous good deeds, his gifts and charitable donations, his preaching the dharma, his exemplary conduct—did all this go to his head? In all this was he seeking glory and fame—as most ancient, and for that matter modern, rulers did? Was this all simply a vanity project? It appears that Ashoka may have been mindful of such accusations. In Rock Edict X, as I have already noted, he takes it head on, telling his audience why he may, in fact, seek glory and fame but only for one reason—so that, seeing his glory, his people may seek to emulate him in the practice of dharma.

> The Beloved of Gods, King Piyadasi, does not consider glory or fame as offering great benefits, with this exception—whatever glory and fame the Beloved of Gods, King Piyadasi, seeks, it is so that in the present and in the future people may observe obedience to dharma and follow my teaching of dharma. It is for this reason, the Beloved of Gods, King Piyadasi, seeks glory or fame.

The recognition, the inner awareness of one's own shortcomings is an essential component of a dharmic life. Ashoka's comments on human nature, prone to see one's own virtues but blind to one's sins, in Pillar Edict III are reminiscent of many similar passages in religious scripture from around the world, including the Biblical statement that one sees the mote in someone else's eye but not the beam in one's own.[10]

> One sees only what is good, thinking: 'I have done this good thing.' One does not see as well what is bad, thinking: 'I have done this bad thing,' 'This, indeed, is what is called immoral action.' But this is quite difficult to recognize. Yet, clearly, this is how one should see it: 'These are what lead to immoral action, namely: rage, cruelty, anger, pride, and envy. By reason of these may I not bring about my downfall.'

Ashoka is sensitive to human suffering. This was perhaps instilled into him when he was educated by Buddhist monks on the fundamentals of Buddhist doctrine. A foundational principle of Buddhism is that human life is defined by suffering—*duḥkha*. An ability to recognize this and to empathize with this basic human condition is an essential ingredient in a life devoted to dharma. Writing in the aftermath of the immense suffering cause by his disastrous war in Kalinga, Ashoka in Rock Edict XIII is self-reflective and philosophical:

> Even people who are well cared for and whose love is undiminished, when misfortune strikes their friends, companions, associates, and relatives, it causes injury to those very people. This is the common plight of all human beings, and it is deemed grievous by the Beloved of Gods.

Ashoka's exemplary life was anchored in the principle of generosity. He repeatedly requests his officers to identify worthy recipients for his gifts. A main feature of his numerous 'dharma tours' was the distribution of gifts to the needy and to ascetics. But all that, he says in Rock Edict XI, is little, for 'there is no gift comparable to the gift of dharma'.

---

10 Gospel of Matthew, 7.4.

PART FOUR

Pāṣaṇḍa
Ashoka the Ecumenist

ONE THING WE CAN SAY WITH CERTAINTY ABOUT ASHOKA IS THAT he was a devout Buddhist. Evidence from both Ashoka's own edicts and from other literary and inscriptional sources shows that there were several other parallel religious organizations during his time. Ashoka himself mentions two, the Jains and the Ajivikas. Like the Buddhists, these also had historical founders and consisted mainly of celibate mendicants. Then there was the much older Brahmanical tradition where membership was hereditary, and marriage and procreation were central elements of its orthopraxy, although there were segments that adopted a way of life involving itinerancy, celibacy and mendicancy. And there were, of course, other local and regional beliefs and practices, the 'popular religions' of the day.

What did Ashoka make of this remarkable religious diversity within his empire? How did he as emperor deal with that religious diversity?

One way humans attempt to make sense of and organize perceived diversity in any area of experience is to create categories within which the diverse elements can be systematized and conceptualized. The penchant to classify is a deeply human trait. So, we have the categories of animal, plant, bird and the like. What we in the modern world and speaking English or another Western language have come to call 'religion' is precisely such an overarching category that attempts to define a cluster of human activities, beliefs and emotions. The singular 'religion' subsumes many historical traditions such as Buddhism, Christianity, Hinduism and Islam. Human categories, especially 'religion', can be and often are imprecise and lead to misunderstanding. Yet, we continue to use them both in scholarship and in normal discourse. It is important to remember, however, that in using the label 'religion' we are dealing with a humanly created category and not an independent reality out there. It is a product of the human mind rather than a natural or historical entity.

Ashoka uses a category quite similar to 'religion' in order to comprehend what can be called 'organized religious groups', taking 'organized' in a very loose sense, groups that people of the time could identify demographically. And it is Pasanda (Sanskrit: *pāṣaṇḍa*). Pasandas, then, were recognizable religious groups that, Ashoka tells us, were spread throughout his empire. I think we can take Pasanda to parallel our category of religion, even though upon closer examination there are significant differences.

Religious diversity in Ashoka's empire was certainly not limited to groups called Pasandas. There were local and regional religious beliefs and practices, local gods and goddesses, local religious experts and local places of worship and pilgrimage. Ashoka refers to these in passing. He was not a fan of these local forms of popular religiosity. The next three chapters deal with Ashoka's attitude to, interaction with, and, to some degree, control of both these kinds of religions.

Beyond these pre-existing religious configurations, we saw in the preceding chapters Ashoka's total and passionate devotion to his conception of dharma. We can, within this context, think of Ashoka's dharma as a kind of new religion—what I have called the 'cult of dharma'—he was attempting to propagate. It was not an exclusivist religion but one I will call a 'civil religion', a religion that hovers above all others, a religion to which all the people of his empire can belong without renouncing their allegiance to their preferred Pasanda.

Recently two philosophers, Rajeev Bhargava and David Wong,[1] have proposed conceptualizing—or theorizing—this Ashokan dharma

---

1   Bhargava 2022; Wong 2020.

within the framework of 'harmony'. The concept of harmony (*he*) is central to Confucian philosophy, but it is not prominent within Indian moral discourse in which there is not even a special or technical term for it. As Bhargava and Wong have pointed out, however, this category captures the various dimensions and nuances Ashoka ascribes to dharma. Individuals, Wong has argued, are understood 'in terms of the relationships they have with others and in the contexts of their activities' (Wong 2020: 142). This relational dimension of dharma is extended to groups: a Pasanda, Ashoka claims, can foster its moral and religious life only in dialogue with other Pasandas. Harmony does not obliterate the individual, however; it raises the individual to a new and higher level where it blends into a harmonious whole with others. Wong uses the metaphor of a soup where different ingredients blend into a harmonious and delicious whole. Harmony with others within an individual's orbit defines his progress in dharma. Likewise, harmony among Pasandas is essential for their growth in dharma. It is also essential for social harmony within the kingdom. That is the essence of Ashoka's ecumenism.

11

Religious Diversity

ASHOKA AND PASANDAS

T HE TERM 'PASANDA' IS NOT CONFINED TO ASHOKA, BUT ITS EARLIEST
documented use is in Ashoka's inscriptions. The term is found
in early Brahmanical, Buddhist and Jain literature in Sanskrit and
a variety of Prakrits. The extant examples, however, are from texts
postdating Ashoka. The common feature in all these later usages is
the significant semantic shift the term underwent. Ashoka uses it as a
neutral classificatory term carrying positive connotations: Pasandas were
good and valuable organizations. In its later usage, however, with some
notable exceptions,[1] the term takes on a pejorative meaning—we are
not a Pasanda, but the others are. It is usually the religious communities
different from the one to whom the writer belongs that are branded
Pasanda. It signifies 'the other', accentuating the pejorative tone of the

---

1 In early Jain scriptures we find the expression *parapāsaṇḍa*, 'other Pasanda',
indicating that there may have been a parallel expression, 'our Pasanda'
(*svapāsaṇḍa*), used self-referentially with respect to the Jain ascetic
community. See Kendall W. Folkert (1993: 294–99). Folkert (p. 299) cites
Rudolf Hoernlé's conclusion: 'The word *pāsaṇḍa* has, with the Jains, no bad
sense. It means generally "the adherent of any religion," especially of their
own. Hence, with the Brāhmans, it came to mean "an adherent of a false or
heterodox religion"; with them *pāsaṇḍa* is equal to the Jain *para-pāsaṇḍa*.'

term. It is often used as an insult, in much the same way as terms such as 'atheist' and 'heretic' are hurled at each other in religiously oriented communities. Thus, translators of these later texts usually use expressions such as 'heretical sect' to translate Pasanda.[2]

This semantic history is a mirror image of the path 'religion' took in the West. Within Christian theological circles, Christianity as revealed truth was contrasted to 'religion', which was viewed inevitably as false or inadequate. A recent essay by James Fowler states this principle boldly: 'The need of the hour is to distinguish and differentiate between "religion" and Christianity,' and he cites the famous Swiss theologian Karl Barth's adage: 'The revelation of God is the abolition of religion.'[3] Yet, both within scholarly circles and in common public discourse, 'religion' has become an umbrella concept encompassing *all* religious traditions, including Christianity. It transitioned from identifying the other to encompassing the all. Pasanda went in the opposite direction, transitioning from a neutral and all-encompassing category in Ashoka's vocabulary to becoming a derogatory term to brand the other.

The term 'Pasanda' has several Prakrit and Sanskrit variations.[4] Its etymology is obscure and disputed. The probability is that it came into Prakrit and Sanskrit through a local north-eastern language, possibly of Munda derivation. It may thus have been a term that originated from what has been called 'Greater Magadha', broadly the area in and surrounding modern Bihar. It was the heartland not only of Ashoka's empire but also of the major new religions, such as Buddhism, Jainism and Ajivika, all of which Ashoka refers to as Pasanda. It is important to note, however, that, in Ashoka's usage, the term also encompasses the

---

2   Wendy Doniger (1971: 271) notes: 'The Sanskrit term most closely corresponding in negative tone as well as in denotation to the English "heretic" is *pāṣaṇḍa*.' For the most detailed account of the semantic development of this term in early Indian history, see Brereton 2019.

3   James Fowler, 'Christianity Is NOT Religion', Christ in You Ministries, http://christinyou.net/pages/Xnotrel.html (posted 1998; accessed 17 May 2021). See also Brereton 2019: 23.

4   *pāsaṃḍa, prasaṃḍa, paṣaḍa,* and in Pali: *pāsaṇḍa.* In Sanskrit, it is *pāṣaṇḍa,* also written sometimes as *pākhaṇḍa.*

Brahmin community, which had a much broader footprint across India. The term took a while, however, to enter the Brahmanical vocabulary. It is missing in all the early Vedic and post-Vedic texts, including the four early Dharmasutras. It is also absent in the grammatical literature, especially the major commentary that Patanjali wrote in the middle of the second century BCE, which is a mine of cultural information. It makes its appearance in Brahmanical texts only around the beginning of the Common Era.[5] Its original home, however, was within the Prakrits.

Taking all the available evidence into account, Joel Brereton presents this fruitful summary of what 'Pasanda' meant during Ashoka's time:

> First, especially in literature from around the beginning of the common era, *pāṣaṇḍa* is not always used pejoratively, but it can have a neutral sense or even a positive one that it has in the Aśokan inscriptions. This is true in both Brahmanical and non-Brahmanical literature. Second, *pāṣaṇḍas* are communities of religious adepts, who practiced some sort of religious discipline. Third, members of these religious communities lived not only in close proximity with one another but also near populated areas, on which they likely depended for their support. And fourth, *pāṣaṇḍas* are associated with rules and doctrines that govern what they do—the dharma of the *pāṣaṇḍa*.[6]

We could expand on Brereton's description of Pasanda with a few queries regarding Ashoka's own understanding of the category as presented explicitly or implicitly in his writings on it. I will first give schematically all these passages before commenting on them.

---

5   It is used in the *Vaikhānasa Gṛhyasūtra*, 5.9: 4, 13; *Atharvaveda Pariśiṣṭa*, 64.4.9, as well as in Manu's Law Code and the Mahabharata.
6   Brereton 2019: 28.

Chart 11.1
Ashoka on Pasandas

1: ROCK EDICT V

Now, in times past dharma-mahamatras did not exist at all. But, thirteen years after my royal consecration, I established the dharma-mahamatras.

They are occupied with all the Pasandas for the establishment of dharma and, by the increase of dharma, for the welfare and wellbeing of dharma-devotees among the Greeks, the Kambojas and Gandharas, the Ristikas and Pitinikas, and also among others along the western frontiers.

2: ROCK EDICT VII

The Beloved of Gods, King Piyadasi, desires that all Pasandas may reside everywhere. For, all of them desire self-restraint and purity of heart.

3: ROCK EDICT XII

The Beloved of Gods, King Piyadasi, pays homage to all Pasandas, to those who have gone forth and to those staying at home, with gifts and with various acts of homage.

No gift or homage, however, is as highly prized by the Beloved of Gods as this: namely, that the essential core may increase among all Pasandas. But the increase of the essential core takes many forms. This, however, is its root, namely, guarding speech—that is to say, not paying homage to one's own Pasanda and not denigrating the Pasandas of others when there is no occasion, and even when there is an occasion, doing so mildly. Homage, on the other hand, should indeed be paid to the Pasandas of others in one form or another. Acting in this manner, one certainly enhances one's own Pasanda and also helps the Pasanda of the other.

When someone acts in a way different from that, one hurts one's own Pasanda and also harms the Pasanda of the other. For, should someone pay homage to his own Pasanda and denigrate the Pasanda of another wholly out of devotion to his own Pasanda, thinking, that is, 'I'll make my Pasanda illustrious'—by so doing he damages his own Pasanda even more certainly.

Therefore, meeting one another is, indeed, excellent. That is—they should both listen to and take guidance from each other's dharma. For this is the wish of the Beloved of Gods. That is—all Pasandas should become highly learned and follow good discipline. And no matter which of these they may be devoted to, they should acknowledge: 'No gift or homage is as highly prized by the Beloved of Gods as this: namely, that the essential core may increase among all Pasandas.'

Large numbers, furthermore, have been dispatched for this purpose—dharma-mahamatras, mahamatras overseeing women, officers in charge of farms, and other classes of officers. And this is its fruit: enhancement of one's own Pasanda and making dharma illustrious.

4: ROCK EDICT XIII

But this is deemed even more grievous by the Beloved of Gods, that Brahmins or Sramanas, or other Pasandas or those staying at home and dwelling there who are well cared for—among whom are established obedience to authority, obedience to mother and father, obedience to elders, and proper regard to friends, companions, associates, and relatives, and to slaves and servants, and firm devotion—that they endure there the injury, killing, or deportation of their loved ones ... There is no land, furthermore, except among the Greeks, where these classes—Brahmins and Sramanas—are not found. Yet even where they are not found, there is no land where human beings are not devoted to one Pasanda or another.

5: PILLAR EDICT VI

To all classes of people, likewise, I pay close attention. To all Pasandas I have paid homage with various acts of homage. But individual visits in person is what I consider as paramount.

6: PILLAR EDICT VII IV

As to my dharma-mahamatras also—they are occupied with various matters that are beneficial, that is to say, both to those who have gone forth and to those staying at home. And they are occupied also with all Pasandas, that is to say—I have ordered them to be occupied with matters relating to the Sangha; I have likewise ordered them to be occupied also with Brahmins and Ajivikas; I have ordered them to be occupied also with the Nirgranthas; I have ordered them to be occupied also with various Pasandas—different mahamatras with different Pasandas according to the special features of each. But my dharma-mahamatras are occupied with these and with all other Pasandas.

Taken together, these writings of Ashoka on Pasandas show how the term was generally understood during his time, and how Ashoka may have in subtle and not-so-subtle ways redefined the category of Pasanda.

The most obvious expansion of the category is the inclusion of Brahmins. In later literature—Brahmanical, Buddhist and Jain—we rarely, if ever, encounter passages that view Brahmins as constituting a Pasanda. There are a couple of exceptions noted by Brereton,[7] but their exceptional nature underscores the fact that Brahmins are not normally included within the category of Pasanda. This is understandable, because even in Ashoka the primary reference of Pasanda is to communities of celibate mendicants, to the 'gone forth' (*pravrajita*) in Ashoka's terminology. Although, as we will see, some Brahmins also adopted this lifestyle, they were, by and large, 'stay-at-home' individuals, that is, householders (*gṛhastha*). Brahmanical texts celebrate the centrality of the householder within Brahmanical dharma. Ashoka's inclusion of Brahmins within the category of Pasanda is implied in passage no. 4: 'Brahmins and Sramanas, or other Pasandas'. The clearest and most explicit inclusion of Brahmins is in passage no. 6. There, Ashoka gives a list of four kinds of Pasandas, and the second in the list is the Brahmin. The inclusion of Brahmins hints at the possibility, if not the likelihood, that Ashoka is deliberately reshaping the contours of this category. In fact, there are other features of Ashoka's conception that also indicate such a reconceptualization. The likelihood that Ashoka's use of the term Pasanda to include Brahmins—and perhaps also lay adherents—shows that his broadening of the semantic compass of the term was deliberate, and that it had repercussions with respect

7   See Brereton 2019: 25–26.

to Brahmins and their self-definition as exceptional within society and religion, the so-called 'Brahmanical exceptionalism'.

Another feature of the Ashokan reconceptualization of Pasanda is its association with the 'stay-at-home', the *grhastha*—often rendered as 'householder', a translation liable to misunderstanding. There is a difference of scholarly opinion as to what sort of association Ashoka envisaged. Was it full membership? Did he think that Pasandas had two kinds of members, the 'gone forth' and the 'stay-at-home'? Or was the connection of the latter to Pasanda less formal; some sort of a connection short of full membership— akin to the 'lay' and 'clergy' distinction in contemporary religions? This may be the association that the Upasakas, within whose numbers Ashoka counts himself, had with the Buddhist Sangha. My own view, which I will develop more fully later, is that Ashoka's statements support the first kind—if not full membership, then at least a strong association. It is not necessary to assume that *every* Pasanda had both these kinds of members. It could well have been that some Pasandas had only the 'gone forth', while others had only the 'stay-at-home', and still others had both kinds of members.

The question of membership raises another issue regarding what Pasanda meant for Ashoka. There is no doubt that the term referred first and foremost to religious professionals and virtuosi. In passage no. 4, there is the statement 'Brahmins and Sramanas, or other Pasandas'. Its obvious meaning is that Brahmins and Sramanas constituted Pasandas, while there may have been other Pasandas besides these. In the same passage, he makes this interesting demographic observation:

> There is no land, furthermore, except among the Greeks, where these classes—Brahmins and Sramanas—are not found. Yet even where they are not found, there is no land where human beings are not devoted to one Pasanda or another.

He acknowledges that the north-western regions where Hellenistic Greeks had settled in the wake of Alexander's conquest did not have the two demographic groups Sramanas and Brahmins. But he adds, 'there is no land'—presumably including land owned by Greek kings—'where human beings are not devoted to one Pasanda or another'. So, Ashoka appears to assume that the category of Pasanda was much broader and more universal that the other two categories. The Greek translation of this very edict renders Pasanda as *diatribē*, generally glossed as 'philosophic school'. Later Greek authors expand its semantic range and relate it to the school of Moses and Christ (that is, Judaism and Christianity).[8] If the Greek translator had some insight into what Pasanda may have meant to Ashoka and his officials for whom he worked, then we can see Pasanda as a category that is broader than simply ascetic or monastic communities and comes closer to what we would call today a 'religion'.

Some light is thrown by Ashoka's remarks in Rock Edict V given in passage no. 1, where the activities of dharma-mahamatras relating to Pasandas extend into Greek and other foreign lands:

> They are occupied with all the Pasandas for the establishment of dharma and, by the increase of dharma, for the welfare and wellbeing of dharma-devotees among the Greeks, the Kambojas and Gandharas, the Ristikas and Pitinikas, and also among others along the western frontiers.

The category of people 'devoted to dharma' appears here to parallel Pasanda. Were these also Pasandas in Ashoka's eyes? It appears so.

So conceptualized, we can see how lay followers and partisans of a particular religious doctrine, ethical philosophy or charismatic leader may, indeed, be included within the rubric of Pasanda. Accordingly, Upasakas would, perhaps, belong to or be associated with the Buddhist Pasanda. Consequently, the Pasanda pluralism that Ashoka acknowledges and even celebrates can be seen as what today we would call 'religious pluralism'.

Ashoka calls such Pasanda associates *gṛhastha*, literally, 'stay-at-home'. Significantly, this is the earliest recorded occurrence of the term which was to become so commonplace in later Indian literature. This significant historical fact was not known until 2015 when the historian of ancient

---

8   See Brereton 2019: 29.

India Stephanie Jamison discovered the hitherto unknown history of this term and category while she was researching the history of the householder in Brahmanical literature on dharma, the Dharmashastras. She explains her discovery this way:

> I set about digging up what I could and figuring out how to frame what I thought was going to be a fairly predictable and predetermined assignment. Since I'm a philologist above all, the first thing I thought to do was to examine the word—*gṛhastha*—where it appears and what it means in texts older than dharma texts. I figured that this was just necessary due diligence, that these facts were generally known, and that nothing much would come of it. But, as it turns out, it seems no one had bothered to look at the word (at least no one I could unearth), and when one does, some unexpected things emerge. The first unexpected thing I came across was, in fact, absence.[9]

This term, so central to the Brahmanical project that created the dharma texts, is conspicuous by its total absence in the entire Sanskrit literary corpus—the Vedas and ancillary literature—composed over a millennium or more; until, in fact, the time of Ashoka. We can say with a fair degree of certainty that *gṛhastha* was a neologism invented around the fourth or third century BCE to identify a new social and religious reality. The common translation of this term as 'householder' misses the whole point for the invention of the term. A *gṛhastha* is not any married man with home and family. He is a special kind of individual who has decided to 'stay at home' while pursuing a religious path parallel to and contrasting with that of an ascetic who has 'gone forth', the *pravrajita*. The 'stay-at-home' is an individual given to what may be called 'inner-worldly asceticism'. Ashoka associates him with the Pasandas. Stephanie Jamison summarizes well the conclusions of some pathbreaking studies on this topic:

> The implications of this word history are quite striking, at least to me. It indicates that the *gṛhastha-*, so thoroughly embedded verbally

---

9 Stephanie Jamison 2019: 3–4.

in the orthodox Brahmanical dharma texts and so explicitly the foundation of the social system depicted therein, is actually a coinage of and a borrowing from śramaṇic discourse, which discourse, at this period, was conducted in various forms of Middle Indo-Aryan [= Prakrit]. The *gṛhastha*, literally the 'stay-at-home,' is thus defined against a contrastive role, that of an ascetic of no fixed abode and no domestic entanglements … This contrastive pairing implies that the householder of the Hindu dharma texts was not simply a married man and *pater familias* in what we might, anachronistically, consider an essentially secular role, but a man with a religious life equivalent to that of a wandering ascetic—but a religious life pursued and fulfilled within the context of a sedentary family existence.[10]

It is gratifying for a biographer of the emperor that it is Ashoka who provides the earliest glimpse of this new form of *homo religiosus*, the 'stay-at-home'. What we can say with certainty is that the religious diversity of his empire included people who undertook to live a life dedicated to religious pursuits by adopting an itinerant and mendicant mode of life, and others who did the same while staying at home.

Ashoka gives the most detailed account of Pasandas in passage no. 6 from Pillar Edict VII. He says that the jurisdiction of his dharma-mahamatras extends to all Pasandas, and goes on to list five, no doubt the most prominent ones during his time. He refers to the Buddhist Pasanda as Sangha, the only place, apart from Minor Rock Edict I, where Ashoka uses an emic technical term, showing that he is a Buddhist quite conversant with the Buddhist vocabulary. In the second line he gives a pair: Brahmins and Ajivikas. This pairing probably indicates that in Ashoka's eyes these two traditions had close links. The extensive study of the Ajivikas by the historian of ancient India A.L. Basham supports this link.[11] Ashoka's patronage of the Ajivikas is shown also in the three

---

10 Jamison 2019: 18–19.

11 Basham concludes: 'A close connection between the Brāhmaṇa and the Ājīvaka is indicated by Asoka's classification of the sects.' And again: 'It is evident that he [Ashoka] considered the Ājīvakas to be more closely related

Barabar Hill Cave Inscriptions where he says that he donated the caves
to the Ajivikas. As Balcerowicz has shown, the Ajivika tradition was a
more prominent religion in the second century BCE than Jainism and
attracted more political support.[12] The religious tradition of the Ajivikas
gradually became weaker and probably disappeared by the end of the first
millennium of the Common Era.[13]

Ashoka refers to the religious tradition better known as Jainism by its
more ancient name 'Nirgrantha' (Prakrit: *nigaṃṭha*) in this edict. We do
not encounter the Jains in any other part of Ashoka's writings.

Ashoka's own keen interest in the Pasandas can be put down to
two main reasons. First, a transactional one—he wanted them to be
instruments in the propagation of his new dharma. This would have been
an obvious move because they had rules and doctrines that constituted the
dharma of Pasandas. What better way to spread the word than to recruit
for that purpose the religious groups dedicated to dharma, groups that
already had adherents and commanded widespread respect within the
population at large. The very ambiguity of the term 'dharma' may have
incentivized the Pasanda groups. Propagating dharma could have been
seen as one way of propagating their own religion. The second reason
was more practical and political: there was a need to keep interreligious
rivalry and conflict to a minimum. I will discuss this in greater detail in
the next chapter.

The first time Ashoka uses the word 'Pasanda' is in passage no. 1,
where it is closely connected to the new office of dharma-mahamatra
he had recently created. We have already seen the broad mandate these
high-ranking officials had to establish dharma in every corner of the
empire. They even had the authority to enter the inner chambers and
living quarters of the royal family—of Ashoka's own brothers and sisters.
One of the main targets of their mission was the Pasandas. Two points
in this passage are worth noting. First, Ashoka assumes that Pasandas

---

to the orthodox brāhmaṇas than were the Jainas.' A.L. Basham 1951: 149;
see also p. 131.

12 See Balcerowicz 2016.

13 Basham 1951: 184–86.

are present in the culturally distinct areas in the north-western frontier region, including the Hellenistic kingdoms.

The second point to note is the use of 'all' with reference to Pasandas. Ashoka uses the expression 'all Pasandas' in all but one of the passages cited above. I think Ashoka is using the word deliberately to show that he works with *all* Pasandas, that he is not playing favourites. Rock Edict V also reveals that Ashoka began working with Pasandas very early in his dharma campaign. This campaign started twelve years after his royal consecration, and the appointment of dharma-mahamatras to work with Pasanda groups was made the very next year.

In passage no. 5, Ashoka speaks about his close relationship with Pasandas: 'To all Pasandas I have paid homage with various acts of homage.' The emphasis is on 'all', and acts of homage included the distribution of gifts. He was a patron of Pasandas. But he goes on in the very next sentence to say that, rather than simply give gifts, what he really wants to do is to visit to them personally: 'But individual visits in person is what I consider as paramount.' His personal visits to 'all' the Pasandas, once again, indicate his desire to treat them all equally. Still, the question remains: what did these visits entail? Visiting implies a geographical location, and the entirety of a given Pasanda could not dwell in a single location. These Pasandas, as exemplified in the Buddhist monastic establishments, lived a dispersed life. Did he visit *all* the places where members of a given Pasanda lived? That would have been next to impossible. The meaning probably is that he visited at least some centres—maybe the major ones—of each Pasanda, so that word could get around that the emperor had visited their Pasanda.

The word used by Ashoka for 'acts of homage' is *pūjā*, a term much in use even today in India within the context of divine worship. This kind of homage is not simply verbal or bodily—kneeling, bowing and the like—but also involves giving gifts. Ashoka refers tangentially to his gift-giving in the Queen's Edict. We can be sure that he supported the Buddhist monastic establishments with donations. But he was ecumenical in this respect. His gifts extended to other Pasanda communities as well. In Rock Edict VIII, in the context of his 'dharma tours', Ashoka states explicitly

his charitable activities with respect to religious communities and the
needy: 'During it the following take place: paying visits to Sramanas and
Brahmins and making gifts to them, paying visits to elderly people and
providing monetary support to them.'

We have three richly adorned cave dwellings given to Ajivikas
recorded in the three Barabar Hill Cave Inscriptions (Fig. 17). These caves
were excavated manually in granite rock. It must have involved a lot of
labour, technology and money. Harry Falk comments on all three aspects
involved in the construction of these cave dwellings:

> Whoever has visited these caves know that their technology is
> absolutely breathtaking. The rooms not only have perfectly rounded
> roofs and skillfully designed huts inside two caves, but all surfaces
> have been given such a polish that the walls shine like mirrors. These
> extremely polished walls reflect every sound inside the room, so that
> even the click of a camera resounds like thunder … because of the
> extreme hardness of the stone the production of these caves must
> have been very costly.[14]

A significant royal proclamation is found in passage no. 6, and it concerns
the residence of Pasandas. Ashoka says: 'The Beloved of Gods, King
Piyadasi, desires that *all* Pasandas may reside everywhere. For, *all* of
them desire self-restraint and purity of heart.' I will discuss in detail the
implications of this order in the next chapter, but here I want simply to
point out that, once again, he refers to 'all' Pasandas, and gives a reason
why he is permitting them to live freely everywhere in his kingdom.

In passage no. 4 two major religious categories are subsumed under
Pasanda. They are Sramana and Brahmin.[15] These two terms are used
most frequently in the compound *śramaṇabrāhmaṇa*, indicating that it
formed a commonly used category to refer to religious people as a whole.
Ashoka uses this compound twenty times, much more frequently than
Pasanda. As we have seen, this dual category is a constant feature in

---

14 Falk 2008: 245.

15 For an explanation, see Norman 2012a: 122.

Ashoka's definitions of dharma. Donations to this group are a central feature of his dharma.

This composite category, however, preceded Ashoka. The Greek envoy Megasthenes visiting Pataliputra during the time of Ashoka's grandfather, Chandragupta, mentions it in the context of his ethnographic description of the demography in and around Pataliputra. It continued to be used after Ashoka. Its use by the grammarian Patanjali in the middle of the second century BCE to illustrate a grammatical rule shows that the compound had become commonplace.

The rule is enunciated by the grammarian Panini (2.4.9): a Dvandva compound, that is, a coordinative compound containing two or more nouns is inflected in the dual or plural, and the gender is that of the last member. But when two members of such a compound, Panini tells us, are in permanent opposition to each other, the compound is put in the singular and in the neuter gender. Patanjali[16] gives examples of such Dvandva compounds where the two members are in perpetual opposition to each other. One such example is *śramaṇabrāhmaṇam*, 'Sramana-Brahmana'. This use of the compound as a grammatical example—such examples are normally taken from ordinary speech—shows two things. First, and obviously, this compound was in regular and normal use by the speakers of Sanskrit during the second century BCE. Second, Patanjali, and more broadly the Sanskrit grammarians of the time, viewed the two members of the compound, Sramanas and Brahmins, as antagonistic to each other. I will deal with the latter point in the next chapter.

The Brahmins were a group of ritual specialists closely associated with the Vedas, even though their demography may have been much more complex than normally imagined. A few characteristics stand out, especially in comparison with its companion Sramana. Brahmins were (1) hereditary: a person is born a Brahmin; (2) most Brahmins were married householders (*gṛhastha*), even though there were segments of that community who became 'gone forth' (*pravrajita*) persons with a lifestyle similar to that of Sramanas; (3) they participated in economic

---

16 Patañjali (Poona: Bhandarkar Oriental Research Institute, 1962–72), I: 476, line 9.

activities, even though receiving gifts, often for ritual services, was a central part of their livelihood; (4) memorizing the Vedic texts and their daily recitation and study were central features of their life; (5) finally, being poor, living simple lives, and not being avaricious were parts of their moral philosophy. This view of what constitutes a 'Brahmin' has been questioned recently by the historian Nathan McGovern (2019), who takes the term to be fluid and contested. Even Buddhists and Jains claimed to be 'true' Brahmins. Yet, I think Ashoka takes this demographic category to be clear and different from, if not necessarily opposed to, Sramanas.

Sramanas did not constitute a single group.[17] Many individual religious groups and traditions are encompassed within this umbrella term. In Ashoka's list of four Pasandas given in passage no. 6, three— Buddhist Sangha, Ajivika and Nirgrantha (Jains)—fall within the rubric of Sramana. Most, if not all, Sramanas have historical founders, who are viewed in each tradition as the individual who has discovered the ultimate truth that will liberate humans from their life of suffering and rebirth. At least some of them had sacred places associated with the life of their founders, such as the holy Buddhist sites that Ashoka visited. Sramanas (1) were celibate; (2) renounced domestic life; (3) lived an itinerant life, at least ideally, even though by the time of Ashoka many of them may have lived in monastic settings; (4) vowed to poverty, they begged for their food every day and were not permitted to hoard; (5) gave up the use of fire, thus having to beg cooked food; and (6) either went naked or were dressed in distinctive ochre robes, ideally consisting of rags.

The Sramana communities did not get new members through natural reproduction, as Brahmins did. They depended on people converting to their way of life and entering their ascetic institutions voluntarily. The very existence of these communities thus depended on their outreach to the world and on their missionary activities. They recruited members from almost all classes of society, thus opening their membership to everyone. This was quite different from Brahmins, who remained a closed community. To be a Brahmin meant to be born a Brahmin. The openness

---

17 Christopher Beckwith's (2017) contention that *śramaṇa* referred solely to Buddhist monks is misconceived and erroneous.

of Sramana organizations made it easier for them to spread across India and, as in the case of Buddhism, beyond India to other parts of the world. Sramanas thus were not territorially or ethnically circumscribed. At least some Sramana traditions, such as the Buddhist and the Jain, welcomed women into their monastic orders, thus creating a parallel women's order. It was one of the world's oldest—if not *the* oldest—voluntary organizations for women outside of marriage.

Ashoka's Pasanda, then, encompassed both these types of religious individuals and communities—Sramanas and Brahmins. There may have been others as well because Ashoka twice refers to 'other Pasandas'. A glimpse at the rich diversity of Sramana communities is provided in the important Buddhist scriptural text *Sāmañña-phala Sutta*. In this discourse on the fruits of living the Sramana life, the Buddha mentions six founders of Sramana religions: (1) Purana Kassapa: the Buddha ascribes to him a fatalist doctrine. A man who kills, robs and rapes commits no sin. (2) Makkhali Gosala: he was the founder of the Ajivika community. Like Purana, Makkhali denied any cause for the purity or sinfulness of humans. (3) Ajita Kesakambali: denied any benefit in giving gifts or doing meritorious deeds; there is no life after death. (4) Pakudha Kaccayana: there are seven elements, which are stable and unchanging. So, nothing we do can have any effect on them. If a man cuts off another's head, he does not take life; the sword simply passes between the seven elements. (5) Nigantha Nataputta: the historical founder of the Jain tradition. (6) Sanjaya Betatthiputta: adhered to an absolute scepticism. Is there another world? He would say: 'I do not say that it is so, and I do not say that it is otherwise.'

The Buddhist account is formulaic, but it points to the rich diversity of religious beliefs and philosophical opinions among Sramanas. Some even subscribed to materialist positions. Diversity was also a feature of the Brahmin communities, although it is less documented and often ignored in scholarship. The system of four orders of life (*āsramas*) recorded in the earliest of the Dharmasutras, that of Apastamba, probably contemporaneous with Ashoka, gives us a glimpse: Brahmins could live permanently as students residing at the houses of their teachers and be

dedicated to a life of learning. They could get married and live at home
as *grhasthas*, 'stay-at-home'. Brahmanism is the only tradition in which
the 'stay-at-home' aspect occupies such a central position. Brahmins
could also live ascetic lives either as forest hermits (*vānapratha*) living
in forest hermitages, or as 'gone forth' itinerant mendicants, living lives
very similar to that of Sramanas. This fourfold classification, no doubt,
masks internal diversities within each, especially the last two. Later
texts mention the 'stay-at-home' householders as having various ascetic
practices, especially with regard to food. One text[18] gives nine kinds of
such householders on the basis of their food habits:

1. *Saṇṇivartinī*: cultivating a small plot of land lent by its owner.
2. *Kauddālī*: ploughing near a place of water and cultivating bulbs, roots, fruits and vegetables.
3. *Dhruvā*: obtaining food by presenting oneself with a yoke in front of houses in a village.
4. *Sampraksālanī*: living on what one obtains daily.
5. *Samūhā*: living on the grains one can sweep up from places where grain is grown.
6. *Pālanī*: also called *Ahiṃsakā* ('not hurting'), living on husked rice or seed one obtains from virtuous people.
7. *Śiloñchā*: living on what one obtains by gleaning.
8. *Kāpota*: living like a pigeon (*kapota*), picking up single grains with just two fingers.
9. *Siddhecchā*: obtaining cooked food from virtuous people when one becomes old or sick.

We are thus presented with a bewildering variety of ascetic lifestyles.
Some of them may have been based on individual preferences. But many
of them represented the way of life, the dharma, of various organized
Pasanda groups.

Hints at the diversity of the Sramanas are found in the writings of
Megasthenes. He says that some Sramanas lived in the forest, subsisting

---

18 *Baudhāyana Dharmasūtra*, 3.2.1–19.

on wild fruits and leaves, and wearing clothes made of tree bark. Others provided medical services and lived on alms received from householders.

The way Ashoka managed this great religious diversity within his empire both in the interest of maintaining peace in his kingdom and as an instrument of his dharma mission is the topic of the next chapter.

ASHOKA AND POPULAR RELIGION

Ashoka was not a populist—at least as far as religion was concerned. He directed his messages at the Pasandas, the elite, organized and philosophical religions. A major component of his dharma consisted of people giving gifts to these organized religious groups represented by Sramanas and Brahmins. Yet, I think it is a safe assumption that most ordinary people in Ashoka's realm followed beliefs and practices that we would call, for want of a better term, popular or folk religion. In this section, I want to explore Ashoka's views of such beliefs and practices and his policies towards them.

Now, there is no hard and fast boundary separating the 'higher' forms of religion from the 'popular'. As we will see, some of the practices frowned upon by Ashoka became part of the Brahmanical ritual repertoire. Ashoka's own view appears to be that popular ritual practices are outside the realm of what he called Pasanda. They were local, probably practised by the lower strata of society and—here Ashoka is explicit—by women. So, the popular seems to be gendered. The popular also, in Ashoka's mind, is associated with practices like animal sacrifice that went against the central tenet of Ashoka's dharma: not killing, ahimsa.

Ashoka, as we have already seen, connects such popular religious expressions with festivals and auspicious occasions. He comments on fairs in the very first of his major inscriptions, Rock Edict I.

Here no living creature is to be slaughtered and offered in sacrifice. And no festivals are to be held, for the Beloved of Gods, King Piyadasi, sees much evil in festivals. There are, however, some festivals that the Beloved of Gods, King Piyadasi, considers good.

As I noted in Chapter 9, the prohibition of festivals or fairs is related to the ritual killing of animals that were associated with such religious gatherings. The term for fair or festival is '*samāja*', and it relates to any kind of social and religious gathering of people at particular times of the year. Such festive gatherings are commonplace in India today, as they were during Ashoka's time. We obtain a glimpse into what may have transpired at such festivals in Kautilya's *Arthashastra.* Consumption of liquor was a major feature on such occasions. We gather this from Kautilya's statement that 'during festivals, fairs, and excursions' the state should grant a liquor licence for four days.[19] The background to this provision is that the manufacture and sale of liquor was a state monopoly. This was relaxed during certain times of celebration, such as a festival. On such occasions people could manufacture, transport and consume liquor without state intervention and payment of taxes. One way for the state to outwit forest people was through adulterated liquor during a festival:

> An agent operating undercover as a tavern keeper should outwit forest people with drink mixed with coma-inducing juices on the occasion of selling or presenting liquor during a rite for gods or ancestors, a festival, or a fair.[20]

Festive gatherings were also occasions for commerce. Traders exhibited their wares for sale. Kautilya thinks that this would be a good pretext for the king to make some money: the king gets one of his agents to act as a trader and display large amounts of goods. He then collects gold and money using his goods as collateral. Perhaps they get people to advance money towards a future purchase. Then these 'traders' will be robbed at night, absolving them of any liability.[21]

The book on dharma by Apastamba also gives us glimpses into the nature of festivals and the Brahmanical attitude towards them. Twice he forbids Brahmins from attending festivals. If someone happens to run across one, he should simply leave after walking around it clockwise, the

---

19 Kautilya, *Arthaśāstra*, 2.35.36.
20 Kautilya, *Arthaśāstra*, 13.3.56.
21 Kautilya, *Arthaśāstra*, 5.2.50–51.

common gesture of reverence to sacred objects, persons and places, once again indicating the presence of religious ceremonies during festivals.[22] It was not just Ashoka who looked down upon such festivals; Brahmins did that too.

A Buddhist text, probably post-Ashokan, nevertheless throws light on what people generally thought would happen at a festival. A young man goes to one thinking: 'Where's the dancing? Where's the singing? Where's the music? Where are the stories? Where's the applause? Where's the drumming?'[23] Given their religious nature, some of these festivals may have been held on hilltops that were considered sacred. As we have seen, many sites of Ashoka's Minor Rock Edicts are on such hilltops with caves. Buddhist sources also speak of 'hilltop festivals'. The account of six monks—who always seem to get into trouble—going to see a festival is instructive:

> Now at that time there was a festival (*samāja*) on a mountaintop in Rajagaha. The group of six monks went to see the festival on the mountaintop. People spread it about, saying: 'How can these recluses, … come to see dancing and singing and music like householders who enjoy pleasures of the senses?' They told this matter to the Lord. He said: 'Monks, you should not go to see dancing or singing or music.'[24]

So, much else other than religious rituals took place at these gatherings. Ashoka, like the Brahmins and Buddhists, and perhaps all the Pasandas, looked down upon this sort of bacchanal feasting.

Ashoka notes: 'The Beloved of Gods, King Piyadasi, sees much evil in festivals.' This is especially so because they were occasions for slaughtering animals to be offered in sacrifice. The original words Ashoka uses for slaughtering sacrificial animals are noteworthy, because, as we have seen in Chapter 9, they are probably taken directly or indirectly from

---

22 *Āpastamba Dharmasūtra*, 1.3.12; 1.32.19–20; see also *Vasiṣṭha Dharmasūtra*, 12.40.

23 *Dīgha Nikāya*, III: 183 (*Sigalovāda Sutta*, 10).

24 *Vinaya Piṭaka*, II: 107–08. Translation from I.B. Horner.

the Vedic Brahmanical vocabulary. Even though Ashoka never mentions animal sacrifice or even the performance of rituals in connection with Brahmins, it is clear that this prohibition would have affected the central ritual activity of Brahmins. Vedic sacrifice involved the killing and offering of animals.

The second concept through which Ashoka intersects with popular religious practice is *maṅgala.* This is a very common term in the Indian religious vocabulary and refers to any rite or ceremony intended to ensure a favourable outcome. Often called 'auspicious ceremonies', they are performed mainly on important occasions, such as a marriage, birth of a child and setting out on a journey. Unlike festivals, here there is no blood, sex or liquor. These auspicious ceremonies are pretty tame domestic affairs. Yet, Ashoka does not look favourably on them. He does not condemn them outright, but he thinks they are trivial and frivolous, the kind of thing that women would like to do—revealing his sexist side! In Rock Edict IX, Ashoka compares his dharma to these auspicious rites:

> People perform auspicious rites of diverse kinds—during an illness, at the marriage of a son or daughter, at the birth of a child, when setting out on a journey. On these and other similar occasions, people perform numerous auspicious rites. At such times, however, womenfolk perform many, diverse, trifling, and useless auspicious rites.
>
> Now, clearly, auspicious rites are going be performed. But, equally clearly, such auspicious rites bear little fruit.

Ashoka's rhetorical style is quite elegant. He begins by stating the facts: people normally perform various kinds of auspicious rites at significant moments in their lives; women are prominent in promoting such rites. He then moves to render an evaluation of such rites. He calls them trivial and useless. The semantic spectrum of the term he uses, *kṣudra,* ranges from small, petty and trivial, to more negative connotations such as low, vile and vulgar. I prefer to see here a meaning closer to the former, especially because there is no outright condemnation of these practices, in contrast to the festivals.

Having said that, he circles back to say that he is not prohibiting these rites; only stating their relative triviality. The statement 'auspicious rites are going to be performed' seems a bit peculiar, given his criticism of these rites. I feel that the gerundive used here, *kartavyam* ('should be performed') probably has a concessive meaning rather than injunctive: 'auspicious rites *may* indeed be performed'. He concedes that people will probably continue to perform these rites, irrespective of what the emperor may say. But he wants to draw them into a discussion and self-reflection: these rites, on which they spend a lot of effort and money, actually bear little fruit. There is a much better kind of auspicious rite that bears great fruit, a rite they should aim at performing, and he calls it 'auspicious rite of dharma'—*dharma-maṅgala*:

> But this, clearly, is what bears copious fruit, namely, the auspicious rite of dharma. It consists of the following:
>
> > proper regard toward slaves and servants, reverence toward elders, self-restraint with respect to living beings, and giving gifts to Sramanas and Brahmins.
>
> This and anything else like it are called 'auspicious rite of dharma'.

Here Ashoka undertakes a reinterpretation, a reimagining, of what a proper 'auspicious rite' should consist of. It is the practice of the Ashokan dharma. In his attitude towards these popular rites, Ashoka seems to be following the Buddhist point of view. As already noted in Chapter 6, a Buddhist text recommended by Ashoka disparages such rites:

> The Lord said: 'For whom ceremonies (*maṅgala*) are rooted out, as also meteors, dreams, and signs; the monk who has completely abandoned the blemish of ceremonies—he shall wander properly in the world.[25]

In stark contrast to Ashoka's and Buddhism's belittling of these auspicious rites, Brahmanical texts of roughly the same period took them seriously and attempted to incorporate them into the Brahmanical ritual

---

25 *Suttanipāta*, verses 359–75.

repertoire. The early Brahmanical ritual writings focused on the major Vedic rituals requiring several ritual specialists; they were elaborate and expensive. Around the time of Ashoka, as the historian Timothy Lubin has explained, a new class of ritual texts came to be composed. They were called '*gṛhyasūtra*' and they dealt with rites performed in a domestic setting. Many of these rites were of the 'auspicious' kind. 'Aśoka's examples of ceremonies (*maṃgalam*) that are vulgar and pointless—the life-cycle rites of marriage, conception, and birth, and the rites for the sick and for setting out on a journey—figure prominently in the Gṛhya codes, where they are sometimes even called *maṅgalāni*.'[26]

Indeed, like Ashoka, Apastamba's code of domestic rituals ascribes to women the knowledge of these auspicious rites and advises his readers to learn them from women.[27] Apastamba's dharma code also, after describing the funeral ceremonies, tell his readers to 'do whatever else women ask them to do'.[28] But here the knowledge and experience of women are valorized, not disparaged. Indeed, Timothy Lubin considers that Brahmanical ritual codes focused on domestic rites were composed around the same time as Ashoka was writing his edicts.

> A concomitant aim of that canon was the extension of Vedic ritual forms and Brahmin expertise into the realm of popular ceremonial that had previously lain beyond their purview. In Aśoka's RE IX we see those practices depicted as folklore and womanly foolishness not rising to the level of dhamma, while in the Gṛhyasūtras a similar roster of rites, described in similar terms, is explicitly validated by some section of the Brahmins' community as dharma.[29]

We see here, once again, the Brahmanical community—or at least sections of it—splitting from Ashoka on the matter of popular rites and women's roles in them.

---

26 Lubin 2013: 36.
27 *Āpastamba Gṛhyasūtra*, 1.12.14–15. See Lubin 2013: 37.
28 *Āpastamba Dharmasūtra*, 2.15.9.
29 Lubin 2013: 39.

Ashoka's attitude towards rituals associated with popular religion, therefore, is mixed at best. Some he condemns and prohibits, such as killing animals for religious offerings, and all the reprehensible activities that go on at festivals. On the other hand, he has a benevolent, though dismissive, attitude towards common auspicious ceremonies. He does not think that they do much good, yet he is tolerant with regard to them.

Overall, however, Ashoka has little patience with these popular expressions of religiosity, especially the common domestic and communal ritual repertoire, at least some of which involve activities that are diametrically opposed to Ashoka's dharma. His focus in the quest for ecumenism and the mass dharma education of the people is on the organized sector of religion, the Pasandas.

12

Ecumenism

RELIGIOUS PLURALISM, WE SAW IN THE PREVIOUS CHAPTER, WAS A feature of the society over which Ashoka presided. This is evident in the multiplicity of Pasandas—both the religious professionals and the laity aligned with and supporting them—that Ashoka speaks about and speaks to in his inscriptions; these were summarized in Chart 11.1. Ashoka names four major Pasandas; the number of local religions may have been legion. The way Ashoka dealt with the multiplicity of religions in his empire is the focus of this chapter.

I use the term 'ecumenism' to characterize Ashoka's efforts to encourage concord, harmony, mutual respect and cooperation among the Pasandas. Some justification may be needed for my use of this term, whose usage is connected to Christianity. The *Encyclopaedia Britannica* defines ecumenism as a 'movement or tendency toward worldwide Christian unity or cooperation. The term, of recent origin, emphasizes what is viewed as the universality of the Christian faith and unity among churches.'[1] Many terms used in common language or scholarship have such origins, including the very category of 'religion'. That is a reason to be careful but not to reject all such terms outright. I think, mutatis mutandis, Ashoka's vision both for Pasandas and for a worldwide adherence to dharma can be encapsulated in the term 'ecumenism'. The

---

1 'Ecumenism', *Encyclopaedia Britannica*, 18 December 2019, https://www. britannica.com/topic/ecumenism; accessed 24 May 2021.

term has its origin in the Latin *oecumenicus*, 'general, universal', from the original Greek *oikoumenikos*, 'from the whole world'. The term indicates an attitude that promotes universal unity. This is similar to the Sanskrit adage *vasudhaiva kuṭumbakam*, 'one's family is, in truth, the whole world'. This is the meaning of ecumenism that we can, with full justification, associate with Ashoka. He believed that beneath and beyond the apparent differences among Pasandas, there was a fundamental unity expressed in the term 'dharma'.

To search for unity implies an underlying diversity, a diversity that is often characterized by hostility and antagonism. Such, indeed, was the relationship among Pasandas that we can gather from the available sources, both Brahmanical and Buddhist.[2] In Chapter 8, I cited verses from the Buddhist anthology *Aṭṭakavagga* of the *Suttanipāta*, which is considered to represent the oldest stratum of the Buddhist canon and certainly pre-dates Ashoka. It contains some interesting admonitions to Buddhist and perhaps other ascetics. These verses tell them not to engage in debates about whose dharma is true or the best; better to leave such debates alone. I repeat here a few representative verses already cited:

> They call their own dharma the highest; the dharma of others the lowest.
> Some call a dharma the highest; others call the same the lowest.
> They call someone from another sect a fool with impure dharma.
> If you do not know my dharma you become an animal; this is how they speak.[3]

Some Brahmanical texts like to lump together Pasandas and other nefarious and disreputable classes of people, a didactic technique often used by these texts to denigrate by association. So, the very famous

---

2   Rajeev Bhargava (2014: 184) also draws attention to this background of interreligious conflict: 'I hope to have shown the deeply mistaken character of the view that religious interaction in Asoka's period of rule was relatively trouble free and that he must have had an easy time finding common ground among followers of different schools of thought.'

3   *Aṭṭakavagga* of the *Suttanipāta*, verses 904, 903, 893, 880.

Brahmanical law code of Manu composed several centuries after Ashoka has this telling verse:

> The king should quickly banish from his capital gamblers, theatrical performers, entertainers, Pasandas, people engaged in illicit activities, and liquor vendors. When these clandestine thieves remain in a king's realm, they constantly harass his decent subjects with their illicit activities.[4]

The poor Pasandas seem to get it from both sides. For Buddhists, Pasandas are always the 'other', false ascetics preaching false doctrines. When evil Mara, the god of death, sees a shaven-headed Buddhist nun, he asks her to which Pasanda she belongs. The nun seems to be offended by this question, and retorts:

> Pasandas who are outside of this [that is, Buddhist order]
> find satisfaction in false views.
> I do not choose their dharma.
> They are not skilled in dharma.[5]

But there is particular vitriol aimed at Brahmins. One passage[6] paraphrased by the historian of Buddhism Oliver Freiberger compares dogs favourably to the Brahmins of Buddha's day. It reviews the 'five ancient dharmas' of Brahmins, which are seen today among dogs but not Brahmins:

> First, in the past Brahmins held the principle to go to Brahmin women only, not to non-Brahmin ones; today they go to both. Dogs, however, even now only go to female dogs, not to females of other species.

---

4   Manu's Code of Law, 9.225–26. See also Kauṭilya's *Arthaśāstra* 2.4.13.
5   *Saṃyutta Nikāya*, I, 133–34. Translation based on Brereton 2019: 22. For further sources, see T.W. Rhys Davids et al. *The Pali Text Society's Pali-English Dictionary* (London: Luzac, 1966) under *pāsaṇḍa*.
6   The passage summarized is *Aṅguttara Nikāya* III.221–222, sutta 191. See *The Numerical Discourses of the Buddha*, tr. Bhikkhu Bodhi (Boston: Wisdom Publications, 2012), pp. 800–801.

Second, Brahmins of old used to approach a Brahmin woman only in the proper season, not at other times. Today's Brahmins do it anytime, while dogs approach she-dogs only during the proper season. Third, in old times Brahmins did not buy or sell Brahmin women; they engaged in getting together for the sake of companionship by mutual consent only. Today they do any of these things, while dogs behave like the Brahmins of old. Fourth, while in the past Brahmins did not engage in accumulating wealth, grain, silver and gold, they do it now; dogs do not. And the fifth principle Brahmins held in times of old was that they sought for food for the evening meal in the evening and for the morning meal in the morning. Today Brahmins eat their fill, as much as possible, and then go ahead and eat the remainder. Again, today's dogs act like the Brahmins of old.[7]

This was the kind of antagonism among the Pasandas with which Ashoka probably had to contend. This background and context are important for understanding Ashoka's writings about the Pasandas and his ecumenical undertakings.

We saw in the previous chapter Ashoka's repeated use of the phrase 'all Pasandas', setting the scene for his ecumenical endeavours. In his language, he is attempting to blur inter-Pasanda distinctions. He is speaking to all of them. He tells them that he values them all. The second passage in Chart 11.1 taken from Rock Edict VII underscores this point: he permits all Pasandas to live anywhere within his empire. He says: 'The Beloved of Gods, King Piyadasi, desires that all Pasandas may reside everywhere.' The question is why Ashoka had to issue this order. Why did he feel the need to explicitly permit Pasandas to live anywhere they liked?

According to some scholars, the sociological background to this imperial proclamation was the conflicts among Pasandas. The political theorist Rajeev Bhargava summarizes their point of view:

Asoka effectively grants these [Pasanda] leaders permission to travel freely everywhere in the kingdom to provide them an opportunity to teach and convert each other. Asoka impartially grants this privilege

7   Freiberger 2009: 63.

to religious teachers of all pashandas. It is likely that the edict became necessary because mutual interaction and the attempt to preach [one's] own ethics to others had begun to cause severe friction, leading to the birth of local rules forbidding one pashanda from communicating with or, worse, entering into the territory of another pashanda.[8]

It is certainly possible that some religious organizations may have sought to establish areas of exclusivity, sort of religious ghettos. We know that Brahmins did, in fact, have such exclusive zones with state sanction. Such Brahmin areas of villages and towns are common in later India. In the idealized layout of a fort city described by Kautilya, Brahmins are allocated residences in the northern section: '[I]n the northern direction should be the residences of the deities of the city and deities of the king, and workers in metal and gems, as well as Brahmins.'[9] It is not unreasonable to assume other religious groups also sought such exclusive zones.

Yet, I think there is more to Ashoka's statement about where Pasandas may reside. The history of state control of ascetic groups in ancient India may throw some light on the historical and sociological background to Ashoka's order. The ancient Indian book on politics and governance, Kautilya's *Arthashastra*, contains some interesting insights into how a king should limit the areas of his kingdom open to certain kinds of ascetic groups. For example, Kautilya forbids such groups from living in what he calls *janapada*, the countryside, where much of the agricultural land and state-controlled forests were located. The only kind of ascetic permitted in those lands is the forest hermit: 'He should not let the following settle in his countryside: any kind of "gone-forth" (*pravrajita*) other than forest hermits.'[10] Even in towns and cities, the areas where Pasandas were allowed to reside were strictly regulated. The following statements of the *Arthashastra* show the suspicion with which Pasandas were regarded by state authorities.

---

8   Bhargava 2014:185.
9   Kautilya, *Arthashastra*, 2.4.15.
10 Kautilya, *Arthashastra*, 2.1.32.

The residences of Pasandas and Chandalas [outcastes] are on the outskirts of the cemetery. (2.4.23)

Those in charge of religious rest houses should give lodgings to Pasandas and travellers after informing the authorities. (2.36.5)

Hermits and Pasandas should live in a large compound without disturbing each other. (3.16.33)

The Pasandas, according to Kautilya, were either relegated to areas outside a town close to the cemetery, or, if they found lodging in specially designated religious rest houses, appropriately called *dharma-āvasatha*, the managers of these houses had to inform the local authorities.

As in the passage from Manu I cited above, Pasandas were associated by Kautilya with some unwholesome characters, as we see in this instruction to secret agents in charge of security within cities:

Secret agents deployed on roads and in roadless tracts should arrest anyone with a wound, carrying harmful tools, hiding behind a package, agitated, overcome by intense sleep, or tired from travel, or any stranger within or outside the city, in temples, holy places, woods and cemeteries.

Likewise, inside the city they should carry out searches in empty houses, workshops, taverns, places for selling boiled rice and cooked meat, gambling halls and Pasanda residences. (2.36.13–14)

Kautilya's remarks are even more significant because most are made while dealing with other topics. Apart from the statement about residing near cemeteries, all others *assume* that Pasandas were living in undesirable and suspicious locations, not in respectable neighbourhoods. They were not permitted to 'live everywhere'.

That may have been the background for Ashoka's bold statement ordering his bureaucracy to permit all Pasandas to reside wherever they wish. This must have been a welcome change of state policy as far as many of the Pasandas were concerned, with the possible exception of Brahmins. The reason Ashoka offers in Rock Edict VII for this change of policy is significant: 'For, all of them desire self-restraint and purity of heart.' The term for 'self-restraint' is *sayama* (Sanskrit: *saṃyama*). As we will see, self-restraint is something Ashoka sees as a central element in the spiritual life of Pasandas. The term I have translated as 'heart' is *bhāva*. This term has a broad meaning relating to the inner life of a person: spirit, soul, inner self and the like. Taken together, these two virtues—self-restraint and purity of heart—are desired, according to Ashoka, by all Pasandas, and anchor their spiritual journey and their way of life, which Ashoka defines as dharma. Ashoka's hope was that such Pasandas living close to the ordinary people, the *jana*, in contrast to the extraordinary people who constitute Pasandas, may become models of behaviour for those people. In the same edict where he permits Pasandas to live everywhere, he continues with his wishes for the ordinary people:

> But the common people (*jana*) have diverse yearnings and diverse passions. They carry out all or just a part. Even the giving of copious gifts, however, is clearly paltry when there is no self-restraint, purity of heart, gratitude and firm devotion.

The second sentence, 'carry out all or just a part', probably refers to dharma. Here he identifies inner virtues, including self-restraint and purity of heart, as the indispensable foundation for the practise of dharma. The ordinary people can learn these from the Pasandas living among them. That seems to be the gist of Ashoka's message, and a possible reason for permitting Pasandas to 'live everywhere' in his kingdom. The cities and the countryside are now open to these religious communities. They are not relegated to ghettos.

In Rock Edict XII, Ashoka addresses the Pasandas directly and makes explicit what Pasanda ecumenism is and how it can be achieved. As is the custom for Ashoka, he begins the message with a salutation honouring *all* Pasandas. Coming from the emperor himself, this must have meant a great deal to his audience. It was meant to win them over. The message, moreover, is addressed to both the ascetic communities (the 'gone forth', *pravrajita*) and the household communities associated with Pasandas (the 'stay-at-home', *gṛhastha*).

The Beloved of Gods, King Piyadasi, pays homage to all Pasandas, to those who have gone forth and to those staying at home, with gifts and with various acts of homage.

After this exchange of pleasantries, Ashoka gets down to business. He tells the Pasandas to shape up—no more bickering, no more lashing out at one another, no more intemperate and vituperative language. Turn inwards, look at your own selves, and see the defects and evil tendencies that bedevil each one of you. This is where Ashoka tries to do two things at once: the Pasandas must live up to the lofty ideals of their religion, and they should respect and learn from each other. This is the path to Ashokan ecumenism.

   He begins with a gentle move away from his initial salutation, but like a good writer and rhetorician, he connects the introductory statement with the body of his message using the term 'homage' that anchored his salutation. I want to pay you homage, to regale you with gifts and donations. But you know what—all that is trivial. What I really value, the great favour I ask of you, is that you pay attention to the 'essential core' of your religious life, the reason why you adopted the Pasanda mode of life in the first place. The term 'homage' acts as the thread that weaves the whole text. Here is Ashoka:

No gift or homage, however, is as highly prized by the Beloved of Gods as this: namely, that the essential core may increase among all Pasandas. But the increase of the essential core takes many forms. This, however, is its root, namely, guarding speech—that is to say, not paying homage to one's own Pasanda and not denigrating the Pasandas of others when there is no occasion, and even when there is an occasion, doing so mildly. Homage, on the other hand, should indeed be paid to the Pasandas of others in one form or another. Acting in this manner, one certainly enhances one's own Pasanda and also helps the Pasanda of the other.

   When someone acts in a way different from that, one hurts one's own Pasanda and also harms the Pasanda of the other. For, should someone pay homage to his own Pasanda and denigrate the Pasanda of another wholly out of devotion to his own Pasanda, thinking, that is, 'I'll make my Pasanda illustrious'—by so doing he damages his own Pasanda even more certainly.

There is a lot to unpack in this dense statement. First, what does Ashoka mean by 'essential core'? The original word is '*sāla*', and it has been seen by many as the Prakrit equivalent of the Sanskrit '*sāra*', meaning the essential and best part of anything—core, pith, essence, quintessence. There is, however, no scholarly consensus that the Prakrit *sāla* is the same as the Sanskrit *sāra*.[11] A clue is found in the Greek translation of this term using the Greek equivalent of dharma, namely, '*eusébeia*'. I think, whatever the etymology and semantic range of this term, what Ashoka meant by it is dharma, or something very close to it: that is, the core undertaking of all Pasandas. And this was the understanding of those who undertook its translation into Greek. This conclusion is supported by what Ashoka says in Rock Edict V with regard to the work of dharma-mahamatras among Pasandas: 'They are occupied with all the Pasandas for the establishment of dharma and, by the increase of dharma, for the welfare and happiness of dharma-devotees.' Strengthening of dharma parallels strengthening of the essential core: the same term, '*vaḍhi*', strengthening or increase, is used in both places. So, the first and most basic request of Ashoka is that all Pasandas make sure that they pay attention to the ultimate reason why they became Pasandas, namely, the pursuit of dharma—that dharma continues to grow among them, that each individual endeavours to grow in dharma.

That is all well and good. But how does a Pasanda go about accomplishing this? Ashoka comes down next to the nitty-gritty: Pasandas must give up their usual one-upmanship, their claim that their dharma is better than that of others, their disparagement of others. Be nice to each other! Tolerance in word and deed is the absolute minimum demanded

---

11 For a discussion of the issues relating to the etymology and meaning of *sāla*, see Brereton 2019: 30–32. I agree with Brereton that by *sāla* Ashoka likely meant dharma or something close to it. Norman (2012a: 122) notes: 'All sects must listen to each others' *dhamma*, so that there may be an increase of *sāla* (which I take to mean "communication") between them.'

by the ecumenical spirit, the lowest common denominator. But more is required, and more is demanded of them.

Growth in dharma, Ashoka tells the Pasandas, can take many forms; dharma is a complex moral order. But the indispensable foundation for any growth in dharma—the root from which the sprouts grow—is just one thing: guarding one's speech, controlling the tongue.[12] This concept jumps out of the pages of Ashoka's writings as a pivotal notion in his intellectual project. Ashoka brings back 'homage' into the discussion of guarding one's speech: paying homage—evidently in words—to one's own Pasanda and using disparaging language to characterize the Pasanda of others amounts to failure to guard one's speech. It exemplifies the disregard of the very root of one's progress in dharma. In such a situation there can be no growth in dharma. Such Pasandas defeat the very purpose and foundation of Pasanda life.

Ashoka here sounds like an exasperated teacher or parent trying to get the blockheads to understand the implications of their words and actions. When one praises one's own Pasanda and denigrates those of others, Ashoka takes pains to explain, it boomerangs and hurts one's own Pasanda. Someone may think that boastful language will make his Pasanda illustrious, but in reality 'he damages his own Pasanda even more certainly'. Such behaviour tells the world that growth in dharma is absent in that person's Pasanda. And such behaviour is not going to attract new converts. When one controls one's speech, is modest in one's praise of one's own Pasanda, and generous in praising the Pasandas of others, on the contrary, 'one certainly enhances one's own Pasanda and also helps the Pasanda of the other'. The focus on controlling one's speech brings to mind an adage given in the wisest and most entertaining of Indian books of wisdom, the *Panchatantra:*

---

12 Ashoka uses the same metaphor of root in Separate Edict I where he points to the root of various proclivities and moral failings among officials: 'One fails to act in this manner due to these proclivities: envy, quick temper, cruelty, haste, lack of zeal, laziness and lethargy ... The *root of all this* is being always free of quick temper and haste.'

Struck by an arrow or cut by an axe,
Even when a forest fire burns it up,
    a tree mends itself.
But a wound that is caused by cutting words
    can never be healed.[13]

This is ecumenism at work, but there is more. Ashoka goes further. True ecumenism demands not just the minimum: tolerance, living in harmony, not using insulting language. No, ecumenism requires more, much more.[14] Living an ecumenical life alongside other religions demands one to converse with others, to learn from others, to educate oneself in the dharma of others. It requires an activist and positive agenda. Ashoka calls such fellowship and interaction '*samavāya*', which means meeting one another, getting together, consorting with each other. The virtues Ashoka talks about, especially the control of speech, lead to this positive outcome. Members of different Pasandas should meet one another, either informally or at formal meetings, to discuss their dharma, their beliefs and practices. This is the third segment of Ashoka's message:

> Therefore, meeting one another is, indeed, excellent. That is—they should both listen to and take guidance from each other's dharma. For this is the wish of the Beloved of Gods. That is—all Pasandas should become highly learned and follow good discipline. And no matter which of these they may be devoted to, they should acknowledge: 'No gift or homage is as highly prized by the Beloved of Gods as this: namely, that the essential core may increase among all Pasandas.'

Here too Ashoka uses language effectively. First, he defines 'meeting one another', the major concept of this section: one should 'both listen to and take guidance from each other's dharma'. Meeting one another is not merely a social visit or a casual get-together. It is far deeper and more

---

13 *Panchatantra*, Book 3, verse 53; Olivelle 1997: 120.

14 For an extended discussion of this point, that Ashoka's message requires the Pasandas to go beyond 'tolerance' to actively engage with each other, see Rajeev Bhargava 2014.

serious. It involves 'listening' and 'taking guidance'—the two original terms are '*suneyu*' (literally: they should listen) and '*susūseyu*' (literally: they should desire to listen). The second term developed a secondary—and gradually the standard—meaning of being obedient. That is the meaning this term has in Ashoka's definitions of dharma: obedience to mother and father, for example. We can see how it developed that meaning if we look at the English expression 'listen to' someone. So, to the native hearer both these terms carry similar and reinforcing meanings: to listen, to listen to, and finally to learn. That is how, Ashoka tells them, you become 'highly learned'. And the term for learned is '*bahu-suta*' (literally: much heard, that is, one who has heard, that is, learned, a lot). The connection between hearing and learning relates to the ancient method of instruction: the student sits in front of the teacher and listens to him, learns by heart what he has heard, and then is able to repeat what he has learned. One becomes a 'much heard', that is, a 'highly learned' person, only by carrying on dialogues with others and learning from them, says Ashoka. You cannot hear much or learn a lot by simply listening to yourself or to your own group. You have to expand your horizon.

So, the goal of becoming a highly learned Pasanda can be accomplished only by following Ashoka's version of Pasandic ecumenism. The implication is profound: each individual Pasanda cannot make its members highly learned in isolation, but only through conversations, interactions and dialogue with members of other Pasandas. A further implication is that not a single Pasanda possesses the complete dharma, the complete truth. This is quite stunning when we consider that Ashoka himself was a devout Buddhist Upasaka.

Ashoka's compositional skills are admirable. He began the body of his message in part two with the hope that 'the essential core may increase among all Pasandas'. He concludes it in part three with the very same hope and the same expression: 'the essential core may increase among all Pasandas'. This is the most excellent gift that Ashoka can bestow on the Pasandas, far richer than material gifts. It is his gift of dharma and a reiteration of his statement in Rock Edict XI: 'There is no gift comparable to the gift of dharma.'

He ends this elegant piece of writing with a concluding paragraph about the dispatch of dharma-mahamatras and other officials to further his ecumenical mission.

> Large numbers, furthermore, have been dispatched for this purpose—dharma-mahamatras, mahamatras overseeing women, officers in charge of farms, and other classes of officers. And this is its fruit: enhancement of one's own Pasanda and making dharma illustrious.

The final prediction about the outcome of Ashoka's efforts—'enhancement of one's own Pasanda and making dharma illustrious'—brings us back to the topic of dharma. A Pasanda can flourish and become eminent only if their dharma is also illustrious.

We do not know what these dharma-mahamatras did when they were working with a particular Pasanda. Ashoka does not provide details. There are hints that their interactions may have been intense and perhaps intrusive. In Pillar Edict VII, as we have seen in passage no. 6 of Chart 11.1, he says that he has dispatched different dharma-mahamatras to different Pasandas, and he mentions the Buddhists, Brahmins, Ajivikas and Jains. Whatever form their work took, one thing is clear: Ashoka's ecumenism was top-down. The idea was his, and he wanted to instil it among the Pasandas.

But we get only one side of the story. The Pasandas themselves do not provide any information about how they reacted to what they may have perceived as Ashoka's high-handed interference in their internal affairs. The fact that he did interfere, however, is evident from the Schism Edict we explored in Chapter 6. There, Ashoka tells his mahamatras to take direct action to expel Buddhist monks and nuns who cause dissension in a monastery. The work of dharma-mahamatras was probably not that of a religious police force, yet it seems to have been overly intrusive. The Pasanda groups, which prized their independence and flaunted their direct access to ultimate religious truth, likely were not fans of these bureaucrats interfering in their lives and communities.

How successful was Ashoka's ecumenical campaign among the Pasandas? That is difficult to gauge. There are tantalizing hints, nevertheless, that there was resistance, especially among the Brahmins, who are counted among the Pasandas by Ashoka. As we saw in the previous chapter, the very expression Sramana–Brahmana, so common in Ashoka's vocabulary, became a prime example used by later Sanskrit grammarians to illustrate a kind of compound word in which the two terms are diametrically opposed to each other. The Sramanas and Brahmins, in the view of these grammarians, are irreconcilably opposed to each other. We should also note that in numerous Vedic texts composed by Brahmins living in the Brahmanical heartland of the middle Gangetic plain, the region of Magadha was viewed as barbaric and outside the Brahmanical cultural world. These texts even mock the speech patterns of these 'eastern' people, who pronounce 'r' as 'l'—precisely the way we have seen in Ashoka's eastern inscriptions.[15] Nothing good can come out of Magadha, whether it is the Sramanic religions like Buddhism or a preacher of morality like Ashoka.

As I have already noted, there is one Brahmanical text devoted to the elucidation of Brahmanical dharma that is roughly contemporaneous with Ashoka. It is the Dharmasutra of Apastamba. An interesting text from several aspects, it contains the earliest documented evidence for the system of four ashramas (*āśrama*s) or modes of religious life, a system that, along with the system of four social classes (*varṇa*s), came to define the Brahmanical religion in post-Ashokan times. In the context of the four ashramas, it is also the first Sanskrit text to use the term '*gṛhastha*', stay-at-home, with respect to the Brahmanical householder, and in opposition to the homeless mendicant, the 'gone forth' (*pravrajita*). So, its statements on dharma are significant—with all due caveats—as a possible commentary on or a counterpoint to Ashoka's own take on dharma. At least that is how I will approach it.

Unlike earlier Brahmanical texts, Apastamba begins his book with a basic question: How do we come to know the true dharma? It is the central epistemological issue at the heart of all discourses on dharma. For Buddhists, the cardinal rule is the words of the Buddha (*buddhavacana*). That alone guarantees the truth of dharma. Apastamba has a different

---

15 For a study, see Hans Hock 1991.

take: 'We shall explain the accepted customary dharmas. The authority
for them is acceptance by those who know the dharmas, and the Vedas.'[16]
Here, the Sanskrit term for 'authority' is '*pramāṇa*', which is also the
term used in philosophy for means of knowledge, such as perception
and inference. So, how we come to know dharma is the acceptance or
agreement by 'people who know dharmas' that a particular action is
dharma. This seems to be tautological: to get to know dharma one must
get to know people who know dharma. The final statement that the
means of knowing dharma is the Vedas tells us that those who know
the dharmas are the same as those who know the Vedas. Such people
are, by definition, Brahmins. The use of the plural 'dharmas' (Sanskrit:
dharmān) contrasts with Ashoka's use of the singular. For Ashoka, dharma
is a singular ethical philosophy with multiple ethical principles. For
Apastamba, dharmas are many, and they consist of Vedic injunctions
on the performance of various ritual and religious actions. Apastamba's
epistemology of dharma upholds what has come to be called 'Brahmanical
exceptionalism', a far cry from Ashoka's ecumenism, the humility to learn
from one another.

There is another passage where Apastamba seems to directly confront
the kind of dharma instruction that Ashoka revelled in. Not just anyone
has the capacity to teach dharma, Apastamba seems to be saying:

> Let him not become vexed or easily deceived by the pronouncements
> of hypocrites, crooks, infidels and fools. The Dharma and Adharma
> do not go around saying, 'Here we are!' Nor do gods, Gandharvas or
> ancestors declare, 'This is Dharma and that is Adharma.' An activity
> that Aryas praise is Dharma, and what they deplore is Adharma. He
> should model his conduct after that which is unanimously approved in
> all regions by Aryas who have been properly trained, who are elderly
> and self-possessed, and who are neither greedy nor deceitful. In this
> way he will win both worlds.[17]

---

16 *Āpastamba Dharmasūtra*, 1.1.1–3.
17 *Āpastamba Dharmasūtra*, 1.20.5–9.

The term 'adharma' is the negative form of dharma—the non-dharma, the opposite of dharma. Apastamba personifies dharma and adharma here. They do not advertise themselves. Even divine beings are unable to declare what is dharma and what is not dharma. Dharma can only be learned from observing the conduct of people called 'Arya', a term that each religious tradition of the time attempted to define to support its own views. For Apastamba, Arya is a male Brahmin who is elderly, well-trained—no doubt in the Vedas—and virtuous. It is the conduct of these individuals, and their consensus and verbal approval that determines what is dharma and what is not. There is a bit of venom in Apastamba's advice to his readers: don't be duped by 'the pronouncements of hypocrites, crooks, infidels and fools'. Did he have Ashoka in mind, or perhaps the Buddha?

No ecumenical sentiment is evident in Apastamba's writings on dharma. We do not know what intellectuals of other Pasandas thought. But if the Brahmanical reaction was in any way representative, Ashoka's pleas may have fallen on mostly deaf ears. The later histories of these same Pasandas, which we will examine in the Epilogue, seem to support such a conclusion.

Yet, all may not have been lost. Ashoka left his mark on the way both ordinary people and intellectuals viewed dharma. We have seen that the very reason Apastamba thought about writing a book on dharma may have been Ashoka and his popularization of this cornerstone of his moral philosophy. Pre-Ashokan Brahmanical tradition had not focused much on this concept. Now Brahmanical intellectuals were scrambling to salvage dharma from 'hypocrites, crooks, infidels and fools'. And in the process, they seem to have absorbed some of Ashoka's own innovative ideas about dharma.

First, dharma defines a universal moral philosophy applicable to all, even to people living in countries and cultures outside India. Brahmanical moral philosophy was very much contextual: your dharma was defined by who you were—woman or man, married or not, what caste you belonged to, and so on. In later theology this kind of ethic is called *svadharma*, 'dharma specific to an individual'. Yet, we have instances of Brahmanical authors teaching a universal dharma applicable to all. Here is Apastamba in perhaps one of the earliest such forays into dharma as a universal ethic:

> Refraining from anger, excitement, rage, greed, perplexity, hypocrisy and malice; speaking the truth; refraining from overeating, calumny and envy; sharing, liberality, rectitude, gentleness, tranquility, self-control, amity with all creatures, Yoga, Arya-like conduct, benevolence and contentment.[18]

This, Apastamba says, is applicable to all the ashramas, and perhaps to all humans. This, arguably, is the legacy of Ashoka.

Even though we have little information about how Ashoka's ecumenical initiatives were received by the Pasandas themselves, Ashoka himself considered these initiatives central to his dharma project. Co-opting these organized and disciplined groups of devoted religious adepts to further his mission of creating a morally grounded population would have seemed to him a no-brainer.

---

18 *Āpastamba Dharmasūtra*, 1.23.6.

13

Civil Religion

ASHOKA HAD A COMPLEX RELATIONSHIP WITH RELIGION. BY NOW, this much must be clear to the reader who has ploughed through the last dozen chapters. We do not know what sort of religious upbringing Ashoka had as a child. Traditionally, his father and grandfather have been viewed as followers of or influenced by the Pasanda traditions of the Jains and the Ajivikas. Living in the region of Magadha, he was bound to have been influenced by the new ascetic religions emerging in that part of India. So, when as an adult he became a Buddhist Upasaka, he was still operating within the broader ascetical religious traditions that have their roots in his home territory of Magadha. As a Buddhist, he maintained good relations with other Pasanda groups. We explored that in the previous two chapters.

But Ashoka went further than simply remaining within the orbit of the organized religions of his time. He did something none of his predecessors had done—indeed, no king before or after him had done either in India or possibly elsewhere in the world. He founded a new universalist kind of religion based on a specific understanding of the central concept of dharma. It had the characteristics of a religion with a focus on moral philosophy, doctrines relating to destiny after death, and even a kind of cult with the liturgical reading of Ashoka's writings on specific holy days of the annual liturgical calendar. It also had the characteristics of a political movement and philosophy, with the mobilization of his extensive government bureaucracy in its service, and even the creation of a whole new government department of dharma-mahamatras solely devoted to his dharma project.

What are we to make of this new religious initiative of Ashoka? How are we to understand it? Or, to use a term much loved by scholars today, how can we theorize it? In other words, what sort of a theoretical structure would best explain what Ashoka was aiming to do, linking the religious, the moral and the political inherent in his conception of dharma?

Using religion to legitimize the political power of kings and rulers is commonplace in world history. Kings may claim divine ancestry, proclaim themselves to be gods, or simply invoke a heavenly mandate. In ancient India, the Sanskrit term '*deva*', which is related to the Greek '*theos*', Latin '*deus*' and English 'divine', is used for both gods and kings. All that is unremarkable.

But Ashoka is doing something quite different. He is not claiming to be a god or to have divine parentage or sanction. He is not even using a particular religion to support his legitimacy. His propagation of dharma has nothing to do with the legitimacy of his own kingship. He is doing something else, something that has more to do with his people than with himself.

Here, it is useful to posit the distinction between 'state' and 'people'. This distinction is made mostly in the context of modern democracies, and some may feel that it is inapplicable to ancient polities. The political philosopher Charles Taylor comments:

> A modern democratic state demands a 'people' with a strong collective identity. Democracy obliges us to show much more solidarity and much more commitment to one another in our joint political project than was demanded by the hierarchical and authoritarian societies of yesteryear … To form a state, in the democratic era, a society is forced to undertake the difficult and never-to-be-completed task of defining its collective identity.[1]

---

1   Charles Taylor 2014: 67–68.

Yet, it is not only in modern pluralistic nation-states that the need to 'constitute' a people with a collective identity becomes necessary for a state to remain viable. Pluralistic states containing people with diverse ethnic, linguistic, religious and even culinary backgrounds dispersed over a large geographical area are found historically in several parts of the world, including China and India during the Mauryan empire. When the Qin and Han dynasties had to rule a unified China, and when the Mauryan kings, especially Ashoka, had to incorporate populations with vastly different cultural, religious and linguistic backgrounds—from Afghanistan to Bengal to Karnataka—they ran into problems similar to those of modern nation-states: how to constitute a 'people' that would owe allegiance to the state represented by the emperor. Force and coercion, though necessary, were not sufficient.

The ancient Indian political theorist Kautilya is clear-eyed about the importance of a satisfied and loyal population for the safety and prosperity of a kingdom. Kautilya uses two terms for 'people' of his ideal kingdom: 'prajā' (meaning progeny, child and subject, a term used also by Ashoka) and 'prakṛti' (meaning the people as the basis and source of the kingdom). When the people are disaffected and unhappy (virakta), Kautilya tells us, the kingdom becomes weaker and a target for attack by neighbouring kings: 'When his subjects are disaffected … it will be possible for me to overpower him.'[2] On the other hand, polities are strong and stable when their people are loyal and devoted (anurakta).[3] Kautilya advises a king not to initiate hostilities against such a kingdom.

What were the means available to ancient states to create a loyal and satisfied people, an 'imagined community'? I think, in the case of Ashoka at least, the method to constitute a people, mutatis mutandis, paralleled those deployed in many modern nation-states, a method that has been called the creation of a 'civil religion'. I want to suggest that the category of 'civil religion', although it was created within the context of modern nation-states, may yet be useful, at least for heuristic purposes, to theorize

---

2   Kautilya, *Arthaśāstra*, 2.6.38. See also 7.4.15.

3   Kautilya, *Arthaśāstra*, 7.4.16; 7.8.11; 7.14.10.

Ashoka's dharma project. This project aimed at transforming his subjects into a 'people' in Taylor's sense.

The expression 'civil religion' was coined by the eighteenth-century French political philosopher Jean-Jacques Rousseau and made famous in the twentieth century by the American sociologist Robert Bellah.[4] This civil religion is not identified with any organized religion or sect that may operate within a society, even though themes and symbols derived from them may be used within the civil religion. A civil religion can thus rise only in a relatively complex society where multiple religions coexist, as in Ashoka's India with its many Pasandas. Nonetheless, it contains some aspects of a religion. Bellah, in the context of the United States of America, points to such rituals and religious elements as a national flag, a national anthem, a national holiday, founding fathers, a constitution as a quasi-scripture and the like. These elements, however, will be different in different societies and historical situations. One central symbol is 'god' for the American version of civil religion, a term which means so much and so little that individuals can fill it with the meaning they want. With reference to the use of 'God' in John F. Kennedy's inaugural speech, Bellah notes:

> He did not refer to any religion in particular. He did not refer to Jesus Christ, or to Moses, or to the Christian church; certainly he did not refer to the Catholic church. In fact, his only reference was to the concept of God, a word almost all Americans can accept but that means so many different things to so many different people that it is almost an empty sign.[5]

This is precisely why 'God' is such a central and convenient concept for the American version of civil religion, and why 'In God We Trust' can be printed on every American dollar bill without rousing opposition.

I propose that Ashoka's dharma project and his ecumenism can be understood as an attempt to build a 'people' with a sense of belonging

---

4   Jean-Jacques Rousseau 1792; Robert Bellah 1970.
5   Bellah 1970: 170.

to a larger community, the Mauryan empire, through the creation of an Ashokan civil religion. In the case of this civil religion, the place of 'God' in Bellah's analysis is occupied by 'dharma'. We have already explored the religious dimensions of dharma, a term that had come to define the core of Buddhism and many other Pasandas, as well as of the moral and otherworldly doctrine propagated by Ashoka. If dharma did not have this resonance already among at least a large segment of the population, his use of the term would have been ineffective. Yet, like Bellah's 'God', dharma was somewhat of a vacuous concept into which individuals and groups could read whatever content they desired. Ashoka's definitional elements are broad moral principles eliciting widespread acceptance; nobody could be opposed to them. Dharma had the potential to become all things to all people. It could thus serve as a core value around which all the people of the empire, irrespective of their differences, could unite and create an 'imagined community'. The civil religion of dharma was a religion that could encompass and transcend particular religions that Ashoka refers to as Pasandas.

I recognize that some may view the use of the theoretical category 'civil religion' as anachronistic when applied to a polity that existed two millennia ago. Yet, despite the dangers of anachronism, I think this category provides a useful lens to peek into Ashoka's preaching of the cult of dharma precisely because it helps us understand the common features of two entirely disparate societies. Rajeev Bhargava has used the modified category of 'civil ethic' to eliminate 'religion', which he finds problematic in the context of ancient India. Still others have preferred the category of 'political theology'. Whatever term we may prefer, some such broader and theoretical category is useful to understand and explain Ashoka's propagation of dharma within his empire.

The aim of Ashoka's dharma project was to create a moral population with cultivated virtues that informed their relationships to significant others within their social universe, a moral cultivation that leads to happiness both here and in the hereafter. Ashoka believed that a state full of such moral and model citizens would be prosperous, peaceful and righteous. There would be no need for prisons, police, armed struggles and injury to living beings. He may even have believed—much like the slogan today that democratic nations do not initiate wars—that if other countries abided by dharma there would be no wars. There would be universal peace, harmony and prosperity. Ashoka's civil religion thus had an international dimension as well, perhaps even a nascent theory of international relations.[6]

The very 'canon' of Ashoka's writings inscribed on stone served as a textual basis, a form of scriptural authority, for this civil religion. There was both an iconic and a performative aspect to these inscribed texts. We have already seen that Ashoka in some of his writings requires that they be read aloud publicly on sacred days of the liturgical calendar. It is not improbable that all his major edicts were intended for public and quasi-religious recitations. The existence of a civil liturgical calendar is indicated also in Pillar Edict V, where, as we saw in Chapter 9, the killing of fish and animals, castration of bulls and the branding of horses and bulls are forbidden on holy days. Adherence to dharma, Ashoka tells his people, secures happiness both in this world and the next. The only way to ensure heaven is to abide by the requirements of dharma.

Ashoka's civil religion was not in opposition to or in competition with the organized religions of his day, the Pasandas. Their domains and missions were different. Ashoka professes his support of and affection for all Pasandas. His wish is that all of them live in harmony with each other. The Pasandas, who were already dedicated to their respective dharmas, were strategic partners of Ashoka for the propagation of his own universal dharma. Unlike the American version, Ashoka's civil religion had also an otherworldly dimension. Abiding by dharma ensures heaven after death. This heaven is a generic after-death beatitude, distinct from the specific goals formulated by the religions of his day.

There were, however, some specific religious beliefs and practices that Ashoka's civil religion opposed and sought to replace. We have seen

---

6   See the papers by Rajeev Bhargava, Patrick Olivelle and Upinder Singh in the volume from the collaborative project on international relations by Chinese and Indian scholars: Amitav Acharya, Daniel A. Bell, Rajeev Bhargava and Yan Xuetong, eds, *Bridging Two Worlds: Comparing Classical Political Thought and Statecraft in China and India* (Berkeley: University of California Press, 2022).

his opposition to and disparagement of some folk religious practices, such as animal sacrifices, festivals and auspicious rites. This position exhibits the subtle influence of the moral teachings of ascetic religions, especially the Jain and the Buddhist. Ahimsa was a central tenet of these religions. Ashoka adopted it as the anchor of his moral philosophy, even though such a stance went against the practices of some religions, such as Brahmanism and possibly local cults, that authorized ritual killing of animals.

One significant result of Ashoka's civil religion is the replacement of what may be termed 'Brahmanical exceptionalism' with a policy of equal regard for all Pasandas and the encouragement of ecumenism. The displacement of Brahmins from their privileged position within the social and political hierarchy was clearly one of the major consequences of Ashokan reforms.

Rajeev Bhargava, who has investigated Ashoka's thought as a political philosophy, refers to claims that Ashoka 'formulated a conception of the proto-secular state in India', and that 'Asoka's tolerance towards all religions was the forerunner of the policy of religious neutrality associated with secularism'.[7] Although such claims, as Bhargava notes, are often overdrawn and anachronistic, he sees Ashoka's reconceptualization of dharma as 'a major attempt to introduce norms of civility among rival followers of major systems of beliefs and practices, to forge an order where potentially conflicting religious and philosophical groups could enjoy principled coexistence'.[8]

Following Bhargava, I see Ashoka's strong advocacy of ecumenism among Pasandas as a significant ingredient in the formulation of a civil religion aimed at constituting a people, a people who would have a sense of belonging to a common polity on the basis of dharma. Ashoka's unique definition of dharma was meant, among other things, to provide a common ethical and religious basis for belonging to the Ashokan state. As such, the simple establishment of harmony among Pasandas could not have been a sufficient basis. It required more than harmony. It required

---

7   Bhargava 2014: 174. See also Bhargava 2022b.
8   Bhargava 2014: 175.

the Pasandas both to engage in fruitful dialogue with other Pasandas as fellow co-religionists and to become missionaries in Ashoka's dharma project. This is the reason he tells the Pasandas to strengthen their dharma, to attend to the essential core of their religious life, a core that consists of dharma. As we have seen elsewhere, Ashoka here engages in sleight of hand. The ambiguity of dharma allows him to speak at the same time about the deepest doctrines of each Pasanda and about his own programme of civil religion: both are dharma. Drawing the Pasandas into Ashoka's dharma web was a clever move. Whether it was successful is quite another matter. We have little evidence either way. But, as we will see later, if Ashoka was ever able to establish an ecumenical spirit among the Pasandas, it was short-lived.

In dealing with Ashoka's dharma project, it is easy to become cynical. He was, after all, a politician. All this was probably a political ploy, an administrative strategy. Romila Thapar is right to admonish against it: 'Aśoka's *dhamma,* it would seem, provided an ideology of persuasive assimilation. It arose as much from his personal conviction of Buddhist teachings as from the wider discussion of ethical precepts and from demands of imperial policy.'[9] His personal convictions, nevertheless, were broader than the merely Buddhist. There was something very personal, very 'Ashokan', in his dharma project. He reveals himself as a visionary not overly constrained by his Buddhist identity.

That dharma for Ashoka was not simply a political strategy—although it certainly was that—is indicated by repeated admonishment that following his dharma ensures felicity after death in the next world. He is deeply concerned about the spiritual welfare of his people. Even in as common a matter as judicial execution, he orders a three-day delay in carrying it out so the prisoners can perform religious rites in preparation for their death and afterlife.

That Ashoka's dharma project was not simply a civil religion—it was definitely that too—is demonstrated by the international dimension of his dharma mission. A civil religion is bounded by the territory of the state in which it operates. To use a modern example, the Indian and the

---

9   Thapar 2000: 436.

American flags can be symbols of a civil religion, but their symbolism will not extend to Pakistan and Canada. When Ashoka sends envoys to propagate dharma among his neighbours to the west and the south, he is doing something that transcends a simple civil religion. He is making a statement that the Ashokan dharma has a universal appeal and fills a universal need. Besides promoting the spiritual and ethical welfare of the people of the world, the Ashokan dharma, he believed, was a vehicle for international peace and prosperity.

We have no way of measuring to what degree Ashoka's promotion of a civil religion was effective in creating an imagined community, in forging an identity among his people beyond ethnic and regional divides, an identity as subjects of the Ashokan empire, as the 'children' (*prajā*) of Ashoka. His letters to his senior and mid-level officials that they should do his bidding and follow his instructions hint at the possibility that there may have been resistance to his pet projects within the imperial bureaucracy itself. The historian, however, is deprived of evidence from the 'other side'. We see the world through the lens provided by Ashoka's writings, which is bound to be distorting. No independent account is available.

Epilogue
Ashoka's Legacy and the Unravelling of the Ashokan Experiment

ASHOKA CASTS A LONG SHADOW OVER THE *LONGUE DURÉE* OF INDIAN history, even when his silent impact is unacknowledged or unknown. The figure of Ashoka rarely, if ever, comes to mind when people reflect on the centrality of 'dharma' in Indian religion and culture, the primacy of the moral principles of vegetarianism and ahimsa, or the multiplicity of scripts in South and Southeast Asia. Rabindranath Tagore writing Bengali poetry in the early twentieth century, Sri Lankan Buddhist monks writing the Buddhist chronicle *Mahavaṃsa* in the Sinhala script, Tamil poets writing Sangam poems in the old Tamil script, Cambodian kings commissioning inscriptions engraved in the Khmer script on Angkor Wat, and even Bollywood wordsmiths writing Hindi film scripts in Devanagari—we can be sure that none of them felt any connection to Ashoka, none thought they were part of Ashoka's legacy. But they were. And so are a billion people of South and Southeast Asia whenever they put pen to paper, when Indians extol vegetarianism, or when Mahatma Gandhi preached non-violence. Long before vegetarianism went mainstream in India and across the world, Ashoka was known as the 'vegetarian king'.

In numerous areas of language, culture and religion we can—with the benefit of hindsight—see the impact of this unique ruler on India's long history. That is the unseen and mainly forgotten legacy of Ashoka.

Yet, that was not the legacy Ashoka sought. In the last piece of writing he left to posterity, Pillar Edict VII, Ashoka expresses his hope that the dharma project he initiated 'may endure as long as my sons and grandsons, as long as the moon and sun'. The very last words he left to posterity at the conclusion of Pillar Edict VII are *cilaṭṭike siyā*, 'so it will last a long time'. That was the legacy he sought, the fame he craved. It was a legacy that was denied to him.

The Ashokan experiment of governance anchored in a universalist moral philosophy and religious ecumenism was unique and unprecedented in world history. An idealist at heart, he worked single-mindedly for over a quarter of a century to further that goal. The reasons may be many, but this unique political, philosophical and religious experiment did not last many years—let alone until the moon and sun—following Ashoka's death.

The year of Ashoka's death is disputed, but I will accept the conclusion of Romila Thapar that he died in 233 or 232 BCE. That would make his reign roughly thirty-six years long. There is little clarity as to what happened in the years and decades following Ashoka's passing. Much of the historical writing about this period is conjectural and based on information in texts produced many centuries after Ashoka. These sources, both Buddhist and Brahmanical, give conflicting information about the names of Ashoka's successors and the durations of their reigns. Romila Thapar provides the following line of succession with the respective years of their reigns:[1]

Dasharatha	8 years
Samprati	9 years
Shalishulka	13 years
Devavarman	7 years
Shatadhanvan	8 years
Brihadratha	7 years

1 For a detailed and balanced account of Mauryan rule after the death of Ashoka, see Romila Thapar 1961: 182–217.

Brihadratha was the last ruler of the Mauryan dynasty. He was assassinated around 181–180 BCE by his army general Pushyamitra, who founded the successor dynasty of the Shungas. With that, the Mauryan rule of India lasting about 137 years came to an end, along with Ashoka's dream of a world governed by dharma. As Romila Thapar says:

> As compared to other early empires, such as the Achaemenid, Han, Roman, the Mauryan was short-lived. Rising with the conquest of Candragupta and reaching its peak with his grandson Aśoka, it seems to have declined rather rapidly after this. As an imperial structure it survived at most for a century.[2]

Ashoka's sons and grandsons, about whom he writes so wistfully, did not measure up to their father and grandfather in vision or imagination, in skill or competence. Their reigns were also short-lived. The territory may also have been divided among different pretenders. They were not avid writers like their illustrious ancestor. They left behind no engraved letters, except for a couple of donative inscriptions.

It is likely that Ashoka imagined himself to be a trailblazer inaugurating a new dispensation, a new era of moral living and governance in accordance with dharma—an end to conflicts and wars and an era of world harmony founded on dharma. He did not claim an ancestry like other ancient kings did. He did not invoke the names of his father or grandfather. He measured time from his consecration as king. His wish, perhaps, was that the world would also reckon years from that day, probably in 268 BCE. His hope, frequently expressed, was that his children and grandchildren would continue his mission. That was not to be.

The death of the ecumenical experiment along with his own death would have caused deep sorrow to Ashoka. It also changed the course of Indian history. We cannot be sure how successful Ashoka's ecumenism was in bringing together the various Pasandas, replacing rivalry with cooperation, even during his lifetime. But any hope for such a course was dashed when he died, and his successors were unable or unwilling to pursue the Ashokan project. The Ashokan experiment would lie hidden

---

2   Thapar 1987: 6.

beneath words inscribed on stone that no one could or cared to read—
until the middle of the nineteenth century, two millennia after Ashoka
wrote them.

The death of Ashoka's ecumenism is evident in how Ashoka was
remembered or forgotten in the Buddhism and Brahmanism of the
succeeding centuries. It may also signal the fact that, however much
Ashoka may have tried, his top-down effort at ecumenism did not
fully penetrate the Pasanda communities themselves. It was never fully
internalized or implemented by them. The best we can say is Ashoka was
far ahead of his times, perhaps ahead by a couple of millennia.

The collapse of Ashokan ecumenism is revealed in the efforts by the
Brahmanical and Buddhist traditions to depict the 'ideal' king either in
implicit contrast to Ashoka or modelled after him. The two Brahmanical
Sanskrit epics, the Mahabharata and the Ramayana, depict two ideal
kings, Yudhisthira and Rama, both ruling according to dharma, and both
intensely devoted to Brahmins. They placed the Brahmins at the head
of their respective kingdoms and ruled the country according to their
advice. The two long epics, however, never invoke the name of Ashoka.
The Brahmanical tradition by and large cancelled Ashoka from historical
memory, except for a few passages in some Puranic lists of kings. Yet, as
many recent scholars have pointed out, Yudhisthira stands in contrast
to Ashoka—a silent but eloquent contrast.[3] The epic scholar Madeleine
Biardeau has argued forcefully that the composition of the Mahabharata
is connected to Ashoka: 'We have posed from the beginning, as our
fundamental hypothesis, a causal rapport between the conversion of
Aśoka and the composition of the *Mahābhārata*.'[4] The scholar of Indian
epics James Fitzgerald presents the most forceful comparison of the two
kings, the historical Ashoka and the epic Yudhisthira, a literary creation

3   See Nick Sutton 1997. For the Ramayana, see Sheldon I. Pollock, *The
    Rāmāyaṇa of Vālmīki: An Epic of Ancient India*, Vol. II (Princeton: Princeton
    University Press, 1986), pp. 23–24, 71.
4   Biardeau 2002, II, p. 747 (Alf Hiltebeitel, trans., 'Buddhism and the
    Mahābhārata: Boundary Dynamics in Textual Practice', in *Boundaries,
    Dynamics and Construction of Traditions in South Asia*, ed. Federico Squarcini
    [Florence: Firenze University Press, 2005], p. 109).

of Brahmins intent on depicting the ideal king who is 'brahmaṇya', devoted
to Brahmins:

> I have long believed that Yudhiṣṭhira ... is a literary creation designed
> by a literary theo-philosophical artist for the purpose of giving others
> a new vision of a new world of possibilities. And for many years I have
> suspected that Yudhiṣṭhira was designed as a refutation, or at least a
> rebuttal, of the emperor Aśoka.[5]

If for Brahmins the ideal king is one, who—like Yudhisthira and unlike
Ashoka—is always devoted to the welfare and supremacy of Brahmins,
then for Buddhists it is a king who emulates Ashoka in his singular
devotion to the Sangha and Buddhism. As the anthropologist Stanley
Tambiah notes: 'The manner in which the early Buddhist conception
of kingship and polity was realized ... in the epochal reign of Emperor
Asoka ... was to constitute the great precedent and model for some of the
emergent polities of South and Southeast Asia.'[6] Max Deeg, moreover,
notes the way both Indian and Chinese kings modelled their rule after
Ashoka, calling him 'a model ruler without a name'. In India, we have the
Kushana king Kanishka, who is 'narratively molded into an ideal Buddhist
ruler according to the blueprint of Aśoka's legendary biography, as a
second Aśoka'.[7] There is the sixth-century Chinese Emperor Wu, a ruler
'who wanted to act in an ideal Buddhist way by constructing himself as
another Aśoka ... Emperor Wu erected numerous relic *stūpas*, took part
in proto-archaeological searches for Aśokan *stūpas*'.[8] As the historian
Chongfeng Li has noted, China is dotted with two kinds of sculpture
relating to Ashoka:

> The first type consists of Buddha images reputed to be made by King
> Aśoka or by his daughter, and [the] second type consists of portrait-

---

5 James L. Fitzgerald 2004: 136–37.
6 Stanley Tambiah 1976: 5.
7 Max Deeg 2012: 365.
8 Max Deeg 2012: 370.

images of King Aśoka commissioned by Buddhist monks and laymen, which are meant to honour his contributions to Buddhism.[9]

Both these depictions of the ideal king from two opposing perspectives share a common theme: a king should not be neutral in interreligious rivalries like the Ashoka we have come to know through his own words. They also signal the end of Ashokan ecumenism.

A glimpse into Buddhist triumphalism projected back to Ashoka is found in the writings of a distinguished Buddhist monk named Ashvaghosa (first–second century CE). He was probably a well-educated Brahmin before becoming a Buddhist and a monk. His special talent was poetry. He wrote two epic poems (*kāvya*)—the earliest such works extant in Sanskrit—one of which was the *Buddhacarita*, 'Life of the Buddha'.[10] Significantly, this biography of the Buddha ends not with the Buddha's death but with the birth and activities of Ashoka and his building projects:

> In course of time king Aśoka was born, who was devoted to the faith … The Maurya took the relics of the Seer from the seven Stupas they had been deposited and distributed them in due course in a single day over eighty thousand majestic Stupas, which shone with the brilliancy of autumn clouds.[11]

So, one of the earliest accounts of the Buddha's life ends with Ashoka viewed as the person responsible for the spread of Buddhism across the Indian subcontinent. Ashoka represented the triumph of Buddhism.

This triumph was nowhere more celebrated than in Sri Lanka, where the chronicles tout the close and direct connection of Sri Lankan Buddhism to Ashoka and the missionary activities of his son and daughter. The oldest inscriptional corpus of the island bears witness to the co-option of Ashokan ideals of kingship by Sri Lankan monks and

---

9   Chongfeng Li 2012: 380.

10 For a translation of this work, see Olivelle 2008.

11 Translation with modification of Johnston (Chapter XXVIII, verses 63, 65): E.H. Johnston, ed. and trans., *Aśvaghoṣa's Buddhacarita or Acts of the Buddha* (Delhi: Motilal Banarsidass, reprint, 1998).

kings, with several rulers adopting the Ashokan title of *devanampiya*, 'The Beloved of Gods'. Max Deeg concludes his survey of Ashoka's influence on Asian kings with the assessment: 'The examples discussed here should be enough to demonstrate that the cultural memory of Aśoka was strong enough to establish him, in his legendary form, as an ideal Buddhist king.'[12]

An interesting piece of evidence underscores the end of Ashoka's ecumenical venture. This evidence comes in the form of an act of vandalism and forgery frozen in time on the very same rocks on which Ashoka engraved his generous gifts of cave dwellings to ascetic communities. Three of these are located in the Barabar Hills in Gaya district of Bihar. They were given by Ashoka to the Ajivikas, an ascetic community that Ashoka mentions in Pillar Edict VII. The donative inscriptions on these caves record the word '*ājīvikehi*', 'to the Ājīvikas' (see Appendix). But in all three locations this word has been totally or partially chiselled out by a new community of rival ascetics who took possession of the caves sometime after Ashoka.[13] Here we have an ancient example of 'cancel culture'. The forgery here is implicit, because the new owners did not substitute their name for the original donee. That final step is taken by one Buddhist sect when it inserted its name after erasing the name of the original sect. Harry Falk has identified the substitution of 'Sarvastivada' for the original 'Sammatiya' on the stone fencing at Sarnath, which was originally at Lumbini, the Buddha's birthplace. And on the Ashokan pillar at Sarnath, we have the opposite: 'Sammatiya' is substituted for 'Sarvastivada'.[14]

The final nail in the coffin of Ashoka's ecumenism was the change in the semantics of the term 'Pasanda', which was the key term in Ashoka's ecumenical undertaking. In the post-Ashokan period, as we have seen, the term is used regularly in the pejorative sense to refer to one's religious opponents.

---

12 See Deeg 2012: 372.
13 See Hultzsch 1925: 181; Falk 2008.
14 See Falk 2006: 212.

A glimmer of hope that ecumenism was not completely dead is revealed in the Hathigumpha cave inscription of Kharavela in precisely the same region of Kalinga conquered by Ashoka. The dating and interpretation of this inscription, which is poorly preserved, are quite uncertain. It has been dated to the first century CE.[15] The significant point is that at the end of this inscription the king is described as *savapāsaṃḍapūjako*—'one who honours all Pasandas'. Here, we may detect an echo of Ashoka and his consistent statements about honouring '*all* Pasandas'.

The other example of an ecumenical experiment in India comes 1,800 years later when the Mughal emperor Akbar initiated the 'Din-i Ilahi', or 'Religion of God', as an ecumenical religion rising above the divides of Islam, Hinduism, Christianity, Buddhism and the like. He himself converted to this new religion for a new enlightened polity. But, just like Ashoka's, Akbar's experiment did not outlast his death by many years.

The memory of Ashoka, however, remained not just in the literary tradition of later centuries, but also in the archaeological and inscriptional remains. As the art historian Monica Zin (2018) has shown, Ashoka is depicted at Kanaganahalli in sculpture dated between the first century BCE and the second century CE. The Satavahana rulers who sponsored this project were aware of Ashoka's prestige. As Zin (2018: 550–51) notes: 'Placing the kings around "Aśoka," and the Buddhist symbols at his side, accords the Sātavāhanas not only the prestige of being depicted with Aśoka in a prominent position of the *stūpa*, but also implicitly represents them, like Aśoka himself, as Buddhist rulers.'[16] Also in the second century CE, Rudradaman refers to Ashoka by name in his inscription at Girnar engraved right by the edict of Ashoka himself.

The memory of a reimagined Ashoka spread throughout Asia, especially in the Buddhist countries. This journey of the king across the expanse of south and Southeast Asia has recently been traced by Nayanjot Lahiri (2022).

---

15 D.C. Sircar 1986: 213, n. 1.

16 For a detailed discussion of royal power inscribed in art and architecture, see Upinder Singh 2022.

As the 'imagined Ashoka' flourished, the Ashoka disclosed in his own writings remained hidden until, as I noted in the Prologue, James Prinsep, a British colonial officer, was able to decipher the script and open this particular book to the world. This inscriptional Ashoka spawned a new burst of creative activity within the leadership of the newly emerging Indian state, as it attempted to shed the shackles of colonialism and build a new independent India. At the forefront of this march was Jawaharlal Nehru, the Prime Minister in-the-making.

The historian Bhagwan Josh in a perceptive essay on the reimagination of Ashoka in the emergent postcolonial Indian state cites the French historian Amaury de Riencourt: 'In Jawaharlal Nehru India found a remarkable reincarnation of emperor Aśoka.'[17] It was the discovery of Ashoka that took Nehru—as he was attempting to discover India—on a long journey of bonding Ashoka firmly to his nation-building project. Reading the words of Ashoka and seeing the monuments he built, Nehru was filled with pride as he wrote in 1931—on 26 January, which the Congress Party celebrated as Independence Day—from a British prison to his young daughter Indira quoting the eulogy of Ashoka by H.G. Wells I cited in the Prologue. For a man devoted to a secular state, it is telling which of Ashoka's words he chose to cite. They are a paraphrase of Ashoka's advice to the Pasandas to respect and cooperate with each other, found in Rock Edict XII: 'All sects deserve reverence for one reason or another. By thus acting a man exalts his own sect and at the same time does service to the sects of others.'[18]

Fast forward to 1947, and deliberations regarding the modifications to the national flag. Nehru asked for a 'slight change' from the spinning wheel to a simple wheel, the *chakra*. He notes that his mind goes back to a specific wheel, 'the one at the top of the capital of the Aśoka column'. He continues: 'I am exceedingly happy that in this sense indirectly we have associated with this flag of ours not only this emblem but in a sense the name of Aśoka, one of the most magnificent names not only in India's

---

17 Bhagwan Josh 2012: 400 (citing Amaury de Riencourt, *The Soul of India* [London: Jonathan Cape, 1961], p. 367).

18 Cited in Josh 2012: 399.

History but in world history.'[19] Bhagwan Josh summarizes the long journey that created a new Ashoka for a new India:

> Immediately after Independence in 1947, two emblems dominated public and private space in India. From every teaspoon, plate, and teapot in an ambassador's household to the face of every railway engine, from the stamp paper in every court of a small town legalizing every little economic transaction to the currency note of the lowest denomination in every Indian pocket, the omnipresence of Aśoka as the presiding deity of the Indian nation-state cannot be ignored.[20]

The magnificent Sarnath capital with four lions was co-opted by the new Indian state as the national emblem on 26 January 1950, the day the now-independent country adopted a new Constitution. And the State Emblem of India (Prohibition of Improper Use) Act of 2005 puts the connection of the state to the Ashokan lion capital in legal terms:

> [N]o person shall use the emblem or any colourable imitation thereof in any manner which tends to create an impression that it relates to the Government or that it is an official document of the Central Government, or as the case may be, the State Government, without the previous permission of the Central Government or of such officer of that Government as may be authorised by it in this behalf.

The lion capital of Ashoka is now ubiquitous in India (Fig. 9, 10, 11), whether someone is licking a stamp or purchasing something with a coin or paper currency. A bronze replica of the lion capital now sits atop the new parliament building in Delhi.

There is a parallel between the Buddhist and modern Indian reimaginations of Ashoka. Both find in him an ideal ruler—the former because he ushered in the triumph of Buddhism, and the latter, at least in Nehru's vision, because he supported the equality of all religions, with

---

19 Josh 2012: 403.
20 Josh 2012: 394.

the state refusing to take sides. Ashoka's ecumenical project lived on in Nehru's vision for his newly independent country.

The reimagining of Ashoka is part of his legacy, a legacy over which he could exert no control. At some of it he would have looked with amusement. Much of it he would have strongly disapproved of. We can guess what he would have thought when the new Indian state adopted his emblems as mere icons without much commitment to his basic ethical principle of dharma. But, I imagine, he would not have been displeased that his latest reimagination took place within the territory over which he had once ruled. Nor that the founding fathers of the new nation spread across what was once his empire sought to be supportive of the diverse religious traditions flourishing in the land but to favour none, as he had sought to do two millennia ago.

Appendix
Ashoka's Inscriptional Corpus

T HE INSCRIPTIONS ARE ARRANGED, MORE OR LESS, IN A chronological order, except for the donative inscriptions and the Aramaic and Greek inscriptions from Kandahar, which are given just prior to the Pillar Edicts. Given that not all the inscriptions are dated, the order is tentative. The dates given for undated edicts are thus uncertain, but sufficiently close to be helpful.

ORDER OF THE EDICTS

Minor Rock Edicts I and II
Rock Edict Series
Separate Edicts I and II
Buddhist Inscriptions: Bairat and Schism Edicts
Donative and Miscellaneous
Queens, Barabar I, II and III, Lumbini, Nigali-sagar
Aramaic and Greek Edicts
Pillar Edict Series

Minor Rock Edict Series

Minor Rock Edict I has been discovered at the following sites:
Ahraura, Bairat, Brahmagiri, Delhi, Erragudi, Gavimath, Gujarra,

Jatinga-Ramesvara, Maski, Nittur, Paligundu, Panguraria, Rajula-
Mandagiri, Rathanpurwa, Rupnath, Sahasram, Siddapur and
Udegolam. Minor Edict II is added at the following sites: Brahmagiri,
Erragudi, Nittur, Jatinga-Ramesvara, Rajula-Mandagiri, Siddapur and
Udegolam. For the location of these sites, see the Map. The translation
is based on the edition of Paul Kent Andersen (1990).

MINOR ROCK EDICT I

Undated; possibly June 257 BCE

A key word in this edict is 'striving'. Ashoka uses this term in several
of his other edicts as well with reference to both spiritual striving
in the context of dharma and Ashoka's striving to help his subjects
with material and spiritual benefits. Here, for the first time, Ashoka
explicitly refers to his becoming not just a Buddhist but a Buddhist
lay devotee, technically called Upasaka. Many elements of this edict
are obscure, including the meaning of 256. The edict as inscribed at
different locations contains many textual variants. It is noteworthy
that the term 'dharma' does not occur in this edict. For further
discussion, see Chapters 5 and 10.

From Suvarnagiri, at the direction of the prince and of the mahamatras,
the mahamatras of Isila, after wishing them good health, should be told
the following:
**(The above preamble is found only at Brahmagiri and
Siddhapur)**

The Beloved of Gods proclaims the following:

It has been over two and a half years since I have been an Upasaka. But
for one year I did not strive vigorously. It was over a year ago, however,
that I approached the Sangha and began to strive vigorously.[1]

---

1 Although the technical terms 'Upasaka' and 'Sangha' can refer to the devout
laity and the monastic organization of any ascetic religion, such as the Jain,
I think it is very likely that here the terms are used in a Buddhist sense. See
Chapter 5.

But during that time men in Jambudvipa,[2] who were unmingled with gods, were made to mingle with them.[3] For that is the fruit of striving. This can be achieved not only by eminent people, but even lowly people if they strive are indeed able to attain even the immense heaven.

This promulgation has been promulgated for the following purpose— so that both the lowly and the eminent may strive, that the frontier people also may come to know it, and that this striving may endure for a long time. And this matter will spread and spread immensely—spread at least one and a half times more.

This promulgation has been promulgated on completing 256.[4]

(The following supplement is found at Rupnath, Panguraria and Sahasram)

Furthermore, have this matter inscribed on rocks as circumstances permit. And wherever there are stone pillars, you should have it inscribed on stone pillars.

MINOR ROCK EDICT II

Undated; possibly between 257 and 256 BCE

In this edict, Ashoka for the first time brings up the topic of dharma and presents a definition of it. This was probably an oral directive that Ashoka sent out as an addendum or supplement—perhaps as a corrective—to Minor Rock Edict I. It points to his adoption of a new moral philosophy of dharma to anchor his outreach to the population, a message different from that adopted in Minor Rock Edict I. This edict has been badly preserved at the various locations, which poses difficulties to both editor and translator. It is discussed in Chapters 8 and 9.

---

2   Literally, 'island (or continent) of the rose apple'. The appellation generally refers to the land mass of the Indian subcontinent.

3   At some locations the reading is: 'gods who were unmingled with men were made to mingle with them'. For an explanation, see Schmithausen 1992: 130–37.

4   The reference is probably to the completion of a journey of eight months undertaken by Ashoka. See Chapter 5 for an explanation.

(Erragudi Version)

The Beloved of Gods proclaims the following:

What the Beloved of Gods says should be carried out. The rajuka officers should be ordered: they are now to issue orders to the people of the countryside, as also to rastrika officers.

Mother and father should be obeyed. Elders, likewise, should be obeyed. Living creatures should be treated with compassion. Truth should be spoken. These are the attributes of dharma that should be practised.

Thus should you[5] order at the direction of the Beloved of Gods.

You should similarly enjoin those who are elephant-riders, investigators, horse-trainers[6] and Brahmins: 'You should similarly instil in the resident students their obligation to abide by that which is the common standard of old'; 'All the respect that is due to a teacher is due to mine.' Likewise, just as towards the male relatives of the teacher, so also should they comport themselves as appropriate towards his female relatives. Likewise, towards resident students they should comport themselves as appropriate, according to the common standard of old, so that this common standard of old would become abundant. In this manner, you should order the resident students and admonish them.

Thus does the Beloved of Gods order.
Inscribed by the scribe Chapada.

Major Rock Edict Series

This series of fourteen edicts has been discovered at nine locations: Dhauli, Erragudi, Girnar, Jaugada, Kalsi, Mansehra, Sannati,

---

5   The antecedent of 'you' is unclear. It appears that the edict was sent to the princes and mahamatras of southern centres such as Suvarnagiri. If that is so, 'you' here may refer to these high officials.

6   These categories of individuals, especially the second *karanaka*, are difficult to identify, and it is unclear why they have been singled out here. Some have suggested that they have apprentices, but there surely were other professions also which had apprentices. For an interpretation, see Gaál and Tóth 2018.

Shahbazgarhi and Sopara, even though in some only fragments are visible. Their geographical locations are given in the Map. At Dhauli and Jaugada, Rock Edicts XI, XII and XIII are omitted, and two Separate Edicts are added. For a discussion of this series as an anthology, see Chapter 3. The translations of Rock Edicts, unless otherwise stated, are based on the edition of Ulrich Schneider (1978).

ROCK EDICT I

Undated; in or soon after 256 BCE

This very first of the Rock Edict anthology focuses on ahimsa, not injuring, not killing living beings. Its two parts focus on two different kinds of killing. The first deals with ritual killings, both in Brahmanical sacrificial offerings and in folk religious festivals and rituals. The second deals with killing for procuring food, and Ashoka uses the example of his own household and kitchen. At the time of writing this edict, animals were still being killed in his own kitchen, showing the complexity of the prohibition Ashoka envisages. A case could be made that this text is composite, made up of the two parts possibly taken from two different letters of Ashoka and here integrated under the topic of ahimsa. In its original setting, perhaps Ashoka described the kinds of festivals that he considered good. This edict is discussed in Chapters 9 and 11.

This writing on dharma has been made to be inscribed by the Beloved of Gods, King Piyadasi.

Here[7] no living creature is to be slaughtered and offered in sacrifice. And no festivals are to be held, for the Beloved of Gods, King Piyadasi,

---

7   The reference 'here' is unclear. It could be taken literally as referring to the places where the inscription is located. Sometimes Ashoka uses 'here' to refer to Pataliputra, the capital city where he was composing his edicts (see Rock Edict V). I think it is more likely that in this edict 'here' refers to Ashoka's territory, and the term is used with that meaning in Rock Edict XIII. For a discussion of the two parts of this edict, see Vigasin 1997–98.

sees much evil in festivals. There are, however, some festivals that the Beloved of Gods, King Piyadasi, considers good.

Formerly, in the kitchen of the Beloved of Gods, King Piyadasi, many hundreds of thousands of creatures were slaughtered every day to prepare stews. But now when this writing on dharma is being inscribed only three animals are slaughtered to prepare stews: two peacocks and one game animal,[8] and the game animal[8] also not always. Even these three animals are not going to be slaughtered in the future.

ROCK EDICT II

Undated; in or soon after 256 BCE

> The theme of this edict is the provision of medical services and medicinal plants. Ashoka considers his initiatives in these areas as central to his mission of propagating dharma both within his empire and in neighbouring countries. Note the rhetorical repetition of 'everywhere' four times, twice paired with 'wherever'. They underscore the universality of his dharma mission, repeated elsewhere as well. His medical diplomacy constitutes some of the good works about which Ashoka reminisces in Pillar Edict VII (iii). This edict is discussed in Chapter 10.

Everywhere—in the territory of the Beloved of Gods, King Piyadasi, as well as in those at the frontiers, namely, Codas, Pandyas, Satiyaputras, Keralaputras, Tamraparnis, the Greek king named Antiochus, and other kings who are that Antiochus's neighbours—everywhere the Beloved of Gods, King Piyadasi, has established two kinds of medical services: medical services for humans and medical services for domestic animals.

Wherever medicinal herbs beneficial to humans and domestic animals were not found, he had them brought in and planted everywhere.

---

8   The term 'miga' (Sanskrit: mṛga) used here can refer more specifically to a deer, which is the paradigmatic game animal. My translation, however, leaves the term open to a broader interpretation.

Likewise, wherever root vegetables and fruit trees were not found, he had them brought in and planted everywhere.

Along roads he had trees planted and wells dug for the benefit of domestic animals and human beings.

ROCK EDICT III

Undated; in or soon after 256 BCE

> Ashoka here uses the term 'sādhu' as an exclamation at the end of each phrase in the definition of dharma. In addition to its lexical meaning of 'good' and 'excellent', this term developed an exclamatory use corresponding to 'Yes!', 'Well done!', 'Bravo!' and the like. This term is picked up again in Rock Edicts IV, IX and XI. For the history of this term, especially within Buddhism, and for a discussion of this edict, see Chapters 9 and 10.

The Beloved of Gods, King Piyadasi, proclaims the following:

Twelve years after my royal consecration, I issued this order. Everywhere in my territory yukta officers, rajuka officers and pradesika officers should set out on circuit every five years for this purpose: in order to give the following instruction in dharma, as also for other tasks.

Obedience to mother and father—excellent! Giving gifts to friends, companions and relatives, and to Brahmins and Sramanas—excellent! Not killing living beings—excellent! Spending little and accumulating little—excellent!

And the Ministerial Council shall order the yukta officers to register this—giving the rationale and adhering to its provisions.

ROCK EDICT IV

Dated 256 BCE

> Note the repeated use of the term 'increase', vaḍhi, a term that also means 'growth'. Ashoka uses this and related terms frequently elsewhere in his writings. They refer broadly to increase or growth,

depending on the context. In the first sentence the term refers to activities of previous kings cast in a negative light. In the next paragraph it is used positively with reference to Ashoka's own activities. The term is used a total of seven times in this brief edict; it serves to bring a rhetorical unity to Ashoka's essay. In this paragraph Ashoka uses very loose and slightly disjointed syntax, quite common in oral compositions. This edict is discussed in Chapters 9 and 10.

In times past, for many hundreds of years, the following only continued to increase: the slaughter of living beings, the injuring of creatures, disrespect towards relatives, and disrespect towards Sramanas and Brahmins.

But now, due to the practice of dharma by the Beloved of Gods, King Piyadasi—the sound of drums, the sound of 'Ah! Dharma!', displays of celestial chariots, elephants, fiery shafts and other heavenly forms—having shown these to the people, the kinds of things that did not exist for many hundreds of years, today these same things have increased through the instruction in dharma provided by the Beloved of Gods, King Piyadasi:

> Not slaughtering living beings, not injuring creatures, proper regard towards relatives, proper regard towards Sramanas and Brahmins, obedience to mother and father, and obedience to the elderly.

These, as also many other kinds of the practice of dharma, have increased.

And indeed, the Beloved of Gods, King Piyadasi, will continue to bring about the increase of this very practice of dharma. And the sons, grandsons and great-grandsons of the Beloved of Gods, King Piyadasi, will further make this practice of dharma increase until the end of the eon. Abiding in dharma and good conduct, they will provide instruction in dharma. For, this is the paramount task—to provide instruction in dharma. The practice of dharma, however, is not possible for a man devoid of good conduct.

So, to increase this endeavour and not to diminish it—that is excellent!

This has been written for the following purpose: that they should apply themselves to its increase and not countenance its diminution. This was written by the Beloved of Gods, King Piyadasi, twelve years after his royal consecration.

ROCK EDICT V

Undated; in or soon after 256 BCE

> This edict has two parts. The first notes how difficult it is to do good. In a bit of self-praise, Ashoka relates this to the good deeds he has already done, suggesting that he is the first person to have done so. The second part is dominated by the new office he created: dharma-mahamatra. This edict, thus, may also be a composite. But thematically the two sit well together. The description of the duties of dharma-mahamatras appears to offer a definition of this new bureaucracy. For the names of places and peoples listed here, see the Glossary and the Map. This edict is discussed in Chapters 10 and 11.

The Beloved of Gods, King Piyadasi, proclaims the following:

It is difficult to do good. He who is the first to embark on doing good has done something difficult to do. I, on the other hand, have done many good things. Therefore, if my sons and grandsons, and my descendants beyond them until the end of the eon, abide by this in the same manner, they will do the right thing. But he who neglects[9] here even a part, he will do the wrong thing. For the bad is something that readily proliferates.

Now, in times past dharma-mahamatras did not exist at all. But, thirteen years after my royal consecration, I established the dharma-mahamatras.

They are occupied with all the Pasandas for the establishment of dharma and, by the increase of dharma, for the welfare and wellbeing of dharma-devotees among the Greeks, the Kambojas and Gandharas, the Ristikas and Pitinikas, as also among others along the western frontiers.

---

9   The term used here could be causative: 'cause the neglect of even a part'.

They are occupied with Bhatamayas, Bambhanibhiyas,[10] the destitute and the elderly for their welfare and wellbeing, and for the removal of obstacles from dharma-devotees.

They are occupied with prisoners to render them support, to remove obstacles and to set them free when they find: 'This one has to care for family and children'; or 'This one has an obligation'; or 'This one is elderly'.[11]

They are occupied everywhere, here and in outlying cities, with the inner chambers of my brothers and sisters, as well as with other relatives.

'This one is fervent with regard to dharma' or 'this one is established in dharma' or 'this one is devoted to gifts'—thus they are occupied everywhere in my territory with dharma-devotees.

These are the dharma-mahamatras.

For the following purpose has this writing on dharma been inscribed—that it may endure for a long time, and thus my children may act in conformity with it.

ROCK EDICT VI

Undated; in or soon after 256 BCE

Ashoka uses two key expressions here: 'affairs (or business) of the people' and 'everywhere/at all times'. These are repeated in different contexts throughout the edict. Unlike kings of the past, Ashoka intends to attend to the affairs of his subjects at all times. Like the father he claims to be, his time is totally at the disposal of his children,

---

10 These two terms, as Schneider (1978: 128) says, are 'still inexplicable and should therefore not be translated at all'. For attempts to interpret them, see Alsdorf 1960: 260f; K.R. Norman 1966: 117; 1967: 164–66. Given their connection with the destitute and the elderly, they probably refer to social groups needing the assistance of the state.

11 The terms used and the syntax of this sentence are not clear. It is likely that, as Schneider (1978: 130) has noted, the three kinds of assistance given to prisoners correspond to the three situations that the dharma-mahamatras identify among the prisoners under their care.

his subjects. Only by fulfilling this obligation to all his subjects can he be free from his 'debt', the debt he owes to his people. Two other ideas also emerge: 'exertion' and 'striving', two concepts central to Ashoka's mission and already mentioned in Minor Rock Edict I. Here, as in the previous two edicts, Ashoka stresses the novelty of what he is doing: nothing like this has ever been done before. This edict is discussed in Chapters 2 and 10.

The Beloved of Gods, King Piyadasi, proclaims the following:

In times past, this practice did not exist: to bring up at any time the affairs that needed attention or related information. But this is what I have done.

At all times—whether I am eating, in my inner chambers, in my private quarters, at the farm, in a vehicle or in a park—everywhere informants should inform me about the people's affairs. And everywhere I myself attend to the affairs of the people.

Whatever order I issue orally, furthermore, whether it relates to a donation or a proclamation, or else to an urgent matter that is assigned to the mahamatras—in connection with such a matter, if there is a dispute or deliberation in the Council, it should be reported to me immediately everywhere and at all times.

Thus have I ordered.

For, I am never complacent in exerting myself and in carrying the affairs to a conclusion. For, I consider the welfare of all the people as my responsibility. The root of that, again, is exertion and carrying the affairs to a conclusion. For there is no task more important than working for the welfare of the whole world.

And whatever striving I have made, it is for this: that I may become freed from my debt to creatures, that I may procure wellbeing for them in this world, and that they may attain heaven in the next.

Now, this writing on dharma has been inscribed for the following purpose: that it may endure for a long time, and thus my sons and grandsons may strive for the welfare of the whole world. But this is truly difficult to accomplish without utmost striving.

ROCK EDICT VII

Undated; in or soon after 256 BCE

> This brief edict permitting all Pasandas to reside everywhere in
> Ashoka's territory implies that this may not have been so in the past.
> That ideally all Pasandas seek self-restraint and purity of heart is
> repeated in Rock Edict XII. This feature of Pasanda life is contrasted
> to that of ordinary people, who are swayed by passions and desires,
> and who are not as single-minded in their pursuit of dharma as are
> the Pasandas. This edict is discussed in Chapters 11 and 12.

The Beloved of Gods, King Piyadasi, desires that all Pasandas may reside
everywhere.[12] For, all of them desire self-restraint and purity of heart.

   But the common people have diverse yearnings and diverse passions.
They carry out all or just a part.[13] Even the giving of copious gifts,
however, is clearly paltry when there is no self-restraint, purity of heart,
gratitude and firm devotion.

ROCK EDICT VIII

Undated; in or soon after 256 BCE

> In this short edict, Ashoka once again contrasts his behaviour to that
> of his predecessors. They undertook outings to pursue recreational
> activities such as hunting. Ashoka's outings are for the purpose of
> dharma alone. The same term, *yātā* (Sanskrit: *yātrā*), is used for both
> kinds of tours. Although he speaks only about his visit to the Buddha's
> place of enlightenment, implicit here is that he was in the habit of

---

12 The order of the words in the sentence complicate its syntax. What Ashoka
    probably meant was to permit all Pasandas to reside anywhere they chose
    within his kingdom.

13 Ashoka does not tell us of what they carry out only a part. The reference is
    probably to what Ashoka expects the people to do, probably the dharma. This
    topic is mentioned in Rock Edict V, and fully explored in Separate Edicts I
    and II.

undertaking dharma tours to assist his subjects and to teach them dharma. This edict is discussed in Chapters 5 and 10.

In times past, Beloveds of Gods [= kings] used to set out on recreational tours. During these, hunting and other such enjoyments took place.

But, the Beloved of Gods, King Piyadasi, ten years after his royal consecration, set out to Enlightenment.[14] Through that came about the dharma tour.

During it the following take place: paying visits to Sramanas and Brahmins and making gifts to them, paying visits to elderly people and providing monetary support to them, paying visits to people of the countryside, providing instruction in dharma and in germane questions about dharma.

This gives greater enjoyment to the Beloved of Gods, King Piyadasi; the other is but a fraction.

ROCK EDICT IX

Undated; in or soon after 256 BCE

> This edict presents a good example of how Ashoka attempts to show that folk ritual practices are of little significance. In contrast, his own practice of dharma bears everlasting fruit. Note Ashoka's literary sleight of hand when he calls dharma itself the best kind of auspicious rite (*maṅgala*), thus grafting his new religion of dharma on to the old folk practices called *maṅgala*, paralleling the double entendre of *yātrā* in the previous edict. This edict is discussed in Chapters 2, 10 and 11.

The Beloved of Gods, King Piyadasi, proclaims the following:

People perform auspicious rites of diverse kinds—during an illness, at the marriage of a son or daughter, at the birth of a child, when setting

---

14 The term here is '*saṃbodhi*', which literally means enlightenment. There is a difference of opinion as to whether Ashoka set out on an inner journey in quest of enlightenment or set out to the place or the tree where the Buddha gained enlightenment. I have opted for the second: 'Enlightenment' as a place name: see Chapter 6.

out on a journey. On these and other similar occasions, people perform numerous auspicious rites. At such times, however, womenfolk perform many, diverse, trifling and useless auspicious rites.

Now, clearly, auspicious rites are going be performed. But, equally clearly, such auspicious rites bear little fruit.

But this, clearly, is what bears copious fruit, namely, the auspicious rite of dharma. It consists of the following:

Proper regard towards slaves and servants, reverence towards elders, self-restraint with respect to living beings, and giving gifts to Sramanas and Brahmins.

This and anything else like it is called an 'auspicious rite of dharma'.

Therefore, a father, son, brother, master, friend, companion or even a neighbour should say: 'This is excellent! This auspicious rite of dharma should be performed until the object is achieved.'

From here the text continues in two recensions. The first is found at Dhauli, Jaugada and Girnar, and the second at Erragudi, Kalsi, Mansehra and Shahbazgarhi.

[First Recension]

'Even when it is achieved, I will perform this again.'

For other auspicious rites are of questionable efficacy—perhaps one may achieve the objective and perhaps one may not. And it pertains only to this world here. This auspicious rite of dharma, on the other hand, is timeless. Even if one does not achieve the objective here, yet endless merit is produced in the hereafter. If, on the other hand, one achieves the objective here, thereby both are obtained—here that objective and hereafter endless merit is produced by means of that auspicious rite of dharma.

[Second Recension]

Furthermore, it has been said: 'Giving gifts is excellent.' But there is no gift or favour comparable to the gift of dharma or the favour of dharma.

For that reason, however, a friend, well-wisher, relative or companion should clearly counsel on particular occasions: 'This ought to be done. This is excellent. By this it is possible to attain heaven.' For what is more important to do than this by which heaven is attained?

ROCK EDICT X

Undated; in or soon after 256 BCE

> This edict contains a significant reflection on glory and fame, central quests of kings and warriors. As 'auspicious rites' (*maṅgala*) of the previous edict, so here Ashoka makes fame a vehicle for his dharma mission. Also note the return of the term 'strive', prominent in Minor Rock Edict I and Rock Edict VI, a term that is central to Ashoka's understanding of how to live a virtuous life and how to lead an effective administration. The statement at the end of the edict that one must strive 'forsaking everything' may imply an exhortation to undertake a renunciate mode of life. This edict is discussed in Chapters 2 and 10.

The Beloved of Gods, King Piyadasi, does not consider glory or fame as offering great benefits, with this exception—whatever glory and fame the Beloved of Gods, King Piyadasi, seeks, it is so that in the present and in the future people may observe obedience to dharma and follow my teaching of dharma. It is for this reason, the Beloved of Gods, King Piyadasi, seeks glory or fame.

Whatever the Beloved of Gods, King Piyadasi, strives to do, however, all that is solely for the sake of the hereafter, so that everyone would have few hazards. But this is the hazard: lack of merit.

This is difficult to do, however, for either a low-class person or a high-class person without utmost striving, giving up everything. But between them, it is clearly more difficult to do for a high-class person.

ROCK EDICT XI

Undated; in or soon after 256 BCE

As 'auspicious rites' in Rock Edict IX and 'fame' in Rock Edict X, so here the word Ashoka latches on to is 'gift'. The centrality of giving gifts—generosity and hospitality—in ancient Indian culture in general, and especially in Ashoka's definitions of dharma, is well known. But here he downplays the significance of material gifts to place his preaching of dharma, which is his 'gift of dharma', at the centre as the most important gift a person can make. This edict is discussed in Chapters 9 and 10.

The Beloved of Gods, King Piyadasi, proclaims the following:

There is no gift comparable to the gift of dharma—the praise of dharma, the distribution of dharma, the bond through dharma. From that follows:

Proper regard towards slaves and servants; obedience to mother and father; giving gifts to friends, companions and relatives, and to Sramanas and Brahmins; and not killing living beings.

A father, son, brother, master, friend, companion or even a neighbour should say this: 'This is excellent! This is to be carried out.'

If someone carries it out, he gains this world and generates endless merit in the hereafter—by this gift of dharma.

ROCK EDICT XII

Undated; in or soon after 256 BCE

It is in this edict that Ashoka addresses the topic of Pasandas most directly and in greatest detail, as also the two groups of religious people: the 'gone forth' (*pravrajita*) and the 'stay-at-home' (*gṛhastha*), topics that are of great significance to Indian religious history.[15]

---

15 The topic of Pasandas and the 'stay-at-home' have been studied in detail in the edited volume of essays: Olivelle 2019. See, especially, Brereton's essay on Pasandas in that volume.

A central concern of Ashoka with respect to interactions among various religious groups is 'guarding speech'. The 'essential core' here likely refers to dharma. Ashoka plays with the terms for 'listen to' (or obedience), 'learn' and 'learned'—all derived from the Sanskrit/Prakrit verbal root 'to hear'. The only way that members of the Pasandas can become 'highly/much learned', literally 'much heard' (*bahu* = many, much; *suta* = heard) is by hearing and listening to a wide variety of people and doctrines. They can become 'highly learned' only by cooperating with and listening to other Pasanda groups. Showing Ashoka's rhetorical skills, the main section of the edict begins and ends with the same expression: 'No gift or homage is as highly prized by the Beloved of Gods.' This edict is discussed in Chapters 11 and 12.

The Beloved of Gods, King Piyadasi, pays homage to all Pasandas, to those who have gone forth and to those staying at home, with gifts and with various acts of homage.

No gift or homage, however, is as highly prized by the Beloved of Gods as this: namely, that the essential core may increase among all Pasandas. But the increase of the essential core takes many forms. This, however, is its root, namely, guarding speech—that is to say, not paying homage to one's own Pasanda and not denigrating the Pasandas of others when there is no occasion, and even when there is an occasion, doing so mildly. Homage, on the other hand, should indeed be paid to the Pasandas of others in one form or another. Acting in this manner, one certainly enhances one's own Pasanda and also helps the Pasanda of the other.

When someone acts in a way different from that, one hurts one's own Pasanda and also harms the Pasanda of the other. For, should someone pay homage to his own Pasanda and denigrate the Pasanda of another wholly out of devotion to his own Pasanda, thinking, that is, 'I'll make my Pasanda illustrious'—by so doing he damages his own Pasanda even more certainly.

Therefore, meeting one another is, indeed, excellent. That is—they should both listen to and take guidance from[16] each other's dharma. For

16 The terms '*suneyu*' and '*susūseyu*' generally mean 'listen/hear' and 'obey'. I think Ashoka is using the sound similarity and the etymology (both coming

this is the wish of the Beloved of Gods. That is—all Pasandas should become highly learned and follow good discipline. And no matter which of these they may be devoted to, they should acknowledge: 'No gift or homage is as highly prized by the Beloved of Gods as this: namely, that the essential core may increase among all Pasandas.'

Large numbers, furthermore, have been dispatched for this purpose— dharma-mahamatras, mahamatras overseeing women, officers in charge of farms, and other classes of officers. And this is its fruit: enhancement of one's own Pasanda and making dharma illustrious.

ROCK EDICT XIII

Undated; in or soon after 256 BCE

> In this, the most self-reflective of his writings, Ashoka explores the terms for conquering and conquest: *vijita*, *vijaya*, and finds, once again, a way to lead the reader back to dharma. There is a higher kind of conquest that we must aspire to, and that is *dharma-vijaya*, conquest achieved through dharma, or perhaps the conquest of dharma. Normal conquests through force of arms result in death, destruction and mental anguish, as happened during Ashoka's conquest of Kalinga. This edict is discussed in Chapters 2, 9 and 10.

Eight years after the royal consecration of the Beloved of Gods, King Piyadasi, the Kalingas were conquered. People deported from there numbered 150,000; those killed there totalled 100,000; and almost that many died.[17] Thereafter, now that the Kalingas have been secured, the

---

from the Sanskrit root √*śrū*, to hear/listen) to good effect—the hearer/reader would note the double meaning of the second word. It is doubtful that Ashoka would have wanted one Pasanda to actually obey other Pasandas. Likewise, in the next sentence he uses the term '*bahusutā*', generally meaning 'learned', but here also connected to the previous two words both in sound and in etymology.

17 The meaning of the term '*bahutāvatake*' is not altogether clear. It probably means 'almost as many', as noted by Norman 1972 in *Collected Papers* I: 150, and Schneider 1978: 117. This meaning is confirmed by the Greek translation

intense study of dharma, love of dharma and instruction in dharma occupy the Beloved of Gods.

This is the regret that the Beloved of Gods has after conquering the Kalingas. For, conquering an unconquered land entails the killing, death and deportation of people. That is deemed extremely painful and grievous by the Beloved of Gods. But this is deemed even more grievous by the Beloved of Gods, that Brahmins or Sramanas, or other Pasandas or those staying at home and dwelling there who are well cared for—among whom are established obedience to authority, obedience to mother and father, obedience to elders and proper regard to friends, companions, associates and relatives, and to slaves and servants, and firm devotion—that they endure there the injury, killing or deportation of their loved ones. Even people who are well cared for and whose love is undiminished, when misfortune strikes their friends, companions, associates and relatives, it causes injury to those very people. This is the common plight of all human beings, and it is deemed grievous by the Beloved of Gods.

There is no land, furthermore, except among the Greeks, where these classes—Brahmins and Sramanas—are not found. Yet, even where they are not found, there is no land where human beings are not devoted to one Pasanda or another. Therefore, of the number of people who were killed, died and were deported among the Kalingas, today even one-hundredth or one-thousandth part of that would be deemed grievous by the Beloved of Gods.

And further, should someone commit an offence today, if it can be forgiven the Beloved of God thinks he should be forgiven. And even the forest people living within the territory of the Beloved of Gods—he conciliates them also and persuades them to be favourably disposed. And he also tells them of the remorse, as also the power, of the Beloved of Gods, so that they may become contrite and never engage in killing.[18] For,

___

of this edict in Kandahar II. Others take the expression to mean 'many times that number'.

18 Here, Ashoka is asking the forest people (*aṭavi*) to be like him—to be remorseful of past deeds and to keep to the path of ahimsa. Others have translated: 'and may not get killed', thus making this a statement about

what the Beloved of Gods wishes for all creatures is this: freedom from injury, self-restraint, impartiality and gentleness.

This, however, is deemed the foremost conquest by the Beloved of Gods, namely, conquest through dharma. This again has been secured by the Beloved of Gods here and among all the neighbouring lands—as far as 600 *yojanas*[19] where the Greek king named Antiochus resides; and, beyond that Antiochus, the four kings named Tulamaya, Antekina, Maka and Alikasundale;[20] and, consistently,[21] the Codas, the Pandyas, and as far as Tamraparni. Likewise, here in the king's domain, among the Greeks and Kambojas, the Nabhakas and Nabhapanktis, the Bhojas and Pitinikas, the Andhras and Paladas—everywhere they follow the instruction in dharma of the Beloved of Gods.[22]

Even where envoys of the Beloved of Gods do not go, after hearing the discourses on dharma, the ordinances and instruction in dharma of the Beloved of Gods, they conform to dharma, and they will conform to it in the future. In this manner, this conquest has been secured everywhere. In all cases, however, the conquest is a source of joy. So, joy has been secured by the conquest through dharma.

But that joy, clearly, is fleeting. Only what is done for the hereafter, the Beloved of Gods thinks, bears great fruit.

And it is for this purpose that this writing on dharma has been inscribed, to wit, that my sons and grandsons may not think that a new realm is worth conquering, that they find pleasure in kindness and lenient

---

Ashoka's ability to kill the forest people if they do not behave. I think both grammatically and contextually the latter interpretation is less likely.

19 This is likely to be a distance of 4,320 kilometres. See Chapter 2 for a more detailed discussion.

20 These have been identified as Ptolemy II Philadelphus of Egypt (285–247 BCE), Antigonus Gonatas of Macedonia (276–239 BCE), Magas of Cyrene (death dated to between 258 and 250 BCE), and the last either Alexander of Corinth (252–244 BCE) or Alexander of Epirus (272–255 BCE).

21 The meaning appears to be that Ashoka worked with these southern areas constantly, as opposed to his endeavours among the Hellenistic kingdoms of the northwest where his efforts may have been more sporadic.

22 For these geographical locations, see the Glossary and the Map.

punishment in their own territory, and that they consider the only real conquest to be conquest through dharma, for that is conquest in this world and the next world. And may every pleasure be pleasure through dharma—for that is pleasure in this world and the next.

ROCK EDICT XIV

Undated; in or soon after 256 BCE

> This last statement of the Rock Edict anthology functions as a coda and parallels the beginning of the very first edict with identical words. The two thus act as bookends to the anthology. This coda makes it clear that not all of Ashoka's writings have been engraved, and some have been given in abbreviated form.

This writing on dharma has been made to be inscribed by the Beloved of Gods, King Piyadasi. It is given in greatly or moderately abbreviated form or in greater detail, for not everything is suitable for every place. For, my territory is vast, and I have written a lot. And I will always have still more written. Some of it has been repeated over and over again because of the charm of various topics, so people would act accordingly. Here and there, however, some may have been written incompletely either bearing the region in mind, or taking a particular reason into account, or due to the fault of the scribes.

Separate Rock Edict Series

Undated

The two edicts in this series have been discovered at two locations, Dhauli and Jaugada, both in Odisha, called Kalinga during Ashoka's time. A third version found recently at Sannati is badly preserved. Some have called these 'Kalinga edicts', but, although found in Kalinga and addressed to officials of Tosali and Samapa located in Kalinga, they are not exclusively addressed to the people of Kalinga. Ashoka mentions the prince and mahamatras of Ujjain and Taxila, located far from Kalinga. Sannati is also outside of that region. Although I follow the traditional numbering of the two edicts, Separate Edict I is actually the second of the two, and Separate Edict II is the first; I have given them in that sequence.[23] The readings at the two sites differ. For the translations I have used the Dhauli version, supplemented where necessary by the Jaugada. For a detailed study of these two edicts, see Alsdorf (1962), on whose edition this translation is based.

Two central themes emerge in these two edicts. The first is the trope of the king as the father and his subjects as children, a trope found in Ashoka's other writings as well. The second is the debt that officials owe to the emperor. This way of describing the obligations of imperial officers is found only in the Separate Edicts, even though Ashoka's own debt to his subjects is mentioned elsewhere as well.

The Separate Edicts are discussed in Chapters 2 and 10.

SEPARATE EDICT II (= FIRST EDICT)

At the direction of the Beloved of Gods,[24] the prince and mahamatras at Tosali[25] are to be instructed.[26]

Whatever I set my eyes on, that I seek to carry out through action and to realize through appropriate means. And I consider this to be the principal means in this matter—to give you instruction.

All men are my children. Now, what I desire for my children, namely, that they be provided with complete welfare and wellbeing in this world and the next, the same do I desire for all men.

It might occur to the frontier people outside my territorial jurisdiction: 'What are the king's intentions with respect to us?' This

23 The strongest evidence for this comes from Sannati, where Separate Edict II is given immediately after Rock Edict XIV.
24 The parallel passage in the Jaugada version reads: 'The Beloved of Gods says thus.'
25 The Jaugada version omits the prince and reads: 'Mahamatras at Samāpā.'
26 It is unclear who precisely is to carry these instructions to the mahamatras. The likely candidate is the group of people called *puruṣa* ('men'), who are the personal emissaries of Ashoka (see Pillar Edicts I, IV, VII).

alone is my wish with respect to the frontier people—they should gain the conviction:

This is what the Beloved of Gods wishes: 'They should not fear me but have confidence in me. They will obtain wellbeing alone from me, not grief.'

They should also know this:

'The Beloved of Gods will forgive us what can be forgiven.'[27]

At my behest, they should practise dharma and gain this world and the next.

For this purpose am I instructing you—that I may be freed from my debt through this, namely, by instructing you and by informing you of my wish, which is my firm resolution and unshakeable pledge. So, by doing this you must fulfil your task and reassure them, in order that they may gain the conviction:

'The Beloved of Gods is just like a father to us. The Beloved of Gods has compassion for us just as he has for himself. To the Beloved of Gods, we are just like his own children.'

After I have given you my instructions and informed you of my wish, I will have done my duty for the country. For you are up to this task: to inspire confidence in them, to procure welfare and wellbeing in this world and the next. Acting in this manner, moreover, you will attain heaven and be freed from your debt to me.

And for this purpose has this writing been inscribed here—so that the mahamatras may display constant effort at inspiring confidence and at fostering the practice of dharma among those frontier people. And this writing should be listened to during every four-month season on the days of the Tishya constellation. Even in between the days of the Tishya when an opportunity presents itself, even a single individual, if he so wishes, may listen to it. Acting in this manner, you will be able to carry it out fully.[28]

---

27 The same statement is made with regard to forest people in Rock Edict XIII.

28 This expression is elucidated in Separate Edict I (= #2), where Ashoka speaks of the average, exceptional and perfect performance by his officials.

SEPARATE EDICT I (= SECOND EDICT)

At the direction of the Beloved of Gods,[29] the mahamatras of Tosali,[30] who are the judicial officers of the city, are to be so instructed.

Whatever I set my eyes on, that I seek to carry out through action and to realize through appropriate means. And I consider this to be the principal means in this matter—to give you instruction. For, you take care of many thousands of living beings with the thought, 'Would that we gain the affection of men.'

All men are my children. Now, what I desire for my children, namely, that they be provided with complete welfare and wellbeing in this world and the next, the same do I desire for all men. But you do not realize how far-reaching this matter is. Perhaps one officer may realize it, and he too only partially, not fully.

For, you must look into this—'Are they well cared for?'—constantly. If a single officer learns of someone's imprisonment or torture, the result is that for no reason his imprisonment happens to be terminated, whereas many others continue to suffer. In such cases, you must aspire: 'We will keep to the middle way.'[31] One fails to act in this manner due to these proclivities: envy, quick temper, cruelty, haste, lack of zeal, laziness and lethargy. So, you must aspire: 'May these proclivities not develop in us.' The root of all this is being always free of quick temper and haste. Anyone who is lethargic should pull himself up and get going, proceed and advance.

Whoever among you looks at it the same way should tell each other:

Look, such and such are the instructions of the Beloved of Gods. Carrying them out fully yields great reward, while failure to carry them out fully brings great misfortune. For, by carrying them out improperly one gets neither heavenly favours nor royal favours.

---

29 The parallel passage in the Jaugada version reads: 'The Beloved of Gods says thus.'

30 Samāpā in the version at Jaugada.

31 The middle way probably refers to the 'impartiality in judicial proceedings and impartiality in imposing punishments' mentioned in Pillar Edict IV.

The average performance of this task brings a double reward; how much more, then, when it is carried out to an exceptional degree! If you carry it out fully, however, you will attain heaven and you will be freed from your debt to me.

This writing, furthermore, should be listened to on the day of the Tishya constellation. Even in between the days of the Tishya, when an opportunity presents itself, even a single individual may listen to it. And acting in this way, you will be able to carry it out fully.

For this purpose has this writing been inscribed here, so that judicial officers of the city may at all times see to it that the people are not shackled or subjected to torture without reason. And also for this purpose I will dispatch every five years a mahamatra who is neither harsh nor fierce, and who is gentle in his actions in order to find out whether they are acting according to my instructions.

From Ujjain also, furthermore, the prince should dispatch for this purpose an individual of the same type—and he should not let three years pass without doing this. Likewise, also from Taxila. When these mahamatras set out on a tour without neglecting their own tasks, they should find out also whether they are acting according to the king's instructions.

MESSAGES TO THE BUDDHIST SANGHA

The Bairat Inscription

Undated

> Inscribed on a stone at Bairat, now exhibited at the Asiatic Society in Kolkata.
>
> Although this letter of Ashoka's has been discovered only in one location, it is likely that it was sent to Buddhist monasteries in different parts of the country. Ashoka uses very polite language—a language used by laypeople when addressing monks—yet he makes it very clear that he expected monks of these monasteries to follow his 'wishes', the gentle way Ashoka often couches his commands. Note that he does not use his formal title 'the Beloved of Gods' in his

letter, but simply calls himself 'king of Magadha'. I use the edition of
Schneider (1982). This inscription is discussed in Chapter 6.

Piyadasi, the king of Magadha, having paid his respects to the Sangha,
extends his wishes for your wellbeing and comfort.

It is known to you, Venerable Sirs, my esteem for and faith in the
Buddha, the dharma and the Sangha. Whatsoever, Venerable Sirs, the
Lord Buddha has spoken, all that has been well-spoken indeed. But,
Venerable Sirs, what I see as embodying the statement 'Thus the True
Dharma will long endure',[32] I take the liberty to state that—namely,
Venerable Sirs, these discourses on Dharma:

> *Vinayasamukase* (Exaltation of Monastic Disciplinary Rules),
> *Aliyavasāni* (Lineages of Noble Ones), *Anāgatabhayāni* (Future
> Dangers), *Munigāthā* (Sage's Poem), *Moneyasūte* (Discourse on
> Sagehood), *Upatisapasine* (Upatissa's Questions), and *Lāgulovāde*
> (Advice to Rahula) relating to falsehood,

spoken by the Lord Buddha.[33]

These discourses on Dharma, Venerable Sirs—I wish that large numbers
of monks and nuns will listen to them repeatedly and reflect on them, so
also male Upasakas and female Upasikas. For this reason, Venerable Sirs,
this has been inscribed, so that they will know my intention.

Schism Edict

Undated

> Versions of this edict are found inscribed on pillars at Allahabad-
> Kosambi, Sanchi and Sarnath. Parts of the inscribed text are

---

32 It was E. Hardy (1901) who first suggested that this was a quotation from
Buddhist scripture and alluded to *Aṅguttara Nikāya* (III; pp. 247). Ashoka says
that even though *all* of the Buddha's discourses are well said, the discourses
he enumerates here are the ones that will actually make the prediction 'Thus
the True Dharma will long endure' come true.

33 There have been numerous attempts to identify these seven texts within the
Pali canon: Winternitz 1972: 606–09; Norman 2012a: 141–42; Schmithausen
1992: 113–17. For a discussion, see Chapter 6.

unreadable and mutilated at all three locations. I use the reconstructed edition given by Alsdorf (1959). This edict is discussed in Chapter 6.

(Allahabad-Kosambi Version)

The Beloved of Gods orders: the mahamatras of Kosambi should be instructed—

[*Sanchi and Sarnath versions add*: 'The division of the Sangha by anyone should not be tolerated.']

The unity of the Sangha has been instituted [*Sanchi version adds*: 'as long as my sons and great-grandsons, as long as the moon and the sun']. In the Sangha, no division is to be tolerated. Whoever divides the Sangha, be it a monk or a nun, that person should be made to put on white clothes and to reside in a non-monastic residence.

Sarnath Supplement

At Sarnath, what appears to have been a 'cover letter' to the officials is also inscribed. It sheds light on what Ashoka expected his officials to do with respect to ensuring discipline within the Sangha. The translation is based on the edition of Hultzsch (1925).

This decree should be communicated in this form both to the Sangha of monks and to the Sangha of nuns.

The Beloved of Gods says the following—

Let one copy of this edict remain with you, deposited in the bureau, and have one copy of it deposited with the Upasakas. And let these Upasakas go on every Uposatha day so that trust may be developed in this decree; and consistently on every Uposatha day let respective mahamatras go to the Uposatha ceremony so that trust may be developed in this decree and attention paid to it.

And as far as your jurisdiction extends, you should dispatch officers everywhere adhering to the provisions of this directive. Likewise, adhering to the provisions of this directive, you should have officers dispatched to all the areas around forts.

MISCELLANEOUS AND DONATIVE INSCRIPTIONS

Queen's Edict

Undated

> This letter of Ashoka to his senior bureaucrats was probably never
> intended to be inscribed. It found its way to the Allahabad Pillar thanks
> to an overzealous local official. It deals with some accounting practices
> relating to donations made by members of Ashoka's household. This
> edict is discussed in Chapter 3.

At the direction of the Beloved of Gods, the mahamatras everywhere
should be instructed:

> Whatever gift is given there[34] by the second queen—a mango grove,
> garden, almshouse or anything else at all—it is credited to that queen.
> You should credit it to the second queen, that is, Kaluvaki, the mother
> of Tivala.

Barabar Hill Cave Inscription I

Dated 256 BCE

King Piyadasi, twelve years after his royal consecration, donated this
Nigoha cave to the Ajivikas.

Barabar Hill Cave Inscription II

Dated 256 BCE

King Piyadasi, twelve years after his royal consecration, donated this cave
in the Kalatika Hill to the Ajivikas.

---

34 The reference of this term (*hetā*) is unclear, but it probably refers to
the localities overseen by the mahamatras in which the donations were
distributed.

Barabar Hill Cave Inscription III

Dated 249 BCE

> The translation is based on the reading established by Harry Falk
> (2006: 266; and 2008).

King Piyadasi, nineteen years after his royal consecration, came to Jalutha,
on which occasion he donated this cave, Supriyeksa, to the Ajivikas.

Lumbini Pillar Inscription

Dated 248 BCE

The Beloved of Gods, King Piyadasi, twenty years after his royal
consecration, came in person and paid reverence.

Saying, 'Here was born the Buddha, the Sakya sage,' he had a stone
fence constructed and a stone pillar erected.

Saying, 'Here was born the Lord,'[35] he made the village of Lumbini
tax-free and to have a one-eighth portion.[36]

Nigali-sagar Pillar Inscription

Possibly 248 BCE

The Beloved of Gods, King Piyadasi, fourteen years after his royal
consecration, enlarged the stupa of Buddha Konakamana to double its

---

35 This is a citation of the Buddha's own words predicting pilgrimages to places
associated with the four major events in the Buddha's life: birth (Lumbini),
enlightenment (Bodh Gaya), preaching the first sermon (Sarnath) and death
(Kushinara). See *Mahāparinirvāṇasūtra*, Waldschmidt 1951, p. 388 (§41.7–8).
For a discussion of the Buddhist pilgrimage practices that underlies Ashoka's
statement, see Schopen 1987 (in 1997, pp. 115–18).

36 Falk (2012) has argued that the 'one-eighth portion' refers to the remains of
the Buddha interred in the stupa at Lumbini.

size. (And twenty years)[37] after his royal consecration, he came in person and paid reverence, and had a stone pillar[38] erected.

Panguraria Inscription

Undated

> The translation is based on the reading established by Harry Falk (1997).

The king named Piyadasi, when he was a prince and living with his consort, came to this place while he was on a recreational tour.

ARAMAIC AND GREEK EDICTS

KANDAHAR I: Bilingual

Undated

Aramaic

When[39] ten years had passed to him who is Lord Piyadarśi the king, he practised truth (= dharma). From then on, he has reduced disease for all the people and demolished all hostile things. And joy arises over the whole land. In addition to this, with respect to the food of our lord the king, very little killing is done. Seeing this, all the people refrained (from killing). And in the case of those who caught fish, those people abjured that. Likewise, with respect to those who were trappers, they have refrained from trapping. People are obedient to their mothers and fathers and to elders, as destiny has laid out to them. And there is no

---

37 Here, the words for the years are missing and have been reconstructed on the basis of the Lumbini inscription.

38 There is a lacuna here, and the words have been reconstructed.

39 In this translation I was assisted by my colleague Professor Na'ama Pat-El, an expert in Aramaic, at the Department of Middle Eastern Studies at the University of Texas at Austin, and by the previous translations by Itō 1977: 156–61; and Garbini, in Carratelli and Garbini 1964: 41–62.

judgment of people. This has benefited all the people and will continue
to benefit them.

Greek

When[40] ten years had been completed, King Piodasses [= Piyadasi]
disclosed piety [= dharma] to men. And from that time, he has made men
more pious, and everything thrives throughout the whole world. And
the king abstains (from killing) living beings, and other men, as also the
king's hunters and fishermen, have refrained from hunting. And if some
lacked self-control, they have gained self-control to the extent that they
could. And they became obedient to their father and mother and to their
elders, in contrast to the past. And by so acting on every occasion in the
future, they will live better and more happily.

KANDAHAR II

Undated

Greek

The first half of the Greek translation is based on Rock Edict XII.

... piety[41] [= dharma] and self-control in all the schools [= Pasanda]. Self-
control is especially a matter of controlling one's tongue. And they should
neither praise themselves nor criticize other schools for anything, for that
is hollow. It is better to try to praise other schools and not to criticize
them in any way. By keeping to that, they will enhance their reputation
and win over others. By flouting that, their reputation will suffer, and

---

40 Translation based on the one provided by my colleague Professor Michael
   Gagarin, an expert in early Greek epigraphy, at the Department of Classics of
   the University of Texas at Austin. I have also benefited from the translation
   by Carratelli (Carratelli and Garbini 1964: 32). See also Maniscalco 2018:
   252–53; Scerrato 1958.

41 Translation based on the one provided by Michael Gagarin. See also
   Schlumberger and Benveniste 1965; and Maniscalco 2018: 256–57.

they will be disliked by others. Those who praise themselves and criticize others merely feed their self-love; wishing to outshine others, they end up causing more harm to themselves. It is proper that they admire one another and learn from each other. By doing that they will know more, and each person will communicate to others what he knows. And to those who practise this we must not be afraid to say these things, so that they always persevere in piety [= dharma].

The second half of the Greek translation is based on Rock Edict XIII.

In the eighth year of his reign, Piodasses conquered Kalinga. 150,000 people were captured and deported, 100,00 were killed, and almost as many died. Since that time, mercy and compassion have taken hold of him and weighed him down. Just as he has decreed the abstention (from killing) living beings, so has he established and organized zeal for piety [= dharma]. And what has caused even more grief to the king is this. All those who lived there, Brahmins or Sramanas or others who practised piety—those who lived there who had to be mindful of the interests of the king, who revere and respect their teacher and their father and mother, who love and not deceive friends and companions, and who treat their slaves and servants with as light a hand as possible—if one of those among them who behaved like this had died or been deported, the others also felt the impact of this, and the king is terribly distressed by all this. And that among other peoples, there is…

KANDAHAR III

Undated

Prakrit in Aramaic Transliteration with Aramaic Translation
Only a fragment of this inscription is preserved. The translation below is from Gikyo Itō (1969).

All whatever is good, indeed, has been done by me. (To this) the whole world has conformed. Therefore, they have promoted (or increased) as well … the one obedient to his own mother and to his own father, the one obedient to teachers, the one respectful to Brahmins and the Sramanas, the one conforming to the elders, the one respectful of humbles and the slave.

—

I have not given here Ashoka's Aramaic inscription of Taxila. The authenticity of the Taxila inscription has been disputed. Falk (2006: 252) observes: '[T]here is no hint in the text itself that it was produced by orders of Aśoka. The only thing that is certain is that it mentions his name.'

Pillar Edict Series

The first six of the Pillar Edict series, just like the Rock Edict series, constitute an anthology. They have been discovered at six locations: Allahabad, Araraj, Mirath, Nandangarh, Rampurva and Delhi-Topra. The seventh edict is added on the Delhi-Topra pillar. The translations are based on the edition of Hultzsch (1925).

PILLAR EDICT I

Dated 242 BCE

The central theme of this first of the Pillar Edict series is how people can practise dharma. It requires, first, utmost personal effort and exertion (see 'striving' in Minor Rock Edict I and Rock Edict X); it is not an easy thing to do. Second, it requires governmental assistance in the form of Ashoka's personal instruction and example, efforts of his dharma-mahamatras and other personal emissaries, and the work of frontier officials—the last, perhaps, in the case of people who are not fully integrated into the Ashokan state. This edict is discussed in Chapters 2 and 10.

The Beloved of Gods, King Piyadasi, proclaims the following:

This writing on dharma has been made to be inscribed by me twenty-six years after my royal consecration.[42]

What pertains to this world and the next is difficult to procure except through utmost love of dharma, through utmost circumspection, through utmost obedience, through utmost fear and through utmost exertion. But, indeed, through my instruction this concern for dharma and love of dharma have increased day by day, and they will continue to increase. And my personal emissaries also—the high-ranking, the low-ranking, and the mid-ranking—conform to it and procure it, and they are able to inspire the wavering. So also do the frontier mahamatras, for this is the directive—protecting according to dharma, governing according to dharma, bestowing wellbeing according to dharma and guarding according to dharma.

PILLAR EDICT II

Dated 242 BCE

The edict has two distinct parts. The first continues the theme of dharma from the previous. Here, Ashoka says: 'Dharma is excellent!', using the multivalent term '*sādhu*', which was used in Rock Edict III in the context of the components of dharma. As opposed to Rock Edict III, the acts comprising dharma are given here as abstract virtues.

The second part of the edict turns to Ashoka's good deeds. He speaks of the gift of sight he has bestowed. The meaning of 'sight' (or 'eye') has been disputed, but I think it is a preamble to Pillar Edict III, where verbs for 'seeing' occur four times. It is the sight provided by dharma that Ashoka has bestowed. This extended meaning of sight is prevalent in Buddhist texts. Through enlightenment the Buddha gained perfect sight and insight into truth. The 'gift of life' probably refers to the prohibition of animal slaughter mentioned in Pillar Edict V. This edict is discussed in Chapters 3 and 9.

---

42 This opening statement of the Pillar Edict series parallels the opening of Rock Edict I.

The Beloved of Gods, King Piyadasi, proclaims the following:

Dharma is excellent! But what is the extent of dharma? Few evil acts, many good deeds, compassion, gift-giving, truthfulness and purity.

I have also given the manifold gift of sight. I have conferred various benefits on bipeds and quadrupeds, on birds and aquatic animals, even up to the gift of life. And I have also done many other good acts.

For the following reason have I had this writing on dharma inscribed, so that people may conform to it and that it may endure for a long time. And he who will conform to it fully does what is well done.

PILLAR EDICT III

Dated 242 BCE

> This closes the first half of the Pillar Edict series. Its first part picks up the theme of seeing and sight, which Ashoka introduced in the previous edict. We now recognize that the sight he conferred is not normal vision, but the ability to see good and evil within oneself. The second part picks up the thread of the opening sentence of Pillar Edict I, dealing with what is beneficial for a person in this world and the next—which is the practise of dharma. This edict is discussed in Chapter 10.

The Beloved of Gods, King Piyadasi, proclaims the following:

One sees only what is good, thinking: 'I have done this good thing.' One does not see as well what is bad, thinking: 'I have done this bad thing'; 'This, indeed, is what is called immoral action.' But this is quite difficult to recognize. Yet, clearly, this is how one should see it: 'These are what lead to immoral action, namely: rage, cruelty, anger, pride and envy. By reason of these may I not bring about my downfall.'

This is, without question, what one should see: 'This is for my benefit in this world, while this is for my benefit in the next world.'

PILLAR EDICT IV

Dated 242 BCE

> This edict is devoted almost entirely to the duties of a class of mid-level bureaucrats called rajukas, who were probably deployed in villages and the countryside. A subtext seems to run through this piece of writing. Some officials may not have always followed the king's wishes and orders. He is sending his 'personal emissaries'—literally 'my men'—to make sure that his orders are obeyed. Ashoka is especially concerned about the impartial dispensation of justice, a topic that he explores also in his Separate Edicts. Ashoka strikes a personal note about the people being his children whose care has been entrusted to the rajukas, as a father might entrust the care of his children to an experienced nurse. This edict is discussed in Chapters 2, 3, 9 and 10.

The Beloved of Gods, King Piyadasi, proclaims the following:

This writing on dharma has been made to be inscribed by me twenty-six years after my royal consecration.

Within the population, my rajuka officers[43] take care of many hundreds of thousands of living beings. I have given them independent authority to grant rewards and to impose punishments, in order that rajuka officers may carry out their tasks with confidence and without fear, and bestow welfare and wellbeing on and grant favours to the people of the countryside. They will know how to bestow wellbeing and how to inflict pain. Through dharma-devotees, furthermore, they will exhort the people of the countryside, so that they may gain the benefits of this world and of the next.

The rajuka officers must also submit to me. They will also submit to my personal emissaries who know my wishes. And these emissaries will also exhort them, so that the rajuka officers will be able to gratify me.

Just as one feels confident in entrusting one's child to a proficient nurse, knowing, 'She is a proficient nurse. She is able to take good care

---

43 See the Glossary for the identity of these officials.

of my child', so I have appointed the rajuka officers for the welfare and wellbeing of the people of the countryside.

That the rajuka officers, being fearless and confident, may carry out their tasks unperturbed—for this reason I have given them independent authority to grant rewards and to impose punishments. For this is what is to be desired: there should be impartiality in judicial proceedings and impartiality in imposing punishments.

My practice, moreover, has extended as far as this: for men who are confined in prison, on whom the sentence has been passed, and who have received the death penalty,[44] a stay of three days is granted. Their relatives will make them reflect on what provides protection for their lives. Having been made to reflect on the fact that their lives end in death, they will give gifts for the sake of the world beyond, or they will perform fasts.

For this is my wish, that when the time has expired, they may gain the world beyond, and that the manifold practice of dharma, self-restraint and distribution of gifts may increase among the people.

PILLAR EDICT V

Dated 242 BCE

> This edict expands on Ashoka's statement in Pillar Edict II that he has conferred benefits on animals and birds 'even up to the gift of life'. Many of the animal species listed here are difficult to identify. This edict is discussed in Chapters 2 and 9.

The Beloved of Gods, King Piyadasi, proclaims the following:

Twenty-six years after my royal consecration, I made the following species exempt from being slaughtered—parrots, myna birds, whistling

---

44 Norman (1975b) interprets the term 'vadha' as corporal punishment rather than capital punishment. Although that meaning of the term is found in Indian legal literature, I do not think Norman is right here. If this passage dealt with what he calls 'after-prison care', Ashoka could have said so in a more direct manner.

teals,[45] sheldrakes, ruddy geese, the red-billed leiothrix, malkohas, Indian oriole, tortoise, soft-shell turtle,[46] water snake,[47] Gangetic dolphin, Samkuja fish,[48] pangolin,[49] flying fox,[50] Simale,[51] Samdaka,[52] Okapinda,[53] turtle dove, white pigeon and village pigeon, as well as all quadrupeds that are neither useful nor edible.

---

45 I have followed Dave (2005) in identifying some of these birds. For whistling teals (*alune*), p. 450; for red-billed leiothrix (*naṃdīmukhe*), p. 32; malkoha (*gelāṭe*), p. 140; Indian oriole (*aṃbākapīlikā*), pp. 77–78. Yet, Dave (p. 78) himself admits that these identifications are very tentative, calling them 'the still unsolved bird-names in the Edict of Aśoka'. For some of the other species, I have benefited from the work of Norman 1967b. These identifications, however, are very tentative and uncertain.

46 Also called Ganges softshell or Indian softshell turtle (*Aspideretes gangeticus*). See J.C. Daniel, *The Book of Indian Reptiles and Amphibians* (Mumbai: Bombay Natural History Society and Oxford University Press, 2002), pp. 32–33. For the identification of *duḷi* and *anahikamacche*, see Norman 1967b: 28.

47 For this identification, see Norman 1967b: 28.

48 These have been identified as skate fish, and as dugong (sea-cows) by Norman, but neither of these inhabit fresh water. Our assumption is that Ashoka is dealing with fish that would be encountered by normal people in Magadha, and not fishermen who operate along the coasts.

49 For this identification, see Norman 1967b: 29.

50 The identity of *paṃna-sase* is unclear. Suggestions include squirrel and snake (Norman).

51 The Sanskrit form '*sṛmara*' occurs in Kauṭilya's *Arthashastra* (2.17.13). It is probably some form of large game animal, possibly a deer, because it is valued for its skin. It is quite unlikely that Ashoka would prohibit the killing of common deer, which was the paradigmatic object of the hunt in ancient India. In Rock Edict I, further, Ashoka says that a game animal was killed in the royal kitchen every day. Norman (1967b: 30) suggests a black snake or cobra.

52 Sometimes identified as a bull ritually released, or as a lizard (connected to the Hindi *sāṇḍā*; see Norman 1967b: 30).

53 The meaning is unclear. Given the etymology ('eating house food'), it could be an animal finding food in houses, possibly a house lizard. I think Norman's (1967b: 31) suggestion that it is an adjective qualifying the following entry is doubtful; normally in lists each item is independent.

Those nanny goats, ewes and sows that are pregnant or nursing the young are exempt from slaughter, as also the young before they are six months old. Cocks should not be caponed. Chaff containing living beings should not be burnt. One should not set a forest on fire without reason or for killing. Animals should not be fed to animals.

Fish are exempt from slaughter and should not be sold on the three full-moon days at the beginning of each season, on the full-moon day of Tishya, on the three days of the fourteenth and fifteenth of a fortnight and the first day of the next fortnight, and on every Uposatha day. During these same days other animal species living in elephant forests and fishery preserves should not be killed.[54]

On the eighth day of each fortnight, on the fourteenth and fifteenth days of a fortnight, on the Tishya day, on the Punarvasu day, on the three full-moon days at the beginning of each season and on festival days, bulls should not be castrated, and goats, rams, pigs and other animals that are subject to castration should not be castrated.

On the Tishya day, on the Punarvasu day, on the full-moon days at the beginning of each season, and on the fortnight following the full-moon day of each season, horses and bulls should not be branded.

It has been twenty-six years after my royal consecration, and during this period prisoners have been released twenty-five times.

PILLAR EDICT VI

Dated 242 BCE

> The central topic of this edict is 'welfare and wellbeing'. This dual goal is a primary concern of Ashoka also in his other writings. In the second paragraph, note the verb 'I pay close attention', which occupies a central position at the opening and at the end. This edict is discussed in Chapters 3, 8 and 10.

---

54 For these calendrical days, see the Glossary.

The Beloved of Gods, King Piyadasi, proclaims the following:

After I had been consecrated for twelve years, I had my writing on dharma inscribed for the welfare and wellbeing of the people, so that by not transgressing that writing they may obtain an increase of dharma in various ways.

Knowing this is the way for the welfare and wellbeing of the people, I pay close attention, just as to my relatives, so also to those who are near and to those who are far. Knowing how I may bring such wellbeing, I ordain accordingly.

To all classes[55] of people, likewise, I pay close attention. To all Pasandas I have paid homage with various acts of homage. But individual visits in person is what I consider as paramount.

I had this writing on dharma inscribed twenty-six years after my royal consecration.

PILLAR EDICT VII

Dated 241 BCE

> This edict appears to have been an afterthought, given that it is inscribed only on the Delhi-Topra pillar. Further, its engraving was carried out after the pillar had been erected with the first six Pillar Edicts already inscribed (see Chapter 4). It also has a format quite different from the first six, with the introductory statement 'The Beloved of Gods, King Piyadasi, proclaims the following' repeated seven times. It has the hallmarks of an anthology of several of Ashoka's previous messages in abbreviated form. I have given lower-case Roman numerals to identify individual segments.
>
> The key word of the first segment is 'increase' or 'growth'.[56] People's growth refers to their prosperity, which can only be secured

---

55 In Rock Edict XIII the term '*nikāya*' refers to Brahmins and Sramanas.

56 The original term is '*vaḍhi*' (Sanskrit: *vṛddhi*), which occurs frequently in the edicts. Elsewhere, I have translated it as 'increase', but in this edict I use 'grow' and 'growth' because the peculiar syntax here makes 'increase' inappropriate.

fully if they grow in dharma. Ashoka uses noun–verb combinations of common derivation to stress his actions. It is difficult and awkward, but not impossible, to replicate these combinations in English: 'increase through the increase', 'promulgate promulgations'. This edict is discussed in Chapters 2, 3, 4, 6, 7, 10 and 11.

(i) The Beloved of Gods, King Piyadasi, proclaims the following:

Kings who lived a long time ago had this desire: 'How can the people grow through their growth in dharma?' But people did not grow through a corresponding growth in dharma.

On this point, the Beloved of Gods, King Piyadasi, proclaims the following:

Here's what occurred to me. Though kings of long ago had this desire: 'How can the people grow through a corresponding growth in dharma', yet people did not grow through a corresponding growth in dharma.

So, by what means will the people comply? By what means will people grow through a corresponding growth in dharma? By what means could I lift them up through growth in dharma?

On this point, the Beloved of Gods, King Piyadasi, proclaims the following:

Here's what occurred to me. I will promulgate dharma-promulgations. I will prescribe dharma-prescriptions. Having listened to that, people will comply, they will be lifted up, and they will assuredly grow through growth in dharma. For this purpose, I have promulgated dharma-promulgations and decreed diverse kinds of dharma-prescriptions, so that my numerous personal emissaries, who are occupied with the people, will exhort them and fully explain to them. Also, rajuka officers—who are occupied with many hundreds of thousands of living beings—they too have been ordered by me: 'In such and such manner, exhort the people to be devoted to dharma.'

(ii) The Beloved of Gods, King Piyadasi, proclaims the following:

Reflecting on this very matter, I have made dharma-pillars, established dharma-mahamatras and issued dharma-promulgations.

(iii) The Beloved of Gods, King Piyadasi, proclaims the following:

Along roads, furthermore, I have had banyan trees planted to provide shade for domestic animals and humans; I have had mango orchards planted; and I have had wells dug at intervals of 8 K [about 28 km] and constructed rest houses.[57] I have had numerous watering places constructed at different locations for the benefit of domestic animals and humans. But this benefit is really trivial. For, previous kings, as well as I, have gratified the people with various gratifications. But I have done this so that they may conform to the observance of dharma.

(iv) The Beloved of Gods, King Piyadasi, proclaims the following:

As to my dharma-mahamatras also[58]—they are occupied with various matters that are beneficial, that is to say, both to those who have gone forth and to those staying at home. And they are occupied also with all Pasandas, that is to say—I have ordered them to be occupied with matters relating to the Sangha; I have likewise ordered them to be occupied also with Brahmins and Ajivikas; I have ordered them to be occupied also with the Nirgranthas; I have ordered them to be occupied also with various Pasandas—different mahamatras with different Pasandas according to the special features of each. But my dharma-mahamatras are occupied with these and with all other Pasandas.

(v) The Beloved of Gods, King Piyadasi, proclaims the following:

These, as well as many other top officials, are occupied with the distribution of gifts, that is to say, from me and from the queens, and within the whole of my inner chambers. In many different ways, they

---

57 The Prakrit term has sometimes been translated as 'flights of steps', so people will have easier access to the water. Others have taken the term to mean a 'rest house' where pilgrims could spend the night. See Hultzsch 1925: 135 for a discussion. Jason Neelis (2011: 188–89, n. 12) supports 'rest house', an interpretation I have followed.

58 This section of the edict has been analysed in Chapter 11.

establish spheres of contentment[59] right here[60] and in the provinces. I have ordered them to be occupied with the distribution of gifts from my boys also and from other princes from the queens, for the purpose of promoting noble acts of dharma and conforming to dharma. For noble acts of dharma and conforming to dharma consist in this—that compassion, gift-giving, truthfulness, purity, gentleness and goodness will grow among the people.

(vi) The Beloved of Gods, King Piyadasi, proclaims the following:

For, whatever good deeds I have done, people have conformed to them and continue to adhere to them. Thereby they have grown and will continue to grow by means of the following: obedience to mother and father, obedience to elders, deference to the aged, and proper regard to Brahmins and Sramanas, to the destitute and distressed, down to slaves and servants.

(vii) The Beloved of Gods, King Piyadasi, proclaims the following:

But this growth in dharma among the people has grown by just two means: through regulations with respect to dharma and through persuasion. Of these two, however, regulations with respect to dharma do little, while a lot is accomplished through persuasion. Regulations with respect to dharma consist of these directives of mine: such and such species are exempt from slaughter,[61] as well as the many other regulations with respect to dharma that I have issued. But through just persuasion there's a lot more: people's growth in dharma has grown to the point of not injuring creatures and not killing living beings.

Now, this has been done so that it may endure as long as my sons and grandsons, as long as the moon and sun, and so that people may

---

59 The reading and the meaning of this sentence is far from clear, with much of the main verb missing. Hultzsch translates: '[they are reporting] in divers ways different worthy recipients of charity both here and in the provinces.'
60 That is, in the capital Pataliputra.
61 See above the beginning of Pillar Edict V.

defer to it. For, by deferring to it in this manner one gains this world and the next.

Twenty-seven years after my royal consecration I have had this writing on dharma inscribed.

This is what the Beloved of Gods directs: 'This writing on dharma should be recorded wherever there are stone pillars or stone slabs, so that it will last a long time.'

Glossary

NOTE: Many of the geographical areas and ethnic groups mentioned by Ashoka cannot be identified with any degree of precision and certainty. Some of them, such as Gandhara, Coda and Pandya, have medieval and modern counterparts. See the Map for their approximate geography.

Ajivika   An ascetic religious group that flourished during Ashoka's time. It was founded by Makkhali Gosala, a contemporary of the Buddha, and espoused a rigorous regimen of ascetic practices, including going naked. The tradition is associated with 'determinism' (*niyati*), leaving no room for human effort and volition. See Chapter 11 and Basham (1951).

Andhras   An ethnic area in south-central India, related to the modern Andhra.

Bhojas   An ethnic area in west-central India, around the Narmada river.

Codas   Also spelled Colas, an ethnic area in south-eastern India, in the northern part of Tamil Nadu.

Gandhara   An ethnic area in the north-western region of the subcontinent. It became a centre of Buddhism a few

	centuries after Ashoka, developing a vibrant literary and artistic tradition.
Jambudvipa	Literally, 'island/continent of the rose apple', the term referring to the land mass of the Indian subcontinent.
Kalinga	The region broadly coinciding with modern-day Odisha (Orissa). Ashoka's conquest of this region is described in Rock Edict XIII.
Kamboja	An ethnic area in the northwest of the subcontinent.
Keralaputra	The region broadly coinciding with the modern-day state of Kerala.
Konakamana	The name of a previous Buddha. Ashoka erected a pillar at Nigliva in his honour and visited his birthplace.
Mahamatra	The highest rank in the Ashokan bureaucracy. The mahamatras were probably part of Ashoka's chancery in Pataliputra as well. Individuals of this rank were also located in population centres throughout the empire with authority over those regions. See Chapter 2.
Nabhapanktis	An ethnic group in the north-central region of the subcontinent.
Nirgrantha	The other name by which the Jain religious organization was known during Ashoka's time. See Chapter 11.
Paladas	An ethnic region in central India to the east of the Bhojas.
Pandyas	An ethnic region in the far southeast of the subcontinent, south of the Codas.
Pasanda	A classificatory term referring to the various organized religious groups during Ashoka's time, including the Brahmins, Buddhists, Jains and Ajivikas. See Chapter 11.
Pitinikas	An ethnic group in the west-central region of the subcontinent.
Piodasses	The Greek spelling of Piyadasi.

Pradesika	An official in the Ashokan state bureaucracy, mentioned only once, in Rock Edict III. There, the pradesika is listed last, preceded by rajuka and yukta. This appears to indicate that he ranked lower than the other two, although Thapar (1961:105–11) thinks that he outranked the other two.
Punarvasu	The name of a particular lunar asterism in ancient Indian astronomy; the two brightest stars in the Gemini constellation.
Rajuka	A mid-level official in the Ashokan state bureaucracy. In Rock Edict III, the yukta is listed first, followed by the rajuka and the pradesika. This appears to indicate that the rajuka ranked higher than the pradesika and lower than the yukta. See Chapter 2.
Rastrika	An official in the Ashokan state bureaucracy ranking below the rajuka. He was probably located in the countryside and villages.
Ristika	An ethnic group located in the upper reaches of the Indus River system.
Sakya	The clan to which the Buddha belonged.
Sangha	In Ashoka's writings, the term refers specifically to the Buddhist monastic order, including monks and nuns. In other early Indian texts, Sangha can refer to any kind of corporate body, including political confederations. See Chapter 6.
Satiyaputra	An ethnic group located in the south-central region of the subcontinent.
Sramana	A generic term referring to individuals belonging to ascetic religious groups, including Buddhists, Jains and Ajivikas, but excluding Brahmins.
Stupa	A funerary mound to commemorate a deceased person, especially the round architectural mounds with the relics of the Buddha.

Tamraparni	Another name for Sri Lanka.
Tishya	Also called Pushya or Pausha, Tishya is a particular lunar asterism (*nakṣatra*) in ancient Indian astronomy, of which there are twenty-seven. The moon passes through each during a month. It also corresponds to a month, December–January in the modern calendar. The full moon days falling within the Tishya constellation are considered especially sacred.
Upasaka	A lay Buddhist man, in a special way a devout and committed lay Buddhist. A Buddhist woman is referred to as Upasika (*upāsikā*). See Chapters 5 and 6.
Uposatha	Sacred days in the lunar calendar, generally the full moon and new moon days, when the monks gathered for a communal recitation of the rules for monastic living. See Chapter 6.
Yona	Derived from Ionia, the Indian term referred in general to the Greeks, but more specifically to the Hellenistic Greek states established in the West Asian regions, including what are today Afghanistan and Iran.
Yukta	An official in the Ashokan state bureaucracy, mentioned only once in Rock Edict III. There, the yukta is listed first, followed by the rajuka and the pradesika. This appears to indicate that he ranked higher than the other two, although Thapar (1961:105–11) thinks the last listed, pradesika, outranked the other two.

Bibliography

For a comprehensive bibliography of studies pertaining to Ashoka, see Falk 2006, pp. 13–54.

Adrados, F.R. 1984. 'Aśoka's Inscriptions and Persian, Greek and Latin Epigraphy.' *Amṛtadhārā: Professor R.N. Dandekar Felicitation Volume*, ed. S.D. Joshi. Delhi: Ajanta Publications, pp. 1–15.

Allchin, F.R., and K.R. Norman. 1985. 'Guide to the Aśokan Inscriptions.' *South Asian Studies* I: 43–50.

Allen, Charles. 2012. *Ashoka: The Search for India's Lost Emperor.* New York: Overlook Press.

Alsdorf, Ludwig. 1959. 'Aśokas Schismen-Edikt und das dritte Konzil.' *Indo-Iranian Journal* 3: 161–74.

———. 1960. 'Contributions to the Study of Asoka's Inscriptions.' *Bulletin of the Deccan College Research Institute* 20: 249–75.

———. 1962. *Aśokas Separatedikte von Dhauli und Jaugada.* Akademie der Wissenschaften und der Literatur. Wiesbaden: Steiner.

Andersen, Paul Kent. 1990. *Studies in the Minor Rock Edicts of Aśoka.* Freiburg: Hedwig Falk.

Asher, Frederick M. 2006. 'Early Indian Art Reconsidered.' In Olivelle (ed.) 2006, pp. 51–66.

Balcerowicz, Piotr. 2016. *Early Asceticism in India: Ājīvikism and Jainism.* London: Routledge.

Basham, A.L. 1951. *History and Doctrines of the Ājīvakas: A Vanished Indian Religion.* London: Luzac.

———. 1967 [1954]. *The Wonder That Was India: A Survey of the History and Culture of the Indian Sub-continent Before the Coming of the Muslims.* 3rd edition. London: Sidgwick & Jackson.

———. 1979. 'Saṃbodhi in Aśoka's 8th Rock Edict.' *Journal of the International Association of Buddhist Studies* 5: 81–83.

———. 1982. 'Asoka and Buddhism—A Reexamination.' *Journal of the International Association of Buddhist Studies* 5: 131–43.

Bechert, Heinz. 1982. 'The Importance of Aśoka's So-Called Schism Edict.' *Indological and Buddhist Studies: Volume in Honour of Professor J.W. de Jong on His Sixtieth Birthday*, eds L.A. Hercus et al. Canberra: Faculty of Asian Studies, pp. 61–68.

Beckwith, Christopher I. 2015. *Greek Buddha: Pyrrho's Encounter with Early Buddhism in Central Asia.* Princeton: Princeton University Press.

Bellah, Robert. 1970. 'Civil Religion in America.' *Beyond Belief: Essays on Religion in a Post-Traditional World.* New York: Harper and Row, pp. 168–89. Originally published in *Daedalus*, Vol. 96 (1967): 1–21.

Bhargava, Rajeev. 2014. 'Beyond Toleration: Civility and Principled Coexistence in Asokan Edicts.' In *Boundaries of Toleration*, eds Alfred Stepan and Charles Taylor. New York: Columbia University Press, pp. 173–202.

———. 2022a. 'Harmony as a Collective Virtue in Ashokan Inscriptions.' In *The Virtue of Harmony*, eds Chenyang Li and Dasha Düring. New York: Oxford University Press, pp. 68–92.

———. 2022b. 'Asoka's Dhamma as a Project of Expansive Moral Hegemony.' *Bridging Two Worlds: Comparing Classical Political Thought and Statecraft in China and India*, eds Amitav Acharya et al. Berkeley: University of California Press.

Biardeau, Madeleine. 2002. *Le Mahābhārata: Un récit fondateur du brahmanisme et son interprétation*, two volumes. Paris: Seuil.

Bloch, Jules. 1950. *Les inscriptions d'Asoka.* Paris: Société d'Édition 'Belles Lettres'.

Bosworth, A.B. 1996. 'The Historical Setting of Megasthenes' Indica.' *Classical Philology* 91: 113–27.

Brereton, Joel. 2019. '*Pāṣaṇḍa*: Religious Communities in the Aśokan Inscriptions and Early Literature.' In Olivelle (ed.) 2019, pp. 20–42.

Bronkhorst, Johannes. 2007. *Greater Magadha: Studies in the Culture of Early India.* Leiden: Brill.

———. 2011. *Buddhism in the Shadow of Brahmanism.* Leiden: Brill.

———. 2016. *How the Brahmins Won: From Alexander to the Guptas.* Leiden: Brill.

Buddruss, Georg. 1964. 'tenatā/tenada im 8. Felsedikt des Aśoka.' *Münchener Studien Zur Sprachwissenschaft* 16: 5–12.

Carratelli, G. Pugliese, and G. Garbini. 1964. *A Bilingual Graeco-Aramaic Edict of Aśoka.* Roma: Istituto Italiano per il Medio ed Estremo Oriente.

Chakrabarti, Dilip K. 2011. *Royal Messages by the Wayside: Historical Geography of the Asokan Edicts.* New Delhi: Aryan Books International.

Cribb, Joe. 2017. 'The Greek Contacts of Chandragupta Maurya and Ashoka and Their Relevance to Mauryan and Buddhist Chronology.' *From Local to Global: Papers in Asian History and Culture*, Vol. III, eds Kamal Sheel, Charles Willemen, and Kenneth Zysk. Delhi: Buddhist World Press, pp. 3–27.

Dave, K.N. 2005. *Birds in Sanskrit Literature*, revised edition. Delhi: Motilal Banarsidass.

Deeg, Max. 2012. 'Aśoka: Model Ruler Without a Name?' In Olivelle, Leoshko, and Ray (eds) 2012, pp. 362–79.

Deshpande, Madhav M. 2009. 'Interpreting the Aśokan Epithet *devānaṃpiya*.' In Olivelle (ed.) 2009, pp. 19–43.

Doniger, Wendy. 1971. 'The Origin of Heresy in Hindu Mythology.' *History of Religions* 10: 271–333.

Dutt, Sukumar. 1960. *Early Buddhist Monachism.* London: Asia Publishing House.

Dyson, Tim. 2018. *A Population History of India: From the First Modern People to the Present Day.* Oxford: Oxford University Press.

Eggermont, Pierre Herman Leonard. 1956. *The Chronology of the Reign of Asoka Moriya.* Leiden: Brill.

Exler, Francis Xavier J. 1923. *The Form of the Ancient Greek Letter: A Study in Greek Epistolography.* Washington, DC: Catholic University of America.

Falk, Harry. 1993a. *Schrift im alten Indien: Ein Forschungsbericht mit Anmerkungen.* Tübingen: Gunther Narr.

———. 1993b. 'The Art of Writing at the Time of the Pillar Edicts of Aśoka.' *Berliner Indologische Studien* 7: 79–102.

———. 1997. 'The Preamble at Pāṅgurāriā.' *Bauddhavidyāsudhākaraḥ, Studies in Honour of Heinz Bechert on the Occasion of His 65th Birthday*, eds Petra Kieffer-Pülz and Jens-Uwe Hartmann. Swistal-Odendorf: Indica et Tibetica Verlag, pp. 107–21.

———. 2006. *Aśokan Sites and Artefacts: A Source-Book with Bibliography.* Mainz am Rheim: Philipp von Zabern.

———. 2008. 'Barabar Reconsidered.' *South Asian Archaeology 1999*, ed. Ellen M. Raven. Groningen: Egbert Forsten, pp. 245–51.

———. 2012. 'The Fate of Aśoka's Donations at Lumbini.' In Olivelle, Leoshko, and Ray (eds) 2012, pp. 204–16.

———. 2013. 'Remarks on the Minor Rock Edict of Aśoka at Ratanpurwa.' *Jñāna-Pravāha Research Journal* 16: 29–49.

Ferro-Luzzi, Gabriella Eichinger. 1981. 'Abhiṣeka: The Indian Rite that Defies Definition.' *Anthropos* 76: 707–42.

Fitzgerald, James L. 2004. *The Mahābhārata: 11 Book of the Women, 12 The Book of Peace Part One.* Chicago: University of Chicago Press.

Folkert, Kendall W. 1993. *Scripture and Community: Collected Essays on the Jains*, ed. John E. Cort. Atlanta: Scholars Press.

Fox, Robin Lane. 2004 (1973). *Alexander the Great.* New York: Penguin.

Freiberger, Oliver. 2009. 'Negative Campaigning: Polemics Against Brahmins in a Buddhist *Sutta.*' *Religions of South Asia* 3.1: 61–76.

Fussman, Gérard. 1982. 'Pouvoir central et régions dans l'Inde ancienne: le problème de l'empire maurya.' *Annales. Histoire, Science Sociales* 37: 621–47.

———. 1987–88. 'Central and Provincial Administration in Ancient India: The Problem of the Mauryan Empire.' *Indian Historical Review* 14: 43–72 (English version of 1982).

———. 1988–89. 'Les premiers systèmes d'écriture en Inde.' *Annuaire du Collège de France 1988–1989: Résumé des cours et travaux*, pp. 507–14.

Gaál, Balázs, and Ibolya Tóth. 2018. 'Some "Major" Trends in Aśoka's Minor Rock Edicts.' *Acta Orientalia Academiae Scientiarum Hung* 71: 81–97.

Gagarin, Michael. 2008. *Writing Greek Law.* Cambridge: Cambridge University Press.

Gomez, Louis. 1976. 'Proto-Mādhyamika in the Pāli Canon.' *Philosophy East and West* 26: 137–65.

Goyal, S.R. 1979. 'Brāhmī: An Invention of the Early Maurya Period.' *The Origin of Brahmi Script*, eds S.P. Gupta and K.S. Ramachandran. Vol. 2. Delhi: DK Publications, pp. 1–52.

Guha, Sumit. 2001. *Health and Population in South Asia: From Earliest Times to the Present.* New Delhi: Permanent Black.

Guruge, Ananda. 1993. *Aśoka, the Righteous: A Definitive Biography.* Colombo: Ministry of Cultural Affairs and Information.

Halbfass, Wilhelm. 1983. 'Kumārila on Ahiṃsā and Dharma.' *Studies in Kumārila and Śaṅkara.* Studien zur Indologie und Iranistik, Monographie 9. Reinbek: Dr Inge Wezler Verlag für Orientalistische Fachpublikationen, pp. 1–26.

Hardy, E. 1901. 'On a Passage in the Bhabra Edict.' *Journal of the Royal Asiatic Society* 33: 311–15.

Hinüber, Oskar von. 1989. *Der Beginn der Schrift und frühe Schriftlichkeit in Indien.* Mainz: Akademie der Wissenschaften und der Literatur.

———. 2010. 'Did Hellenistic Kings Send Letters to Aśoka?' *Journal of the American Oriental Society* 130: 261–66.

———. 2012. 'Linguistic Experiments: Language and Identity in Aśokan Inscriptions and in Early Buddhist Texts.' In Olivelle, Leoshko, and Ray (eds) 2012, pp. 195–203.

Hock, Hans. 1991. 'Dialects, Diglossia, and Diachronic Phonology in Early Indo-Aryan.' *Studies in the Historical Phonology of Asian Languages,* eds William G. Boltz and Michael C. Shapiro. Amsterdam: John Benjamins, pp. 119–59.

Hultzsch, Eugen. 1925. *Inscriptions of Asoka: Corpus Inscriptionum Indicarum I,* new edition, Vol. 1. Oxford: Clarendon Press. Reprint. Delhi: Indological Book House, 1969.

Huntington, Susan, and John Huntington. 2014. *The Art of Ancient India: Buddhist, Hindu, Jain.* Delhi: Motilal Banarsidass.

Irwin, John. 1973. '"Aśokan" Pillars: A Reassessment of the Evidence.' *Burlington Magazine* 115: 706–20.

———. 1974. '"Aśokan" Pillars: A Reassessment of the Evidence—II: Structure.' *Burlington Magazine* 116: 712–27.

———. 1975. '"Aśokan" Pillars: A Reassessment of the Evidence—III: Capitals.' *Burlington Magazine* 117: 631–43.

———. 1976. '"Aśokan" Pillars: A Reassessment of the Evidence—IV: Symbolism.' *Burlington Magazine* 118: 734–53.

———. 1983. 'The True Chronology of Aśokan Pillars.' *Artibus Asiae* 44: 247–65.

Itō, Gikyo. 1969. 'An Indo-Aramaic Inscription of Asoka from Quandahār: Japanese with English Summary.' *Gengo Kenkyu* (Kyoto) 55: 1–13.

———. 1977. 'A New Interpretation of Aśokan Inscriptions, Taxila and Kandahar I.' *Studia Iranica* 6: 151–61.

Jamison, Stephanie. 1996. *Sacrificed Wife/Sacrificer's Wife: Women, Ritual, and Hospitality in Ancient India.* New York: Oxford University Press.

———. 2007. *The Rig Veda Between Two Worlds.* Paris: Édition-Diffusion de Boccard.

———. 2019. 'The Term *Gr̥hastha* and the (Pre)history of the Householder.' In Olivelle (ed.) 2019, pp. 3–19.

Jamison, Stephanie W., and Joel P. Brereton (trans.). 2014. *The Rigveda: The Earliest Religious Poetry of India,* three volumes. New York: Oxford University Press.

Janert, Klaus L. 1967–68. 'Recitations of Imperial Messengers of Ancient India.' *Adyar Library Bulletin* 31/32: 511–18.

———. 1973. 'About the Scribes and Their Achievements in Aśoka's India.' *German Scholars on India: Contributions to Indian Studies*, Vol. 1. Varanasi: Chowkhamba, pp. 141–45.

Jayaswal, Vidula. 1998. *From Stone Quarry to Sculpturing Workshop: A Report on the Archaeological Investigations Around Chunar, Varanasi and Sarnath.* Delhi: Agam Kala Prakashan.

———. 2004. 'Aśokan Pillars: Medium, Chiseling & Composition.' *The Ananda-vana of Indian Art, Dr Anand Krishna Felicitation Volume*, eds N. Krishna and M. Krishna. Varanasi: Indica Books, pp. 35–46.

———. 2012. 'Mauryan Pillars of the Middle Ganga Plain: Archaeological Discoveries of Sarnath-Varanasi and Chunar.' In Olivelle, Leoshko, and Ray (eds) 2012, pp. 229–57.

Jerryson, Michael. 2013. 'Buddhist Traditions and Violence.' *Oxford Handbook of Religion and Violence,* eds Mark Juergensmeyer et al. New York: Oxford University Press, pp. 41–66.

Josh, Bhagwan. 2012. 'Aśoka, Historical Discourse, and the Post-Colonial Indian State.' In Olivelle, Leoshko and Ray (eds) 2012, pp. 394–408.

Karttunen, Klaus. 1989. *India in Early Greek Literature.* Studia Orientalia, 65. Helsinki: Finnish Oriental Society.

———. 1997. *India and the Hellenistic World.* Studia Orientalia, 83. Helsinki: Finnish Oriental Society.

Khanna, Ashok. 2020. *Ashoka, the Visionary: Life, Legend and Legacy.* New Delhi: Bloomsbury.

Kosmin, Paul J. 2014. *The Land of the Elephant Kings: Space, Territory, and Ideology in the Seleucid Empire.* Cambridge, Massachusetts: Harvard University Press.

Kubica, Olga. 2013. 'Edicts of King Piyadassi (Aśoka) in the Context of Ethnicity.' *Proceedings of the 1st Annual International Interdisciplinary Conference,* 2013, pp. 723–33.

Lahiri, Nayanjot. 2015. *Ashoka in Ancient India*. Cambridge, Massachusetts: Harvard University Press.

——. 2022. *Searching for Ashoka: Questing for a Buddhist King from India to Thailand*. Delhi: Permanent Black.

Legge, James. 1886. *The Travels of Fa-Hien*. Oxford: Clarendon Press.

Li, Chongfeng. 2012. 'Aśoka-type Buddha Images Found in China.' In Olivelle, Leoshko, and Ray (eds) 2012, pp. 380–93.

Ling, Trevor. 1976. *The Buddha: Buddhist Civilization in India and Ceylon*. Harmondsworth: Penguin.

Lingat, Robert. 1989. *Royautés bouddhiques. Aśoka et la fonction royale a Ceylan*. Paris: Editions de l'Ecole des Hautes Etudes en Science sociales.

Lubin, Timothy. 2013. 'Aśoka's Disparagement of Domestic Ritual and Its Validation by the Brahmins.' *Journal of Indian Philosophy* 41: 29–41.

Majumdar, Susmita Basu, Soumya Ghosh, and Shoumita Chatterjee. 2017. 'Scribe, Engravers and Engraving of the Aśokan Edicts: A Critical Analysis of the Edicts in the Southern Territory.' *Pratna Samiksha: A Journal of Archaeology* 8: 135–60.

——. 2019. 'Separate Rock Edicts of Aśoka.' *Pratna Samiksha: A Journal of Archaeology* 10: 53–73.

Maniscalco, Francesco. 2018. 'A New Interpretation of the Edicts of Aśoka from Kandahar.' *Annali di Ca' Foscari. Serie Orientale* 24: 238–63.

McClish, Mark. 2019. *The History of the Arthaśāstra: Sovereignty and Sacred Law in Ancient India*. Cambridge: Cambridge University Press.

McGovern, Nathan. 2019. *The Snake and the Mongoose: The Emergence of Identity in Early Indian Religion*. New York: Oxford University Press.

McHugh, James. 2021. *An Unholy Brew: Alcohol in Indian History and Religion*. New York: Oxford University Press.

Neelis, Jason. 2011. *Early Buddhist Transmission and Trade Networks: Mobility and Exchange Within and Beyond the Northwestern Borderlands of South Asia*. Leiden: Brill.

Norman, K.R. 1966. 'Middle Indo-Aryan Studies VI.' *Journal of the Oriental Institute, Baroda*. 16: 113–19 (1990–2001 *Collected Papers* 1: 77–84).

———. 1967a. 'Notes on Aśokan Rock Edicts.' *Indo-Iranian Journal* 10: 160–70 (1990–2001 *Collected Papers* 1: 47–58).

———. 1967b. 'Notes on Aśoka's Fifth Pillar Edict.' *Journal of the Royal Asiatic Society of Great Britain and Ireland*, pp. 26–32 (1990–2001 *Collected Papers* 1: 68–76).

———. 1970. 'Some Aspects of the Phonology of the Prakrit Underlying the Aśokan Inscriptions.' *Bulletin of the School of Oriental and African Studies* 23: 132–43 (1990–2001 *Collected Papers* 1: 93–107).

———. 1972. 'Notes on the Greek Version of Aśoka's Twelfth and Thirteenth Rock Edicts.' *Journal of the Royal Asiatic Society*, pp. 111–18 (1990–2001 *Collected Papers* 1: 144–55).

———. 1975a. 'Studies in the Epigraphy of the Aśokan Inscriptions.' *Studies in Indian Epigraphy (Bharatiya Purabhilekha Patrika)* No. 2, pp. 36–41 (1990–2001 *Collected Papers* 1: 214–19).

———. 1975b. 'Aśoka and Capital Punishment: Notes on a Portion of Aśoka's Fourth Pillar Edict.' *Journal of the Royal Asiatic Society*, pp. 16–24 (1990–2001 *Collected Papers* 1: 200–13).

———. 1976. 'Notes on the So-Called "Queen's Edict" of Aśoka.' *Studies in Indian Epigraphy* 3: 35–42 (1990–2001 *Collected Papers* 2: 52–58).

———. 1978–79. 'Middle Indo-Aryan Studies XII.' *Journal of the Oriental Institute (Baroda)* 28: 78–85 (1990–2001 *Collected Papers* 2: 20–29).

———. 1982. 'Aśokan *silā-thambha*-s and *dhamma-thambha*-s.' *Ācārya-vandanā: D.R. Bhandarkar Birth Centenary Volume.* Calcutta, pp. 311–18 (1990–2001 *Collected Papers* 2: 224–32).

———. 1983. 'Notes on the Ahraura Version of Aśoka's First Minor Rock Edict.' *Indo-Iranian Journal* 26: 277–92 (1990–2001 *Collected Papers* 2: 250–68).

———. 1985. *The Rhinoceros Horn and Other Early Buddhist Poems* (Sutta Nipāta). London: Pali Text Society.

———. 1987a. 'Aśoka's "Schism" Edict.' *Bukkyogaku Semina* (Buddhist Seminar [Otani]) 46: 1–34 (1990–2001 *Collected Papers* 3: 191–218).

———. 1987b. 'The Inscribing of Aśoka's Pillar Edicts.' *India and the Ancient World: History, Trade and Culture before A.D. 650, Professor P.H.L.*

Eggermont Jubilee Volume, ed. G. Pollet. Leuven: Dept. Orientalistiek, pp. 131–39 (1990–2001 *Collected Papers* 3: 173–82).

———. 1990–2001. *Collected Papers,* Vols I–VII. Oxford: Pali Text Society.

———. 1994. 'A Note on *silāvigaḍabhīcā* in Aśoka's Rummindei Inscription.' *Buddhist Forum* III, pp. 227–37 (1990–2001 *Collected Papers* 6: 31–46).

———. 1997–98. 'Aśoka's Thirteenth Rock Edict.' *Indologica Taurinensia* 23–24: 459–84.

———. 2012a. *A Philological Approach to Buddhism: The Bukkyō Dendō Kyōkai Lectures 1994.* Berkeley: Institute of Buddhist Studies.

———. 2012b. 'The Languages of the Composition and Transmission of the Aśokan Inscriptions.' In Olivelle, Leoshko and Ray (eds) 2012, pp. 38–62.

Olivelle, Patrick. 1993. *The Āśrama System: The History and Hermeneutics of a Religious Institution.* New York: Oxford University Press.

———. 1997. *The Pañcatantra: The Book of India's Folk Wisdom.* Oxford: Oxford University Press.

———. 2005. *Language, Texts, and Society: Explorations in Ancient Indian Culture and Religion.* Florence: University of Florence Press.

———. (ed.) 2006. *Between the Empires: Society in India, 300* BCE *to 400* CE. New York: Oxford University Press.

———. 2008. *Life of the Buddha: Buddhacarita by Aśvaghoṣa.* Clay Sanskrit Library. New York: New York University Press.

———. (ed.) 2009a. *Dharma: Studies in Its Semantic, Cultural, and Religious History.* Delhi: Motilal Banarsidass.

———. (ed.) 2009b. *Aśoka, in History and Historical Memory.* Delhi: Motilal Banarsidass.

———. 2012a. 'Material Culture and Philology: Semantics of Mining in Ancient India.' *Journal of the American Oriental Society* 132: 23–30.

———. 2012b. 'Aśoka's Inscriptions as Text and Ideology.' In Olivelle, Leoshko, and Ray (eds) 2012, pp. 157–83.

———. 2013. *King, Governance, and Law in Ancient India: Kauṭilya's* Arthaśāstra. New York: Oxford University Press.

———. 2016. 'Economy, Ecology, and National Defense in Kauṭilya's *Arthaśāstra.' Indigenous Historical Knowledge: Kautilya and His Vocabulary*, eds Pradeep Kumar Gautam et al. New Delhi: IDSA and Pentagon Press, pp. 3–15.

———. 2017. 'The Medical Profession in Ancient India: Its Social, Religious, and Legal Status.' *eJournal of Indian Medicine* 9: 1–21.

———. (ed.) 2019. *Gṛhastha: The Householder in Ancient Indian Religious Culture.* New York: Oxford University Press.

———. 2022. 'Mining the Past to Construct the Present: Some Methodological Considerations from India.' *Bridging Two Worlds: Comparing Classical Political Thought and Statecraft in China and India*, eds Amitav Acharya et al. Berkeley: University of California Press.

———. 2023. 'To Kill or Not to Kill: The Hermeneutics of the Ethical Axiom *ahiṃsā.' Science and Society in the Sanskrit World: Studies in Honor of Christopher Z. Minkowski*, eds Toke Lindegaard Knudsen et al. Leiden: Brill.

Olivelle, Patrick, Janice Leoshko, and Himanshu Prabha Ray (eds). 2012. *Reimagining Aśoka: Memory and History.* Delhi: Oxford University Press.

Parasher-Sen, Aloka. 1991. *Mlecchas in Early India: Attitudes Towards Outsiders Upto AD 600.* Delhi: Munshiram Manoharlal.

———. 2004. '"Foreigner" and "Tribe" as Barbarian (*Mleccha*) in Early North India.' *Subordinate and Marginal Groups in Early India*, ed. Aloka Parasher-Sen. Delhi: Oxford University Press, pp. 275–313.

Pargiter, F.E. 1913. *The Purana Text of the Dynasties of the Kali Age.* Reprint. Varanasi: Chowkhamba Sanskrit Series Office, 1975.

Parker, Grant. 2012. 'Aśoka the Greek, Converted and Translated.' In Olivelle, Leoshko, and Ray (eds) 2012, pp. 310–26.

Rahula, Walpola. 1966. *History of Buddhism in Ceylon*, second edition. Colombo: MD Gunasena.

Ray, Himanshu Prabha. 2008. 'Interpreting the Mauryan Empire: Centralized State or Multiple Centres of Control?' *Ancient India in Its Wider World*, eds Grant Parker and Carla Sinopoli. Ann Arbor: University of Michigan Press, pp. 13–51.

Rezavi, Syed Ali Nadeem. 2009–10. 'Antiquarian Interests in Medieval India: The Relocation of Ashokan Pillars by Firuzshah Tughluq.' *Proceedings of the Indian History Congress,* 2009–10, pp. 994–1010.

Rousseau, Jean-Jacques. 1792. *The Social Contract, Or Principles of Political Right.* Amsterdam.

Salles, Jean-François. 2012. 'Environmental Changes in North Bengal: An Opportunity for the Mauryas?' In Olivelle, Leoshko, and Ray (eds) 2012: 258–79.

Salomon, Richard. 1995. 'On the Origin of the Early Indian Scripts.' Review essay. *Journal of the American Oriental Society* 115: 271–79.

——. 1998. *Indian Epigraphy: A Guide to the Study of Inscriptions in Sanskrit, Prakrit, and the Other Indo-Aryan Languages.* New York: Oxford University Press.

——. 2007. 'Ancient India: Peace Within and War Without.' *War and Peace in the Ancient World,* ed. Kurt A. Raaflaub. Oxford: Blackwell, pp. 53–65.

——. 2009. 'Aśoka and the "Epigraphic Habit" in India.' In Olivelle (ed.) 2009, pp. 45–52.

Sasaki, Shizuka. 1989. 'Buddhist Sects in the Aśoka Period (1): The Meaning of the Schism Edict.' *Bukkyo-kenkyu – Buddhist Studies* XVIII: 181–202.

——. 1992. 'Buddhist Sects in the Aśoka Period (2) – *Saṃghabheda* (1).' *Bukkyo-kenkyu –Buddhist Studies* XXI: 157–176.

——. 1993. 'Buddhist Sects in the Aśoka Period (3) – *Saṃghabheda* (2).' *Bukkyo-kenkyu – Buddhist Studies* XXII: 167–199.

Scerrato, Umberto. 1958. 'An Inscription of Aśoka in Afghanistan: The Bilingual Greek-Aramaic of Kandahar.' *East and West* 9: 4–6.

Scharfe, Hartmut. 1971. 'The Maurya Dynasty and the Seleucids.' *Zeitschrift für die vergleichende Sprachforschung* 85 (2): 211–25.

Schlingloff, Dieter. 2013. *Fortified Cities of Ancient India: A Comparative Study.* London: Anthem.

Schmithausen, Lambert. 1992. 'An Attempt to Estimate the Distance in Time Between Aśoka and the Buddha in Terms of Doctrinal History.' *The Dating of the Historical Buddha,* ed. Heinz Bechert. Göttingen: Vanden Hoeck & Ruprecht, pp. 110–47.

———. 2000. 'Buddhism and the Ethics of Nature: Some Remarks.' *Eastern Buddhist* (New Series) 32.2: 26–78.

Schlumberger, D., and E. Benveniste. 1965. 'A New Greek Inscription of Asoka at Kandahar.' *Epigraphia India* XXXVII: 193–200.

Schneider, Ulrich. 1978. *Die grossen Felsen-Edikte Aśokas: Kritische Ausgabe, Übersetzung und Analyse der Texte.* Wiesbaden: Harrassowitz.

———. 1982. 'The Calcutta-Bairāṭ Edict of Aśoka.' *Indological and Buddhist Studies: Volume in Honour of Professor J.W. de Jong on his Sixtieth Birthday,* eds L.A. Hercus et al. Canberra: Faculty of Asian Studies, pp. 491–98.

Schopen, Gregory. 1997 (1987). 'Burial *Ad Sanctos* and the Physical Presence of the Buddha in Early Indian Buddhism: A Study in the Archaeology of Religions.' *Bones, Stones, and Buddhist Monks: Collected Papers on the Archaeology, Epigraphy, and Texts of Monastic Buddhism in India.* Honolulu: University of Hawai'i Press, pp. 114–47.

———. 2004. 'What's in a Name: The Religious Function of Early Donative Inscriptions.' *Buddhist Monks and Business Matters: Still More Papers on Monastic Buddhism in India.* Honolulu: University of Hawai'i Press, pp. 382–94.

Sealy, Irwin Allan. 2012. *Asoca: A Sutra.* Delhi: Penguin.

Seneviratna, Anuradha. 1994. *King Aśoka and Buddhism: Historical and Literary Studies.* Kandy: Buddhist Publication Society.

Singh, Upinder. 2012. 'Governing the State and the Self: Political Philosophy and Practice in the Edicts of Aśoka.' *South Asian Studies* 28: 131–45.

———. 2017. *Political Violence in Ancient India.* Cambridge, Massachusetts: Harvard University Press.

———. 2021. *Ancient India: A Culture of Contradictions.* New Delhi: Aleph.

———. 2022. *Inscribing Power on the Realm: Royal Ideology and Religious Policy, c. 200* BCE*–300* CE. 28th J. Gonds Lecture. Amsterdam: Royal Netherlands Academy of Arts and Sciences.

Sircar, D.C. 1986 [1954]. *Select Inscriptions Bearing on Indian History and Civilization,* Vol. I., third edition. Delhi: Asian Humanities Press.

———. 1967 [1957]. *Inscriptions of Aśoka,* second edition. New Delhi: Publications Division, Government of India.

Smith, Monica L. 2005. 'Networks, Territories, and the Cartography of Ancient States.' *Annals of the Association of American Geographers* 95(4): 832–49.

Smith, Monica L., et al. 2016. 'Finding History: The Locational Geography of Ashokan Inscriptions in the Indian Subcontinent.' *Antiquity* 90: 379–92.

Smith, Vincent. 1901a. *Asoka: The Buddhist Emperor of India*. Rulers of India Series. Oxford: Clarendon Press.

———. 1901b. 'The Identity of Piyadasi (Priyadarśin) with Aśoka Maurya, and Some Connected Problems.' *Journal of the Royal Asiatic Society of Great Britain and Ireland*, pp. 827–58.

Strong, John S. 1983. *The Legend of King Aśoka: A Study and Translation of the Aśokāvadāna*. Princeton: Princeton University Press.

———. 2012. 'The Commingling of Gods and Humans, the Unveiling of the World, and the Descent from Trayastriṃśa Heaven.' In Olivelle, Leoshko, and Ray (eds) 2012, pp. 348–61.

Squarcini, Federico. 2019. 'Selling Tolerance by the Pound: On Ideal Types' Fragility, Aśoka's Edicts and the Political Theology of Toleration in and beyond South Asia.' *Philosophy and Social Criticism* 45: 477–92.

Sugandhi, Namita. 2013. 'Conquests of Dharma: Network Models and the Study of Ancient Polities.' *Archeological Papers of the American Anthropological Association* 22.1: 145–63.

Sutton, Nick. 1997. 'Aśoka and Yudhiṣṭhira: A Historical Setting for the Ideological Tensions of the *Mahābhārata*?' *Religion* 27.4: 333–41.

Tambiah, Stanley. 1976. *World Conqueror and World Renouncer: A Study of Buddhism and Polity in Thailand Against a Historical Background*. Cambridge: Cambridge University Press.

Taylor, Charles. 2014. 'How to Define Secularism.' In *Boundaries of Toleration*, eds Alfred Stepan and Charles Taylor. New York: Columbia University Press, pp. 59–78.

Thapar, Romila. 1960. 'Aśoka and Buddhism.' *Past & Present* 18: pp. 43–51.

———. 1961. *Aśoka and the Decline of the Mauryas*. Reprint. New Delhi: Oxford University Press, 1998.

———. 1987. *The Mauryas Revisited*. Calcutta: Bagchi and Co.

———. 2000. *Cultural Pasts: Essays in Early Indian History.* Delhi: Oxford University Press.

———. 2012. 'Aśoka: A Retrospective.' In Olivelle, Leoshko, and Ray (eds) 2012, pp. 17–37.

Tieken, Herman. 2000. 'Aśoka and the Buddhist *Saṃgha:* A Study of Aśoka's Schism Edict and Minor Rock Edict I.' *Bulletin of the School of Oriental and African Studies* 63: 1–30.

———. 2002. 'The Dissemination of Asoka's Rock and Pillar Edicts.' *Wiener Zeitschrift für die Kunde Südasiens* 46: 5–42.

———. 2006. 'Aśoka's Fourteenth Rock Edict and the *Guṇa mādhurya* of the Kāvya Poetical Tradition.' *Zeitschrift der Deutschen Morgenländischen Gesellschaft* 156/1: 95–115.

———. 2012. 'The Composition of Aśoka's Pillar Edict Series.' In Olivelle, Leoshko, and Ray (eds) 2012, pp. 184–94.

———. 2023. *The Aśoka Inscriptions: Analaysing a Corpus.* Delhi: Primus Books.

Trautmann, Thomas. 1971. *Kautilya and the Arthaśāstra.* Leiden: Brill.

———. 2012. *Arthashastra: The Science of Wealth.* New Delhi: Penguin.

———. 2015. *Elephants and Kings: An Environmental History.* Chicago: University of Chicago Press.

Vetter, Tilmann. 1990. 'Some Remarks on Older Parts of the Suttanipāta.' *Earliest Buddhism and Madhyamaka,* eds D.S. Ruegg and L. Schmithausen. Leiden: Brill, pp. 36–56.

Vigasin, Alexei. 1997–98. 'Some Aspects of Aśokan Edicts.' *Indologica Taurinensia* 23–24: 501–05.

Walder, Heather. 2018. 'Inscription Carving Technology of Early Historic South Asia. Results of Experimental Archaeology and Assessment of Minor Rock Edicts in Karnataka.' *Walking with the Unicorn: Social Organization and Material Culture in Ancient South Asia: Jonathan Mark Kenoyer Felicitation Volume,* eds Dannys Frenez et al. Oxford: Archaeopress, pp. 605–22.

Waldschmidt, Ernst. 1951. *Das Mahāparinirvāṇasūtra.* Part III. Berlin: Akademie Verlag.

Welles, C.B. 1934. *Royal Correspondence in the Hellenistic Period: A Study of Greek Epigraphy.* New Haven: Yale University Press.

Wells, H.G. 1951 (1920). *The Outline of History: Being a Plain History of Life and Mankind,* revised edition. London: Cassell.

Winternitz, Maurice. 1972 (1927). *A History of Indian Literature,* Vol. II, trans. S. Ketkar and H. Kohn. New Delhi: Oriental Reprint Corporation.

Wong, David. 2020. 'Soup, Harmony, and Disagreement.' *Journal of the American Philosophical Association* 2020: 139–155.

Wright, J.C. 2000. 'Aśoka's 256-Night Campaign.' *Journal of the Royal Asiatic Society,* third series, 10: 319–39.

Zin, Monika. 2018. 'Kanaganahalli in Sātavāhara Art and Buddhism.' *Journal of the International Association of Buddhist Studies* 41: 537–55.

Zysk, Kenneth G. 1991. *Asceticism and Healing in Ancient India: Medicine in the Buddhist Monastery.* New York: Oxford University Press.

Index